Like a Brazen Wall

The Battle of Minden, 1759, and its Place in the Seven Years War

Ewan Carmichael

Helion & Company

For Alexandra and Alistair

Helion & Company Limited
Unit 8 Amherst Business Centre
Budbrooke Road
Warwick
CV34 5WE
England
Tel. 01926 499619
Email: info@helion.co.uk
Website: www.helion.co.uk
Twitter: @helionbooks
Visit our blog at http://blog.helion.co.uk/

Published by Helion & Company 2021
Designed and typeset by Mach 3 Solutions Ltd (www.mach3solutions.co.uk)
Cover designed by Paul Hewitt, Battlefield Design (www.battlefield-design.co.uk)

Cover: Advance of Napier's 12th Foot against the cavalry of the Régiment du Roi. (Artwork by Patrice Courcelle © Helion and Company 2021)

ISBN 978-1-913336-58-5

British Library Cataloguing-in-Publication Data.
A catalogue record for this book is available from the British Library.

For details of other military history titles published by Helion & Company Limited, contact the above address, or visit our website: http://www.helion.co.uk

We always welcome receiving book proposals from prospective authors.

Contents

Preface

When Prince Ferdinand of Brunswick rode towards the village of Hahlen, on the edge of Minden Heath, before dawn on 1 August 1759, his plan was already in danger of unravelling. The commander of a combined allied force, of Germans and Britons, tasked with protecting Hanover from two French armies acting in concert, he had already experienced his enemy stealing a march on him. Three weeks earlier, the two French armies had interposed themselves between him and Hanover by capturing and occupying strong positions in and around the fortress of Minden. From there they could control the vital crossings over the River Weser, which were a mere 60 kilometres from Hanover.

In response, Ferdinand's plan had been to lure the stronger French forces out from behind their defences by spreading his own force thinly to provide what appeared to be an irresistibly weak target, but which would rapidly march to concentrate as soon as the French began to move. The effect was intended to be like the closing of a net. The dispersed allied force, having studied and prepared the routes to be used, would be able to assemble faster than the enemy could break out from behind his defences, but the plan all hinged on early warning and passage of information. To facilitate this, Ferdinand had ordered a series of picquets to be posted to provide early notice of French movement.

Unfortunately for Ferdinand, a series of unfortunate mistakes by his subordinates had allowed the enemy to gain an advantage of several hours in a plan where time was critical. When Ferdinand had been woken at about 3:00 a.m., the French were already on the verge of occupying positions which he himself had previously identified as vital to the success of his own plans.

Quickly mounting and cantering off in the dark, and accompanied by only one orderly, he immediately headed to Hahlen, a village on which he would anchor the right of his line. However, on his way he passed through the village of Hartum where he learned from the picquets there that the enemy had second-guessed him and that two battalions of French infantry were already beginning to infiltrate Hahlen, a mere 2,000 metres distant. For his plan to succeed, it was essential that Hahlen be recaptured, and quickly, to protect the right flank of his army as it marched forward to concentrate.

Ordering the small force in Hartum forward to drive the French out of the adjacent village at all costs, he turned to hasten the assembly of the remainder of his army. As he did so, he heard the first rumble of cannon fire from the extreme left of his line as it too came under attack by the French. His situation could barely have worsened, but it was not long before the sound of gun fire reached him from a position to his rear. In fact, this new threat was coming from the direction of his own headquarters.

The Seven Years War spanned the globe, to the extent that it has frequently been described as the 'first World War'. It was fought between most of the, then, great powers, European protagonists, on land and at sea, in North America, the Caribbean, the Mediterranean, Western Europe, Central Europe, India and Africa. While the scale of the wars against Louis XIV may have overshadowed the Seven Years War, those were arguably reflections of a traditionally balanced status quo. The importance of the Seven Years War was that it caused permanent change in the geo-political limits of European politics, expanding to embrace global politics.[1]

The Battle of Minden took place on 1 August (Lammas day) 1759, Britain's *Annus Mirabilis,* during the Seven Years War. 1759 was an incredible year of multiple British victories which, as they balanced in Europe and the colonies, and on land and sea, contributed significantly to the growth of the British Empire.

The Battle of Minden was fought between, on one side, the French with a sizeable contingent from Saxony and, on the other, a composite mix of British and allied German states. The popular images of the battle include six British infantry battalions, intimately supported by gallant artillerymen, stolidly advancing against the mass of French cavalry, and soldiers plucking roses to adorn their caps and drums. Whilst resulting in an allied victory, there are many aspects of the French operations which demand respect and are worthy of study. The battle and the operations leading up to it provide lessons in leadership, command and control, communications, understanding of terrain, manoeuvre, deception, concentration of force, mutual support, liaison with allies and discipline.

The aim of this book is to review the Battle of Minden. Because of the central role of the British contingent, much of the strategic context will be from a British perspective: why were the British manoeuvring about the European Continent as part of a combined, allied army? The achievements of the British foot and artillery have been justifiably celebrated over the centuries. This book echoes that celebration, but also attempts to set a new balance: reviewing the role of the British horse, and its controversial commander, Lord George Sackville; appropriately applauding, where due, the dash and élan of their French opponents who are worthy of respect; examining the enduring challenges of multinationality by thinking of the relationships between Britain and her German allies; critically reviewing the role of the leader by reconsidering the strengths and weaknesses of Prince Ferdinand of Brunswick.

For those readers who would rather dispense with the strategic considerations, coverage of the campaign begins at page 67, while the accounts

1 E.B. Carmichael, 'British Strategy', *Seven Years' War*, <http://www.kronoskaf.com/syw/index.php?title=British_Strategy> (accessed 9 February 2019).

of the tactical preparations begin at page 104. Given that British musketry was such a vital factor in the final outcome, a review of that aspect has been included at page 198. The Seven Years War took place simultaneously around the globe. In order to assist the reader to better understand this simultaneity, some charts with comparative timelines are included at page 225.

Clausewitz, the great Napoleonic-era military thinker, wrote that war has a dynamic all of its own, recognizing that the combatants become engaged in a struggle in which passion, friction and chance all play a role. The outcome is far from predictable. One of Clausewitz's most important insights about war's nature is that it is a reciprocal activity: the enemy gets a vote too.[2] The reality, and indeed the only certainty, of combat is that there will be casualties. Commanders and soldiers, on both sides, learn the pain of this lesson to their cost. Not all armchair generals appreciate it however, so this book will draw out some the medical arrangements made in advance of battle and the human impact.

The commonly recognized dates of the Seven Years War are that it began on 17 May 1756, with the declaration of war between France and Britain, and ended on 15 February 1763 when Saxony sued for peace with Prussia. However, the causes were rooted in the outcomes of previous wars, and there had been a slide towards conflict over colonial trade, most noticeably in North America and India. A further factor was the readjustment of protective alliances. The new alliance between Britain and Prussia did not endure the conflict. By the end of the Seven Years War, Prussia was the dominant power in the Germanies, Russia likewise in Eastern Europe, while Britain's place as a maritime imperial power was confirmed. However, the war had sapped much of the energy of the protagonists and various commentators have suggested that the seeds of the American Revolution had been sown through the requirement to pay for the defence of the American colonies by taxation. Furthermore, the conditions left by the Seven Years War in France may have contributed to the French Revolution.

2 C.P.G. Clausewitz, *On War* (Princeton: Princeton University Press, 1989), pp.87, 122, 149.

Acknowledgements

It is generally accepted form that authors thank their editors and publishing staff for their efforts. In this case, Dr Andrew Bamford deserves more than that, for inviting me to write on a subject which fired my imagination as a boy and which became a passion as I joined the British Army, eventually being posted to 11th Armoured Brigade on Minden Heath during the 'Cold War'. I am grateful to Patrice Courcelle, for bringing the men and the battle to life through his delightful artwork, and to George Anderson for his skilful mapping.

First and foremost, thanks are due to Richard Couture, the custodian of a remarkable *Seven Years' War* website, Kronoskaf, a resource which grows by the day and is freely open to all (please support it and consider donating towards it). Effectively it is peer-reviewed. Richard went above and beyond the call of duty by painstakingly translating most of the French sources, many of which are in archaic, pre-revolutionary language. He conscientiously burnt a lot of midnight oil, grappling with the twin challenges of language and of the outlook of an era. I have taken the considerable liberty of lightly adapting his work in order to render it marginally more straightforward to read and to introduce relevant military terms. Richard also introduced to me to Jean Louis Vial, steward of the *Nec Pluribus Impar* website, and Frédéric Aubert, both of whom selflessly shared their French primary sources.

Dr Yolande Hodson, a leading authority on the history of British military maps and survey, was generous with her time and advice. Through her good offices, I was privileged to have advance sight of The Royal Collection Trust's forthcoming on-line catalogue of King George III's Military Maps which are preserved in the Royal Collection at Windsor Castle. At the time of writing, the site looks accessible and highly attractive.

Dr Christopher Duffy will be unaware of this, but he reinforced my enthusiasm for black powder while I sat at his feet in the War Studies department at the Royal Military Academy Sandhurst. Other members of that department have now gone onto a military academic Valhalla where, no doubt, they exchange tales of derring-do over quarts of claret. More recently, I have enjoyed comparing views on Frederick the Great with Dr Duffy at the Royal Military Academy Sandhurst's War Discussion Group, and thank him for chivalrously responding to my, probably naïve, questions on Saxon rifles.

I am grateful to Lord Robert Sackville-West for his pointers on his ancestor's papers and for his gracious offer of further assistance.

Two groups of which I am, or have been, a member deserve mention. The International Guild of Battlefield Guides, formed by the late, and deeply missed, Professor Richard Holmes, exists to raise the standard of battlefield guiding. Its members are unfailingly generous in sharing material. To that end, Frank Baldwin deserves mention for some valuable documents on the parallel battle at Gohfeld, while Duncan Cook, Graeme Cooper and Anthony Rich are always refreshing on the black powder era. There really is no substitute for getting out on the ground with like-minded enthusiasts. The author is willing to lead tours of Minden and Gohfeld, given sufficient planning time, and can be contacted through the Guild. Likewise, members of the 36th Regiment of Foot, of Lace Wars, seek to recreate the life of the eighteenth century soldier. This is a fascinating experience in terms of the sheer friction of existing and operating in the field.

I wish to thank Emma White for contacts with the National Army Museum. I came rather late to the Society for Army Historical Research: I must recommend its journal, under the meticulous editorship of Dr Andrew Cormack, which is accessible to non-members via the JSTOR system.

When researching a multinational battle, it is a particular pleasure to be able to thank experts from the other nations. I am grateful to WOII Christoph Lechermann of the Bundeswehr, working in the International Branch of the British Army Headquarters who promptly put me in touch with Angelika Nawroth of the Zentrum für Militärgeschichte und Sozialwissenchaften der Bundeswehr in Potsdam. Angelika kindly led my quest onto Katja Hartmann of the Militärhistorisches Museum der Bundeswehr in Dresden, an expert in small arms.

In Minden, I have had generous support from Anita, who sourced my Roy/Schley map, from Christa Rosentreter and from Heinrich Gieseking, on whose farm the Todtenhausen redoubt was and where, in particularly dry weather, it is still possible to see changes in the soil which reflect the gun positions. Harmut Zettwitz challenged my Anglo-centric view of the battle back in 1989, and caused me to look at why the monument to the battle is at Todtenhausen. Thank you, too, to the staff of the Mindener Museum and also the Preussen Museum, regrettably temporarily closed at the time of writing. I am also grateful to both Drs Warmke of Haddenhausen, who provided coffee and cake on a hot day, as Alexandra and I hunted for a French gun platform.

The book is dedicated to my children Alexandra and Alistair, both patient and stalwart Battle of Minden explorers. It was with Alexandra that we rediscovered the French gun platform in a back garden at Biemke, while Alistair risked life and limb, mounting various pieces of street furniture to capture horseman's-eye views in some of my photographs.

Lastly, and vitally, I thank my wife Carol for her unfailing and patient support.

1

Setting the Scene and Working Definitions

The aim of this book has been to review the Battle of Minden in order to achieve a more accurate balance of what happened in reality. Hailed as one of the great battles of the British infantry (and justifiably so), the net effect of this has been to downplay the truth that those brave and effective infanteers played only a part in an allied coalition. Modern British battlefield tourists often puzzle over why the monument to the battle is not where the British foot won 'undying glory'. It has long been assumed in the United Kingdom that the British infantry faced the French main effort. In fact, a review of the French commander's orders reveals that his intentions were completely different. Similarly, the vital contribution played by the British artillery, whilst still commemorated and celebrated by the Royal Regiment, has often been marginalised.

As Minden is principally celebrated in Britain, most effort has gone into getting that balance right from a British perspective. What was at stake and why were British soldiers committed to battle on Minden Heath? It is assumed, with the deepest respect and affection for French and German readers, that most readers of this work will be Anglophones. As a result, in attempting to restore an appropriate balance, greater emphasis is given to strategic aims, operational concerns and tactical issues from the British point of view. That said, it is hoped that Francophones will appreciate the respect with which the former enemy is treated.

It is a truism that the winners get to write the history. The character and role of the various commanders has often been skewed and exaggerated. Prince Ferdinand of Brunswick was hailed as a military genius. He was certainly gifted, possessing keen operational instincts, and yet a review of his tactical communications once engaged reveals all too human shortcomings. Sackville, the much-maligned commander of the British contingent, and of an allied cavalry column during the battle, was court-martialled at his own request. His reputation was damned for a while, and yet a review of the evidence suggests that he was not totally blameworthy. On the French side, Broglie failed to press home his attack on what was meant to be the main effort, and was later castigated by Napoleon for it. Yet it was his commander, Contades, whose reputation suffered the more.

Grand strategy might be described as marshalling large means in pursuit of medium to long-term ends. Modern thinking suggests that it is a 'course of action that integrates ends, ways and means to meet policy objectives'.[1] Identifying and articulating national interests and objectives is the key to this.

It is frequently assumed that Britain was a unit, with unified opinion and leadership, but that was not necessarily the case. Who did Britain's strategy 'belong' to? In the politics of the day, national policy might be shaped by the Ministry, a term taken to mean all the ministers of a government, including the cabinet and junior ministers alike. The King chose his ministers, yet the Commons could deny them the funds they required. The post of Prime Minister was evolving. There were several incumbents during the course of the war, but strong characters in parliament, not necessarily in government, could sway both popular opinion and national policy. This mix was further complicated by perceptions of what 'the Mob' would tolerate, and of what constituted 'Patriotism'. These diverse perspectives made achieving a consistent view of interests and war aims difficult.

In the modern narratives of some of the countries which provided theatres of the war, their portion of the Seven Years War may have a name specific to the war conducted in that theatre (for example, The French-Indian War of 1754-63 in North America, and the Third Carnatic War of 1757-63 on the Indian sub-Continent). To avoid confusion, it should be noted that the dates of these theatre conflicts do not conform precisely to the core events of the more common title, the Seven Years War.

Occasionally the term 'Atlanticism' will be used which, for the purposes of this book, is intended to capture a sense of British, non-Continental (that is, non-European) interests which might, by preference, focus on North America and Canada. There was considerable debate about Britain's identity. Her leaders and vociferous parts of her population were torn between an Atlanticist and a Continental, European identity.

'Patriotism' was a phenomenon particularly recognizable in Britain, understandably perhaps given her island separation and also ethnic and religious differences from the Continent. Commentators described the dominant moral traits of the English as violence and patriotism. The bellicose English hated the French, but they hated everyone else too, a view described half a century later by the military philosopher Clausewitz as 'hostile feelings'.[2] It is challenging to translate eighteenth century patriotism into a contemporary equivalent. Politically, patriotism tended to be the stance of a group of disenchanted Whigs. Christopher Duffy describes most people's lives being limited by a spirit of '*campanilismo*' and of social divisions, but public interest and opinion were high.[3]

With place names and titles, I have been inconsistent, often using the English version as would have been used in Britain, so Brunswick and

1 Royal College of Defence Studies, *Thinking Strategically* (Shrivenham: British Crown Copyright, 2010), p.8.

2 Clausewitz, *On War*, p.138.

3 C. Duffy, *The Military Experience in the Age of Reason* (London: Wordsworth, 1998), pp.7-9.

Hanover rather than Braunschweig and Hannover. I have, however, used modern local spellings for other names. I hope that the reader will bear with me in this.

Two of the principal characters in this story have remarkably similar, and potentially confusing titles. Prince Ferdinand of Brunswick was the allied commander. The grandson of Ferdinand Albert I, the first Duke of Brunswick-Bevern, but the fourth son of the second Duke. For him, I have used 'Ferdinand' or 'Prince Ferdinand'. His nephew, another Ferdinand, the Hereditary Prince, Karl Wilhelm Ferdinand, was a subordinate commander but heir to the third Duke. For him, I have used his title 'the Erbprinz'.

Modern students of Minden have been left a rich legacy in terms of military mapping. In particular, several talented cartographers took part in the battle and were enabled by Prince Ferdinand to create lasting records of the battle, and these were made while memories were still fresh. Two stand out for the quality and precision of their work. William Roy was both a lieutenant in the British 51st Regiment of Foot and an ensign, promoted to captain on 10th September 1759, in the Corps of Engineers. Prince Ferdinand was understandably keen to celebrate his achievement and 'was pleased to require that plans of it should be presented to him by the various engineers in the army'.[4] Roy volunteered and, in addition to a very accurate map of the terrain, superimposed a succession of flaps showing the changing dispositions of the forces as the battle progressed.[5] The Prince was so pleased with the result that Roy was appointed to his personal staff soon after. Roy's plan was engraved, etched, printed and sold by Thomas Major, engraver to King George II. It appears to have been released on 29 February 1760, which happened to be the first day of the trial of Lord George Sackville for disobeying orders during the battle. Versions of Roy's map were made available in French, engraved by the Dutch engraver, Jakob van der Schley, also in 1760. The other great mapper was Friedrich Wilhelm von Bauer, variously described as a Quarter-Master General, a colonel, and as a captain (in a letter to Holdernesse, the Prince describes him as a captain), a Prussian cavalryman whose map Ferdinand may actually have preferred. It was released in 1759, before Roy's. The notable feature of Bauer's map is that it shows far more of the surrounding landscape, providing a wider topographical context.

Mapping was also available to the combatants before the battle. The Hanoverian military engineers, Anton Heinrich du Plat and George Josua du Plat, created maps in 1757 showing the campsites of George II's German troops at Dankersen and Holzhausen as well as those of the allied army.[6] In the period immediately before the battle, when Prince Ferdinand instructed the allied commanders to reconnoitre their approach routes onto Minden Heath, at least one British artillery officer left a record of having examined his route, comparing the ground with his map.

4 Y. Hodson (2019), 'Minden. At last!', E-mail (22 September 2019), quoting Sir James Campbell, who knew Roy and who was present at the battle, aged 13.

5 Royal Collection (Map) K.Mil. RCIN 732111-a(1).

6 Royal Collection (Map) K.Mil. RCIN 732019, 732020.

2

The Strategic Context

By the mid-eighteenth century, Spain's period of glory as a colonial power was beginning to wane, allowing France and Britain the opportunity to compete for supremacy. This was particularly so in North America, where French attempts to contain British colonies to a narrow eastern coastal strip created friction between the two rival nations. This friction had smouldered where their territories abutted against one another, and had already evolved into skirmishing over the previous five years. The French territories in Louisiana, Illinois and Canada needed only the Ohio country to create a chain which would simultaneously bottle up the British colonies and enable further French expansion inland. At the same time as this geographical containment, France also created alliances with the local Native American tribes, using them as proxies to attack British interests.

Should war break out on the European Continent, France was prepared to use the vulnerability of Hanover as a lever against Britain. However, France's policies were complicated by the personal goals of King Louis XV, supported by *Le Secret du Roi*, his personal system of private diplomacy which was outwith the control, and even at times the knowledge, of the Foreign Minister. While France in general sought the expansion of its colonies, Louis sought to compete with Austria and Russia for influence in Poland, Sweden and Turkey. In particular, he wanted to see a relative, Louis François de Bourbon, as king of Poland, which was contrary to stated French policy of pushing forward the House of Saxony within Poland.

Meanwhile, Austria and Russia sought to curb the power of Frederick II (the Great) of Prussia, slicing off Silesia and restoring it to Austria, giving East Prussia to Poland in return for the Polish Duchy of Courland which would pass to Russia. Frederick was to be limited to his Electorate in Brandenburg. To these ends, Austria and Russia had formed a defensive alliance on 2 June 1746 which was to protect them, and Poland, in the event of attacks by Prussia or Turkey.

The potential support by France of Prussia was a limiting factor on Austrian aggression. Equally though, Frederick appreciated that he would alienate France by attacking either Saxony or Polish West Prussia. However, were he to join with France in an attack on Hanover, he might make himself vulnerable in turn to a combined attack by Austria and Russia.

British Policy and Positioning

Sir Edward Grey, Britain's longest serving twentieth century Foreign Secretary, dismissed the notion of 'far-sighted views or large conceptions or great schemes' as guiding Britain's foreign relations.[1] However, it would be inappropriate to assume an altogether random foreign policy-making process, subject only to short-term needs, without some concept of grand strategic objectives. What were deemed as Britain's vital national interests?

'The ultimate object of statesmen in London and Versailles was to maintain or increase security, power and influence in Europe'; in short, they had identical core interests.[2] Beyond this core, their interests were often opposed, but directly related.

Sir Winston Churchill was of the opinion that for 400 years the foreign policy of England had been to oppose whatever was the strongest, most dominating power on the Continent. In the eighteenth century, Europe was viewed as a tremendous field of forces, which were liable to become unstable unless they were held in equilibrium. The principle itself tended to come into operation of its own, being self-adjusting through the British policy of maintaining equilibrium by throwing her weight on the scale in favour of the weaker side.[3]

An enduring aim of the policy of Great Britain was the preservation of the 'Liberties of Europe', which could only be protected by frustrating attempts by any power, or group of powers, to dominate Europe so that they could dictate to lesser states. The prime example of such a domineering force within Europe would be the Bourbon Alliance, which resulted in Britain necessarily making compacts and alliances in order to balance power. Balancing power was conducted as a means of self-preservation, and protecting the nation's vital interests, and not out of a spirit of altruism.[4]

Certain patterns emerge from study of Britain's past history of external relations. At least four elements emerge of a foreign policy which helped to underpin Britain's international position.[5] The first element was the use of armed force to project British power, not only to protect the Empire but also to contain, through blockade (or the threat of it), any Continental European power attempting to achieve dominance or hegemony. The second strand, both underwriting armed force but also contributing to 'hard power', was wealth or financial capacity: in the eighteenth century, Britain had distinct advantages through her possession of colonies and her trade. The third element of British global strategy was closely related, the potential to sustain a major war effort through mobilizing colonial resources, including raw materials and manpower reserves. Closely linked to these 'hard power' elements was an important diplomatic component: alliances, and indeed

1 T.G. Otte, '"It's What Made Britain Great": Reflections on British Foreign Policy, from Malplaquet to Maastricht', in T.G. Otte (ed.), *The Makers of British Foreign Policy* (Basingstoke: Palgrave, 2002), p.2.

2 D. Baugh, *The Global Seven Years War 1754-1763* (Harlow: Longman, 2011), p.1.

3 L.L. Claude, *Power and International Relations* (New York: Random, 1965), pp.43-47.

4 Otte, '"It's What Made Britain Great"', pp.3-4.

5 Otte, '"It's What Made Britain Great"', pp.2-3.

wider diplomacy, during both peace and wartime. It was through diplomacy that alliances could be achieved with other powers, or groups of powers, in order to contain any nations threatening Britain's communications links at sea, or impinging on the independence of the Low Countries, both of which were of strategic relevance, or seeking Continental hegemony. This is the first indication that there was a complex relationship between Britain's extra-European interests and her European commitments.

A consistently important enabler was 'Sea Power', or 'all that tends to make a people great upon or by the sea'. Sea power came not just from possessing a fighting navy, but resulted also from a suitable geographical situation and a character that made for trade and for colonisation. The impulse to trade by sea was vitally the 'prime foundation of sea-power, which grows and dies with it'.[6] Foreign trade, and the wealth generated by it, underpinned the ships, seamen and naval force of the nation. There was a complex but symbiotic relationship between naval strength, a merchant fleet, wealth for ship-building and paying for the seamen who supplied the fighting ships, and the transports which conveyed land forces around the globe. Furthermore, sea-power provided the wealth which propped up the leagues and confederacies of previous monarchs, and which limited French ambitions. So, commerce and the protection provided by the navy were mutually interdependent.

Britain's wars tended to fall into one of three broad categories. First, a reflection of the age, were small wars with 'weak or savage' powers which may not have depended on maritime trade.[7] Here land forces were dominant and control of the seas was not being competed for, so the active strategic role of the Navy in co-operation was clearly negligible.

The second type, described by Clausewitz as a war of 'limited object', was where Britain, possibly as part of an alliance, came into conflict with another power contesting ownership of land or maritime rights overseas.[8] Here the naval role was in support of land forces in the disputed territory, protecting them from counterstroke, impeding enemy reinforcement, sustaining them and protecting them in transit. At that stage in history, it would not be normal to defeat a great power solely at sea. Nelson himself said it was to be 'regretted that England could not decide the fate of Empires by action at sea'.[9] In the Seven Years War in North America, the role of the Royal Navy was securing maritime superiority to enable the British Army to reach the territory in dispute, and then operate with minimal external interference from Brest. The fleet's strategic role lay in securing the line of communications of the Army, the outcome, or 'decision', being accomplished on land.

The third group was of wars of coalitions, in which a group of Powers, including Britain, opposed another great group: what amounted to the world was at war, a sort of 'hegemonic war'.[10] In such great conflicts the situation was different in that Britain could not, and did not, predominate in the main

6 H.W. Richmond, *National Policy and Naval Strength* (London: Longmans, 1928), pp.161-166.
7 Richmond, *National Policy*, pp.32-33.
8 Clausewitz, *On War*, pp.601-616.
9 Richmond, *National Policy*, pp.33-36.
10 R.N. Lebow, *Why Nations Fight* (Cambridge: Cambridge University Press, 2010), pp.95-96.

theatre of operations. British forces constituted a fraction of the armies in that theatre. In such operations of treaties of alliance between Continental powers, military strength on land might be roughly balanced. Britain's small land force contribution was sufficient only to contribute to that balance and was insufficient to alter the situation decisively. In the absence of decision, such conflicts tended to be protracted and generated great internal debate about the conduct of British strategy. Should Britain deploy an army to the Continent, perhaps as a subordinate part of a larger Continental army, with the Royal Navy in a defensive role? Should Britain act as a maritime power, providing mobility to the army and multiplying its size? Should Britain consummate her command at sea, using the army as an amphibious force and depriving the enemy of maritime commerce and all the supplies which that would involve? This debate, which could be described as that between supporters of Continental operations against the Maritime, or Atlanticist, school featured prominently during the Seven Years War. In terms of Britain's involvement with Europe, the period 1740-1763 witnessed a high-water mark of her commitment to the Continent.[11]

At this time, William Pitt the Elder (1711-78), later the First Earl of Chatham, featured significantly as a key figure in the development of British foreign policy. Pitt's role in the prioritisation of 'America or Europe?' debate was profoundly important.

Pitt's stance in the face of political considerations was not always consistent. During the Seven Years War, he was one of the two Secretaries of State responsible for the conduct of foreign policy between December 1756 and April 1757, and between July 1757 and September 1761. For the remainder, Pitt was a severe critic of the government and of Britain's foreign policy.[12] He frequently worked in concert with Thomas Pelham-Holles, 1st Duke of Newcastle, and Philip Yorke, 2nd Earl of Hardwicke, whose characters complemented his. Newcastle, several times Prime Minister, was honest, subtle and perhaps at his best as a Whig organiser on behalf of others; Hardwicke was the best strategist in the Cabinet and played an intelligent support role.

The political considerations were not always fixed but, in general, Pitt could be viewed as an opponent of giving Europe priority and of the Royal role in formulating foreign policy.[13] In Pitt's view, ministers paid too much attention to George II's concerns, as both King and Elector of Hanover, but also to the possibility of constructing a system of European alliances both to protect Hanover and also to restrain the ambitions of other potential hegemons, most notably France.

Rather, Pitt and the 'Patriot' party offered a sense of national identity and national interest that was not expressed through or in the monarch, but was founded on the notion of Britain as a maritime power with an active

11 J. Black, 'Pitt the Elder and the foundation of an imperial foreign policy', in T.G. Otte (ed.), *The Makers of British Foreign Policy* (Basingstoke: Palgrave, 2002), pp.35-51.

12 Baugh, *Global Seven Years War*, pp.24-30.

13 C. Arnold-Baker, *The Companion to British History* (Tunbridge Wells: Longcross, 1996), p.1009.

trans-oceanic destiny. While such an identity and interest had been provided before, particularly in terms of literary rhetoric, with Pitt they were to assume a central role in the discussion of foreign policy.

At the beginning of the Seven Years War, Britain's national debt stood at £74.6 million. Despite this being a substantial sum, it was one which could be, and had been, managed.[14] One of Pitt's political allies, Phillip Stanhope, the Earl of Chesterfield, in correspondence with a friend noted the general excitement over the announcement of war with France in 1756, 'In my opinion, our greatest danger arises from our expense, considering the present immense National Debt. Where can France annoy us then? I see but two places; in America by slipping over in single ships a considerable number of troops; and next, by keeping us in a state of fear and expense at home.'[15] In his view, the war with France was essentially a no-win situation. Whether Britain won or lost, the cost of fighting the war would only accentuate the debt issue.

Prelude to the Seven Years War

Not only were there armed clashes with the French, outwith Europe, in the years leading up to the commonly accepted date for the start of the Seven Years War, but for the underlying causes of the war the reader must go back several decades. The seeds of future conflict had already been sown as a result of the outcomes of previous ones. Clausewitz advised that defeated states frequently saw peace terms as being a transitory evil.[16]

William III's accession to the British throne in 1689 transformed Britain into a European power, not just through his European connections and commitments, but also through his worldly-wise Dutch entourage. As a result, English politicians were forced to become engaged in European matters. To an extent Britain's interests combined with Dutch interests, beginning to recognize the wider European picture, and coinciding with those of the King in defending the Liberty of Europe against France's hegemonial ambitions.[17]

Britain was the main beneficiary of the 1714 Peace of Utrecht, which brought the War of the Spanish Succession to a conclusion and contained French ambitions through the re-erection of the Dutch 'Barrier', by which the Netherlands should be fortified at Austria's cost to keep the French out, the latter having been forced to destroy her defences and port at Dunkirk.[18] Utrecht restored an emerging balance of power and also the principle of flexibility based on 'alliances and alignments'. Significantly for Britain, she was able to influence a new balance of power in the Mediterranean

14 Jeremy Land, *The Price of Empire: Britain's Military Costs During the Seven Years' War* (Appalachian State University, MA Thesis, 2010), pp.41-42, <https://libres.uncg.edu/lir/asu/f/Land,%20Jeremy_2010_Thesis.pdf> (accessed 1 April 2019).

15 Letter from Lord Chesterfield to Solomon Dayrolles, printed in J. Bradshaw (ed.), *The Letters of Philip Dormer Stanhope, Earl of Chesterfield* (London: Swan Sonnerschein and Company, 1905), p.1146.

16 Clausewitz, *On War*, p.80.

17 Otte, '"It's What Made Britain Great"', pp.3-4.

18 B. Simms, *Three Victories and a Defeat* (London: Penguin, 2007), pp.109-112.

through newly acquired naval bases in Gibraltar and Minorca. Her navy was numerically and organizationally superior to potential European rivals, and it was boosted by a great number of merchantmen and privateers. Almost equally importantly, the Admiralty Board was able to organise and coordinate Britain's global ship movements through information provided by its 'intelligence system'. Furthermore, information gathering on the Stuart Pretender on the Continent gave impetus to the improved institutionalisation of a diplomatic service. The economy played its part too. Import duties and indirect taxation financed Britain's rise to great power status on the back of the military successes. On the other hand, national debt rose substantially. It was as a result of war that Britain changed from a largely free-trade country to a *de facto* protectionist one.[19]

Britain's connections and commitments to the Continent were further reinforced by the Hanoverian accession in 1714. The new King's German interests produced a shift in Britain's European diplomacy. An Anglo-French alliance of 1716 was intended to check Russian and Swedish threats to George's Hanoverian possessions through the diplomatic influence of France in Northern Europe. The French alliance remained important to British foreign policy until the 1730s and yet Britain's main concern lay with trade, commerce and influence, transatlantically with the North American colonies and the West Indies, and looking out in the opposite direction to the East Indies. Whilst Britain and France might both have been prepared to cooperate temporarily in European affairs, both nations' attempts at overseas expansion hampered and undermined each other's maritime trade. Britain's foreign policy became increasingly influenced by the growth of British commerce.[20]

The War of the Austrian Succession (1740-1748) transformed Britain's international position and marked a period characterised by instability in European affairs. Britain's relationship with Europe became complicated by the ensuing Austro-Prussian struggle for mastery of the Continent and the rise of Frederick the Great.[21] Regardless of which side won, the victor would have to become the effective guarantor of Hanover. Hanoverian interests were not automatically pro-Prussian, and Britain joined the conflict on Austria's side principally to counter France. The relationship between Hanover's interest in the Habsburg-Hohenzollern conflict and Britain's continuing commercial and colonial competition with France became tangled. Pitt, in opposition, was convinced that Continental intervention served Hanoverian rather than British interests. In the Commons, on 10 December 1742, Pitt attacked what he claimed were unnecessary alliances and engagement in Continental quarrels, criticizing George II for being most interested in aggrandizing Hanover.[22] Pitt's remarks constituted both a willingness to defend national interests and a powerful attack on George II's conduct. Pitt's own firm convictions and powerful argument in favour of national rights commanded

19 Otte, '"It's What Made Britain Great"', p.4.
20 T. Blanning, *The Pursuit of Glory* (London: Penguin, 2007), pp.109-112.
21 Simms, *Three Victories*, p.279.
22 Black, 'Pitt the Elder', p.36.

popular support and throughout his political career he expressed these in parliament. At a time of intense and rising patriotism, Pitt defined loyalty through the furtherance of national interests rather than arising from Royal initiatives and decreasingly on the defence of the Protestant Succession.[23]

However, in February 1746 Pitt's acerbic criticism of Hanoverian influence stopped when he joined the Government, as Joint Vice-Treasurer of Ireland and then as Paymaster General. He found himself unable to direct government policy and yet having to defend it to the House. As the War of the Austrian Succession progressed, and until its end in 1748, Britain was able to return to a well-worn theme, the defence of the Low Countries.[24]

The results of the war of the Austrian Succession for France had been that her navy had not only been heavily attrited but, even more importantly, its morale had been badly damaged. She had lost over 1,000 merchant ships and her trading companies had suffered grievously. The French East India Company was at rock bottom, and on the brink of insolvency. Sir Alfred Lyall identified that any maritime European power seeking to dominate India in order to achieve supremacy on land would be doomed to fail if it was not able to establish a secure sea line of communications. The net effect of the war which preceded the Seven Years War was to erode that French line of communications through both the loss of such a great part of her fleet, but also the weakening of her trade.[25]

The 1748 peace of Aix-La-Chapelle left one particularly unresolved and unacceptable issue: Louisbourg in Canada, which Britain gave back to France in return for a French withdrawal from the Low Countries. It arose because Lord Newcastle, as the new Northern Secretary, had other pressing concerns: there was anxiety about the Bourbon axis between France and Spain; Britain could overmatch France alone in North America and at sea, but France and Spain combined could draw on Spain's extensive colonies and the preponderance would be reversed. Newcastle was acutely aware that the priority of British foreign policy had to be preventing France from having any naval outlet to the North Sea.[26]

However, Austria was showing disinterest in the arrangement, with the consequent risk that Holland might seek protection from either France or Prussia. A war started by Britain risked driving Holland into the arms of the French, providing Britain's longest standing enemy with several naval bases. Lastly, possibly preying on Newcastle's mind might have been an alliance between France and Prussia dating from 1741 when France agreed to finance 20,000 German troops. That treaty was now due for renewal, and relations between both courts seemed warm. Britain's grave concern lay in Hanover's extreme vulnerability to France. Should Britain be distracted elsewhere, Hanoverian resistance to a far stronger France could quickly crumble unless her neutrality could be assured. In terms of honour, this would be unacceptable as, whilst not actually a British dominion, Hanover did belong

23 Simms, *Three Victories*, pp.300-318.
24 Black, 'Pitt the Elder', p.37.
25 Richmond, *National Policy*, p.173.
26 F. Anderson, *Crucible of War* (London: Faber & Faber, 2000), pp.35-36.

to Britain's King. Further, Hanover did play a part in blocking possession of another stretch of the Continental coast to rivals.[27]

In opposition Pitt had objected to subsidizing foreign troops yet now, rather than furthering secret goals, they were clearly designed to protect British security via the Low Countries. The traditional non-interventionist agenda now seemed less relevant, and Pitt's move into government is interesting in relation to this policy shift. He continued to play an active role in refuting criticism from the opposition that national interests were being ignored.[28] It is perhaps understandable that charges of hypocrisy were levelled at Pitt, but he showed a flexibility which was a realistic response to domestic and foreign circumstances. Even when he had a solid parliamentary majority, Pitt did not evade the unpleasant challenge of explaining the limits of national power. Pitt moved into opposition in 1754, passed over in the ministerial reshuffle, just as Anglo-French relations deteriorated.

Having served under Marlborough in his youth, and famously commanded at Dettingen during the War of the Austrian Succession, King George II became, latterly, something of an armchair general.[29] Out of nervousness for a potential French or Prussian (at that time an ally of France) attack on Hanover, George II attempted to build subsidy-alliances with Hesse-Cassel and Russia. The Duke of Newcastle met Pitt and was able to report: 'There was such a firm resolution, so solemnly declared, both as to persons, and things; that, if complied with, must produce a total change of the present system, both as to measures and men'.[30]

> Pitt said that, if it was expected, that he should take an *active part,* in support of measures, he must be enabled to do it; which he could not think, the calling him to the Cabinet Council, would, in any degree, do. That the House of Commons was now an assembly of atoms; that the great wheels of the machine were stop'd – that *this* could not be thought sufficient to put them in motion…that I did not know the state of the House of Commons; which he might say without vanity, he did, better than anybody…that the business of the House of Commons could not go on, without there was a minister (a subordinate one perhaps) which should go directly between the King and them…that he could not, and would not, take an active part in the House of Commons, without he had an office of advice, as well as of execution;...if he could be induced to part with some part of my sole power; to that I replied, that I know of no such sole power; that my present situation was not my choice, but the King's command.[31]

Pitt's view of the proposed treaty with Russia was that in time of peace it might be approved as a way of preserving that peace, but that, at that time, it was actually in danger of creating a system so disadvantageous to British

27 Julian S. Corbett, *The Seven Years War – A Study in British Combined Strategy* (London: The Folio Society, 2001), p.29.

28 Black, 'Pitt the Elder', pp.35-51.

29 A.C. Thompson, *George II* (Padstow: Yale, 2011), p.277.

30 Black, 'Pitt the Elder', p.38.

31 Black, 'Pitt the Elder', pp.35-51.

interests that it risked alienating the Royal family in the eyes of the people. Newcastle thought it necessary to be prepared to defend Hanover, but that such defence ought to be independent of other Continental considerations. Pitt, recognising the impossibility of this, disagreed, stressing that the British people would resent the consequences of any war entered into on Hanover's account, with dire consequences for the monarchy. Pitt's view was that, rather than indemnify Hanover in advance, it would be preferable to make good any harm done as a result of a brief occupation of Hanover by a foreign Power. Pitt would not back any subsidy treaty with Russia if it would later hinder Britain's ability to fight France. Perhaps unsurprisingly, George II did not want Pitt as Secretary and there was no possibility of an agreement on these terms. Consequently, Pitt was passed over for a Secretaryship of State.[32]

As British commerce expanded, trading stations sprang up which evolved into colonies. The relationship between such settlements and the Navy was symbiotic: the settlements relied on the Navy to contribute towards their security, but the Navy also depended upon the settlements. Ships were not self-supporting: they required to refresh, re-victual and replace other supplies; they required secure harbours and bases in which they could refit. As trading stations and settlements developed into colonies, they also contributed to greater sea-power through the development of both a seafaring population and of trade of their own.[33]

Whenever settlements remained underdeveloped, possibly isolated and having only a proportion of a small population capable of defending itself, such colonies were vulnerable to attack by relatively small forces. On the other hand, those colonies with guaranteed reinforcement could defend themselves and even expand aggressively. Such reinforcement could only come from the parent country, so sea-power provided the means to secure and maintain the maritime link back to Britain. It was due to sea-power that Britain, when conflict escalated, was able to maintain local superiority in the face of French efforts thanks to her strong maritime forces.[34]

Further, sea-power prepared the ground work, providing Britain strong foundations in other parts through trade. British East India trade predated French ingress and encroachment. Unlike the French who were hampered by Royal interference, the relatively unregulated British trade had fostered a scale which gave her a marked advantage later when competition escalated into armed struggle. Britain had more colonies and a larger volume of shipping, both of which provided a competitive advantage, and all this stemmed from a trading impulse.[35]

In the intervening, ostensibly peaceful, years, competition between France and Britain continued in India and North America. In India, Joseph, Marquis Dupleix, the Governor-General of French territories in India, caused tensions which interfered with trade, but he also withheld bad news from Versailles, so he was recalled to France. In North America, collisions between

32 Simms, *Three Victories*, pp.403-405.
33 Baugh, *Global Seven Years War*, p.3.
34 Richmond, *National Policy*, p.163.
35 Baugh, *Global Seven Years War*, pp.66-71.

the French and British colonial levies over disputed frontiers resulted in open combat. During the several years' truce, France had set about attempting to restore some of her sea-power. However, although her trade had revived, the British Royal Navy still had double the number of her warships and an even greater actual superiority in terms of experience and understanding of naval operations. Live operations had filtered out the less able commanders. All these factors gave Britain a preponderance which could not be matched through mere shipbuilding. The combination of numerical strength and ability was to prove particularly potent.[36]

Regarding the situation in North America, the term 'truce' would be a misnomer, as the colonists were virtually uncontrollable by government so distant in the homeland, particularly when egged on by the assertions of the 'Patriot' element in Britain that a struggle for global dominance was afoot.[37] Both countries had skirmished in their colonies for years without a state of war existing between them. Previous clashes with the French in North America had seemed like inconsequential localised squabbles. Britain had had her share of comparative successes and failures in the past without marked change. The difference now was in outlook and vocabulary. Furthermore, the full weight of sea-power could tip the balance beyond limited localised collisions.

In America, the dispute matured as the French tried to impose order in the area between the south shore of Lake Erie and the Ohio's headwaters, an area sought by both Britain and France. Michel-Ange Duquesne came out as Governor of New France with instructions to expel the British from the disputed zone. In doing so, he drove out or imprisoned traders from the English Ohio Company. They had been sent by Company shareholders, influential businessmen of Maryland and Virginia with a concession from the British Crown.[38] The clash was inevitable. A small command under Colonel George Washington was obliged to surrender at Fort Necessity. Although no-one yet realised it, the Seven Years War had started.

The West – Europe and America

As the Canadian conflict smouldered, it is all too easy to reflect with hindsight on Newcastle's unconvincing opening shots compared to Pitt's determination and resolve when the war was at its peak.[39] This is, perhaps, an unfair comparison. There are many subsequent examples of British underinvestment in war effort during the early phases of a large conflict. Pitt's blunt energy was in stark contrast with Newcastle's prim approach, yet Newcastle's strategic lines of development were broadly appropriate. His initial moves were reasonable and, if the energy he injected was inadequate in reality, it certainly seemed proportionate for his perception of the

36 Baugh, *Global Seven Years War*, pp.66-71.
37 P. Kennedy, *The Rise and Fall of Great Powers* (London: Harper Collins, 1989), p.143.
38 Corbett, *The Seven Years War*, p.12.
39 Corbett, *The Seven Years War*, pp.13-14.

challenge on the Ohio. The British were initially surprised by the aggressive initiative and the resourcefulness of the French Canadians and their native allies. Newcastle's 'strategic defensive' from which an offensive might be later launched, his war of 'limited object', suggests that he did not anticipate unlimited war.[40]

How was Britain to act? Would she act offensively or defensively? The decision was to opt for the latter. As it presented itself to Newcastle in 1754, the Ohio affair was a challenge to British citizens' legitimate trade in that buffer zone. It was assumed that such a challenge could not possibly have stemmed from direct orders from France but, rather, as a result of misguided local initiative. Newcastle assumed that a stiff show of force would bring about a prompt denial from Versailles.[41] If, on the other hand, France declared its open support for Duquesne, then the situation was entirely different and, as Newcastle perceptively, and anxiously, wrote to George Keppel, 3rd Earl of Albemarle, 'We then begin the war'.[42] This phrase captures the tragic recognition of the risk involved.

Early in 1755 Major General Edward Braddock sailed with a British naval squadron and 400 men embarked to prevent a sizeable French force of 3,000 from putting in to America. This was designed to isolate Louisbourg. Today such acts would be considered nakedly aggressive, but in the eighteenth century such Colonial operations were considered to be 'hostile intercourse short of war'.[43] To attack Louisbourg blatantly would have been a different matter altogether, a frank act of war. The skill and subtlety of Newcastle's moves was that France could not take exception without admitting her own sins. Newcastle wrote to Albemarle, 'You will try such a turn to these defensive measures as may make the French ministers ashamed to claim of them'.[44]

Newcastle's initial gambit was intended simply to capture some territory in North America. Although recognizing the risks, he did not yet anticipate an unlimited war. Later however, under Pitt, it would become just that – a war which would decide who out of Britain or France would emerge as a power.[45] If Newcastle's initial moves seem modest, it may be that Pitt's heroic reputation became built on an almost unlimited object, that of the destruction of France as a maritime and colonial power.

Early in the conflict the French showed that they were certainly the equals, if not more than a match for, their British opponents in Canada and the Atlantic. Perplexingly, Britain's initial efforts failed. In July 1755 Braddock was defeated through 'absurd adherence to European tactics' at Monongahela.[46] Further, the French fleet, carrying the new Governor-General, Pierre de Rigaud, Marquis de Vaudreil and *Maréchal de Camp*

---

40 Corbett, *The Seven Years War*, p.22.
41 Corbett, *The Seven Years War*, p.13.
42 Corbett, *The Seven Years War*, p.13.
43 Corbett, *The Seven Years War*, p.21.
44 Corbett, *The Seven Years War*, p.21.
45 Baugh, *Global Seven Years War*, pp.79-83.
46 Anderson, *Crucible of War*, p.103.

Jean-Armand, Baron de Dieskau successfully evaded a blocking force under Vice Admiral Edward Boscawen, made successful landfall and then returned to France. Yet another French squadron carried *Lieutenant Général* Louis Joseph, Marquis de Montcalm and a further 1,000 troops from Brest, contributing to his seizing command of the Great Lakes, a vital precursor for further Canadian operations. In November 1755, in the Commons, some Members of Parliament feared that pursuit of the war in the colonies would be ruinous, and that those colonies could be sacrificed and then later recovered as part of a peace settlement. They preferred to use British expenditure to purchase allies in Europe.

Pitt refused, rounding on the Hanoverian foreign policy with its subsidy treaties: 'This unsizable project, impracticable and desperate as it is... will, if fully pursued, bring bankruptcy upon Great Britain'. The vast sums required needed to fund such an idea would be to the detriment of:

> [T]he maintenance of our just and necessary war in North America. And when we consider that such immense issues of money, out-measuring any experiment of past time, are to be supplied by new loans, heaped upon a debt of eighty millions, who will answer for the consequence, or insure us from the fate of the decayed states of antiquity.[47]

Emphasising the role of the Royal Navy, he was critical of the failure to make adequate provision for the defence of North America. He provided a notably Whiggish interpretation of the King's position, 'to load our posterity with intolerable burdens' – that the King owed a supreme service to his people. Consequently, he was sacked as Paymaster and his attacks in parliament made less impact, although he reverted to his stance that the Ministry could not be trusted with either the country or its constitution.

Britain could not go to war without a guarantee of Hanoverian neutrality. Equally, Britain could not ensure Holland's freedom from harm. If those could be made certain, Britain could restrict the war to the colonies and the oceans, both areas where Britain had a preponderance. Then France could probably be forced to agree terms, but this view failed to take account of either Austria's disdain for Britain's previous lacklustre support, or Britain's inability to control Prussia's atavistic ambition. Prussia under Frederick II was emerging as a European great power and a more promising and useful guarantor, initially at least, than Austria of Hanover's security: Britain's 'continental sword'.[48] The 1756 Convention of Westminster of 13 January tied Prussia in to Britain's policy of defensive European alliances.[49]

Austria signed the First Treaty of Versailles with France on 1 May 1756. This 'Diplomatic Revolution' ruined Britain's containment policy towards

47 John Almon (ed.), *Anecdotes of the Life of the Right Honourable William Pitt, Earl of Chatham: And of the Principal Events of His Time: With His Speeches in Parliament, from the year 1736 to the year 1778* (London: L. B. Seeley, 1797), pp.239-241, speech given before Parliament 13 November 1755.

48 Black, 'Pitt the Elder', pp.35-51.

49 Simms, *Three Victories*, pp. 353-354, 403.

France and saw Austria, meant to be the protector of the Dutch 'Barrier', now allied with the hostile camp.

The last war had hardly been over for six years and still loomed large in the consciousness of European statesmen. At the same time, however, there was an unhealed rift between Prussia and Austria. Frederick of Prussia's ambition, coupled with his almost feral sense of self-preservation, was the new and almost unpredictable aspect. For Britain the colonial situation was now complicated by the growing crisis on the continent of Europe. The moment of the colonial dispute coming to a head happened to occur just as Frederick, aiming to prevent an Austrian attempt to regain Silesia, made a pre-emptive strike on Saxony.

War was formally declared between Britain and France on 17 May 1756.

Admiral Byng's failure to prevent the French from capturing the British colony of Minorca in May 1756 provided a surprise reverse, and an opening for Pitt to return to office as Secretary of State when the Duke of Devonshire's Ministry preferred to have Pitt on the inside on its benches rather than criticizing from the outside. As a result, Pitt became the Government's principal spokesman in the House of Commons. Byng's court-martial and subsequent execution, on the grounds that he withdrew in the face of the enemy, reveals another factor, the effect of the London mob. The mob could be ugly, vociferous and aggressive. Angry that Byng's failings would be covered up by his peers, the mob had demanded a scapegoat, threatening, 'Save Byng, and lose your King.'[50]

For Britain, the crisis worsened and became even more complicated as all the British forts and factories in Bengal were captured and Calcutta fell to Siraj-ud-Daulah, the last independent Nawab of Bengal. Worse was yet to come: a feint invasion from Europe was staged in the English Channel; and just as the overall situation seemed to be at its most dire at the end of 1756, Frederick of Prussia launched his Continental war and requested British naval assistance in the Baltic.

Pitt was too weak politically at this time to carry out his 'Patriot' programme, which was intended to block subsidy treaties meant to buy the support of Continental rulers. However, the speech which he wrote on behalf of the King, and which was delivered in Parliament on 2 December 1756 insisted that 'the succour and preservation of America cannot but constitute a main object of my attention and solicitude'.[51]

Pitt's main effort was to be North America. It was imperative to gain the upper hand in Canada, and this could only be achieved through naval superiority which would protect and enable the safe passage of the army. 12,000 troops sailed to invade Canada with an escort of 15 ships of the line. The first staging post was to be Halifax, from which Louisbourg, the door to the St Lawrence, would be retaken. However, on leaving Halifax, the British force discovered a sizeable French fleet which had left Brest and Toulon and was blocking the route. The attack by sea was delayed. Simultaneously, Montcalm was exploiting his advantage and starting to squeeze the land routes to New York. More strenuous efforts were required and the power of the Royal

50 B. Lavery, *Empire of the Seas* (London: Conway, 2012), p.43.

51 Black, 'Pitt the Elder', p.40.

Navy was exerted to protect the sea routes and tighten control of the Atlantic and Mediterranean. Boscawen, now in command of the Canada Squadron, was strengthened. Off Cartagena Admiral Osborn struck a blow against the French Toulon Squadron. Admiral Edward Hawke dispersed yet another fleet in the Aix Roads. Off Halifax, the French squadron which had so successfully prevented the attack on Louisbourg lost its advantage by returning to France.[52]

In spite of Pitt's resolute commitment to the Atlanticist point of view, a French advance into Germany having threatened Prussia's western flank, he had to agree in February 1757 with a request for monies needed to defend Hanover and also its ally, Frederick of Prussia. In order to meet George's obligations to Frederick, a suitable means might be by supporting an Army of Observation made up mainly by Hanoverians and Hessians[53]. Pitt carried this off, in spite of Hanover's unpopularity (the 'despicable Electorate of Hanover') by his emphasis on the necessity for supporting the Protestant hero, Frederick.[54] Prussia was faced by the prospect of simultaneous attacks by four hostile powers from all points of the compass. However, events in Germany did not go to plan and Hanover was overrun by the French in 1757. The Duke of Cumberland, Commander of the Army of Observation, was obliged to sign the Convention of Kloster Zeven, leaving the French in control and incurring the wrath of his father in the process.[55] This demonstrated Hanover's comparative limitations on several counts: by having land borders; by having limited power in diplomacy; and by not having a large army.

Spring and Summer of 1757 saw Pitt's political crisis at its apogee. He lost office, effectively rendering the Government rudderless for three months. The war was not going well, and Britain had lost the initiative on many fronts. Yet Pitt's return to office in Newcastle's ministry in the August restored the vital spark. It came about largely through his reputation with the public. Newcastle entrusted Pitt with additional responsibility and he came to dominate the Cabinet.

Pitt cannot have found the issue of Hanover easy to juggle as he had contradictory obligations to Patriot opinion and to the Government. By the winter of 1757 he had a significant part in creating a political settlement, tying British direction of the defence of Hanover with the Prussian alliance. He had already almost anticipated as much when he had supported the original grant for the Army of Observation in Parliament. Much of the cost of that army now fell to Britain, which also agreed a subsidy for Prussia: George's price for renouncing the Kloster Zeven treaty and re-joining the war. Achieving the necessary parliamentary support for these measures was an indication of Pitt's persuasive powers of oratory, his popularity and ability in strategic communication.[56] Meanwhile Frederick had reversed his dire position through two stunning victories at Rossbach and Leuthen.

52 Anderson, *Crucible of War*, pp.208-209.

53 F.A.J. Szabo, *The Seven Years' War in Europe 1756-1763* (Harlow: Pearson, 2008), p.76.

54 P. Bobbit, *The Shield of Achilles* (London: Allen Lane, 2002), p.132.

55 L. Worsley, *Courtiers. The Secret History of the Georgian Court* (London: Faber & Faber, 2011), p.309.

56 Black, 'Pitt the Elder', p.41.

In Canada, 1758 did not start well. At the tactical level, several early British operations were unsuccessful, not being adapted to local circumstances. Abercromby's failure to capture Ticonderoga had not helped, causing nervousness in the American colonies. However important strategic linkages began to kick-in, contributing to wider success. For example, at sea, having regained maritime superiority through enhanced efforts in the Bay of Biscay, off Gibraltar and off the coast of Canada, Boscawen manoeuvred Major General Jeffrey Amherst, soon to become Commander-in Chief of British forces in America, and 12,000 men onto a position where the combined effects of manpower and ships outnumbered the French opponents in Louisbourg.

On the credit side, lessons were quickly identified and assimilated, allowing later victories. Examples would be trail blazing, light land tactics, and amphibious 'descents', the latter being particularly supported by Pitt. These lessons contributed to the capture of Fort Duquesne and Louisbourg itself. Its fall in August 1758 opened the waterways into the interior depth of Canada. Yet at sea the French squadron off Louisbourg had managed to impose a delay and the season was becoming advanced. The net result was to postpone any attack on Quebec for another year.

However, on the French side the situation was precarious and Canada looked doomed to fall without reinforcement or unless affairs in Europe could impose a general peace.

The East

On the other side of the world, parallel events of equal significance, even if on a smaller scale, were underway in India. Both sides had roughly 2,000 European combatants, but the French had built up a much larger native army through their strenuous political pursuits. Overall, the French had greater political influence and possessed larger territories, mainly through Dupleix's scheming. In spite of those territorial advantages, her sea-power was inferior. The British had a naval squadron in the waters of East India under Vice Admiral Charles Watson. The British East India Company was thriving while its French rival was in danger of catastrophic decline. This imbalance was proved when war broke out.

The disparity in naval strength was all too apparent to the French themselves and they had intended to send a squadron in 1755, but Britain managed to use her stronger sea power to dominate the enemy, drawing and fixing him off course. This was accomplished by trusted, experienced commanders who fully understood their role, what was expected of them and that they could employ initiative. It also highlighted the need for any force to have sufficient elements capable of being commanded and operating independently around the globe. Watson ferried Lieutenant Colonel Robert Clive and an expedition to Calcutta where, in 1757, Clive took revenge for the 'Black Hole', seized Chandernagore from the enemy and expelled them from the province. At Plassey Clive trounced Siraj-ud-Daulah, securing Bengal.[57]

57 Baugh, *Global Seven Years War*, pp.282-295.

On land, however, the French still had capacity to act and to surprise. While the British fleet was elsewhere, France attacked the Coromandel Coast, taking Masulipatam and the Northern Circars.

Pocock, Watson's successor, hounded his French opposite number D'Ache, seizing the French base at Karikal as a launching pad to be able to cling to D'Ache and to cling to him in order to force a conclusive engagement. Under such constant, unremitting pressure D'Ache, fearful for his own communications and supplies, eventually withdrew to the Mauritius, giving up the contest.[58] For the British, the effects were felt almost immediately as the pressure of a twin land and sea attack on Madras was abandoned by the French land force commander, Thomas Arthur, Comte de Lally. On the other hand, the winter monsoons forced Pocock to seek refuge in Bombay in 1758. Lally made another attempt on Madras but without resupply and reinforcement from the sea the siege was raised, while the British had been able to relieve and save the city from the sea. The effect of sucking rival naval forces from one area to another was further demonstrated by drawing de Bussy, a subordinate of Dupleix, from Hyderabad to support coastal operations. This further damaged French standing with the locals. Naval actions were clearly significant factors in the operations themselves, but there was also a wider effect on policy generally.

While Britain had relative freedom of action on the sea to transport her forces from home to India, and then wherever she needed on the Indian coast, as long as she was determined to win she could do. Clive understood this full well, as shown in his correspondence to Pitt in January 1759:

> The superiority of our squadron and the plenty of money and supplies of all kinds which our friends on the coast will be furnished with from this province (Bengal), while the enemy are in total want of everything, without any visible means of redress – an advantage as, if properly attended to, cannot fail of wholly effecting their ruin in that as well as in every other part of India.[59]

58 F. McLynn, *1759, The Year Britain Became Master of the World* (London: Pimlico, 2005), p.187.

59 Richmond, *National Policy*, pp.180-181.

3

The French Army in the Mid-Eighteenth Century

This chapter will use the French Army as a model to describe a typical mid-eighteenth century army.[1] The succeeding chapter will highlight differences between the allies and the French, and also between the British Army and those of the various German states.

A description of a common layout introduces the reader to the three principal arms of the period: the foot, or infantry; the horse, or cavalry; and the artillery.[2] The small arms of the mid-eighteenth century had changed little in the previous 50 years and all armies employed the flintlock musket, with a smooth bore, which, despite being relatively inaccurate and of short effective range, was lethal at close quarters. The pike had been replaced by the long, slim bayonet.

The standard, long-established, tactics fell into two main categories: sieges, the reduction or defence of fortified sites, often following standardised procedures; and doing battle with an opponent in the open field.

The typical sort of fighting of the Seven Years War required high degrees of proficiency and discipline. An army of the 1750s would routinely deploy initially with two, or possibly three, lines of infantry, spaced by about 200 metres. If the flanks were not anchored by a defensible position or by some obstacle such as a high ground or a river, it was common practice to place cavalry on one or both wings: if the flanks were so anchored, the bulk of the cavalry would generally be put behind the infantry, in reserve.[3] Infantry battalions often had their own, organic, light artillery, while the heavier guns would be held to the rear. Light cavalry, if the army had any, might be deployed in advance of the army, providing a scouting function. Elements of the army would be manoeuvred until the climax of musketry at close range, possibly with attempts to turn the enemy flanks with infantry or cavalry.

1 For an overview of this topic, see 'French Army', *Seven Years' War*, <http://www.kronoskaf.com/syw/index.php?title=French_Army> (accessed 15 January–31 October 2019).

2 Digby Smith, *Armies of the Seven Years War. Commanders, Equipment, Uniforms and Strategies of the 'First World War'* (Stroud: Spellmount, 2012), pp 9-17.

3 Smith, *Armies of the Seven Years War*, p.9.

Once the enemy had been sufficiently reduced by attrition, or was showing signs of wavering, the commander might order a bayonet charge to dominate the field.[4]

There were, of course, other functions necessary for success on operations: headquarters; engineering; veterinary; logistic (including the supply and maintenance of materiel, transport, catering); medical; provost; chaplaincy.

The Infantry

Line infantry were the pawns of the battlefield. Relatively inexpensive to recruit, equip and train, the infantry was moderately expendable.[5] As often occurs, the end of the War of the Austrian Succession saw cost cutting measures introduced as reforms: 18 French and several foreign regiments were disbanded, their grenadier companies being retained and amalgamated into the Grenadiers de France; battalions were reduced by cutting their companies from 15 to 13; battalion colours were reduced in number to one, the Colonel's Colour being retained by the first fusilier company of the first battalion.

The standard unit of infantry was, as it remains, the battalion. Each battalion was sub-divided into companies (usually of about 100 men), and further into platoons. By a regulation of 17 August 1757, a French infantry regiment would have one company of grenadiers and seventeen companies of fusiliers providing, in theory, 35 officers and 685 other ranks. In the field, the internal organisation of battalions was adjusted. Companies were paired into platoons (a terminology which seems counterintuitive today), which were further paired into divisions. If the grenadiers were removed to make up a 'converged' grenadier battalion, the picquet company would assume the grenadier role, and another company would be nominated to take its place as second picquet company. It was not until the year after Minden that *Maréchal* Broglie introduced light, or chasseur, companies in his *Instruction pour l'Infanterie* and Smith describes the French as being prepared to put up with smaller companies and squadrons than other armies.[6]

	Left									Right
Companies		2&10	4&12	6&14	8&16	15&7	13&5	11&3	9&1	
Platoons	Picquet	2nd	4th	6th	8th	7th	5th	3rd	1st	Grenadiers
Divisions		2nd		4th		3rd		1st		

Tactical formation of a French battalion deployed Line (*Ordre Mince*)

4 Christopher Duffy, *The Military Experience in the Age of Reason* (London: Wordsworth Military Library, 1998), p.206.

5 For an overview, see R. Chartrand, *Louis XV's Army (2) French Infantry* (London: Osprey, 1996).

6 Smith, *Armies of the Seven Years War*, p.38.

Theoretically of about 720 souls, in reality under-recruitment, sickness, injury, straggling and desertion would see a battalion undermanned. It was not uncommon for a battalion to take to the field with 550 all-ranks (1757 estimate by de Cornillon, the *major général d'infanterie*) or 20 per cent undermanned. Battalions might be grouped together into brigades of three to five battalions, with those battalions belonging in some cases to a single large regiment and in others to two or more smaller ones.

To deal with under-manning practically, instructions were in place for reorganising internally, always aiming to be able to produce a symmetrical body of troops, three deep and of an even numbered frontage. Once platoons had been made up, any soldiers left over might be assigned to the Picquet company.

Many regiments in the French service had existed as private entities long before the Seven Years War, and some retained Royal, or province, titles. Others bore the name of the then colonel-in-chief, who would buy it from, and hold it on behalf of, the sovereign, the title changing with each colonel-in-chief. This entitled the colonel to draw an allowance from the state for the maintenance of the unit. Shrewd, and in some instances dubious, husbandry could mean that a colonel might become rich at the expense of the regiment.

Regiments were distinguished by the colour of their coats and facings, their lace and by the regimental colour. Orders were transmitted by drum beat, each battalion certainly, and company possibly, having several drummers.

In those regiments of multiple battalions, a fairly rigid concept of seniority guided the positions of honour in their placement. This was mirrored down through divisions and platoons, only the grenadiers being permitted some advantageous leeway.

In the War of the Spanish Succession, France had employed, to good effect, troops as skirmishers to suppress the enemy while attacking villages, hedges, woods and vineyards. Whilst this practice had subsequently fallen into neglect, irregular companies had started to be created in the War of the Austrian Succession, and the Seven Years War saw the gradual reintroduction of skirmishing tactics by the French and the adoption of light infantry. Their mode of skirmishing was copied simultaneously as a result of actions in the Balkans and in Canada. Trained to operate in open order and loose formations, skirmishers were of value in piqueting, in skirmishing to the fore, flanks and rear of an army. Units in a skirmishing role were allowed latitude in fire control, frequently being allowed to fire at will.

Line infantry used the muzzle-loading, smoothbore, flintlock musket. French muskets were perhaps slightly more accurate than other nations', but the difference was negligible in practice. The musket had a range of about 300 metres, but realistically an effective range of about 80 metres, although some French authorities recorded from experiments that any shots fired beyond 155 metres would be unlikely to reach a man-sized target without correcting for elevation (Lombard) and that any beyond 233 metres were a complete waste of ammunition (Guibert and Cotty). At 37 metres, the hit ratio was high, virtually 100 percent. At 46 metres, shots would consistently hit a man's torso, and a man's figure at 68 metres. At 91 metres, 25 percent of shots hit the target. An average soldier could achieve a rate of fire of 2-3 rounds per minute, although this would fall off with fouling and misfires, which might account for about one in six attempts. He would carry about 50 shots on his person, with a further resupply held centrally.[7]

To fire in *l'Ordre Mince*, the front rank would kneel on the right knee. The second rank would stand, leaning slightly to the right with their right foot at right angles, eight centimetres behind the left. The third rank would also stand, placing their muskets between the gaps in the second rank and placing their right foot eight centimetres behind the left.

The 1754 regulation described firing by battalion, rank, half-rank, platoon and section. The 1755 ordonnance directed that fire should commence at the battalion's centre and radiate outwards. In reality, fire discipline might sometimes break down, or the men might even be permitted to fire individually at best speed – *Feu de billebaude*.[8] By 1761, Broglie had decided to direct the army to employ volley fire along the whole front of a battalion, using only the front two ranks.

The theory of rate, accuracy and effectiveness of musketry was all very well when conducted in peacetime on flat parade grounds. However, soldiers who have experienced real combat know that shooting becomes far less exact, and that the ground, weather, light conditions and obscuration inevitably have adverse effects. Furthermore, not all soldiers respond at the same rate and with the same precision, so formations can experience gaps or overlaps. Weapon-handling and loading can be prone to error, even with well-drilled troops. Technical malfunctions also occur. If this has been true down the ages, how much more so in an age of pouring powder from cartridges into barrels and priming pans, of the need to ram the powder and ball fully home, of ensuring that the flint is sparking properly? Lastly, there is the human factor, of soldiers under pressure, possibly overwhelmed by fatigue, thirst and the whole experience. The French were fully aware that all of these factors could reduce the accuracy and effect of musketry.

A smoothbore musket is fairly simple and easy to reload, even if relatively inaccurate. Rifling the barrel by cutting spiralled grooves imparts a spin on the round, giving greater accuracy.[9] This technique was not new by the time of the Seven Years War, but it was a more costly process and slowed the reload rate by about 200-300 percent. In consequence, rifles were never on general issue. However, at Minden, a British eyewitness, Lieutenant Hugh Montgomery of the 12th Regiment of Foot, describes grenadiers on the French side having them.[10]

---

7 'French Line Infantry Tactic', *Seven Years' War*, at <http://www.kronoskaf.com/syw/index.php?title=French_Line_Infantry_Tactic > (accessed 15 January 2019 – 31 October 2019).

8 David Blackmore, *Destructive & Formidable. British Infantry Firepower 1642-1765* (Barnsley: Frontline Books, 2014), p.121.

9 K-M. Klass in W. Seele (ed.), *Die Schlacht bei Minden 1759* (Minden: J.C.C. Bruns, 1959), p.56.

10 Quoted in H.C. Wylly, *History of the King's Own Yorkshire Light Infantry* (London: Humphries, 1926), p.48.

For conduct on operations, three successive instructions were issued on 29 June 1753, 14 May 1754 and 6 May 1755.[11] The Seven Years War was a period of tactical experimentation and innovation, including debates over lines versus columns and the employment of skirmishers and battalion guns.

To deploy an army for battle, infantry would depart its encampment and march to its battle positions in column, before deploying into line. Unlike their highly-drilled Prussian opponents, the French infantry were not trained to a peak which easily enabled rapid transition. As a solution, some commanders advocated approaching a battle in six columns which made it slightly more straightforward to form line. On the march, regiments would leave only three paces between platoons. In line, battalions would be separated by only 12 paces.

In battle, and when firing, most European infantry battalions formed lines, three to four ranks deep, the front rank often kneeling to present, and then one or more ranks firing.[12] While four ranks offered good depth against cavalry, the rear rank became slightly redundant in firing, so the Prussians adopted three ranks in 1742, with the French copying them in 1754 and the Austrians adopting the same during the course of the Seven Years War. In the eighteenth century, attempts were being made to experiment with sustaining fire, an important concept given the time between shots during the reload sequence. Options for this included firing by rank, or by subdivisions in order that an element of the battalion would be loaded and ready to fire at all times. In reality, though, this orderly fire control system often disintegrated in combat, with every man loading, firing and reloading as best he could.

Any discussion of the French Army in the Seven Years War ought to include mention of the debate between *L'Ordre Mince* (line) and *L'Ordre Profond* (column). The debate which began in this war was to rumble on in France for the remainder of the century. Those proponents who argued in favour of line, where musket fire was thought to win the engagement, believed that line would allow the maximum number of barrels to be brought to bear. Those in favour of the column believed in the psychological shock created by a column at least six deep, advancing with bristling bayonets.

From 1754 the French line was formalised at three ranks deep. However, that same year at field exercises at the camp at Gray, both formations were practised, *l'Ordre Profond* being used to trial attack against units in *l'Ordre Mince*:

> Being at 120 paces from the enemy, the grenadiers, the picquets and the battalions of the wings moved 20 paces forward, and fired. During this march and this fire, which covered movements in the rear, the three battalions of the centre doubled their ranks, recalling detached troops, and marched at double-step on the enemy line, breaking through its centre.[13]

11 J.L. Vial, 'Formation d'un régiment d'infanterie en bataille durant la Guerre de Sept Ans', *Nec Pluribus Impar*, <http://www.vial.jean.fr/new_npi/achives/archiv.htm> (accessed 15 January–31 October 2019).

12 Duffy, *The Military Experience in the Age of Reason*, p.110.

13 'French Line Infantry Tactic', *Seven Years' War*, at <http://www.kronoskaf.com/syw/index.php?title=French_Line_Infantry_Tactic> (accessed 9 September 2021).

L'Ordre Profond was the preferred formation for an attack on an enemy position, breaking through an enemy line, storming a redoubt or assaulting a village. The attack would be delivered at least six ranks deep, at double pace, and with bayonets fixed. The emphasis was very much on the offensive action, without pausing to fire. The 1753 instruction stated that in training exercises, whilst battalions were to rehearse shooting from three ranks, they must never be allowed to get used to firing from six ranks.

Forming a column six ranks deep had previously been executed through a rather complex series of movements, but the ordonnance of 1755 simplified this considerably with the aim of a smooth transition.[14] It stipulated that an attack column would be formed by doubling up platoons, one in front of the other with no spacing, and that the ideal column would be two battalions together. The centre two divisions would advance together about five metres, and then the wing divisions would close in from the sides, taking up position immediately behind the two centre divisions. The grenadiers and the picquets would remain to the fore of the column, in three ranks which would fire as the column attacked.

As stated, in theory there was to be no firing from six ranks, and yet practical experience showed a need to be able to maintain firing. This was accomplished by the *Feu de Chaussée*, or street-firing, whereby each man at the head of the column would contribute to firing a volley, and then would march rapidly to the rear, to re-form and reload.

L'Ordre Profond was used at Rossbach where French infantry charges in column were effectively halted by rapid, effective fire by the Prussian infantry in line.[15]

The 1755 regulation directed two other situations when the column should be employed: the column of march; and the column of retreat. Broglie was an enthusiast of the column of march, as it permitted rapid deployment in a formation with which one could fight if necessary. Until then, converting from column of route into battle arrangements was rather clumsy. A column of retreat was not optimised for resisting enemy cavalry charges, in the event of which the column would need to re-form into a square.

During the first campaigns of 1757 and 1758, the French Army deployed in battle in two lines, each of three ranks with about 300 paces between the lines.[16]

Officially, for the campaign of 1759, there was a radical change in tactics which was imposed centrally by the Ministry. In April 1759, *Maréchal* Belle-Isle, Minister of War, wrote to *Maréchal* Contades, directing him to organise infantry at camp and in battle in six ranks, and to practise the exercises in six ranks:

---

14 'French Line Infantry Tactic', *Seven Years' War*, at <http://www.kronoskaf.com/syw/index.php?title=French_Line_Infantry_Tactic> (accessed 9 September 2021).

15 Szabo, *The Seven Years' War in Europe 1756-1763*, p.97.

16 'French Line Infantry Tactic', *Seven Years' War*, at <http://www.kronoskaf.com/syw/index.php?title=French_Line_Infantry_Tactic> (accessed 9 September 2021).

> Versailles, 9 April, 1759
>
> Monsieur,
> The King has been informed that in the last two campaigns his troops have only faced the enemy in three ranks. You will recall that, in 1754 when His Majesty ordered a reduction of the four ranks in which the infantry had previously formed, he only intended this to facilitate firing, and he had also ordered that infantry would double its lines to be in six ranks, and that it should practise this. Although the Ordonnance of May 6, 1755, states that infantry will have to manoeuvre in both three and in six ranks, his Majesty's intention was that his regiments should most normally be formed in six ranks when they were ready to fight. And he is advised that the desire to maintain our troops in lines of three ranks to bring fire on an enemy, when there is no obstacle between them and the enemy can only diminish the the ardour of the French soldier, and cause us to lose the advantage we have always from the vivacity of our charge, which must be the more impetuous as the body of troops has greater depth. His Majesty has directed me to have the honour to inform you that his intention is that in order to accustom troops to this formation, they will always march and be arranged in six ranks at all times. The only exception to this is when the case arises that they must fire on an enemy whom it is impossible to close with. Consequently, you are to issue orders to the Colonels of infantry under your command to ensure they practise this regularly.[17]

After the first disastrous campaigns of the war, the Minister wanted to adopt a more offensive tactical formation and the influence of Jean Charles, Chevalier Folard, a student of Caesar and Polybius, is evident. Readers may be amused to read that Folard was elected a member of the Royal Society in London in 1750. *Maréchal* Belle-Isle was his faithful disciple until the end of his life and he appreciated some of his innovative ideas, preferring spirited offensive action in deep order to a musketry battle. In 1750 he had written to Marc René, Marquis d'Argenson, an army reformer and Inspector of Cavalry and Dragoons, 'Our custom was to hold our fire, and to accept the enemy's fire, which we regarded as defeated as soon as we could reach it'.[18]

However, it appears that this arrangement never caught on, so much so that the practice of manoeuvring in three ranks became the standard. Joly de Mezeroy, who served in the French Army during the Seven Years War, a supporter of the deep order, wrote in the introduction to his *Théorie de la Guerre* published in 1777: 'In 1758, *Maréchal* Belle Isle, then Minister of War, issued an order which confirmed charging and manoeuvring at six ranks; but the German style prevailed and the regulation was only ever observed in exercises'.[19]

---

17 Personal communication from Jean-Louis Vial, creator of the *Nec Pluribus Impar* website. E-mail, subject 'Minden 1759' (10 February 2019).

18 Personal communication from Jean-Louis Vial. E-mail, subject 'Minden 1759' (10 February 2019).

19 Personal communication from Jean-Louis Vial. E-mail, subject 'Minden 1759' (10 February 2019).

Maréchal de Contades only partially applied these instructions. At Minden, he placed his infantry in a mixed order, some units in line yet others in column. He ordered each infantry brigade to form its first battalion in column and the remainder in line. In the attack, every battalion was to form column, but to maintain spacing between battalions to form line as needed.[20].

Maréchal Broglie's instructions to the infantry of 1760 and 1761, and those of *Maréchal* Soubise in 1762, were to deploy in three ranks, and this practice lasted until the end of the war.

Influenced by the late *Maréchal* de Saxe, victor of Fontenoy and proponent of manoeuvre, who believed that the strength of infantry lay in its legs, the French infantry introduced the cadenced step under the ordonnance of 1754. Various ordonnances of the 1750s formalised spacing and introduced a complicated range of paces. However, in the field a far more practical *pas de camp* (three feet, or just under one metre) was retained as the standard unit of measure for deploying troops and establishing camps.

It was common practice for each battalion to have its own section of pioneers, who were equipped with carpentry tools to help clear routes, dealing with obstacles and improvising small bridges.

The Cavalry

As the preceding century ended, the doctrine for cavalry was not particularly clear. By the Seven Years War, the 'Caracole', a technique which saw the cavalry circulating while firing and then charging home, had fallen into disuse. The disappearance of the pike and its replacement with the bayonet, and the ponderous loading sequence of the musket, meant that cavalrymen were emboldened to attempt the charge which would shock enemy infantry. Turenne had favoured the *charge en sauvages* (the savage charge) and Condé sought a charge with swords, at the gallop, by large formations. Unlike its Prussian opponents which, by the Seven Years War, had been fully drilled and rehearsed, the French cavalry suffered from a lack of formal instruction.[21]

Part of the reason for this had been the French system of accommodating its cavalry. A regiment would spend one year in a garrison, but the following two years in 'quarters', an arrangement under which regiments were dispersed by company among surrounding villages. There, a less rigorous approach was applied to the military routine. Undoubtedly the troopers and their officers enjoyed the freedom from constraints. The shortcomings of such a lax regime were recognised before the Seven Years War, and remedial instructional camps organised, but not sufficiently so to bring the French to Prussian standards.

20 Jomini, Baron de, *Traité des Grandes Opérations Militaires* (Paris: Magimel, Paris, 1811), Vol.III, pp. 29-40, translated from the French by Richard Couture.

21 For an overview of the French mounted arm, see R. Chartrand, *Louis XV's Army (2) French Cavalry & Dragoons* (London: Osprey, 1996); 'French Heavy Cavalry Tactic', *Seven Years' War*, <http://www.kronoskaf.com/syw/index.php?title=French_Heavy_Cavalry_Tactic> (accessed 15 January–31 October 2019).

The 1755 regulation on cavalry training refreshed the basics up to squadron level and promised more comprehensive regulations in future, but the war overtook this. There were many talented individual experts, including those who had risen through the ranks, and there were some cavalry schools, but there was no centralised cavalry doctrine. Instead, each regiment developed its own independent practices depending on its *Mestre de Camp.* Some regiments never progressed from being mediocre cavalrymen, capable only of charging as individuals at full pelt.

A French cavalry formation needed to accommodate varied levels of expertise in horsemanship. Therefore, regiments would deploy with gaps of about 80 metres between units. However, this would be compensated for by the second line which would overlap and close the gaps in sort of chess board pattern. In this, the French would differ from the Prussians, who usually presented an unbroken wall of horsemen. By 1760, though, Broglie was seeking to emulate the shock effect of the Prussians and directing that the French first line of cavalry should be unbroken while second could have spacing.

Regimental seniority was strictly observed and upheld, even on campaign, where the nature of the ground and obstacles, and also differing levels of fatigue and condition, might have required a more flexible interpretation. So, the positions of honour were invariably taken by those units which felt entitled to them, regardless of how tired their horses were. It was therefore quite possible that a smart regiment would insist on its normal position, even when exhausted, not only falling behind and hindering the rest, but being unable to exploit any opportunities as a result of the horses being blown. It could work the other way though, in that Royal household regiments, exempt from fatigue duties, and mounted on better chargers, might perform with more dash and energy than the average unit.

The French establishment placed the Gendarmerie de France as more senior, after the Maison du Roi, than any other part of the Army. The normal French cavalry regiments, of which there were 60 during the war, were called *Cavalerie Légère*, light cavalry, to distinguish them from the Maison du Roi and the Gendarmerie. Most had two squadrons.

The principal task of cavalry was to provide 'shock' action on the field.[22] The alignment of the front rank was considered crucial to optimize any shock effect on the enemy. It was usual to seek this alignment from the centre of the rank, those troopers on either side of the centre looking in and taking their dressing from it. The two cavalrymen in the very centre would take their cue from, and adjust according to the direction of, the squadron commander out in front, whose responsibility it was to set the correct direction from the middle. Under this system, there was a natural tendency for the troopers on the very extremities of the wings to veer towards the centre, causing crowding and creating disorder. An alternative was to dress by the right.

A French cavalry regiment would typically deploy for battle with two squadrons side by side, albeit once again with a space of about 20 metres. A

22 Duffy, *The Military Experience in the Age of Reason*, p.223.

squadron was expected to deploy with a minimum frontage of 42 men, but seldom in reality more than 48. Each horseman required one metre of space when in close order, so a squadron might take up between 42 and 48 metres. A regiment would therefore take up between 100 and 120 metres frontage.[23]

The regulations of 1754 and 1755 make it clear that the preferred arrangement for cavalry formations was two ranks. It was recognised that having a wider frontage contributed to the shock effect on the enemy, although the wider front made it harder to ensure the correct alignment.[24] The regulations allowed for deployment in three ranks, and even directed training in switching from three to two, and vice versa, in the field. However, the disadvantages of three ranks, notwithstanding the reduction in shock, included that the centre rank found it difficult to maintain a steady pace, being rather at the mercy of the two other ranks between which it was sandwiched. Also, once three became disorganised, it was more difficult to regain control. In reality, as most regiments invariably became undermanned, it was necessary to deploy in two ranks, and it became common practice for troopers to be moved from one company to another to even up the numbers necessary for two ranks, any surplus going into a third, and possibly incomplete, rank.

The charge was normally delivered in as solid a mass as possible, at the trot, breaking into a gallop at the end, when the charge went home. The trot made it easier to maintain control of the formation and to present a solid front, especially under battle conditions with noise, smoke obscuration and if the ground was broken, wet, frozen or strewn with debris. Further, the trot ensured that the mounts were spared and not blown too quickly. There needed to be a sort of 'crescendo' of pace, building speed up to a full gallop just before the moment of impact[25].

As has been noted, there was no single central French cavalry doctrine. However, *Maréchal* de Saxe wrote, prior to his death in 1750:

> When we charge, we must start at a jogging pace from a distance of 100 paces, increasing it as we approach and then break into a gallop; we must press the heels against the horse's sides only at 20 to 30 paces from the enemy, and this must be done by a commanding officer who shouts the order, '*A moi*' ('with me'). We must prepare the cavalry for this, and train it to ensure that this technique becomes second nature, so that it is quick as lightning: we must above all teach them to gallop fully extended. Any squadron which cannot charge 2,000 paces at varied speeds, without breaking up, will never be fit for war. This is the fundamental point: when your cavalry knows how to do that, it will be good, and everything else will seem easy.[26]

23 'French Heavy Cavalry Tactic', *Seven Years' War*, < http://www.kronoskaf.com/syw/index.php?title=French_Heavy_Cavalry_Tactic > (accessed 15 January–31 October 2019).

24 'French Heavy Cavalry Tactic', *Seven Years' War*, < http://www.kronoskaf.com/syw/index.php?title=French_Heavy_Cavalry_Tactic > (accessed 15 January–31 October 2019).

25 Duffy, *The Military Experience in the Age of Reason*, p.224.

26 Maurice Comte de Saxe, *Mes Rêveries. Ouvrage Posthume* (Amsterdam & Leipzig, Arkstee & Merkus, 1757; reprinted London, FB&c Ltd., 2021), p.105.

Maintaining alignment right up to the final moment was important, but a solid front was even more so, even if slightly uneven, as gaps would allow horses to run off line. This could break up the formation, interfere with neighbouring squadrons and cause a multitude of falls in the manner of a steeplechase.

The cavalry was issued with a sword, a carbine, and a pair of pistols. The issue swords were not always of the highest quality of steel, and widely regarded as being too short compared to those of the enemy. In some regiments, metal skullcaps and plastrons were issued.

The French cavalry charged with swords drawn, pistols being reserved for close use in mêlée. In preparation for the charge, swords were carried at the shoulder, with the sword knot on the wrist. Trumpet calls would signal the transition to walk, then trot. A third call would signal the change to a canter, at which point the cavalryman would raise his sword-arm to eye level, virtually fully extended, with a high line and a pronated guard, and the point inclining slightly downwards. As the charge developed to a full gallop, the horseman would raise himself on his stirrups, crouching forwards until the impact.

Dragoons were horse-mounted infantry, although they became increasingly used as medium cavalry. In the periods prior to, and after, the Seven Years War not every man in a regiment had a horse, for reasons of economy. However, in the Seven Years War all were mounted. When dismounted, they could be used as grenadiers in the assault, and as pioneers for clearing and erecting obstacles. Regulations of 18 August 1755 and 1 June 1756 fixed the establishment of a French dragoon regiment at 688, consisting of a regimental staff and four squadrons of 172.[27]

Hussars had first entered French service under King Louis XIV, when Hungarian mercenaries had sought recruitment. Hussars were regular light cavalry whose role was scouting and reconnaissance, and harrying the enemy through opportunistic attacks. The French employment of hussars was not yet as developed as that of Prussia.

Frequently despised for their lack of discipline (the Hussards de Polleresky were disbanded and allocated to other units in 1758 for plundering France's German allies) and cut-throat appearance, they nonetheless could be very dangerous and became experts in skirmishing and invaluable to those armies which used them as eyes and ears.[28] In wartime they were often augmented by 'free companies' of volunteers. A hussar regiment numbered 606, having a regimental staff and four squadrons of 150. Muskets or carbines were employed on vedette and to protect foraging parties.

In general, horses of the French Army were required to be a minimum of 14 hands and one inch in height and of a strong build. In reality, though, the average quality was pretty mediocre. A decent horse would often cost at least double the 250 livres budgeted for purchasing remounts, so there was frequently a shortage of horses. In theory, regiments were to have horses of

27 'French Dragoons Organisation', *Seven Years' War*, <http://kronoskaf.com/syw/index.php?title=French_Dragoons_Organisation> (accessed 15 January–31 October 2019).

28 Duffy, *The Military Experience in the Age of Reason*, p.227.

a mix of ages, to assist in the progressive replacement by remounts, but this policy was seldom adhered to.

Campaigning, and battle, are not generally good for horse health. There is a high wastage rate. Despite this, the French Army just managed to keep sufficient horses for its operational requirements throughout the war. For example, it managed to avoid epidemics of glanders or farcy (infectious ulcerating nodules).[29]

Foraging was a vital part of the life of any cavalryman and fodder was a key input towards the all-important horse condition. The requirement to forage meant that large cavalry formations could seldom be concentrated in one place for too long. In order to gather sufficient food for its needs, the cavalry would need to disperse. From October until June, the Army's *régies* (contractors) were required to purchase and supply dry fodder (in the form of oats and hay). For the remainder of the year, grass was used. In practice, there were always challenges securing sufficient fodder. For example, horses, which themselves would require feeding, would be needed to transport the feed for the main body. In the winter prior to the Battle of Minden, six regiments of cavalry and 20,000 horses had to be sent back to France to meet the feeding supply needs of the Army. This fragile situation could be worsened if lines of communication were severed or if the supplies were spoiled. However, it was an unavoidable requirement if the Army were to function properly.

The Support Arms: Artillery and Engineers

The French artillery had been properly organised as a military force at the end of the seventeenth century, being given a separate organisation.[30] Its personnel had sound professional and practical training. Given free rein, a plethora of gun calibres proliferated but this was rationalised by the first Inspector-General of Artillery, *Lieutenant-Général* Vallière to five: 24-, 16-, 12-, 8- and 4-pounders, thus considerably streamlining the challenge of resupply.[31]

It was the 12-, 8- and 4-pound guns which were most often used on campaign, but they were cumbersome and awkward to shift. Being so, they were frequently overrun and captured by the enemy.

Artillery cannon used solid shot, grape shot or canister. Howitzers and mortars used explosive shells as well as incendiary bombs. Originally painted red, by the time of the Seven Years War, the gun carriages of the French artillery became blue to distinguish them from the brick red of the supply train.

---

29 'French Army Provisioning', *Seven Years' War*, <http://www.kronoskaf.com/syw/index.php?title=French_Army_Provisioning> (accessed 15 January–31 October 2019).

30 For an overview, see Smith, *Armies of the Seven Years War*, pp.12-18.

31 John Mollo and Malcolm McGregor, *Uniforms of the Seven Years War 1756-63* (Poole: Blandford Press, 1977), p.39.

The science of ballistics was employed, particularly when pitted against stationary targets. Gunners were meant to follow theory of factors controlling the flight of shot when aiming their cannon. However, in combat, the eye and the estimate tended to govern. As a generalisation, positional artillery had a range of about 18,000 metres, but a bouncing round might carry on with lethal effect for a further 400 metres.[32] Light artillery had a range of about 1,500 metres, although battalion guns might be manoeuvred forward to within 300 metres of the enemy, providing valuable support to the infantry. Case-shot might be used at a range of about 500 metres.

The mid-eighteenth century saw a sort of arms race, with European nations competing to develop improved artillery faster than rival nations. As Director-General of the Manufacture of Arms in France, Vallière was able to recruit a Swiss, Jean Maritz I, who had invented a water-powered horizontal cannon boring system, into French service. This was a significant technological advance. Also, Bernard Forest de Belidor, conducting research in the Artillery Institute of La Fère, discovered that the standard powder charge of 66 percent of the weight of shot, could be reduced to 33 percent without much reduction in the range achievable. This was significant because it could reduce pressure in the chamber allowing thinning, and hence lightening in weight, of the barrel. Vallière also introduced a new battalion gun in 1757, a light 4-Pounder *à la Suédoise*. Reports suggested that the Swedes and the Russians used just such a gun, and were able to fire a remarkable 10 shots per minute. Just before the Seven Years War, Jean Baptiste de Gribeauval had been appointed by d'Argenson to make a study of the Prussian light artillery, but war commenced before he could do so. Attached to the Austrian Army, which had just overhauled its artillery arm, he was captured by the Prussians, so presumably able to resume the pre-war plan.[33] When he returned to France after the war, he reformed their system.

The artillery was frequently reorganised throughout the war, principally in response to inadequate performance. Such a process was unsettling to that arm. At the start of the war, there was a regimental headquarters and five artillery battalions, each of 10 companies with 72 men. In December 1756 each battalion was reinforced by a company of bombardiers and a company of pioneers and miners.

Artillery trains tended to be cumbersome among all the European armies. Artillery horses were frequently so small and weak that they were sometimes nicknamed the 'sheep'.

Bridging was accomplished by the artillery's Corps du Génie. Prior to 1744, the engineers worked under the King's authority, as *Ingénieurs du Roi*, their tasks being directed by a Director General of Fortifications. As such, they were independent of the Ministry of War. However, in 1755, under the Comte d'Argenson, the War Ministry opened a fortifications and artillery office. Within a short while the King himself was made *Grand Maître et Capitaine Général de l'Artillerie de France*, while an ordonnance of 8 December 1755, created the Corps Royal de l'Artillerie et du Génie, incorporating engineer

32 Duffy, *The Military Experience in the Age of Reason*, p.234.

33 Mollo and McGregor, *Uniforms of the Seven Years War 1756-63*, p.39.

officers in the artillery, and also mining and sapper companies[34]. This union was not necessarily a happy one, with neither side totally at ease with the new arrangement. In 1758, d'Argenson was succeeded as the War Minister by the *Maréchal* de Belle-Isle. He also was not in favour of the amalgamation, which he described as a *hoche-pot* (stew). At an early opportunity in 1758, de Belle-Isle set up a Corps des Ingénieurs (of 320 officers, including 20 directors of fortification and 90 chief engineers), separating the artillery and engineering disciplines.

However, despite having their independence back, the engineers had no troops or labour force: the miners and sappers had not been moved across from the artillery with their officers. This arrangement caused so many practical difficulties and frustrations that a Corps du Génie was created in March 1759, and six sapper companies (of 64, all ranks), along with six miner companies (of 66, all ranks), were regrouped into this from the artillery[35]. However, they remained junior to the artillery in order of precedence, which rankled. On the artillery side, labour companies were incorporated to make up the shortfall.

Support Functions

France's system of logistics was becoming antiquated by the Seven Years War, not having been altered since the reign of Louis XIV. A general preference for the status quo tended to make the acceptance of change difficult. Additionally, the systems were prone to corrupt practices.

The fundamental problem was that there was no central commissariat. Small arms were, however, in reasonably plentiful supply. The state did not manufacture the weapons centrally but, instead, contracted companies to do so in the traditional centres of Charleville and Saint- Étienne. One drawback was that the components were not interchangeable, so gunsmiths were required to effect local repairs. Quality control was overseen to a standard by officers of the artillery. Throughout the Seven Years War production was sufficient that France never needed to import small arms from abroad. The standard musket was the 1754 Saint-Étienne model.

France had no saltpetre factories at a national level, so powder had to be obtained by concessionaires buying it from households where it was made and stored. Despite the potential for this system to break down, it seems that sufficient powder got through to the army.

Bayonets, sabres for grenadiers and swords for fusiliers were all issued by the state. Officers and NCOs were issued standard pattern spontoons and halberds, but it was not uncommon on campaign for these to be abandoned for a musket.

34 'Corps du Génie', *Seven Years' War*, <http://www.kronoskaf.com/syw/index.php?title=Corps_du_Génie> (accessed 15 January–31 October 2019).

35 'French Artillery Organisation', *Seven Years' War*: <http://www.kronoskaf.com/syw/index.php?title=French_Artillery_Organisation> (accessed 15 January–31 October 2019).

Bread was fundamental to the French military diet and the demand was huge: for example, to feed 280,000 men for six years on campaign in Germany. It was supplied by private contractors, *Munitionnaires*, who employed thousands of men and 32,000 horses. A year's budget was 20 million *livres.*

Bread was cooked in brick ovens and issued to the men every four days. The use of brick ovens put the army at a considerable disadvantage against those nations that had already moved on to using portable metal ovens. Not only was a brick oven expensive but, from a tactical point of view, could require up to a fortnight to construct. This would limit the radius of action of the army, putting it at a disadvantage against an army with a more flexible rationing system.

The standard loaf weighed 24 ounces (0.68kg). In theory, in 1758, the weight of each loaf was increased to 28 ounces (0.79kg) but the change never actually occurred due to the intransigent habits of the *Munitionnaires.* Despite failing to comply with this direction and operating a protectionist system, the *Munitionnaires* operated at an unsustainable loss of more than 30% each year and the government owed them 15.5 million livres by 1763[36].

Meat was provided by similar contractors to the *Munitionnaires*, each soldier receiving (in theory) a daily ration of one quarter of a pound (113g) of meat per day.

The use of dry forage in the summer was forbidden, but many officers continued the practice. Officers were allowed to sell surplus forage back to the *régies* in order not to waste hay.

In addition to inadequate logistic planning, the abuse of rations and of fodder were additional challenges. During the winter of 1757, one army drew daily supplies from rear area depots, yet simultaneously also collected and stored supplies locally in forward areas. When the time came to move, its ridiculous excess had to be destroyed. In another example, two neighbouring garrisons had very different experiences: while one had ample supplies, its neighbour had to draw firewood and hay from 30 leagues away.

Spoilage was yet another problem. In May 1758, the garrison of Metz ordered over 7,000 bales of hay. When the hay arrived it was deficient to the tune of 60 percent and, when it was issued, it was so spoiled that most was had to be destroyed.[37]

Dysentery, typhus and fever caused more wastage of manpower than battle injury. During the War of the Austrian Succession, it had been agreed by convention that hospitals should be neutral and could be free to be sited wherever was most appropriate.[38] Sadly, this pragmatic approach agreed between the French and the British was not to be extended to the Seven Years War when Prussia and French were fighting. Now, that hospitals could

36 'French Army Provisioning', *Seven Years' War*, <http://www.kronoskaf.com/syw/index.php?title=French_Army_Provisioning> (accessed 15 January–31 October 2019).

37 'French Army Provisioning', *Seven Years' War*, <http://www.kronoskaf.com/syw/index.php?title=French_Army_Provisioning> (accessed 15 January–31 October 2019).

38 Lt Gen. Sir N. Cantlie, *A History of the Army Medical Department* (Edinburgh: Churchill Livingstone, 1974), p.83, referring to 'A Treaty and Agreement for the sick, wounded and prisoners of war of the auxiliary troops of his Most Christian Majesty and those of his Allies, 28 July 1743.'.

be exposed to capture led to them being relocated when threatened. This, in turn, caused a breakdown of any evacuation system, and regimental surgeons often felt obliged to hold onto their casualties, sometimes for weeks, before they could be properly evacuated. The resulting suffering caused by prolonged journeys, often on unsprung carts over rudimentary roads sometimes resulted in a mortality rate of 30 percent among those wounded survivors.[39]

French surgeons were reported to bleed their patients frequently.[40] Le Dran, the most illustrious French military surgeon of the time (and, interestingly, a member of the British Royal Society), and the first to describe 'shock' in a treatise on battle wounds, was an advocate of primary amputation. A common French practice was for surgeons to perform their rounds with a tub of brandy and syringes, with which they washed wounds, dressing them in dry lint dipped in yet more brandy and covering with 'digestive'.

Officers

Every officer's position in the French Army, excepting the artillery with its technical demands, could be purchased rather than gained through experience and merit. This could result in units being commanded by a boy from a wealthy family. Smith quotes the German historian Archenholz:

> The very subalterns had their mistresses with them, and officers often left their men to accompany them on the march in their carriages. Everything that could contribute to the luxury of the officers was found in the French camp. Balls were given in camp, and officers often left their posts to dance a minuet.[41]

Under the reforms introduced after the War of the Austrian Succession, Louis XV created the *École Militaire* in Paris for 500 sons of the well-to-do. Here they were provided a military education at the nation's expense[42].

The French Character

The French, a 'hot', southern nation were considered to be characterised by an inquisitive nature, by a lively spirit and by weak discipline. They frequently took to looting, drinking and foul language.[43] After the War of the Austrian Succession, the French economy sank, and this was matched by a decline in military performance. However, there was a renaissance under *Maréchal* de Belle-Isle, the new War Minister who insisted on generals setting an example

39 Cantlie, *History of the Army Medical Department*, p.128.

40 Cantlie, *History of the Army Medical Department*, p.85.

41 Smith, *Armies of the Seven Years War*, p.38.

42 'French État-Major Organisation', *Seven Years' War*, <http://www.kronoskaf.com/syw/index.php?title=French_Etat-Major_Organisation> (accessed 15 January–31 October 2019).

43 Duffy, *The Military Experience in the Age of Reason*, pp.18-21.

and raising standards of leadership. The Hugenot, Jakob Mauvillon reports that, as the Seven Years War progressed, there was almost a visible, daily improvement.[44]

The Saxon Corps Serving with the French Army (1758-62)

Early in the war, after Prussia had defeated Saxony, Frederick the Great pressed the Saxon Army wholesale into his service. This did not sit easily with the Saxons, who deserted *en masse*, often as formed units[45]. These '*Reverenten*' numbered almost 7,500 by October 1757. They escaped to Austria and Hungary where, under a subsidies contract of 11.3 million *livres* (5.1 per cent of all the subsidies paid out by France in the war), they were admitted to French service on 11 March 1758.[46] They travelled by a circuitous route through southern Germany to avoid interception by the Prussians, eventually mustering again in Strasbourg in July of that year. They finally reached Contades' army by September 1758 in Westphalia. The Saxons first saw action in French service at Lutterberg on 10 October 1758, where they played a significant part in the French success.

On paper the Saxon contingent had a strength of 10,000 all ranks but, in reality, as the war drew on, this was difficult to maintain through wastage and also through the practical challenges of recruiting.

44 Duffy, *The Military Experience in the Age of Reason*, p.20.

45 Smith, *Armies of the Seven Years War*, p.219.

46 'The Saxon Corps serving with the French Armies 1758-1762', *Seven Years' War*, <http://www.kronoskaf.com/syw/index.php?title=Saxon_Army#The_Saxon_Corps_serving_with_the_French_Armies_1758-1762> (accessed 15 January–31 October 2019).

4

The Allies

The Germans

Prussia

Frederick II, 'the Great', had inherited a large peacetime army from his father in 1740. He quickly turned this parade ground force into a finely-tuned warfighting army. Indeed, he bloodied it to the extent that one regiment consumed 4,474 men in the course of the Seven Years War, suggesting that it had a complete replacement on three occasions.[1]

A key to Frederick's success was his officer corps, dedicated, educated, thorough, and brim full of Protestant work ethic. Frederick required his officers to be noble, although his criteria for that qualification were flexible and could be arbitrary, depending on the needs of the situation.[2] A significant proportion of officers came through the Berlin Cadet Corps, the Corps of Royal Pages or through sponsorship by colonels of regiments, so they had already served a sort of apprenticeship. In comparison with their French or British counterparts, Prussian officers were considered over-serious and rather staid.[3] Young officers were frequently assessed and tested by their colonels, through the writing of essays and reports.

For the other ranks, blind obedience was required, and this was instilled through induction and training, but also by a range of punishments (such as running the gauntlet) for misdemeanours. Discipline was maintained rigidly by a cadre of NCOs, often highly experienced. The rank and file was made up of a mixture of Prussian conscripts and foreign mercenaries. Native recruits came from a cantonal system which paired regiment with the district surrounding its peacetime garrison. Some valuable trades were exempt military service.

---

1 For an overview, see J. Woods, *Armies and Uniforms of the Seven Years War. Vol.1. Prussia, Britain and the Allies* (Leigh-on-Sea: Partizan, 2006), pp.9-38, 161-206

2 Christopher Duffy, *The Army of Frederick the Great* (Newton Abbot: David & Charles, 1974), pp.24-53.

3 Mollo and McGregor, *Uniforms of the Seven Years War 1756-63*, p.10.

On arrival at his new regiment, the recruit was entrusted to an experienced soldier, who was required to introduce him to all aspects of soldiering.[4] On campaign, seven soldiers would make up a tent party, sharing their duties, such as fetching water, hewing wood and cooking. Normally having deductions for rations from their pay of two *thalers* per month, soldiers were issued bread and meat on campaign, but required to buy anything else from the regimental sutler.

Frederick's father set out to create the perfect infantry. In partnership with his drill-master, Prince Leopold of Anhalt-Dessau, Frederick-William I built up an infantry, rehearsed in minute detail in close order drill, and trained to obey unhesitatingly. Turns and wheels on the march were refined for a faster effect while musketry was practised until the rate of fire was the highest in Europe. In terms of appearance, Frederick's father had made a notable break, the *stilbruch,* from the French style which had been slavishly copied throughout Europe.[5] He introduced a new, closer fitting, and shorter coat, whose tightness enforced a very upright bearing. The hair was worn in queue which reached almost to the waist. Whilst the style was mocked initially, Prussian success on operations soon led to them being widely copied. Something unique to the Prussians was the use of embroidered loops on their coats, possibly modelled on the eastern European kaftan, the officers having gold and silver embroidery, with the men having to make do with worsted.

Frederick II's army was not destined for the parade ground alone. Frederick the Great intended that it should be his tool for war. He injected a pace and tempo into his aggressive actions. The Prussians could form faster than any opponents.[6] While old-style commanders would methodically form line well before battle was joined, Frederick could advance to battle efficiently in column, transitioning on the move into line and seeking to gain advantage through never letting the enemy settle. In particular, the employment of battalions advancing in staggered echelons allowed him to engage flanks of that enemy with his celebrated 'oblique order'.[7]

The Prussian battalion would have had a frontage of 150 to 200 paces, fighting in a three-rank line until manpower shortages forced the adoption of two ranks.

In comparison with its French equivalent, the Prussian cavalry was, and indeed had been made as such, the most effective cavalry in Europe. It had not always been so. Prior to the Seven Years War, Frederick had a finely tuned infantry but the cavalry, whilst improving, had not yet reached that pitch and Frederick considered it too ponderous. He set about reforming it with numerous orders and instructions. It was not just Frederick who had made this significant impact. His two great cavalry commanders, Seydlitz and Zieten, had led by example. Indeed, at Leuthen, Frederick had threatened

4 Duffy, *The Military Experience in the Age of Reason*, p.105.

5 Christopher Duffy, *The Army of Frederick the Great* (Newton Abbot: David & Charles, 1974), p.15.

6 Duffy, *The Army of Frederick the Great*, p.88.

7 Duffy, *The Army of Frederick the Great*, p.153-156.

his cavalry that, should any regiment turn away, it would be dismounted and demoted to garrison duties. Frederick had exposed his thinking on the cavalry to the young Comte de Gisors, the son of the *Maréchal* de Belle-Isle during a visit to Silesia in 1754:

> I put my officers in front, out of the ranks, because being in the ranks they become simple cavalrymen and obliged to let themselves be carried away by the torrent of the squadron. I put others behind, to fall on those who would like to flee. I do not permit any interval between my squadrons, because squadrons separated from each other present many flanks to the enemy. I make them charge at full gallop, because fear forces the average men forward, rather than stopping in the middle of the charge, to be crushed by the next squadron. I want that the impetuosity of their charge that forces the enemy to give way before he can fight back…[8]

The Prussian cavalry charged in three ranks until attrition of its manpower forced it to adopt two ranks.

Prince Ferdinand of Brunswick made use of a small Prussian contingent for much of the war. Early in 1758 he petitioned Frederick the Great for reinforcement and received 10 squadrons of dragoons and five of hussars.

Frederick's employment of his artillery was frequently imaginative. He used it to 'soften up' or demoralize his opponents in common with most commanders of his age, but he also used it to fix his enemy while conducting his flanking movements. He used his artillery with a sort of manoeuvrist flair, to 'travel like the wind' to wherever he decided it could be used to best effect.[9] Howitzers were a favourite of his, to the extent of growing in number until they were about one third of his artillery, being employed to seek out enemy units lurking in 'dead ground' – that is to say, out of line of sight.

The calibres of Prussian artillery had been simplified to 24-, 12-, 6- and 3-pounders (the latter being a battalion gun), and 18-, 10- and 7-pound howitzers. 50-, 24- and 10-pound mortars were also available. By 1755, some of the calibres had chambered breeches, although this advance was not without its teething troubles.[10]

Despite the King's enjoyment of artillerism, he tended to regard his artillery officers with disdain, seeing them as mere technicians and preferring not to mix socially with them. They were forbidden to travel abroad in case they should betray technical secrets.

Bilquer, Surgeon General of the Prussian Army, condemned primary amputation, advocating secondary amputation when nature had failed to cure, a method also supported by one of the most famous British surgeons, John Hunter.[11]

8 Duffy, *The Army of Frederick the Great*, p.107.
9 Duffy, *The Army of Frederick the Great*, p.121.
10 C. Rogge, 'Prussian 18th Century Artillery', *Smoothbore Ordnance Journal*, Issue 6 (May 2016), pp.23-60.
11 Cantlie, *History of the Army Medical Department*, p.97.

Hanover[12]

Of the smaller states involved in the Seven Years War, Hanover had a relatively large contingent, with 34 squadrons of cavalry, 29 battalions of infantry, light troops, artillery and engineers, amounting to 29,000 men in 1757. Twelve battalions of foot had been moved to England in May 1757 to shore up the defence of Britain against the threat from France. The men in these units were also subjects of King George II as their Elector, so they were not there as mercenaries and he could order their presence.[13]

The Hanoverian establishment increased by a further five battalions, of which three were pure grenadier battalions formed from the grenadier companies of existing units.[14] They also had a notable strength in light troops, whose numbers grew from 915 to just over 4,000 in the course of the war.

The Hanoverians had a good reputation, being robust and soldierly. Besides, they were Protestant and had frequently served alongside the British for over 60 years. Anecdotally, the two armies got on well together, drinking long into the night and swapping stories, though scarcely able to understand one another. Mirroring the British style, the Hanoverian infantry and Gardes du Corps wore red.

Hanoverian medical arrangements were much praised:

> [T]heir dressings are very neatly drawn lint; wounds are cleaned with fine sponges, soaked in warm water and brandy. Their hospital medicines are carried on a large wagon divided into many different partitions…any particular medicine can be easily got at, the whole easily packed and unpacked. One of their physicians visits the kitchen daily and examines the provision.[15]

Other German Allies

Several smaller states with standing armies were allied to Prussia and Britain: Brunswick-Wolfenbüttel, Hessen-Cassel, Saxe-Gotha and Schaumberg-Lippe. Other German states sided with Austria and France. To an extent these loyalties were dictated by the ruling house's family affiliation, but also by religion and by geography. The size and readiness of the armies was not invariably in direct proportion to the size and wealth of their parent states. The appearance of the armies of these states tended to mirror the major nation which they supported, either Austria or Prussia.

The states allied to Prussia had had experience of combat from the War of the Austrian Succession. However, in the intervening peace, there had been few opportunities to practise and train at much above regimental level. However, their officer corps tended to be organised along Prussian lines, with very similar approaches to professionalism and duty. Likewise, their field organisation, tactics and administration would be easily grasped by another north German officer.

---

12 'Hanoverian Army', *Seven Years' War*, <http://www:kronoscaf.com/syw/index.php?title=Hanoverian_Army> (accessed 10 June 2019).

13 Mollo and McGregor, *Uniforms of the Seven Years War 1756-63*, p.26.

14 Smith, *Armies of the Seven Years War*, p.141.

15 Cantlie, *History of the Army Medical Department*, p.85.

Britain had made use of troops from Hessen-Cassel in 1755 when, under the terms of a defensive alliance, eight battalions had been brought over to Britain. They were no strangers, having previously been used in a similar role in 1746. Frederick II, keen to safeguard his right flank when otherwise engaged, encouraged Britain to maintain a force of German auxiliaries on German soil, so the Hessian battalions returned to form the nucleus of the Army of Observation at Wesel in 1757.

Hessen-Cassel had six regiments of cavalry (four horse, two dragoons), 12 battalions of infantry, and two of grenadiers, 16,500 in all, a significant proportion of which could be loaned to Britain through treaty, and which could be increased at George II's request. The Hessians were highly regarded in Britain, which had employed some 21,570 by the war's end.[16]

In common with the other allies, the soldiers of Brunswick-Wolfenbüttel were also familiar with and to the British, having been engaged under the 1757 treaty of subsidy. They were described as 'noble-bodied, active, handsome, clean, cool, obedient, brave, immoveable fellows'.[17] Their army of 6,000 consisted of six companies of dragoons, two grenadier battalions, eight infantry battalions, and three companies of gunners who crewed the battalion pieces. One hussar regiment, two grenadier battalions and a corps of jägers were added in 1759. The British employed 9,280 by the war's end.

Saxe-Gotha provided a white-uniformed infantry battalion which served in the Hanoverian army. Initially envisaged in a direct combat role, it became an escort to the Hanoverian artillery and pontoon train.[18]

The Electorate of Hanover signed a treaty with Schaumburg-Lippe in 1756, so the troops of the latter were not employed as mercenaries.[19] It provided an artillery contingent, an infantry battalion and 60 mounted and 40 foot carabiniers. William, the Count of Schaumberg-Lippe, was a Hanoverian *General-Feldzeugmeister* (general of artillery). Born in London, he married a daughter of King George I of Britain. He was credited with constructing the first submarine in Germany in 1772. He commanded the allied artillery at Minden.

Britain

In 1759 the British Army was still relatively young.[20] Frequently resented as both a costly institution and a threat to liberty, Parliament frequently sought to curb it. This held true at the end of the War of the Austrian Succession, when it was reduced in size. With the growing threat of a recurrence of war, its establishment had to be re-expanded from a mere 30,000.

16 Mollo and McGregor, *Uniforms of the Seven Years War*, p.27.

17 Mollo and McGregor, *Uniforms of the Seven Years War*, p.28, quoting Major General Lord Pembroke.

18 Mollo and McGregor, *Uniforms of the Seven Years War*, p.28.

19 Mollo and McGregor, *Uniforms of the Seven Years War*, p.28.

20 For an overview see J.A. Houlding, *Fit for Service: Training of the British Army, 1715-95* (Oxford: Oxford University Press, 1981) pp.195-207.

Under the Duke of Cumberland's reforms as Commander-in-Chief from 1748-56, much of the most cumbersome bureaucracy had been stripped away, but the army was still not a model of efficiency, much of its business being controlled by committees. Officership was not an academic pursuit served by a military academy. The British officer tended to be aristocratic and an amateur in officership: whilst it may have been a calling for many more than might be expected as being a by-product of one's station in life, it did not automatically confer values and standards of its own. For the duration of the army's existence, officers of the junior and middle ranks had achieved their position through patronage or wealth, and too many commanders regarded their post as entitling them to an income through perquisites, or perks.[21] The most senior ranks were only attained through following an unbending system of seniority, not a recipe for promoting talent.

Oberst Jakob von Mauvillon on Prince Ferdinand's staff derided the average British officer:

> Their home customs incline them to the indulgencies of life, and nearly without exception, they all expect to have comfortable means of sleep. This disposes them to acts of neglect of duty which would sound incredible if related. To all this is added a quiet, natural arrogance which tempts them to despise the enemy as well as the danger. It is well known how much these people despise all foreigners; this of itself renders their co-operation with troops of other nations very difficult.[22]

One contemporary but far-thinking medical officer, Brocklesby, set on record a view of man-management: 'The well-being of the men and the preservation of their health ought to be a constant serious business and in increasing care of their officers as well as the physicians'.[23] Here was an entirely new conception of the regimental officer's duties, but one which was not yet to be accepted in the army until after the Seven Years War.

Cumberland did much to improve officership, instructing the officer body that it must pay heed to regulations. He did away with much of the *laissez faire,* requiring officers to wear uniform on duty. So, the officers of the British Army were extremely varied, at their best seeking professional expertise and taking their responsibilities extremely seriously, while at their worst refusing to give up individualism and luxury. The one value highly regarded by both officers and men was courage.

A typical infantry regiment would have one battalion of 10 companies, one of which would be the grenadier company. In theory, selected for their height and strength, the grenadier function was now largely redundant, but there was still a place for big, tough men. The grenadier companies of several battalions might be taken away and grouped together as a 'converged battalion', for special tasks. There was also a growing tendency to pick and

21 Alan J.Guy, *Oeconomy and Discipline. Officership and Administration in the British Army 1714-63* (Manchester: Manchester University Press, 1985), pp.101-105.

22 Mollo and McGregor, *Uniforms of the Seven Years War*, p.19.

23 Dr Brocklesby, *Oeconomical and Medical Observations* (London: Becket and de Hondt, 1764), p.21.

put together those fleet of foot, to become a light, or picquet, company. The gradual introduction of light troops into European armies was influenced in two theatres: in south-east Europe, through the Austrian employment of Croats and Pandours, and in North America where the British response to native tribe skirmishing and to French raiding was to use Highlanders and then light companies of marksmen.

The greatest strength of the British infantry was its musketry, which was both disciplined and, by the standards of the day, lethally accurate at the optimum range[24]. Prussian manuals may have made impressions on the armies of Europe, but the British foot had initially learned all about fire control in the wars of Queen Anne, and then experimented almost continuously through subsequent wars.[25] At Minden, the British foot stood its ground and held its fire until the French cavalry was terrifyingly close, shattering its charges.

Here, it may be worth diverting onto the principal instrument used by the British infantry, the Long Land Pattern Musket, affectionately and widely known as 'Brown Bess'.[26] It was introduced in 1718, as a result of an aim of standardising weapons and equipment. Brass fittings were preferred to iron. The components were manufactured in two centres, London and Birmingham, the former making the walnut stocks and brass work, the latter producing the locks and 46-inch barrels. Brought together, assembled and scrutinised for quality, the year of production was stamped on the lockplate. An iron ramrod was introduced in 1750 to replace the original wooden one. Prior to 1760, a Short Pattern Land Service Musket was introduced for Marines, Dragoons and Militia.

The musket had a block-type foresight which doubled as the bayonet lug. There was no official rear sight, although there are records of crude attempts by users to incise a notch to serve as a rudimentary means of alignment.[27] To aim, the firer would line up the rear of the barrel, the sight and the target (the weapon shooting slightly high (five inches at 30 yards; that is 12 centimetres at 27 metres).

User maintenance was officially restricted to unscrewing and cleaning the lock, boiling out the barrel and polishing, more complicated servicing being restricted to artificers. The barrel was tapered slightly to mitigate fouling. A sling, generally buff, was employed although, not being officially issued, might vary with the taste of the regimental colonel. Paintings by Morier show the use of a leather hammerstall to protect the lock.

The ammunition consisted of a ball, officially of 0.69-inch (17.55mm) calibre, although this could vary, and powder made up into cartridges.[28] An extra advantage of a large ball was that enemy ammunition was frequently of smaller calibre, allowing captured ammunition to be used in extremis. The

24 Blackmore, *Destructive & Formidable*, p.70.

25 See also later in this work for analysis of the British musketry at Minden.

26 Houlding, *Fit for Service*, pp.137-148.

27 'British_Line_Infantry_Weapons', *Seven Years' War*, <http://www.kronoskaf.com/syw/index.php?title=British_Line_Infantry_Weapons> (accessed 15 January–31 October 2019).

28 'British_Line_Infantry_Weapons', *Seven Years' War*, <http://www.kronoskaf.com/syw/index.php?title=British_Line_Infantry_Weapons> (accessed 15 January–31 October 2019).

cartridges were premade of 'rag paper' and tied off with hemp or linen string and contained a maximum of 220 grains of powder (14 grams), although this was often less. The quality and reliability of powder was variable. Muzzle velocity would vary with the powder, but might range from 250-350 metres per second (930-1,200 feet per second). The musket flint was another vital component, requiring replacement as it wore down, or even shattered, through use. British flints were of mixed quality, some sparking better than others on delivery.

The musket came with a bayonet, the blade of which was 18 inches (47.5 centimetres) in length and of triangular cross-section. The bayonet was fixed at the muzzle end of the musket by a socket. When mounted, the blade is turned away from the muzzle so as not to hinder continued loading.

In terms of accuracy, the Brown Bess was technically about average relative to the muskets of other powers, the difference being in the discipline and steadiness of its user.

Where the British did learn from the Prussians was on the parade ground, adopting much of their regulation and close order drill with pace-stick and pendulum. Drill is the means by which individual soldiers are instilled with teamwork and discipline: reaction to orders becomes ingrained and instinctive. Additionally, English translations of Prussian drillbooks also dealt with training and manoeuvring larger formations.[29]

Marching under load, carrying his own and also shared equipment, is another significant portion of an infantryman's life. He would frequently be required to carry over 27 kilograms.[30] Under the Duke of Cumberland, the soldier's equipment and clothing was gradually being improved; a goat skin bag or knapsack was issued. Additional pack animals and wagons could be procured at regimental level through contractors, but also perhaps uglily procured at the expense of the local population.

The British cavalry was made up of the Household Cavalry, line regiments of horse and of dragoons. A reform of 1746 aimed at saving money disbanded some of the Horse Guards and converted the three senior regiments of horse into dragoon guards – dragoons in all but name. A light troop was added to some of the dragoon guards and dragoon regiments in 1755, and this innovation was followed by the raising of the 15th Light Dragoons in 1759.

The British horse continued to deploy in three ranks. The era saw changes in cavalry manoeuvre away from individual horses turning on their own ground towards wheeling in divisions.

Recruiting the junior ranks of the army was always a challenge.[31] Attracting soldiers of the ideal sort was almost an impossible challenge, at 20 shillings a month before compulsory deductions.[32] Very few upstanding volunteers stepped forward, despite the offer of a £3 bounty, so sterner measures were relied on. Parishes were rewarded with £2 for every man coerced into service. The balance was topped up to a great extent by magistrates who might spare

29 Houlding, *Fit for Service*, p.204.
30 Mollo and McGregor, *Uniforms of the Seven Years War*, p.21.
31 Houlding, *Fit for Service*, p.119.
32 Guy, *Oeconomy and Discipline*, pp.53-87.

the convicted in return for military service. The reaction to this method of recruitment meant that desertion was a recurring problem.[33]

The roughness of its raw manpower led the army to respond with a range of disciplinary sanctions, which might include corporal and capital punishment. That said, the background range of punishments available in civil society was also harsh by today's standards. Equally, the military diet may have been dull and monotonous, but was probably more nutritious than the routine in civilian life. Rations were delivered by commissaries, and soldiers often pooled their resources, cooking collectively. Every regiment was accompanied by a butcher under contract, and he was required to provide live oxen and sheep, sold at a fixed price and paid for by stoppages from the men's pay. The main meal taken at midday was meant to include one pound (450 grams) of boiled meat, potatoes, root vegetables and greens. Breakfast and supper were gruel or porridge made from oatmeal. The day's ration included one pound (450 grams) of bread.[34]

A novel measure was the attention paid to drinking water. In theory at least, water could be filtered by passing it through a barrel filled with sand into another where it would be collected. If that was not possible, water was to be boiled and cream of tartar or vinegar added to it.

In Britain, the peacetime system of billeting the troops in ale houses and private dwellings was most unsatisfactory; there was no check on the men's health or cleanliness except on parade, and there was no central messing: 'wantoning in lewdness and luxury 'til they have quite lost the spirit of Englishmen'.[35] The only solution to the billeting situation was to build barracks, and this had been started as early as 1739, but by 1762 there were only two permanent army barracks in Britain, one at Chatham and one at Hilsea, and these had been built of salt bricks which attracted humidity. Drainage was inadequate and they were poorly ventilated. It was thought that they 'bred disease and swept off men like a perpetual pestilence'.[36]

The Board of Ordnance oversaw both the Royal Regiment of Artillery and the un-regimented engineers.[37] The Board, a department of the government, procured guns and munitions for the armed forces. Should a phase of operations require a siege train, the Board would allocate, or even raise, units which would come under the direct command of the commander-in-chief.

Initially in Germany, the gunners concentrated on battalion guns, light 3- or 6-pounders, but increasingly through the ideas and influence of the Count of Schaumberg-Lippe, they were employed in larger concentrations and masses. The British employed a range of calibres as field artillery, including heavy 6-pounders, light and heavy 12-pounders, 24-pounders, mortars and howitzers. Under Ferdinand, the artillery trialled a new method of applying itself, it was in fact the emergence of the field battery as we now know it, as the

33 Guy, *Oeconomy and Discipline*, p.127.

34 Cantlie, *A History of the Army Medical Department*, p.125.

35 Guy, *Oeconomy and Discipline*, p.7.

36 Cantlie, *A History of the Army Medical Department*, p.104.

37 'British Line Infantry Weapons', *Seven Years' War*, <http://www.kronoskaf.com/syw/index.php?title=British_Line_Infantry_Weapons> (accessed 15 January–31 October 2019).

tactical fire unit. With guns of such limited range, concentration of fire could only be achieved by enhanced mobility and though this had been realised by Frederick the Great, who introduced horse artillery into the Prussian Army, the British Army was ill equipped to achieve it.

While France's engineers were acknowledged to be among the best in Europe, British engineering was neglected, with only 61 officers, and a company of Miners, almost as an afterthought on the strength of the Royal Artillery.

Any army on the move required a long horse-drawn train which included its artillery, caissons, munitions, rations, camp stores wrapped in oil cloth and officers' personal baggage. Such a train could stretch for miles and was vulnerable. It required careful control to get the correct order of arrival. In Germany each regiment marched with two wagons for the sick and the regimental hospital stores, as well as two wagons for the regimental blankets. In static locations, the routine method of evacuating sick from units to the rear was by means of the bread wagons which delivered bread daily to the different regiments. On the march, the sick were ordered to the hospital wagons in the rear of the column 'if the carriages of their particular regiment cannot carry them' and a 'flying hospital' which was organised to follow any movement.[38]

Flying hospitals had been trialled previously and they provided an essential link between the regimental and the general hospitals, relieving the former of their cases when they were constantly on the move or in action. They could either hold and treat cases, or evacuate them in turn to the general hospitals further in the rear. To be effective they required carry between 200 to 400 sets of bedding, tents and equipment.

On campaign, those units which could not be billeted in villages or farms were required to use tents. In the colder months, these might be thatched over to give some protection from the elements. Hurdles were also improvised as shelters. Deep pit latrines were used and covered with straw. Blankets were only provided on a scale of two per tent, although in winter this could be increased to one per man.

The regimental medical establishment was limited to the regimental surgeon and his mate, both in the clothing of the regiment to which they belonged, with a pack horse and two panniers of medical and surgical equipment, although in theory the regiment would also carry enough bedding and supplies for a 40-bed regimental hospital.[39] At higher formation, a headquarters staff had a physician and a surgeon appointed, and both on equal (a novelty, as previously physicians drew higher salaries) pay at 10 shillings per day. The money to pay for medicines was raised by stoppages from the soldiers' pay, at one penny per month for each private.

Under Cumberland, an important measure was taken for the control and organization of the medical services. It was recognised that previously the physicians who superintended the general hospitals were selected from civil life and had no understanding of military organization and administration,

38 Cantlie, *History of the Army Medical Department*, p.121.

39 Cantlie, *History of the Army Medical Department*, p.65.

yet they thought themselves so superior in education and in status to the surgeons that they would take no guidance from them no matter how ignorant they might be of their duties. Military surgeons, on the other hand, were often highly experienced regular officers, but any efforts to advise the physicians would be jealously rejected. Cumberland, recognising the flaw in such a system, created a board to take advantage of the experience of Regular Officers:

> A Board was established consisting of physicians in the hospitals...the Surgeon General, the principal surgeon and the purveyor to the hospitals, who had it given them in charge conjointly to digest certain rules for regulating all hospital matters, in order that this part of the medical service (including medicines, hospital stores, and other provisions for the sick) might be carried into execution with ability, regularity and despatch.[40]

The British Army of the Seven Years War had both a Physician General (Wilmot), a Surgeon General (Middleton) and an Apothecary General (Garnier). These were not full-time appointments. A significant advance in military medicine was the creation in 1756 of a full-time regular officer based in the London headquarters at Horse Guards, the Inspector of Regimental Infirmaries (Adair).[41] Paid a third more than the Physician and Surgeon Generals, his job title explains the role, to inspect regimental hospitals, checking that medical funding was being appropriately used to buy medicines, that best practice was being maintained by contemporary standards and that stoppages of pay for the hospital were being used to fund a suitable diet for the patients. To prevent abuses where substandard medicines were cheaply bought, any profit being kept by the officer concerned, a formulary was introduced in 1760. These posts were mirrored on the staffs for operations overseas, both in Germany and in North America. Adair was responsible for nominating all surgeons and their mates, although full regimental commissions could be purchased by those doctors with the funds and desire to do so.

The creation of a Director of Hospitals living at the deployed commander's headquarters and overseeing all the hospitals from that centre instead of trying to conduct his operations from the rear was a major step forward. This meant that meant that he would be informed of the commander's intent, ensuring that the necessary medical arrangements could be made in advance. There is also evidence that, for tactical purposes, regimental hospitals came under his control too, with plans being made which included their proposed locations during battle or on arrival in an encampment. Lastly, he was authorised to summon all regimental surgeons for conferences where such plans would be shared and instructions issued. This required the buy-in by all regimental commanding officers. If the flying hospital was to be deployed optimally to support movement, it was vital to plan the current and proposed locations of the regimental hospitals.

---

40 Cantlie, *History of the Army Medical Department*, p.120.
41 Cantlie, *History of the Army Medical Department*, pp.119-138

In reality, the building taken as the Regimental Hospital might have been grim:

> Most commonly the habitation hired for an infirmary has for some time been unoccupied, with the walls all damp, the boarded floors half rotten, and the roof in several places open above…I have indeed seen such a cottage stuffed with 40, 50 or 60, nay with 70 or 80 poor soldiers all lying heel to head, so closely confined together with their own stinking cloathes, foul linen, etc., that it was enough to suffocate the patients as well as others who were obliged to approach them.[42]

42 Brocklesby, *Oeconomical and Medical Observations*, pp.54-55.

5

Minden Personalities

Louis Georges Érasme, Marquis de Contades

Louis Contades was born on 19 October 1704 near Beaufort in Anjou.[1] He entered military service at the age of 16. Fourteen years later, on 10 March 1734, he became the *colonel* of the Régiment de Flandres, but promotion came fast, becoming *brigadier* in October of the same year. He became *maréchal-de-camp* in 1740, and again in the same year, was promoted to *lieutenant-général.*

At the start of the Seven Years War he served under *Maréchal* d'Estrées in the first French attempt to invade Hanover. At Hastenbeck, Contades commanded the first line of the infantry centre. He was nominated as the Governor of Fort-Louis on the Rhine in January 1758, and he replaced the Comte de Clermont as the commander-in-chief of the French Armée du Rhin after the latter's defeat in the Battle of Krefeld. Under Contades, this army crossed the Rhine and began its invasion of Westphalia in concert with Soubise's invasion of Hesse. Contades was appointed *Maréchal de France* on 24 August 1758, but was obliged to re-cross the Rhine, to occupy winter quarters in safety after an unsuccessful campaign.

Unconventionally early in the season, Contades captured Frankfurt-am-Main in January 1759 and was rewarded by being appointed as a Knight of the Ordre du Saint-Esprit. He recommenced

Maréchal Louis George Erasme Marquis Contades, (Public Domain)

1 Career summarised from Smith, *Armies of the Seven Years War*, p.308; 'Contades, Louis Georges Érasme, Marquis de', *Seven Years' War*, <http://www.kronoskaf.com/syw/index.php?title=Contades,_Louis_Georges_%C3%89rasme,_Marquis_de> (accessed 15 January–31 October 2019).

the invasion of Hesse in June and, by mid-July, had captured Minden. Convincingly defeated by Ferdinand of Brunswick at Minden, Contades ceded command of his army to d'Estrées.

By 1763, he was commander-in-chief in Alsace and, in 1788, became Governor of Lorraine. He died in old age on 19 January 1795 at Livry.

Victor François, Duc de Broglie

Broglie was the son of François Marie, the first Duc de Broglie, and although 14 years younger than his superior, shared his birthday, 19 October, with Contades.[2]

Victor François campaigned in the War of the Polish Succession, alongside his father, as a cavalry captain. Participating in the battles of Parma and Guastalla, he progressed to the colonelcy of the Luxembourg Infanterie. In the War of the Austrian Succession, he soldiered under *Maréchal* de Saxe in Bohemia. He was appointed as *Aide-Major Général d'Infanterie* on 1 March 1741 and took part in the storming of Prague in November of that year. He was promoted to *Brigadier* in April of the following year, and to *Major-Général d'Infanterie*, having been twice wounded. He continued to serve, in Bavaria, Haute-Alsace and on the Rhine and, on 1 May 1745, was promoted to *maréchal-de-camp*. Having borne the title comte, he succeeded his father, on the latter's death, as Duc de Broglie. The new duc soldiered, once again, under de Saxe in Flanders in 1746, taking part in the Battle of Rocoux. He returned to Flanders in 1747, participating in the Battle of Lauffeld and, in the following year, took part in the siege of Maastricht. After the war, he was promoted to *lieutenant-général*

Lieutenant-Général Victor François, Duc de Broglie. (Anne S.K. Brown Collection)

When the Seven Years War broke out, Broglie served under *Maréchal* d'Estrées. He took part in the Battle of Hastenbeck on 26 July 1757, after which he was detached to the Prince de Soubise's army. Although this force was heavily defeated at Rossbach on 5 November, Broglie was able to maintain his troops as a capable body and retired in moderate order in the direction of Hanover.

2 Career summarised from Smith, *Armies of the Seven Years War*, p.308; 'Broglie, Victor François, Duc de', Seven Years' War, <http://www.kronoskaf.com/syw/index.php?title=Broglie,_Victor_Fran%C3%A7ois,_Duc_de> (accessed 15 January–31 October 2019).

In the following year, he led Soubise's vanguard into Hesse, but suffered from *Maréchal* de Belle-Isle's antipathy and was prevented from gaining the command of an army. However, while leading Soubise's vanguard, he successfully defeated Prince Johann von Ysenburg at Sandershausen.

In 1759, Broglie served under Contades in Germany, winning the Battle of Bergen against Ferdinand of Brunswick on 13 April. At Minden, he commanded a corps on the right wing of Contades' army. Despite heavy criticism for his perceived lack of determination in driving his attack forward, Louis XV opted to use him to replace Contades as commander-in-chief of that army. In December of the same year, the King appointed him as *Maréchal de France*. He was clearly well thought of, as the Emperor Francis I also raised him to be a Prince of the Empire.

He was the victor at Corbach in 1760, but was defeated at Vellinghausen in 1761 where, despite an agreement to coordinate with Soubise, his hasty and rash actions contributed to the defeat. Disgraced, he was recalled to Court.

After the war, he became Governor of the Trois-Évêchés, and then of Alsace. He returned to military duties and command in 1778, in operations against Britain. By 1789, he was in command of troops around Versailles when the French Revolution erupted. Briefly appointed by the King as Secretary of State for War, five days later he emigrated. His older son Charles-Louis-Victor perished during the Terror. Having commanded the 'Army of the Princes' in Champagne in 1792, when the Austrians and Prussians invaded, he left for Russia in 1797, settling in Riga in 1798. Refusing to return to his homeland, he died in Münster in 1804.

Ferdinand, Prince of Brunswick-Lüneberg-Wolfenbüttel

Born on 12 January 1721 in Wolfenbüttel, Ferdinand was the fourth son of Ferdinand Albert II, Duke of Brunswick.[3] In common with his class and standing in society, he was groomed for a military career. His Brother-in-Law, King Frederick II ('the Great') of Prussia, appointed him as commander of a new infantry regiment, Nr.39, raised in Brunswick for Prussian service.

Ferdinand served as Frederick's aide-de-camp at Mollwitz on 10 April 1741 at the beginning of the War of the Austrian Succession, and at Chotusitz in 1742. Ferdinand was given command of Frederick's Leibgarde Battalion when the Margrave Wilhelm of Brandenburg was killed at Prague in 1744. He was awarded the Prussian Order of the Black Eagle when peace was agreed with Austria. He was promoted to the rank of *Generalmajor* in May 1745 and, the following month, commanded a brigade at Hohenfriedberg.

3 Career summary from Sir Charles Hotham-Thompson, *Operations of the Allied Army under the Duke of Brunswick 1757-1762* (London: T. Jeffreys, 1764; reprinted additional material by Dirk Rottgard Point Pleasant New Jersey: Winged Hussar Publishing, The Nafziger Collection, 2016), pp.213-215; Smith, *Armies of the Seven Years War*, pp.314-315; 'Ferdinand of Brunswick', Seven Years' War < http://www.kronoskaf.com/syw/index.php?title=Ferdinand_of_Brunswick> (accessed 15 January–31 October 2019).

Generalfeldmarschall Ferdinand, Prince of Brunswick-Lüneberg-Wolfenbüttel. (Anne S.K. Brown Collection)

In September his brigade successfully stormed a height, rather poignantly defended by his younger brother Ludwig in Austrian service, during the Battle of Soor. A second brother died by his side during the charge in which five guns were captured. At the Peace of Dresden, King Frederick II and Prince Ferdinand paraded together in Berlin.

Ferdinand remained in close, and trusted, touch with Frederick who acted as his military mentor. Ferdinand was promoted to *Generalleutnant* in 1750, appointed as the Governor of Peitz in 1752, as the Governor of Magdeburg in 1755 and as *Inhaber* (honorary colonel) of the Infanterie Regiment Nr.5 in the same year.

In the opening phase of the European part of the Seven Years War, in 1756, Ferdinand was entrusted with the right of three Prussian columns falling on Dresden. He then led the Prussian vanguard in driving the Saxon Army out of Nollendorf. Again on the right wing, he took part in the blockade of Pirna in September and the Battle of Lobositz in October. Frederick and Ferdinand wintered over in Dresden, where they plotted the future campaign. Ferdinand's successes continued with his capture of Aussig on 23 April 1757 and his able command of a division at Prague on 6 May. He contributed to the preliminaries leading up to Rossbach but did not take part in the battle itself.

Appointed to command the allied army in November, after the Duke of Cumberland's disgrace surrounding the Convention of Kloster Zeven, he found it in low spirits after its capitulation and its defeat at Hastenbeck on 26 July 1757. Taking command at Stade on 9 November, he quickly launched an unseasonal winter attack in Hanover which surprised the French Army at rest. The army he commanded would have posed a challenge to even the most able general. It was a patchwork of troops from various German states and, as its commander, Ferdinand remained answerable to the rulers of those states.

Ferdinand successfully drove the French back across the Rhine by the end of March 1758 in his winter campaign. Newly promoted as *General der Infanterie*, in June he fought the Battle of Krefeld, against a French army under Clermont, deep on the French side of the Rhine. In his attack, he coordinated three separate columns and inflicted 4,000 casualties on his enemy which was, then, prevented from being able to send reinforcements to the Austrians. Although he was unable to maintain his over-extended position and was compelled to withdraw back to Lippe, his successes encouraged the British to send him a force of 8,000. Ferdinand was promoted by Frederick to *Generalfeldmarschall*.

Ferdinand mounted a spring offensive in March 1759, but was beaten at the Battle of Bergen on 13 April. His victory at Minden on 1 August, coupled with the parallel success at Gohfeld, left the French in an untenable position, and they were obliged to give up most of the gains that they had achieved in Germany. King George II of Britain admitted him to the Order of the Garter and the British Parliament gave him a vote of thanks as the 'Victor of Minden'.

Ferdinand inflicted yet another defeat on the French at the Battle of Warburg on 31 July 1760. Despite this he came under increasing pressure, but successfully continued to protect Frederick's rear. The French mounted further pressure on him, threatening him with two armies which amounted to 100,000 men but he forced them to come together through posing his own threat to their lines of communications. Although outnumbered by five to three, he managed to engage and defeat them on 15/16 July at Vellinghausen 1761.

A similar situation arose in 1762 when he, again, faced two larger French armies, defeating one of them at Wilhelmsthal on 24 June. Frederick, hard pressed in the east, genuinely seemed to appreciate Ferdinand's stoical performance in maintaining pressure on the French. After the war was over, in 1763, together they toured the scenes of Ferdinand's successes at Minden, Warburg and Vellinghausen. Ferdinand returned to the Governorship of Magdeburg but the friendship with Frederick became strained, resulting in Ferdinand's resignation from the service of Prussia in 1766. He joined Austrian service in November, becoming a *Feldmarschall*, receiving command of a regiment in Bohemia, and taking possession of a castle at Vechelde. After a period, Frederick and Ferdinand forgot their recent differences and Frederick came to visit him on at least four occasions.[4] He died, unmarried and with substantial debts, on 3 July 1792.

4 Knowles, *Minden and the Seven Years War*, p.56.

Erbprinz Karl Wilhelm Ferdinand, the Hereditary Prince of Brunswick

The eldest son of the Duke of Brunswick and Frederick II of Prussia's older sister, Karl Wilhelm Ferdinand was born on 9 October 1735 at Wolfenbüttel.[5] As a young man, he acquired a taste for travel which was to stay with him in later life, beginning by touring Germany and then France and the Netherlands.

Erbprinz Karl Wilhelm Ferdinand, the Hereditary Prince of Brunswick, depicted here in later life. (Anne S.K. Brown Collection)

He learned his military trade in 1757, initially in the allied Army commanded by the Duke of Cumberland in Westphalia and Hanover. He performed well as a *Generalmajor* at the Battle of Hastenbeck on 26 July, despite it being an allied defeat, personally leading the charge of an infantry brigade and recapturing the central artillery battery. After the awkwardness of Cumberland's capitulation of Kloster Zeven, King George II of Britain secured agreement that the Erbprinz's uncle, Ferdinand of Brunswick, should command the allied army. It was then, almost assumed that the Erbprinz would follow his uncle.

The following years did nothing to tarnish his reputation, and he became known as an exponent of irregular warfare. He performed well in larger battles, such as Minden's companion battle at Gohfeld, at Warburg and Clostercamp.

After the war's end, in 1764, he travelled to England to marry the daughter of the Prince of Wales. In 1766, he visited France, where his former enemies received him respectfully. He went on to Switzerland, where he met Voltaire, and thereafter to Rome and Naples to study antiquities. He and his wife returned to Brunswick, where he served his father, the Duke, and helping relieve the Duchy of debts incurred in the war. In 1779, the Erbprinz defended Troppau in the face of the Austrian Army during the War of Bavarian Succession.

He succeeded his father as the Duke of Brunswick in 1780, and became a notable example of 'benevolent despot': canny, considerate and wise. While providing support and service to the King of Prussia (he was a Prussian *Generalfeldmarschall*) he always tried to keep his Duchy from foreign entanglements.

5 Career summary from 'Karl Wilhelm Ferdinand', *Seven Years' War* <http://www.kronoskaf.com/syw/index.php?title=Karl_Wilhelm_Ferdinand> (accessed 15 January–31 October 2019).

A keen supporter of Prussia's anti-Austrian policy, he joined the 'League of Princes' (the *Fürstenbund*), becoming commander-in-chief of its federal army. In 1787, he led the army which successfully invaded the Netherlands with élan, his campaign being a model example of command.

Bizarrely, he was offered command of the French revolutionary army because of his interest in reform, yet in 1792 he was appointed to lead an Austro-German army to attack revolutionary France. Unfortunately, he was not allowed unfettered command, with the King of Prussia interfering; this led to defeat at Valmy on 20 September. Despite this, the Duke executed an accomplished withdrawal and managed to recapture Frankfurt. In the following year he took command of the army again, this time beating the French at Pirmasens and personally leading the assault on the Kiltrichon Heights, and also inflicting a further defeat on the French at Kaiserslautern. Once again, he found himself stifled by Royal interference and resigned command. Despite this, he was maintained his links with Prussia, acting in a diplomatic capacity. Prevailed upon by Queen Louise of Prussia, he was persuaded to return to command in 1806 but, again, his perennial problem of Royal tinkering adversely affected the performance of the Army. At Auerstadt he received a wound which was ultimately to prove fatal. He died at Ottensen, near Hamburg, on 10 November 1806.

Lord George Sackville

Lieutenant General Lord George Sackville (Anne S.K. Brown Collection)

George Sackville was born on 26 January 1716 to Lionel, the 1st Duke of Dorset, and his wife Elizabeth.[6] Although their third son, his christening was attended by King George I, who became his Godfather. Educated at Westminster School in London, he also became familiar with Dublin, where his father served as Lord Lieutenant of Ireland, during which he became friends with Jonathan Swift and Lord Ligonier. While in Dublin, he graduated from Trinity College and proceeded to serve his father as First Secretary and then as a Member for Portarlington in the Irish House of Commons.

At the age of 21, he joined the British Army as a captain of the 7th Horse. Three years later, he transferred as lieutenant colonel to the 28th Foot, with which he served in the War of the Austrian Succession. A further three

6 Career summary from 'Sackville, Lord George', *Seven Years' War* <http://www.kronoskaf.com/syw/index.php?title=Sackville,_Lord_George> (accessed 15 January–31 October 2019); P. Mackesy, *The Coward of Minden. The Affair of Lord George Sackville* (London: Penguin Books Ltd, 1979), pp. 28-36.

years later he was promoted to colonel. At Fontenoy in 1745, Sackville led his regiment in a bold attack on the French positions where, as a result of his deep penetration, he was captured after being wounded. Taken to Louis XV in person, he was released and permitted to return home. On his recovery, he joined the 20th Foot and took part in putting down the Jacobite Rebellion. Shortly after, he joined the Duke of Cumberland in Flanders, and took up the colonelcy of the 3rd Horse.

A freemason, he rose to be Grandmaster of the Grand Lodge of Ireland in 1751. He married Diana Sambrooke in 1754, with whom he had a daughter, Diana, in 1756.

Promoted to major general in 1755, Sackville was considered for the post of commander-in-chief in North America, but was pipped by Edward Braddock who led the ill-fated Fort Duquesne expedition. Sworn-in to the Privy Council in 1758, Sackville was promoted to lieutenant general and joined the 3rd Duke of Marlborough as his second-in-command for amphibious attacks against the French coastline, including the half-baked Saint-Malo raid.

In July 1758, Sackville supported Marlborough as part of the British contingent sent to Germany to reinforce Ferdinand of Brunswick's allied army, disembarking at Emden and effecting a junction with Imhoff's Corps near Coesfeld. Marlborough's sudden death on 20 October saw Sackville elevated to command the British contingent, although still subordinate to Ferdinand.

At Minden, Sackville's lacklustre performance in command of the allied cavalry on the right wing failed to transform a victory into a total rout. His conduct has been described as 'disgraceful disobedience'.[7] Under a cloud, Sackville was sent home in disgrace while he was replaced as the commander of the British contingent by Lieutenant General the Marquis of Granby.

Bitterly refusing to accept that he had disobeyed orders, Sackville insisted on facing trial by court-martial which he finally achieved in 1760. However, the findings cannot have been to his liking, as the court found him guilty and 'unfit to serve his Majesty in any capacity whatsoever'.[8] The verdict was ordered to be read and entered into the orderly book of every British regiment. King George II also ensured that Sackville's name was struck from the Privy rolls.

By 1765, however, Sackville's return to his former status was begun again when King George III quietly had him added back onto the rolls of the Privy Council. In 1769, Sackville inherited the estates of Lady Elizabeth Germain, whose name he also took on, allowing him to be newly styled as Lord George Germain. Appointed as Secretary of State for the American Department in 1775, Germain had to contend with the American rebellion. His involvement in the Saratoga campaign was, in part through lack of clarity of his orders to Lieutenant General Howe, a failure. The 1781 loss of Yorktown further contributed to tarnishing Germain's reputation and he was persuaded to

7 Lieutenant General Sir R. Savory, *His Britannic Majesty's Army in Germany During the Seven Years War* (Oxford: The Clarendon Press, 1966), p.171.

8 Mackesy, *The Coward of Minden*, p.224.

step down, in return for admission to the House of Lords. Made Baron Bolebrooke, in the County of Sussex and Viscount Sackville, of Drayton in the County of Northampton, this may have been scant consolation as ill-health forced his withdrawal and retirement to his home at Stoneland Lodge in Sussex, where he died in 1785.

August Friedrich von Spörcken

Born to the *Landdrost* (Steward) of Harburg in 1698, August Friedrich von Spörcken was the nephew of the Venetian Field-Marshal Johann Matthias von der Schulenburg.[9] Having benefitted from a good education, including the sciences, he entered military service as an ensign with the Infantry Regiment von Gauvain in 1715. Within a year he transferred to the Hanoverian Guards as a *leutenant*. He married *Gräfin* Kielmansegg in 1729 but was widowed two years later during the birth of the couple's only son.

By 1733, mainly through family connections, Spörcken was an *Oberstleutnant*. He volunteered to serve in the Hanoverian contingent in the War of the Polish Succession. However, his first real experience of combat was to be in the War of the Austrian Succession. Commanding his own regiment of foot, he marched to Brabant in 1742 and took part in the victory at Dettingen in 1743. He campaigned in the Netherlands for the remainder of the war. At regimental command, he sustained a gunshot to the chest at Fontenoy in 1745. Forced to recuperate for nine months, he returned as commander of a brigade. At Rocoux in October 1746, he suffered a blunt wound to the neck. He took part at Lauffeld and was promoted to *Generalmajor* in 1747.

In 1756, as a *Generalleutnant*, he was part of the Hanoverian contingent sent to reinforce Britain against a potential French invasion. That contingent was recalled in 1757 due to the attempted French invasion of Hanover. Spörcken was at Hastenbeck and then had the task of applying the Convention of Kloster Zeven to the Hanoverian Army, much to the disapproval of King George II. After the Battle of Rossbach, generals Zastrow and Spörcken were directed to renew operations against the French. When Ferdinand of Brunswick was invited to take command of the Allied Army in November 1757 Spörcken was given command of the second line, in December of that year participating in the attack on Celle.

During Ferdinand's winter offensive, in February 1758, Spörcken was given the right column, but was switched to the left after the Weser crossing. By the summer, Spörcken was across the Rhine. He commanded the left wing of the allied army at Krefeld and he was promoted *General der Infanterie*.

In 1759, Spörcken was trusted to protect Westphalia when Ferdinand took the remainder of the allied army to Hesse. Spörcken's corps re-joined the allied army in time for the Battle of Minden, where it played a key role in

9 Career summary from 'Sporken, August Friedrich von', *Seven Years* <http://www.kronoskaf.com/syw/index.php?title=Spörcken,_August_Friedrich_von> (accessed 15 January–31 October 2019).

the allied victory. He contributed to subsequent operations in Hesse. In 1760, he was responsible for maintaining communications with Britain via the River Weser and defences in Westphalia. Despite encouragement to remain in a defensive posture while Ferdinand was manoeuvring in Hesse, when Saint-Germain managed to effect a junction with Broglie, Spörcken re-joined the allied army in time to take part in the successful Battle of Warburg. In the winter of 1760, Spörcken was appointed as *Chef* of the Hanoverian Foot Guards.

He suffered mixed fortunes in the latter part of the Seven Years War. He successfully surprised the Saxons at Langensalza but was obliged to withdraw. Frequently consigned to guarding operations, he was blamed for a French attack on one of his subordinates at Neuhaus im Sollinge, and asked to be relieved of command on the grounds of unjustified criticism. Ferdinand agreed but also sent his best wishes. However, it was not long before he was returned to corps command but, in battle, Ferdinand preferred to place his trust in the Erbprinz of Brunswick rather than Spörcken, who was given token command of the first line. Spörcken's last battle of the Seven Years War was at Wilhelmstahl, where his blunders contributed to a failure to trap the French Army.

After the war, he lived in Hanover city, of which he was Governor. Appointed *Generalfeldmarschall* by King George III, he began reform of the Hanoverian Army, focusing on drill and training. He died at Hanover on 12 June 1776.

6

The Operational (or Theatre-Level) Context

Britain's first proper foray onto mainland Europe in the Seven Years War was not a success.

Frederick of Prussia's estimate of French capabilities made him assume that they would be unable to commence operations in Germany before the middle of March 1757. His assumption was that they would not afford more than 50,000 troops. His fortress of Wesel, on the Rhine, had a substantial garrison of six battalions. This would provide sufficient cover and time for his allies to assemble an 'Army of Observation' behind (north of) the River Lippe.[1] The Army of Observation was intended to be a deterrent, never seriously potent enough to be effective or threatening, but sufficient to inflict some damage on an aggressor. However, Britain refused to release any German unit protecting England until replaced by a British one and, as is often the case, the actual assembly took longer than promised.

Matters escalated early in the year. The French insisted that Hanover was to remain quiescent and, worse, maintain at her own expense the routes which the French would use to transit to reach the Prussian front. Additionally, the fortress of Hameln was to be given to Austria, and Hanover was to request approval to move bodies of troops around. Thus insulted, the Elector of Hanover (and virtually automatically, the British King George II) declared war.

The most obvious candidate to command the Army of Observation was the King's (and Elector's) son, William Augustus, the Duke of Cumberland. Not only experienced as a soldier, Cumberland possessed sufficient authority to negotiate with other nations' commanders, and also with Hanover on his father's behalf. Indeed, it was as a Hanoverian general that he was to command the 'Army of his Britannic Majesty'. His orders, issued on 30 March 1757, stipulated that his role was defensive, limited to protecting Hanoverian, Prussian and Hessian dominions from foreign invasion and restricted to the

1 S. Reid, *The Battle of Minden 1759 – The Impossible Victory of the Seven Years War* (Barnsley: Frontline Books, 2016), p.5.

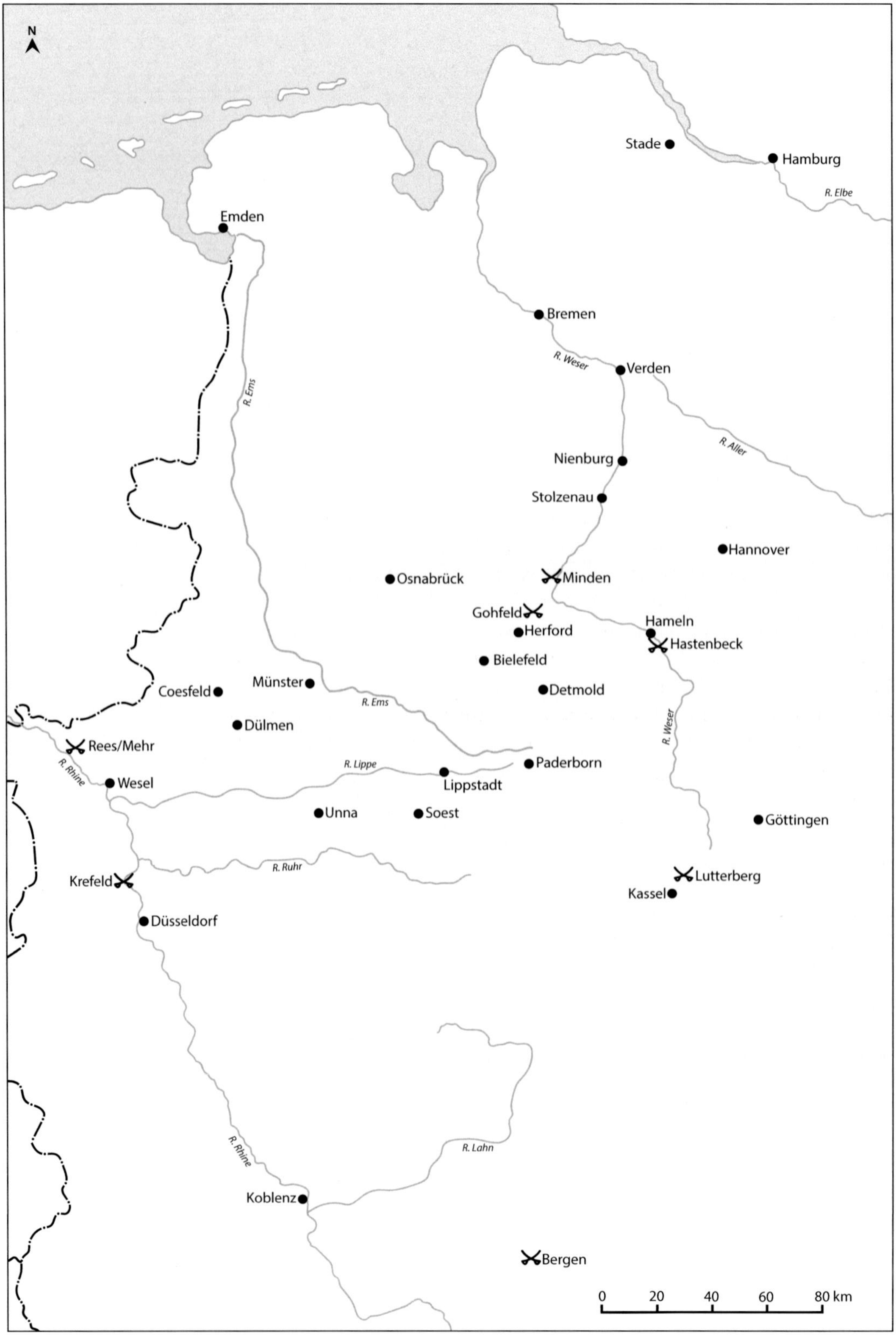

North Germany, showing the theatre of war 1757-1759.)George Anderson © Helion and Company 2021)

use of force only to repulse such an invasion.[2] Rather ambiguously, the orders also noted that France, in penetrating Westphalia, intended solely to reach Bohemia and, that, in such a situation, force was not to be used. In effect, as the possessions which Cumberland was charged to defend lay to the north of the River Lippe, he was presumably expected to infer that, as long as the French transit was restricted to the south of the river, it was to be allowed free passage. Also, the ambiguity of the orders meant that Frederick of Prussia could be endangered, as long as Hanover remained safe.

As it transpired, the French breached any presumed understanding shortly before Cumberland actually received his orders. A party of hussars began a reconnaissance of Geldern, presaging a much larger force, of 135 infantry battalions and 143 cavalry squadrons, than Frederick's estimate had allowed for.[3]

As it was, the Army of Observation was far from assembled. In fact, some elements had not yet left Britain. It was significantly outnumbered by the French. In the face of such overweening force, Frederick's Wesel garrison abandoned the fortress, the six battalions withdrawing eastwards to Lippstadt, near Paderborn, and the guns being moved via Holland to Prussia.

Cumberland arrived in Germany on 14 April and was advised by Frederick's liaison officer, *Generalleutnant* von Schmettau, that if he could head towards Lippstadt and hold the line of the Lippe, then Frederick might be able to send some reinforcements.[4] However, the French had got the bit between their teeth, crossing the Rhine, taking Wesel and capturing Münster by 24 April. In the face of this advancing threat, Lippstadt too was abandoned. However, Zastrow, still in actual command of the Hanoverian Army until Cumberland's arrival, had marched west to Bielefeld to conjoin with the Prussians and assemble a force of 27 battalions of infantry and 20 squadrons of cavalry. Rather than mounting a spoiling attack on the French, who were strung out, he elected to await the arrival of Cumberland, who reached Bielefeld on 3 May. Cumberland barely had time to gather his thoughts for, on the very next day, some of his foraging parties were surprised by the arrival of the buccaneering light troops of Johann Christian Fischer. The Comte d'Estrées, the commander of the French main body, and Cumberland exchanged the sort of pleasantries that commanders exchange when both are set on achieving their objectives. It was suggested that Cumberland could permit the passage of the French, this protecting Hanover's neutrality. He refused.

At this point, the fate of Europe hung in the balance. Frederick had just mauled an Austrian army near Prague, but had insufficient strength to capture the city itself. If the Austrians were to be encouraged to agree a settlement, France could become isolated. Despite this, d'Estrées was ordered by Versailles to press on.

When the French march resumed on 21 May, it was at a much less vigorous pace and it took until 12 June before they were close to the

2 Savory, *His Britannic Majesty's Army in Germany*, pp.13-16.
3 Reid, *The Battle of Minden 1759*, p.8.
4 Savory, *His Britannic Majesty's Army in Germany*, p.20.

Hanoverian picquets on the west side of the Teutoburger Wald. Cumberland's intelligence-gathering was inadequate, so he was taken by surprise when d'Estrées' leading light troops began to envelop both his flanks on the 13th, to the extent of threatening his line of communications via Herford to Minden.[5] Rather than confirm the strength or weakness of these probes, Cumberland decided to withdraw after dark. He and his staff had not, however, made plans for this, still less having communicated them adequately. Not all the units were informed. Chaos reigned. Recognising an opportunity, the French seized it and attacked.[6]

In the confusion, the Hanoverians displayed poor fire discipline, opening up on any movement in the gloom regardless of whether it might have been caused by friendly forces. The Prussians, however, retained their discipline and acted as rearguard, which allowed much of the army to reach Bielefeld. The chaos continued there too, but that served the allies as their French pursuers were unable to resist the temptation provided by the stagnant baggage train.[7] Despite not deserving this relief, Cumberland was able to get most of his force across the River Weser to the relative safety of Hameln on the evening of 16 June. He was, however, still operating with inadequate intelligence and opted to sit it out, leaving the initiative with his opponent. He sent two battalions and two squadrons to Nienburg and the Prussians to Minden to protect his supplies. However, Frederick feared for his units and recalled them in July, causing Cumberland to replace them with two battalions and two squadrons of his own.

Hastenbeck

Despite not having encountered much resistance, d'Estrées resorted to his slower pace until, once again under pressure from Versailles, he resumed the offensive, crossing the Weser at Holzminden. River crossings are potentially risky, creating a vulnerability as the force is astride the obstacle. Cumberland's response was, again, weak. He sent parties up the river to monitor the French but, instead of attacking them while they were unbalanced, resorted to occupying a defensive position on the 286 metre-high Obensberg feature on a woody ridge near Hastenbeck, to the east of Hameln.[8]

The position he selected offered good fields of view and fire but, significantly outnumbered by the French as he was, and judging by his performance thus far in the campaign, there was every chance he would attempt to withdraw again. The disadvantage of his position was that the very steepness of the Obensberg feature would compel him to withdraw off

5 Savory, *His Britannic Majesty's Army in Germany*, p.24.

6 J.W. von Archenholz, *Prussia and the Seven Years War 1756-1763* (Milton Keynes: Leonaur, 2016), pp.51-53.

7 Reid, *The Battle of Minden 1759*, p.9.

8 Digby Smith, *A New History of the Seven Years War* (Godmanchester: Ken Trotman Publishing, 2017), Vol.I, pp.178-179. 'Battle of Hastenbeck', *Seven Years' War* <http://www.kronoskaf.com/syw/index.php?title=1757-07-26_-_Battle_of_Hastenbeck> (accessed 15 January–31 October 2019).

to one of his flanks rather than directly rearwards. This offered the potential for d'Estrées to pin him to the ridge and defeat him.

At dawn on 25 July, *Lieutenant-Général* Chevert was required to fix Cumberland's left wing in the vicinity of Voremberg, by attacking with three brigades. This would allow the Duc de Broglie to cross with his corps from the west bank of the Weser, and further pin Cumberland's right wing. Once Cumberland was well and truly fixed, d'Estrées would launch the decisive attack on the centre.[9]

By the time a thick mist had cleared at about 5:30 a.m., it became obvious that, rather than attempting to withdraw laterally, Cumberland was initially determined to fight from his strong positions. For d'Estrées, this meant that, rather than admit the *coup de grâce*, he was now obliged to launch a frontal assault. In order to achieve this, he would require to commit as many of his resources as possible, which took time. By 5:00 p.m., the time taken to marshal his forces, d'Estrées elected to postpone his attack until the next morning.

An anonymous French officer recorded his experiences:

> Having inspected the positions of the Duke of Cumberland as far as he could, the Marshal decided to advance around the heights, and attack the enemy's left flank. And all his staff officers were in support of this plan. Accordingly, he detached (Note: to the extreme right flank) Monsieur de Chevert at midnight with the Brigades of Picardie, of Navarre, of la Marine, the Volontaires de Flandres and Haynault, and those of the Army (Note: these latter were screening light troops). These three brigades, supported by the Brigade d'Eu, were to attack the enemy's left wing. The success of the day depended on this attack, because it was thought impossible to debouch into the plain, as long the enemy were master of the heights in front of the woods.
>
> The Marquis d'Armentières, who commanded three brigades on the right wing of the French main body, supported by the dragoons on foot, was to advance along the edge of the wood towards the heights. The Brigade Champagne, under the command of Monsieur d'Auerly, and supported by the Brigade Reding was to attack outside the wood. Monsieur Contades commanded four brigades, which were to attack the steep ground between the wood and the village of Hastenbeck, and anything they encountered beyond that. The Marquis de Guerchy and Monsieur de Sainte Pern with the Regiment du Roi, the Grenadiers Royaux and de France, supported by two further brigades and troops from the Palatinate were to assault the village of Hastenbeck itself. The entire cavalry was assigned as general support to the infantry until after the attack had taken place, when it was to debouch onto the plain....
>
> At 5 o'clock on the 26th, the next morning, the enemy started firing from their left flank. Our artillery maintained its dominance, and returned the opposing fire with all possible liveliness and effect... [T]he success of the day hinged on the attack by Monsieur de Chevert. He was not to attack before 9 o'clock; and it was exactly at this time that we heard the first musket shots on our right wing. The

9 Savory, *His Britannic Majesty's Army in Germany*, pp.29-38.

fire then increased, and after a very lively action, which lasted between one and one and a half hours, the enemy was expelled from the hills and from the woods, despite constantly reinforcing their infantry with troops drawn from their right wing.

At the first musket shots of Monsieur de Chevert's attack, the Army started to move forward, the field artillery and the regimental guns to the fore, which crushed the enemy. The Marquis d'Armentières found but little resistance. The Regiment of Champagne encountered fierce opposition, having to pass a ditch in order to get onto a battery of eight pieces that was blocking its advance. Enduring the first salvos, the Regiment was momentarily disordered, but it opened fire and captured the battery in an instant. In the meantime, Monsieur Contades occupied the gap between the wood and village of Hastenbeck with the brigades under his command.

Monsieurs de Guerchy and de St. Pern, who were to attack Hastenbeck village, formed three columns of the Regiments du Roi, the Grenadiers de France and the Regiment Solar, which commenced their advance at the same time the Army started moving. They had hardly approached to within half a cannon shot of the village, when it burst into flames; it was unclear whether this was caused by was the enemy or by our howitzers. It is certain that the enemy was willing to defend it, as they had started to dig trenches. The fire did not prevent the Grenadiers de France from advancing into the village, while the Regiments du Roi and de Solar advanced to the left and to the right of the village. As the Grenadiers de France debouched, they took some canister shots from a distance of barely half a musket shot of the enemy which, however, did little damage. The Commanding Officer, not hesitating a moment, ordered a half turn to the right and rushed the wood, which was still occupied by the enemy who was obliged to abandon a cannon, many knapsacks, entrenching tools, and the like.

By the account I have given of the different attacks, it should be apparent that we had now seized the hills and the village of Hastenbeck, and that the cavalry could debouch in order to attack the enemy on the plain.

How great then was the astonishment of the whole Army, as the Corps of Grenadiers de France was ordered to withdraw into the village of Hastenbeck. Also, the artillery was to retire again past the ravines that lay between the wood and the village. The rather close woods prevented Monsieur de Chevert from close pursuit of the enemy and confirmation of their movements. These withdrew and then took the brigade d'Eu, which was in support of the Brigade of la Marine, "en flanc". The surprise of this unexpected attack, and a persistent fight, forced this brigade to give way to the superior enemy. At the beginning of this attack, the Commanding Officer made off, claiming that he wanted to search for help, but did not return to the battlefield. Instead, he went to the Marshal and announced that he had observed an enemy column of more than nine or ten thousand men turning our right wing. At that news, the Marshal sent all light troops to our camp, to prevent it being looted by the enemy; almost all of the cavalry was moved to the right wing. At the same time he issued orders for the Army to halt, and for the artillery, which had conducted itself so well, to retire. This movement gave the enemy time to withdraw, and perhaps their flank attack was done only to cover their retreat. Monsieur de Guerchy was best placed to observe and comprehend all of this, as he advanced with the Grenadiers de France. He was enraged, as he

> saw such a splendid opportunity for complete victory being wasted. Meanwhile he pursued the enemy with the Grenadiers as best as he could.
>
> At this moment, the Marshal arrived and saw that he had been given false information, and that the enemy was withdrawing. Immediately, but by now too late, he ordered the remaining Grenadiers de France to advance again; the nearby cavalry Brigades of Royal Pologne, and the Carabiniers debouched into the plain, while the Grenadiers de France advanced out of the wood. But the enemy had already crossed the small creek at Afferde, and by 6 o'clock was out of sight. He had even taken the precaution of setting fire to his camp, presumably in order to delay the advance of our cavalry. A single body of infantry could be observed retiring to the right, a regiment of 2 battalions. It seemed to march with speed, but it could still have been caught. However, the Marshal called off any further action.
>
> It is apparent, that the false report given to the Marshal, had saved the opposing army, and I must say that the staff officer who gave it has lost his good name among the troops. One couldn't really describe this action as a full-scale battle because the whole army did not engage "en front". Rather it was a large scale infantry engagement, but one with great honour, considering its courageous conduct in spite of the numerous obstacles it had to surmount… Much credit for the fortune of this day must be assigned to our artillery and to Vallière who had sited it and overseen its action in silencing the enemy guns. The Army camped on the battlefield; it was said that the enemy was retiring to Minden.[10]

The Hameln garrison surrendered on 28 July, the French uncovering 72 pieces of artillery cached there. Its garrison consisted of 1,000 souls, 700 being regular troops and 300 conscripted peasants. The former were forbidden to serve again for at least one year. The latter were informed that if they were ever caught again under arms they would go straight to the gallows. Hameln was considered valuable to the French as a possible future magazine.

Hastenbeck was one of those odd engagements where both sides ought to have performed better, but ultimately victory can go to the side with the stronger morale, and which refuses to be beaten. For this reason, Hastenbeck can be considered as a French victory. Cumberland was not the first commander in history to abandon the field in the mistaken belief that he was losing: indeed, the great Frederick did exactly the same in his first major battle, at Mollwitz. For Cumberland though, despite inflicting greater numbers of casualties on the enemy, he was arguably beaten in his own mind, probably as a result of the impossibility of fully satisfying his irascible father. He withdrew northwards, effectively giving up his defence of Hanover and Brunswick.[11]

In his frustration with his son, King George II, in his role as Duke of Brunswick-Lüneburg, directed him to agree terms which would, at least, protect his army and pre-empt any further French attack on Hanover. Penned

10 C. Rogge, 'Battle of Hastenbeck Account 05', *Seven Years' War* < http://www.kronoskaf.com/syw/index.php?title=Battle_of_Hastenbeck_Account_05> (accessed 4 June 2019). Translation of an account by an anonymous French officer originally published in the *Neues Militärisches Journal*, 1788-1805, Vol.1, Hanover 1788, pp. 220-236.

11 Archenholz, *Prussia and the Seven Years War 1756-1763*, p.53.

in near Hamburg, at Stade on the River Elbe, Cumberland surrendered on 8 September. Under the Treaty of Kloster Zeven, his army was dissolved, the Hessians and Brunswickers forced to make their way homeward, while the Hanoverians went into a sort of suspended animation, neither in captivity nor able to conduct any further action.[12]

Cumberland returned home to face his father's ire. For Frederick too, the prospects seemed bleak, with the Austrians succeeding in occupying Berlin for a spell.[13] Then Frederick succeeded in overturning everything by inflicting a magnificent defeat on a combined Franco-Imperial Army at Rossbach, in Saxony, on 5 November. George, once again in his role as King of Great Britain, overturned his son's surrender and resumed the war with France.

Enter Ferdinand

A fresh commander had to be found, and the role fell to Prince Ferdinand of Brunswick, an officer in Prussian service and Frederick's brother-in-law. Fresh from the victory of Rossbach, Ferdinand insisted on some pre-conditions before agreeing to the role.[14] Most importantly, he refused to become a puppet of the Hanoverian ministry, insisting on being allowed to run the army on his own terms, with complete authority and a budget. He also insisted on having direct access to King George II.

He reached Hamburg, to assume command on 23 November 1757 even before his terms has been formally acknowledged, but found a demoralised force.[15] Worse, the French were reported to be manoeuvring towards him. His cure was to order offensive action, but this late in the season the roads were turning to quagmires and his men and horses were already out of condition. He got as far south as the River Aller, which drains into the Weser, where the French were firmly ensconced on the far bank with no apparent desire to engage in unseasonal combat. In frustration Ferdinand ordered a withdrawal on 24 December, but his remedy had had an effect: the army was starting to learn to trust its new commander; and, having previously been penned-in, it had managed to create some elbow room in which to manoeuvre.[16]

One significant improvement which Ferdinand urgently sought was to increase the capabilities of his cavalry.[17] Arguably, this was something which Cumberland should also have done. Perhaps his performance at the Teutoburger Wald and at Hastenbeck would have been better if he had used his light cavalry as his eyes and ears. Ferdinand asked Frederick for a mounted brigade, both dragoons and hussars. Frederick had gone to great lengths to improve his own cavalry, both for scouting and as a strike force.

12 Savory, *His Britannic Majesty's Army in Germany*, p.39.
13 Smith, *A New History of the Seven Years War*, Vol.I, pp.227-230.
14 Savory, *His Britannic Majesty's Army in Germany*, p.48.
15 Archenholz, *Prussia and the Seven Years war 1756-1763*, p.80.
16 Savory, *His Britannic Majesty's Army in Germany*, p.55.
17 Archenholz, *Prussia and the Seven Years war 1756-1763*, p.134.

In particular, he had instilled a sense of rapid response. As an officer in the Prussian service, Ferdinand was well aware of the shortcomings of these aspects of his own force.

The Prussian cavalry reinforcements were welcome but Ferdinand's force was still relatively small compared to his French opponents. Maintaining a small force on active operations is challenging, and it lacks the resilience needed to absorb shocks. Reinforcements were sought from Britain, which was heavily committed around the globe and so required being given reason to believe that its troops were not going to be needlessly expended. Ferdinand sought to prove himself worthy of such support.

His force's morale was on the up. In contrast, the French were enduring the winter away from home. Morale was poor, and worsening. As an indicator of this, the commander d'Estrées had been replaced by the Duc de Richelieu, soon to be replaced in turn by the Prince de Clermont – seldom a good sign.[18]

Ferdinand began 1758 energetically. He returned to the Aller on 18 February, fixing the French in their positions, while taking the main element westwards to where the Aller joined the Weser, at Verden, capturing a bridge before continuing upriver to Hoya where the Weser could be crossed. Now Ferdinand was able to use his cavalry imaginatively, pushing some Hanoverian hussars across the Weser. The effect of this was to scare the French garrison into hastily abandoning Bremen. This panic became infectious and the local French commander, Saint-Germain, likewise withdrew, as far back as Münster. Similarly, Clermont also withdrew, intending to make a stand at Hameln. This local deflation of the French occupation enabled Ferdinand to set up a secure supply chain along the Weser from Bremen to Nienburg, which then supported operations against Minden.[19] Minden fell to the allies on 15 March after a short siege of two days.

It was now obvious to Clermont that his army was in no fit state to resist, so he decided to retreat back beyond the Rhine. Broglie was directed to abandon Kassel. Ferdinand had done well. Thus far, he had protected Hanover and forced a French evacuation of Westphalia without a major battle, but his army was exhausted and required an operational pause to draw breath and reconstitute.

The allies quickly filled the void left by the French. The liberation of Bremen was coupled with further French withdrawal from Emden under pressure from two warships of the Royal Navy. A scratch occupation force of Royal Marines and British sailors was soon replaced by a British infantry battalion, Brudenell's 51st Foot.[20]

One sole representative of Britain joined Ferdinand's headquarters in advance of further reinforcement, Colonel James Durand. Durand was impressed by Ferdinand, and by 'his politic, cool and clear manner of explaining himself', and yet he also observed another side to Ferdinand's character, one of secrecy: 'he wisely never declares his intention to any body

18 Szabo, *The Seven Years' War in Europe 1756-1763*, p.115
19 Savory, *His Britannic Majesty's Army in Germany*, pp.62-63.
20 Savory, *His Britannic Majesty's Army in Germany*, p.65.

here'.[21] So Ferdinand is shown to be a clear thinker, but also private – arguably to a fault. Ferdinand's preference was to ride almost alone, accompanied only by one aide de camp and a minimal staff. His closest confident was his personal secretary, Westphalen. Subordinate commanders were let in on his plans only at the last moment, and he used sealed, not-to-be-opened-before, orders to maintain secrecy and security. In Ferdinand's army, subordinates were expected to obey, not necessarily to understand. In a multinational coalition, such an approach to allies could have been perceived as offensive and did not engender trust or confidence.

Buoyed up by the British reappearance on the content, but also boosted by fresh supplies, Ferdinand aimed for nothing less than the destruction of his French opponents. Timed to coincide with British amphibious operations on the French coast, he intended to cross the River Rhine and push south, trapping the French against the River Meuse. The British had attempted coastal raiding earlier in the war, inconclusively against Rochefort in 1757 and in June 1758, landing at Cancale before attacking and burning several vessels at St Servan near St Malo.[22] Though hailed as a victory, St Malo was little more than a flea-bite to the French. However, it was hoped that another St Malo adventure would cause the enemy to divert troops there, evening up the disparity in numbers with Ferdinand's smaller force: 'If their design can combine with what I have in hand, the effect will be all the greater'.[23]

Krefeld

Ferdinand's offensive started by violating Dutch territory, using pontoons to cross the Rhine. Clermont feared that Ferdinand was aiming to cross the Meuse as well, so ordered his army to assemble near Wesel to be ready to withdraw across the Meuse. However, Belle-Isle, the French Minister of War, stiffened Clermont and attempted in vain to coordinate his actions with those of the Prince de Soubise commanding a second French army. Clermont adopted a strong defence at Rheinberg which Ferdinand attempted to attack in a rather desultory fashion on the night of 10 June. The French made good their escape from that position on the 12th. Successful withdrawal, however, left the French army in a poor state, with in-fighting between the commanders, not helped by arms-length interference by Belle-Isle. As it was, Ferdinand came up upon Clermont on 23 June at Krefeld. Clermont's force outnumbered Ferdinand's by 47,000 (111 squadrons and 74 battalions) to 32,000 (55 squadrons and 37 battalions).[24]

Krefeld was an awkward battlefield. Command, control and communications were made particularly difficult as it was flat, boggy and its limited visibility was further worsened by a plethora of farms, enclosures and

21 Mackesey, *The Coward of Minden*, p.21.

22 Corbett, *The Seven Years War*, pp.207-208.

23 Corbett, *The Seven Years War*, pp.204-205.

24 Account of Krefeld summarised from Savory, *His Britannic Majesty's Army in Germany*, pp.76-83.

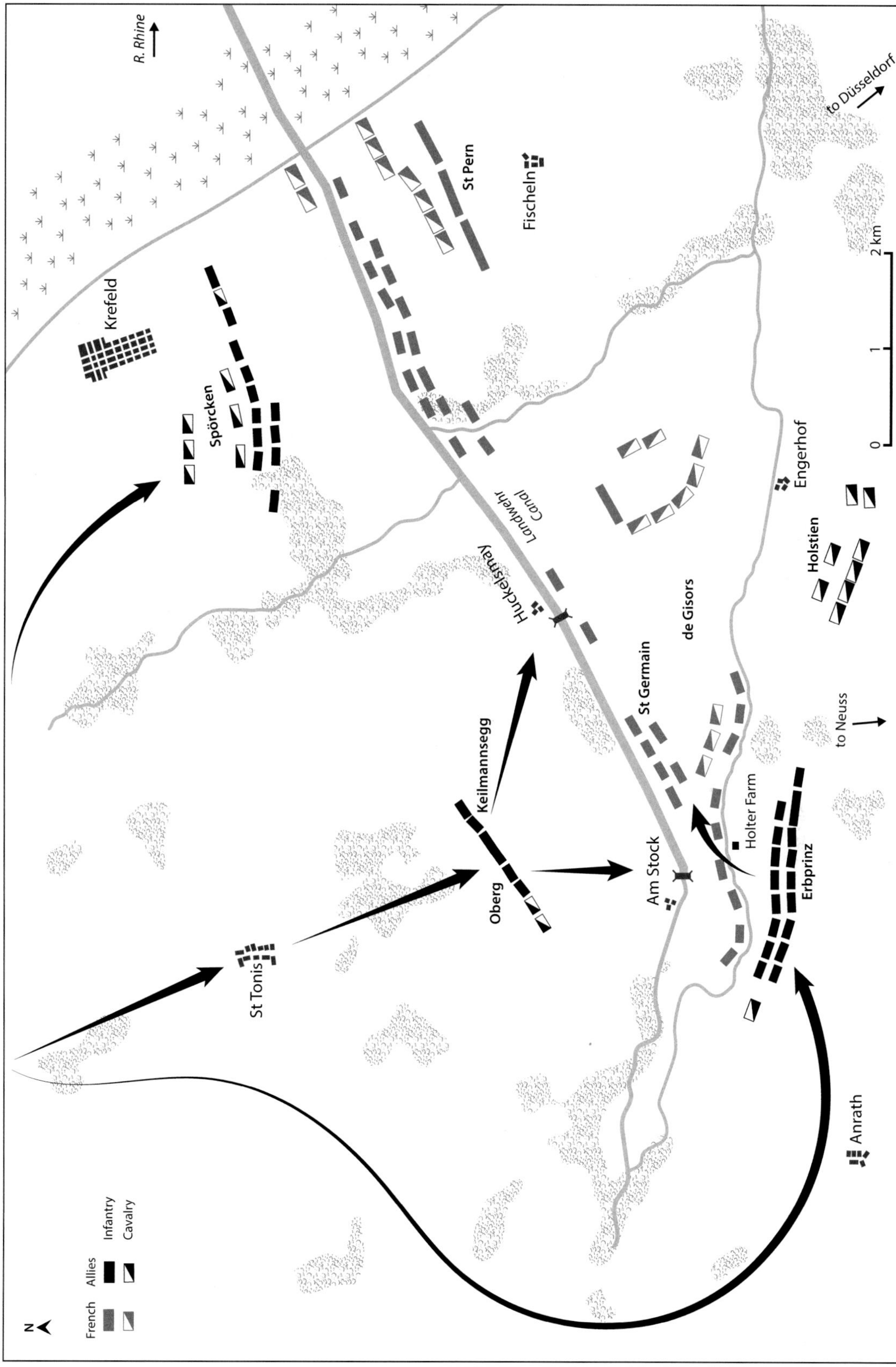

The Battle of Krefeld, 23 June 1758, showing the French defensive position and the allied axes of attack. (George Anderson, © Helion and Company 2021)

copses. A 10-kilometre-long obstacle, the Landwehr,[25] in the form of double walls, four metres high with ditches adjacent, ran south-west from Krefeld.[26]

The French used the Landwehr as a defence line, with the cavalry encamped behind the infantry. Several crossing points were established over the obstacle, each covered by cannon. Their right was partly protected by a large marsh, while the ground on the left was complex terrain, difficult to advance through and retain much control. The village of Anrath, occupied by 400 men of the Légion Royale, was used as a strong point on the extreme left of the line. Two infantry reserves were created, 12 battalions of grenadiers on the right and six battalions of the Brigade Navarre in the centre. Clermont detached 12 battalions and some horse to protect the Rhine between Ürdingen and Düsseldorf. A further 14 battalions were sent to occupy Düsseldorf itself.

Morale in the French camp was good. Clermont assumed that his position was so strong that any frontal attack would be doomed to failure. Of his flanks, he thought his right flank, on the marsh, was the more vulnerable.

Ferdinand gathered his commanders and staff at his tent at 2:00 a.m. on the 23rd to brief them on his plan, which would be confirmed at about 6:00 a.m. when he had managed to reach one of the few patches of higher ground at Sankt-Tönis to survey the ground. He intended to fix the enemy with demonstrations against their right and front-centre, but strike by turning their left flank with the main body of his army.[27]

His own left wing of 23 squadrons and 13 battalions, under *Generalleutnant* von Spörcken, was to advance towards, yet avoid becoming sucked into Krefeld. Further left still were to be light troops (hussars and jägers) which were to attempt to work through the complex terrain out east of Krefeld to seek opportunities to tie down enemy troops on their right.[28]

Ferdinand would lead the right wing of 32 squadrons and 24 battalions in two large columns, via Sankt-Tönis.

Clermont was initially informed that Krefeld was being approached by an allied column at about 6:00 a.m. but continued to believe in the strength of his own situation and refused to take the report seriously.[29]

Ferdinand's approach to Sankt-Tönis caused a French picquet to abandon its outpost. His view from a tower in Sankt-Tönis allowed him to confirm his plans. Spörcken was directed to force the enemy out of Krefeld and then, using artillery, fix the enemy right wing until Ferdinand had managed to

25 Not to be confused with later use of the expression, when it meant militia troops, a Landwehr was a form of land defence, usually with one or more banks, possibly containing several water-filled ditches, as in this case, or a hedge.

26 Prince Adolphus, 1st Duke of Cambridge, *Schlacht bey CREVELT vom 23.ten Junius 1758 zwischen der Alliirten Armée unter dem Befehl Sr Hochfurstl Durchl des Herrn Herzogs Ferdinand und der Franzosischen Arme commandirt vom Grafen von Clermont.* Royal Collection K. Mil. RCIN 732064. Despite being drawn some 34 years after the battle, the young Duke of Cambridge has captured the complexity and awkwardness of the terrain.

27 Smith, *A New History of the Seven Years War*, Vol.II, p.42.

28 Hotham-Thompson, Sir Charles, *Operations of the Allied Army under the Duke of Brunswick 1757-1762* (London: T. Jeffreys, 1764; reprinted Point Pleasant New Jersey: Winged Hussar Publishing, The Nafziger Collection, 2016), pp.33-37.

29 Savory, *His Britannic Majesty's Army in Germany*, pp.79-80.

strike the French right through his outflanking manoeuvre. Spörcken was then to exploit any opportunities presented by Ferdinand's attack.

Generalleutnant Oberg, one of Ferdinand's commanders from the right wing, was to take six squadrons, six battalions and six 12-pounder guns to attack French positions between Hückelsmay and Am Stock, in concert with the main attack[30]. The main attack of 26 squadrons, under *Generalleutnant* Georg Ludwig, Herzog zu Holstein-Gottorp, and 18 battalions, under the Erbprinz, would pass through the village of Vorst and attack the French left wing in the vicinity of Anrath.

At about 8:00 a.m., both wings of the allied army were advancing, albeit that the left, under Spörcken, was crossing the Kleud Marsh towards Krefeld slowly. Clermont continued to believe that the allies would never attack him frontally, and that any movement at that moment was merely providing protection for forage parties. By 9:00 a.m., the French picquet abandoned Krefeld while Spörcken's force occupied the ground to the west of Krefeld.

On the allied right, Ferdinand's wing struggled through close country riddled with scrub and hedges, making heavy going of it. By about 10:00 a.m., Clermont was finally convinced that the Allies were indeed about to attack him frontally, so decided to deploy forwards from his camp, lining the Landwehr and occupying the ditch with his infantry.[31] He situated two lines of cavalry behind his centre. Each section of his line had a reserve element: his right had the Grenadiers de France and Grenadiers Royaux; in his centre was the Navarre infantry; on the left, Carabiniers and dragoons. On his extreme left, at Anrath, he planned to reinforce the 400 men already there of the Légion Royale with a further four battalions. However, Prussian hussars arrived prematurely at Anrath, driving the Légion out after a token show of force. On balance, Anrath could not easily be defended, as it was too isolated from the remainder of the French main defensive position. Arriving back at the French main line, the Légion and the four reinforcing battalions spread the alarm and joined the left wing.

Clermont was beginning to appreciate the developing threat to his left flank. To counter it, he sent four brigades (15 battalions), with 30 squadrons, under Saint-Germain. This force occupied a wood with a wet ditch. As Ferdinand passed near Anrath, he struggled to make sense of the terrain, which was complex, being criss-crossed by hedges and walls. He and his officers climbed a church steeple for better visibility.

The pressure of the allied attack mounted from about midday.[32] Oberg's artillery opened up on the centre at about noon and, half an hour later, Spörcken's artillery also opened up. This fire intensified at 1:00 p.m., yet it did not divert Clermont from lunch.[33] Ferdinand moved his infantry

30 Bauer, Frierich Wilhelm von, *Plan de la BATAILLE de CREVELD done le 23 Juin 1758 contenant les Mouvements de l'Armée alliée deuis le 14 Juin jusqu'au 2.me Juillet 1758.* Royal Collection K.Mil. RCIN 732001.n.

31 Reid, *The Battle of Minden 1759*, p.31.

32 Hotham-Thompson, *Operations of the Allied Army under the Duke of Brunswick 1757-1762*, pp.36-38.

33 Savory, *His Britannic Majesty's Army in Germany*, p.83.

further forward to the wood under supporting artillery fire, and pushed the Malachowski Hussars fully to the right to be able to turn his enemy's flank.

Having completed his lunch, Clermont took stock of his situation. He had previously been more concerned about his right flank and his anxiety had not gone away. Accordingly, he directed his Reserve there. At about this time, Ferdinand's corps was in position and ready to wheel in to the French left flank. Ferdinand's artillery commenced firing at 2:30 p.m. in preparation for a direct attack on the wood which was defended by 15 battalions. Leading from the front, the Erbprinz advanced with eight battalions against a farm complex (Holter Farm) which was vigorously defended by six battalions of the La Marine Brigade. It took 45 minutes for the Erbprinz's force to drive the defenders from the Holter Farm but, before he could fully reorganise and consolidate, La Marine returned with nine further battalions of Saint-Germain's division, which attacked determinedly among the hedges, thickets and a wet ditch.

The very fact that the farmsteads had been so tough to assault was now turned to advantage. The Erbprinz's troops were now in possession of some stout defences. Despite this, he still had to bring forward his second line to be able to defend the newly-taken terrain.[34]

As this part of the battle was still raging, Ferdinand was advised by an officer stationed in the tower at Anrath that further French troops were advancing on his right from the direction of Fischeln. It was critical that he must win on his right before the arrival of these reinforcements. Then some good news: an undefended crossing over the wet ditch had been found a several hundred metres to his left.[35]

On the other wing of the allied army, Spörcken was dithering, uncertain as to Ferdinand's progress, despite the encouragement of one of Ferdinand's aides. His lack of resolve was worsened by the arrival of a hussar with the unwelcome, but inaccurate, report that the first allied attacks on the army's right wing had been unsuccessful. Thus discouraged, Spörcken ordered a withdrawal, although not in such panic as to prevent him attempting to bolster Oberg's corps on his right with two battalions of Hanoverian Foot Guards.

At about 5:00 p.m., Clermont recognised that the situation on his left wing was becoming critical so attempted to commit his reserve, which was behind his right wing. Even if obeyed instantly, it would take quite some time to get across from centre-right to the left wing. However, the situation was worsened by Clermont's aide becoming disoriented and losing time in identifying the reserve.[36]

Meanwhile, the Erbprinz's's grenadiers, with *Generalmajors* Wangenheim and Kielmansegg, managed to force the ditches in the vicinity of the wood. This had an electrifying effect on adjacent units which also started to force

34 Cambridge, *Schlacht bey CREVELT.* Royal Collection K. Mil. RCIN 732064. Again, this map shows the complexity of the obstacles attacked, and then defended, by the Erbprinz.

35 Savory, *His Britannic Majesty's Army in Germany*, p.80.

36 'Battle of Krefeld', *Seven Years' War* <http://www.kronoskaf.com/syw/index.php?title=1758-06-23_-_Battle_of_Krefeld> (accessed 15 January–31 October 2019).

their way across. Ferdinand then ordered Holstein-Gottorp to use the passage which had been found to get round to the rear of the French defenders. Oberg, inspired by the Erbprinz, launched his corps against two passages, at Am Stock and Hucklesmay. Under pressure from both left and right, the French began to abandon their lines. However, the Erbprinz's force, exhausted after its stiff fight through the farms, was taking time to reorganise. On the left, the Hanoverian light troops were making very slow progress through the broken ground.

Between 5:00 p.m. and 6:00 p.m., *Generalmajor* Joachim Christian von Bandemer and four squadrons of dragoons succeeded in getting across the wet ditch at an unguarded passage near Engersdorf. Turning to the north-east, they managed to appear to the rear of the hard-pressed infantry of Saint-Germain. These latter had successfully defended the ditch and their crossing point unsupported against three allied attacks. Having borne the impact of three hours of intense combat, and having taken heavy casualties, Saint-Germain's infantry could have broken. As it was, they were bolstered by the sudden arrival of ten squadrons of French Carabiniers. Badly outnumbered, Bandemer's four squadrons were engulfed by the Carabiniers and the survivors were driven back to Engerhoff and Bötgeshof.

However, in the ebb and flow of battle, the Carabiniers found themselves engaged in turn by *Generalmajor* von Urff leading his own Leib-Regiment and the Leib Dragoons. However, having just crossed the wet ditch, they had not yet managed to deploy properly.

Ferdinand was anxious that the Erbprinz should advance from the wet ditch onto the plain, but the Erbprinz had been fixed in combat for hours and was unable to comply. Riding across to his location, Ferdinand was in a position to observe closely what happened to the reminder of the French Carabiniers with the young Comte de Gisors at their head. They clashed with a force of four Hanoverian and two Hessian battalions under *Generalmajor* von Gilsa.[37] The Carabiniers charged and the German infantry opened fire at 30 paces, destroying the first rank and killing Gisors. Ferdinand knew the French officer and cradled him in his arms while he died.[38] Despite this, one French squadron broke through, forcing Ferdinand to take refuge amongst his infantry, but the rear German rank coolly turned about and finished it off with controlled fire.

During this time, the French reserve had been sent to reinforce their troops behind the Landwehr in the centre. Those Carabinier squadrons which had not gone forward with Gisors were now reinforced by two cavalry brigades, the total force numbering between 14 and 18 squadrons. These were all progressively engaged by more and more German cavalry, mainly dragoons, until 20 allied and 18 French cavalry squadrons were swirling in combat to the north-east of Engerhof. The allies captured a number of standards and kettledrums as the bulk of the French cavalry was forced back. Some of the French managed to rally behind uncommitted squadrons, which Clermont unsuccessfully ordered to counter-attack. While the cavalry battle

37 Savory, *His Britannic Majesty's Army in Germany*, p.81.

38 Archenholz, *Prussia and the Seven Years war 1756-1763*, p.141.

was in progress, the Erbprinz managed to get his infantry back across the ditch and to join up with Oberg's corps.

At about 6:30 p.m., as the successful allied right and centre were advancing, 18 battalions of the French reserve, which contained a preponderance of grenadiers under Saint-Pern, belatedly appeared and prepared to launch a counter-attack. Had this reserve been committed sooner, and been supported by cavalry, a force of this weight could have changed the outcome. As it was, Saint-Pern's late arrival triggered questions about his loyalty.[39] By this time, however, Chevert deemed it too late and ordered a general withdrawal, using the grenadiers to cover the rest of the army.

Ferdinand and Oberg's corps pressed forward, pushing the French grenadiers backwards across the ditch where they briefly attempted to make a stand before retreating in the direction of Neuss. The allied artillery continued to fire on the retreating mass while Ferdinand ordered forward some of his cavalry in pursuit, but the broken terrain was not well-suited and they never managed to catch the enemy.

Belatedly, Spörcken was persuaded to send some of his battalions towards the Landwehr, where they found the French positions and the village of Fischeln deserted. Later still, Ferdinand found most of Spörcken's troops in and around Krefeld. He ordered him forward and to send his cavalry in pursuit of the French, but night was beginning to fall.[40]

On the allies' left wing, Spörcken's leisurely conduct was to prevent the allies from capitalising on the victory. It could, and should, have been a rout. As it was, the three allied corps gathered and slept on the battlefield. The wounded of both sides were mostly gathered at Krefeld, although a French field hospital abandoned at Fischeln was also fully employed.

At a cost of 52 officers and 1,561 men killed, missing and wounded, the Allies captured two colours, five standards, eight cannon and two pairs of kettledrums.[41] The French lost approximately 4,200 killed, missing, wounded or as prisoners. Their cavalry was particularly badly hit, the Carabiniers losing 60 officers and 600 troopers either killed or wounded. Seven other regiments were severely affected, notably the Royal-Rousillon cavalry, which lost its *colonel*, *lieutenant-colonel*, and 21 other officers. The Comte de Gisors who fell at the head of the Carabiniers was the son of *Maréchal* Belle-Isle, the Minister of War.

Krefeld was the catalyst for Britain's wider recommittal to the continent. Under pressure in cabinet, Pitt admitted that it might be possible to spare a force of about 6,000. After some reflection, he realized that the figure might be made up from some of the expensive cavalry otherwise underemployed in England.

Field Marshal Lord Ligonier, the commander-in-chief, was directed to nominate units for operations on the Continent. However, a force made up solely of horse would be unbalanced, so infantry was required also. Two

39 Duffy, *The Military Experience in the Age of Reason*, p.203.
40 Savory, *His Britannic Majesty's Army in Germany*, p.82.
41 Hotham-Thompson, *Operations of the Allied Army under the Duke of Brunswick 1757-1762*, p.39.

commanders for brigades of foot were identified in the shape of Major Generals John Waldegrave and William Kingsley, and their brigades were improvised, using the 51st Regiment of Foot, which was already in Emden, three battalions from the expeditionary force, and the very last two left on English soil. Thoroughly disenchanted with amphibious expeditioning, Marlborough and Sackville volunteered for the new venture, the latter describing himself as 'sick of coasting'.[42] King George II favoured Lieutenant General Thomas Bligh as the commander of the new force, but Marlborough and Sackville managed to elbow him out, leaving Bligh to pick up the pieces from the amphibious operation.

However, the optimism of the situation which pertained immediately after Ferdinand's victory at Krefeld had now been replaced by a far grimmer challenge. Ferdinand may have inflicted a defeat on the French, yet he had been unable to exploit his success.[43] Ferdinand had the unenviable task of opposing not one, but two strong French armies with a numerically inferior force.

No large army of that period could stay concentrated for long because of the demands on one area of sustaining it with fodder and rations. Therefore, Prince Ferdinand's allied army occupied an area which spread from the River Diemel through Paderborn, Lippstadt, Münster to Coesfeld. However, Münster was an essential focus to prevent the French reaching the River Weser from the west, but also to protect the lines of communication with the North Sea and, hence, Britain. Kassel, in Hesse, provided a similar blocking function from the south-west. Between Münster and Kassel was Lippstadt, on the River Lippe, an important link if communications were to be maintained between the two. The rivers Ruhr and Lippe had the potential to facilitate any French advance from the west, while three further rivers, the Ohm, Eder and Diemel had the potential to obstruct any French advance northwards. These strong points and rivers provided a framework for defence and were to be contested throughout the war.

The French western Armée du Rhin under Clermont lay along the River Rhine from its base in Wesel down to Coblenz, and the French southern Armée du Main, commanded by Prince de Soubise, spread north from Frankfurt. After Krefeld, Clermont had managed to extricate the bulk of his army, which fell back on Köln. The collapse of the French occupation laid bare the Austrian Netherlands. This was too tempting an opportunity to ignore, and Ferdinand's force ran amok, occupying Roermond, Charleroi, Louvain and Dusseldorf.

Faced with disaster, as he saw it, Clermont was now a broken reed and he asked to be relieved of command.[44] The French Minister of War, *Maréchal* Belle-Isle, recognised an opportunity rather than disaster: Ferdinand had overextended himself and his lines of communication were now extremely tenuous, being served by only one bridge across the Rhine. Clermont was relieved of command and replaced by *Lieutenant-Général* the Marquis de

42 Mackesey, *The Coward of Minden*, p.31.
43 Savory, *His Britannic Majesty's Army in Germany*, p.85.
44 Savory, *His Britannic Majesty's Army in Germany*, p.86.

Contades.[45] Ordered to ensure the security of Köln from which to mount future offensive operations, Contades struck with alacrity. Recognising the threat, Ferdinand intended to engineer a meeting engagement on some elevated ground at Allrath, just to the north-east of Köln, where a punch should cause his enemy to give pause. Then, in the immediate aftermath, he would aim to break clean and escape northwards. However, Contades' lead elements seized Allrath first, as Ferdinand's force was stuck astride a river crossing. Suddenly, with his opponent vulnerable, Contades' confidence and energy deserted him. He decided to bring up the rest of his army and regain his balance before orchestrating a methodical attack. By the time he was prepared, night had fallen. In the morning Ferdinand's force was nowhere to be seen.

In a manoeuvre of astonishing boldness, rather than withdrawing, Ferdinand had opted to advance further westward, towards Roermond, to threaten Contades' own line of communications. However, his breaking clean had been so successful that Contades had completely lost contact and was unaware of the potential threat which Ferdinand was now posing him.[46] By the time Contades finally learned of Ferdinand's whereabouts, Ferdinand's neck was in a noose of his own making. It would not take much for Contades to advance north, blocking Ferdinand from his bridge over the Rhine, thus trapping him for a denouement.

With Ferdinand's attention so distracted, Belle-Isle took the opportunity to re-direct the other major French army under Soubise, which had been intended for Bohemia, to threaten Hanover.[47] The only force in any position to be able to oppose this was relatively tiny: two squadrons of horse and two battalions of regular foot at Kassel, under *Generalleutnant* Prinz zu Isenburg-Büdingen, albeit reinforced by five squadrons of Hessian cavalry and three militia battalions. Soubise's army comprised 32 squadrons and 39 battalions, dwarfing the opposition. Even Soubise's advance guard, under the command of the very able *Lieutenant-Général* the Duc de Broglie, with 12 squadrons and 14 battalions, outnumbered the defending force. Isenburg-Büdingen prudently elected not to defend Kassel and attempted to withdraw but his force of mixed ability was not capable of rapid manoeuvre. Overtaken near the village of Sandershausen on 23 July, Isenburg was obliged to give battle.[48] Against the talented Broglie, Isenburg's militia collapsed, and he was lucky to be able to extract his regular troops.

Rees/Mehr

Unlike Broglie, Soubise revealed himself to be a self-indulgent courtier rather than a hard-driving commander. He satisfied himself with occupying Kassel, living a relatively comfortable existence there but not further threatening

45 Archenholz, *Prussia and the Seven Years war 1756-1763*, p.141.

46 Savory, *His Britannic Majesty's Army in Germany*, p.90.

47 Reid, *The Battle of Minden 1759*, p.51.

48 Archenholz, *Prussia and the Seven Years War 1756-1763*, p.142.

Hanover, other than to temporarily raid some of the neighbouring towns. Despite this, the government in Hanover was thrown into chaos, evacuating the capital in haste and carrying its documents up to Stade, near the Elbe estuary.[49] The evacuation of Hanover compelled Ferdinand to refocus and to begin his return to his primary role of protecting the city. However, that was not to be straightforward. His only direct route home lay via his own pontoon bridge, which was at Rees on the Rhine, perilously close (18 kilometres) to Wesel, now garrisoned by the French.

Contades simultaneously dispatched *Lieutenant-Général* Chevert up the right bank to capture the pontoon, while he himself attempted to cut Ferdinand off at Dülken, 19 kilometres to the south-east of Krefeld. It would have been a shrewd option, as Ferdinand would have been severely constricted by water obstacles and it could have been a great opportunity. As it was, Contades once again showed a reticence and opted to withdraw to defend Rheindahlen instead, a missed opportunity. Oddly, Contades believed that he had succeeded in escaping being snared by Ferdinand.[50]

Having narrowly missed being blocked at Dülken, Ferdinand used his Prussian cavalry, under Holstein-Gottorp, to screen Contades in Rheindahlen during his onward march to Rees. That march, however, became a trudge as heavy rain came on, turning the roads into quagmires and slowing his progress. Delayed as he was, Ferdinand was beaten to the pontoon by Chevert. Having been sent off hurriedly, Chevert's force of 5,000 was rather mixed.

Ferdinand had prudently left a rearguard of about 3,500 at the bridge, under the command of von Imhoff. As soon as von Imhoff learned of the approach of the French he moved the bulk of his small force two kilometres upstream to a defensive position at Mehr, leaving 500 men on the bridge itself. At the same time, Zastrow came forward with additional troops from Büderich and Rheinberg as hasty reinforcements. A further 1,000 men managed to come from garrison duties in Kleve and crossed the river, but did not advance as far as the scene of the combat.

At 10:00 a.m. on 5 August, Chevert came on at full pelt, but learned that the bridge's defenders had come forward and had deployed in the hedges around the relative heights of the village of Mehr. Additionally, there were two redoubts behind the hedges, which von Imhoff must have already been familiar with.

Von Imhoff had thrown forward on his right the Regiment Stolzenberg into a coppice to enfilade the oncoming French. When the French entered the awkward terrain to his front, von Imhoff's main body was to advance 200 metres to a hedge line and then, as soon as the battalion in the coppice fired from the flank, the main body was to go in with the bayonet.[51]

Chevert originally planned to send *Lieutenant Colonel* de Chavigny, with three companies of grenadiers, light troops and some militia, on towards Rees

49 Reid, *The Battle of Minden 1759*, p.52.

50 Reid, *The Battle of Minden 1759*, p.53.

51 Hotham-Thompson, *Operations of the Allied Army under the Duke of Brunswick 1757-1762*, p.49.

while he personally dealt with Imhoff's force at Mehr. However, he changed his mind, electing instead to send Chavigny directly against a house and post for some 250 of the Allies at the entrance to Mehr.[52] Chevert's artillery fired in support of the advancing French infantry. Following behind Chavigny was the Brigade Brancas on the right and Brigade Reding on the left. Chavigny was successful in driving the allies out, advancing some 300 metres beyond the post.

Chevert ordered the Brigade Brancas to exploit this to envelop the allies' left wing and to engage a strong point which was holding out with vigorous musketry. However, this brigade was channelled to its left by dense hedging belonging to the house just captured by Chavigny. Rather than correct this, Chevert was content to permit this drift to continue as things were hotting up to the left of the left flank brigade, where Imhoff was leading the Stolzenburg battalion in a counter-attack. At about this time, Chevert's attention was being diverted by some militia elements of Chavigny's force which were refusing to advance further and, in some cases, even beginning to melt away.

The attack of the Regiment Imhoff was delivered at bayonet-point. Brigade Reding's response was uncoordinated and disorderly. One panicked and poorly aimed volley was all that the brigade managed before a disordered retreat. Sensing that a tipping point had occurred, Zastrow ordered the allies into a general attack. Despite the efforts of senior French commanders trying to rally the men, the tide washing backwards became infectious and unstoppable.[53] Chavigny's force, depleted by the loss of the militia, also broke, as Chavigny was himself wounded. Finding itself isolated, the Brigade Brancas joined the fleeing mass.

The Dragons du Roi, conducting themselves well, were able to halt the allies just beyond Mehr, allowing the French to retire through the village of Diersfordt and deploy two guns to hold off the Allied columns while a mobile hospital and stragglers caught up. They then withdrew to Wesel. The French had lost 517 (including 11 officers and 354 men as prisoners), 10 guns and several ammunition wagons, at a cost of 200 allies (killed or wounded).

Von Imhoff had saved the bridge, although the torrential downpour, which had delayed Ferdinand on his return march, raised the level of the Rhine requiring the pontoon to be moved downstream.[54] Ferdinand and his force, complete with baggage, had been saved and were able to regain the east bank intact, on 10 August.[55] Contades crossed onto the east bank of the Rhine on 19 August in order to operate in tandem with Soubise, to force Ferdinand back towards Hanover. They were joined by some 8,000 Saxons under Prince Xaver. Prince Xaver of Saxony was also known by the French as the Comte de Lusace and the latter title is used henceforth.

52 'Combat of Mehr', *Seven Years' War* <http://www.kronoskaf.com/syw/index.php?title=1758-08-05_-_Combat_of_Mehr> (accessed 15 January–31 October 2019).

53 Reid, *The Battle of Minden 1759*, p.55.

54 Savory, *His Britannic Majesty's Army in Germany*, p.94.

55 Archenholz, *Prussia and the Seven Years War 1756-1763*, p.144.

The Amphibious Return to Saint-Malo and Saint-Cast

Some desultory raiding at Le Havre, then Cherbourg, kept British amphibious operations ticking over in a moderate manner. These were intended as a diversion which would relieve the pressure on Ferdinand's army, and also keep Frederick content. Even if they failed to draw French forces back from Germany, they might prevent those forces remaining in north-west France from reinforcing those threatening Hanover. Ferdinand was of the view that, 'if their design can combine with what I have in hand, the effect will be all the greater'.[56] Cherbourg was sacked, 35 ships destroyed and 22 brass cannon brought back, to be paraded in triumph in London.

Beginning again in August, a still sizeable British amphibious force had been embarked with the purpose of coastal raiding on Normandy and Brittany. Lieutenant General Bligh had command of nine troops of light Dragoons and 12 battalions, transported and supported by the 109 vessels of Commodore Howe. The next attempt, at the beginning of September, was to be against Saint-Malo. The force having been disembarked, the weather now took a turn for the worse, obliging Howe to shift several kilometres to the west. Bligh was required to rendezvous with the fleet at Saint-Cast.[57]

Bligh's force set out to march the distance, fording a river and taking several days. Having seen off a token French force of about 500, he camped at Matignon, intending to be embarked some five kilometres distant on 11 September.

During the night of 10/11 September, the British force was woken by the Générale, then the Assembly but the drum signals also alerted the French that the British were up to something. The British set off in a single column on the five kilometres route to Saint-Cast. However, the Duc d'Aiguillon had managed to assemble a force and had advanced towards the coast in four columns, three of which were to march to Saint-Cast. The race was now on.[58]

A British rearguard took advantage of some trenches left by the local militia from previous seasons, while the main party reached the beach. The evacuation began as soon as they arrived, under the protection of three bomb-ketches and five frigates.

One of the failings of the boat party was a pedantic return only to their own parent ship, rather than simply transporting the soldiers to the nearest available transport.[59] This wasted time and rowing energy. Additionally, the priorities for loading were wrong: more initial effort was put into carrying off captured livestock, horses, and beef, rather than men. The French were not idle, bringing a battery of 10 guns and mortars into play. Counterbattery fire from the frigates hampered this and also drove any French troops who appeared on the beach to seek cover. However, the French used the cover offered by undulating terrain to form up, ready for their opportunity to attack.

---

56 Corbett, *The Seven Years War*, pp.203-205.

57 Corbett, *The Seven Years War*, p.224.

58 Corbett, *The Seven Years War*, p.225.

59 Reid, *The Battle of Minden 1759*, p.47.

By 11:00 a.m. the bulk, some two thirds, of the landed force had been embarked. Approximately 3,000 remained on shore. At this point, the French left wing under d'Aubigny marched to the attack, despite being fired on by the British frigates. 300 French grenadiers led the attack, followed by three infantry regiments.

The British rearguard of 1,400 guardsmen and grenadiers, under Major General Dury, attempted to cover the lift from the beach by using the sand banks as earthworks. This force gallantly drove off two French attacks but then crumbled when artillery was brought up aggressively against it. The rearguard broke and fled into the sea, struggling to reach the boats. Dury was lost as many of the force were slaughtered, both on the beach and in the surf.[60] Such a number of British boats were destroyed that many crews refused to come inshore, standing off instead, which frustrated Howe who led by example, using his own boat to bring off as many as he could.[61] The accompanying frigates maintained a fire on the French until ordered to desist by their Commodore. At this, French hostility turned almost immediately to sympathy, as the French provided protection to their prisoners and wounded.

The British ground force lost 1,160 killed and wounded, plus 732 taken prisoner, while the Royal Navy lost eight killed and 17 wounded, against 445 French killed or wounded. The disaster at Saint-Cast, in which His Majesty's Foot Guards were mauled, spelled the end of this 'buccaneering' phase.[62] It was to be the last amphibious operation against mainland France for the remainder of the war, but valuable lessons had been learned. It had been hoped that such raids would draw off French forces from Germany. Ferdinand himself was never quite sure that this had been achieved, but the important effect was that French forces guarding the coast could not be considered as a reserve for Germany.[63]

Ferdinand, Back on his 'Home' Bank

Safely back on his home bank, Ferdinand's army was able to reorganise prior to marching eastwards to link up with the newly arrived British contingent.[64] In August 1758, the British contingent of six regiments of cavalry, six battalions of infantry and supporting artillery arrived in Emden to join Ferdinand's army at Coesfeld, bringing the allied army up to a theoretical strength of 66,621 all-ranks. In reality, this amounted to around 40,000 effectives. In addition to the combat arms, a general hospital was also opened in August 1758, every regiment being ordered to send one 'careful' woman, a soldier's wife who followed the drum, to help in the wards. Any woman appointed by her husband's commanding officer and refusing to

60 Reid, *The Battle of Minden 1759*, pp.48-49.
61 Corbett, *The Seven Years War*, p.225.
62 Reid, *The Battle of Minden 1759*, p.41.
63 Corbett, *The Seven Years War*, p.226.
64 Hotham-Thompson, *Operations of the Allied Army under the Duke of Brunswick 1757-1762*, p.49.

attend would be drummed out of the regiment.[65] Dr Winteringham, a senior physician who had previously served with the Duke of Cumberland in the War of the Austrian Succession and who was trusted by him, was appointed as Physician General to the forces in Germany. Mr Young became the Chief Surgeon while a Mr Cathcart, the Head Purveyor, was appointed as Director of Hospitals.

The arrival of the British main body in Europe in early August was hardly the glamorous stuff of picture books. Firstly, the disembarkation occurred piecemeal along the Ems estuary due to a shortage of piers and river pilots. Secondly, once assembled, it was hit by a prolonged and violent rainstorm which turned the onward march into a bedraggled horde, followed by stragglers. When the British finally reached the assembly area at Coesfeld on, or around, 14 August, they were met by a rather smug Hessian, *Generalmajor* Burkhard Wilhelm von Fürstenberg who condescendingly described his own march over 11 days with no delays.[66] It took the best part of a week for both the German and the British baggage to come up. The time must have been well spent by the sergeants getting their soaked men back into shape for, when Ferdinand reviewed the British on 22 August, he expressed his pleasure at their appearance. Perhaps it was all relative, as the British were recently accoutered and the horses were powerful and in good condition. After their own adventures, Germans were also fairly bedraggled, although their weapons were in good order.[67]

As often happens when troops of different nations assemble, there is much curiosity about the other side, with trading, bartering and good-natured joshing. However, there can also be a downside to this, as different interpretations of acceptable behaviour and discipline rub up against each other. Those British veterans of St Malo, brigaded together, started to take liberties by pillaging and trying to misappropriate billets and forage. It was decided to break the emerging pattern, by swapping the 51st Foot with the 23rd Fusiliers. Additionally, a combined pair of German and British lieutenant colonels was tasked to hear and decide on any inter-army disagreement.[68] It was particularly important that the allies should not come to blows and that, on pain of death, they were not to draw swords against one another. Evidence suggests that, despite such rulings, it took time for discipline to settle down to anything approaching a steady state of normality.[69] Some officers may have been complicit in the misbehaviour of their troops, Sir John Whitefoord of the British horse, for example, created his own supply dump at Rheine to prevent his forage being stolen after dark by 'Jews and Hanoverians, both damned pilferers'.[70]

65 Cantlie, *History of the Army Medical Department*, p.123, quoting Historical Manuscripts Commission Report. Various Collections VIII. p.446.

66 Reid, *The Battle of Minden 1759*, p.58.

67 Savory, *His Britannic Majesty's Army in Germany*, p.101.

68 Stephen Wood (ed.), *...By Dint of Labour and Perseverance... A journal recording two months in northern Germany kept by Lieutenant-Colonel James Adolphus Oughton, commanding 1st battalion 37th Regiment of Foot, 1758* (SAHR Special Publication No.14, 1997), p.51.

69 Reid, *The Battle of Minden 1759*, p.59.

70 Reid, *The Battle of Minden 1759*, p.59.

Between the officers of the different nations, there were also differences in approach and style. The Germans, heavily influenced by Prussian norms of devotion to duty, were unimpressed by the studied nonchalance of the British, for whom it was considered inappropriate to appear anything other than gentlemanly: being simultaneously a gentleman and a competent, professional soldier were not, of course, mutually exclusive, but it was 'not done' to appear to be a military swot.

The British commander, Charles Spencer, 3rd Duke of Marlborough, posed challenges of his own. Having muscled-in on the operation with his sidekick, Sackville, displacing the King's preferred choice, he then took umbrage on discovering that von Spörcken of Hanover, once his junior, was now his senior as a *General der Infanterie*. In a fit of pique, he wrote to Pitt, threatening to resign if this were not corrected, effectively forcing through his own promotion to general with a suitable antedate of seniority. This unsubtlety was echoed by both Marlborough and Sackville's arrogance and insensitivity towards their allies. As Britain was underwriting the whole enterprise, Ferdinand had no choice but to accept the situation, but it did not augur particularly well for the future relationship.

Sackville arrived in Germany without the full approval of the King and, given the sensitivity of working closely with allies on their own soil, the King's kindred spirits, this would be a weakness.

In September 1758, the British Headquarters was at Dülmen, south-west of Münster, and regimental hospitals were opened up. Winteringham summoned all regimental surgeons to a conference on 27 September and a General Order was issued: 'The Regimental Surgeons are to provide Regimental Hospitals according to the plan laid down by Dr Wintringham and Mr Burlton, who will report their state to the Duke'.[71] Here is evidence that the medical staff was performing its duties appropriately and that, not only was there a coordinated plan, but also that individual surgeons were being held to maintain standards. This is interesting as previously, those regimental commanding officers who could be bothered, tended to view their hospital as part of their personal fiefdom. Flying hospitals, to support a march, were created at Soest on 21 October and Warendorp on 29 October.

As was common on campaign, the troops were beginning to suffer from bowel problems. In the interests of good hygiene orders were issued that it was forbidden for bread wagons to be used to evacuate those sick with diarrhoea to the flying hospital at Chateau d'Empte. If, however, it became unavoidable, the wagon floors were to be covered by sufficient straw, which was to be immediately burned on arrival. Normally the wagons allocated for the transport of the sick were grouped with the artillery train, being used like a taxi rank and sent out as needed, and returning on arrival back at the camp. It was found that the hospital needed reinforcement so more orderlies and nurses were required, each regiment being obliged to send at least one to d'Empte.[72]

71 Cantlie, *History of the Army Medical Department*, p.123.

72 Cantlie, *History of the Army Medical Department*, p.123.

As the allies were settling down and establishing a working relationship, there was something of an operational pause. For the French, the commanders of both armies sought without much success to coordinate their actions. Contades' army was stretched along the River Lippe between Wesel and Lünen. Soubise took matters into his own hands on 7 September and moved to Göttingen, with the aim of threatening Hanover again. In fact, as part of the coordinated action, he was to be the bait which would fix Ferdinand, allowing Contades to close in, whereupon the two French armies would combine to destroy him. The unfortunate Isenburg, still smarting after Sandershausen, had no option but to withdraw to Hameln. By 12 September, that enterprising French light commander, Fischer, had reached the very walls of Hanover.[73] Despite Belle-Isle's direction to Contades to provide mutual support, the latter sat tight on his own side of the Lippe, providing only vocal encouragement. Having successfully threatened the enemy capital, Soubise became anxious about his own boldness and, feeling overexposed, ordered a withdrawal.

Ferdinand had a gift for seeing opportunities in the face of threats. He quickly recognised the potential vulnerability of Soubise's thrust, and sought to get a force in behind him, recapturing the supply base at Kassel before Soubise could return. Kassel was indeed vulnerable and *Generalleutnant* von Oberg was dispatched with 14,000 troops. The French had a token rearguard force in the city which, rather than choosing to conduct a defence, was on the point of evacuating the city. On 26 September, von Oberg's energetic light troop commander, *Oberst* Lückner, was on the verge of storming straight in, but Oberg hesitated, deciding to summon Isenburg in reinforcement. The delay was fatal, as Soubise was now close by and able to reoccupy the city before Oberg. Rather than withdraw, Oberg loitered, only to be caught and mauled by a rather belated attempt by Contades to provide support to Soubise. Finally stirred into action, Contades had simultaneously distracted Ferdinand by threatening Münster via Hamm on the Lippe, while sending Chevert and the Duc de Fitz-James to reinforce Soubise. This force had caught Oberg on the move at Lutterberg on 10 October.

Lutterberg

Soubise intended to use FitzJames to attack the allies' centre while he enveloped their right and left flanks. This was to take place on a plateau at Sandershausen. However, Oberg was anxious for his lines of communication and, the previous night partly evacuated the plateau, leaving a rearguard to cover his withdrawal as he took his main body through the village of Landwehrhagen on the way to cross the River Fulda near Münden.

Before dawn on the 10th, Chevert commenced his eight-kilometre approach march round the allies' left flank. Broglie, as one of Soubise's subordinates, scouted onto the plateau and recognised that it had largely

73 Szabo, *The Seven Years' War in Europe 1756-1763*, p.184.

been vacated by the enemy. Quickly, Soubise regrouped both his own and FitzJames's corps into six columns which marched on, crossing the Bettenhausen stream and then opening out into eight columns. Broglie, meanwhile, had encountered some Jägers of the allied rearguard who fell back in front of him. Making haste, Broglie pushed on towards Landwehrhagen, through which the allies had passed.

Oberg was aware of the French pursuit and, not relishing having to conduct a withdrawal in contact, arguably one of the most difficult phases of war to conduct effectively, through awkward terrain, decided to halt and make a stand.[74] Just in front of the village of Lutterberg he deployed his foot in two lines with horse as his right wing. His horse on the left was tucked in behind his infantry. Over all, it was not a bad defensive position as, to his front, was a ravine with a marshy bottom which he covered with a few 12-pounders. His right was anchored on a wood, while his left was tethered to a scrubby eminence on which he had placed some 6-pounder guns. The bulk of his artillery was, however, still on its way to Münden.[75]

Broglie had fully caught up with the allies by about 7:00 a.m. and, to interfere with their arrangements while the rest of the French army caught up, bombarded them. Soubise came forward to join Broglie and urged the bulk of his forces to catch up. By 1:00 p.m. the French had reached their positions allocated by Soubise and were ordered to wait for Chevert to attack on the right. When he did so, an hour later, the French artillery opened up all along their line. Chevert's force attacked in three columns, the cavalry to the fore.

Oberg responded by shifting *Generalmajor* Zastrow from the allied right to the left with four squadrons and two battalions. Soubise then launched FitzJames into the attack. At about 2:45 p.m., Chevert's corps reached the allies' left flank, but were met by Zastrow's battalions and halted at bayonet point. Concerned that Chevert could still break through, Oberg continued to send more troops to his left flank, this time four more squadrons and four further battalions of his second line. He also plugged a slight gap between his original left flank and Zastrow's formation with two squadrons of dragoons and two more battalions, again from his second line.

At about 4:00 p.m. Chevert opened fire on Zastrow's force with 42 guns, the signal to begin the attack in earnest. Again, the French infantry was brought to a standstill by Zastrow's bayonets, but Chevert then ordered his cavalry to attack, which it did, breaking Zastrow's formations.[76] Christopher Duffy describes it as a day of glory for the French cavalry, turning the tide of battle, executing sixteen charges and doing great execution.[77]

Chevert's attack was the precursor to a general French advance. The ravine and its wet bottom proved to be less of an obstacle than hoped. Three French infantry brigades and supporting artillery were soon across. The increasing

74 Hotham-Thompson, *Operations of the Allied Army under the Duke of Brunswick 1757-1762*, p.53.

75 Battle summary from Savory, *His Britannic Majesty's Army in Germany*, pp.104-108; 'Battle of Lutterberg', *Seven Years' War*<http://www.kronoskaf.com/syw/index.php?title=1758-10-10_-_Battle_of_Lutterberg> (accessed 15 January–31 October 2019).

76 Hotham-Thompson, *Operations of the Allied Army under the Duke of Brunswick 1757-1762*, p.53.

77 Duffy, *The Military Experience in the Age of Reason*, pp. 116-117.

pressure forced the allies back. Eight squadrons of allied horse attempted to halt Chevert's pursuit. Although it was ultimately fruitless, those squadrons gallantly tried five times to block the French.

Chevert's Saxons managed to fight their way to the scrubby eminence, the Stodberg Hill, where Oberg had sited several batteries. While Saxon grenadiers engaged them frontally, their comrades worked round the side. Together they took the height at bayonet point, and after some desperate fighting, drove off two Hessian battalions and captured six guns. One last allied attempt at a counter-attack was shaken off as further Saxons came onto the hill.

The loss of Stodberg Hill was the straw that broke Oberg's determination to resist further. Under ever increasing pressure from a general advance by the French, he ordered a retreat towards Münden. However, this retreat was not to be straightforward, being forced to retire through a defile which slowed down the escape. The French artillery willingly grasped the opportunity to further hinder their enemy, smashing into retreating allied artillery caissons.[78]

As the French occupied the battlefield, they could see the last elements of the allied cavalry retreating in the gathering gloom, but it was now too late to effect any hot pursuit.

The allies abandoned 28 artillery pieces and lost 1,500 men (killed, missing, wounded and as prisoners). The victorious French army camped on the battlefield while the allies crossed the River Werra that night.

For his victory at Lutterberg, the courtier Soubise was made *Maréchal de France*.

In response to Contades' potential threat against Münster, Ferdinand assembled his forces there. Rather than be dazzled by the threat, again he spotted another opportunity for a counter-offensive. Despite learning of Oberg's failure at Lutterberg, Ferdinand recognised that Contades had weakened his own army by sending reinforcements to Soubise. Ferdinand planned on interposing himself between the two French armies and destroying Contades, as the weaker of the two, before they could conjoin.

He set in train a series of small decoy movements to distract the French and prevent them from concentrating, while he advanced to Lippstadt on 17 October. That night, his cavalry-heavy advance guard bridged the Lippe at Benninghausen. The French commander at Soest, 19 kilometres to the south-west, was taken by surprise by the Erbprinz and Holstein-Gottorp who took 260 prisoners, and then pursued to Werl, whose French garrison also joined the flood of those retreating without inflicting any delay on the pursuers.[79] Their blood up, the Erbprinz and Holstein-Gottorp were almost at Unna when they drew rein and sensibly decided that it might be wise to re-join their supporting infantry, which had trudged in the dark as far as Soest and was now resting.

---

78 Hotham-Thompson, *Operations of the Allied Army under the Duke of Brunswick 1757-1762*, p.54.

79 Reid, *The Battle of Minden 1759*, pp.62-63.

The problem with Ferdinand's approach to manoeuvring and turning threats into opportunities, was that when the scales tipped the other way, the threat could become real. Now Ferdinand risked being trapped on the wrong side of the Lippe between three French forces: Contades who was now approaching from Hamm, just 16 kilometres to the north; Chevert returning from Lutterberg; and a third column under Armentières, marching from the east. In the nick of time, Ferdinand appreciated this and withdrew his army back across the Lippe, but he remained vulnerable. His adventure had left his base of Münster exposed. Contades sent orders to Armentières to divert towards that city. Outnumbering the defenders by about seven-to-one, he had a strong chance of success but, as happened before in this campaign, a pause outside the walls to regain balance for an assault lost valuable time. On 28 October, a hard-riding Holstein-Gottorp arrived back at Münster to discover that Armentières had fled. A token pursuit was mounted, but not for long. Both sides were worn out by their efforts and winter was approaching. It would be entirely reasonable to occupy winter quarters.

When the British went into winter quarters in and around Münster, they opened a general hospital in the city. It was dictated that every sick man admitted to the hospital was to have a pass signed by a field officer but, by December, the returns and accounts were in such a muddle that Mr Cathcart was ordered to sort them out with the assistance of a sergeant from every company with soldiers in the hospital.[80] The Garrison Field Officer of the Day was required to inspect the 'Grand Hospital' daily, accompanied by a Surgeon and a Mate to ensure that the order books tallied, but also to sort out any reasonable complaints by the patients. The Commander-in-Chief was sent a weekly return of the sick.

While Ferdinand had been manoeuvring on the far side of the Lippe, the Duke of Marlborough had succumbed to dysentery and died in Münster on 20 October. His successor as Commander-in-Chief of the British Forces in Germany, Lieutenant General Lord George Sackville, was informed by the Duke of Newcastle. However, the King was not sufficiently pleased with the appointment to grant Sackville the usual privilege of promoting or posting officers within the force to fill vacancies.[81] This patronage was an important aspect of command in the British Army of that era, allowing the commander to give a boost to preferred candidates. Sackville was permitted to make recommendations, which the King would either be pleased to confirm or would not. Newcastle then suggested that Sackville was not to take this curb on his authority personally. However, Sackville felt that the King had indeed diminished his authority and that this was an open indication of his disapproval which must be obvious to all and sundry. It would also be apparent to Ferdinand that something was not quite normal between King George and Sackville.

Sackville was something of a 'marmite' character, appreciated by many of his subordinates, including at one time Wolfe, but prone to rubbing his peers, and some of his superiors, up the wrong way. Previously supported by the

80 Cantlie, *History of the Army Medical Department*, p.124.

81 Reid, *The Battle of Minden 1759*, p.64.

King, his political allegiance to the Prince of Wales, brought him to the King's disfavour.[82] In fairness to the King, though, he did still seem to appreciate Sackville's military ability. In fact, in this aspect, the easy-going Marlborough seemed to have appreciated Sackville's military staffwork, to the extent that he may have hinted to Ferdinand that Sackville would have preferred to have been in charge of the entire allied force, something which the autocratic Ferdinand may not have appreciated. For his part, though, Sackville seems to have admired Ferdinand's intellect.

For Ferdinand, the task of melding the British contingent into his command had been awkward from the beginning. One source of friction was the system of provisioning, in which Hanover paid with cash, but rations and fodder were bought from German contractors who provided poor quality at exorbitant prices. Sackville complained in writing about the cost and waste, which can hardly have endeared him to Ferdinand. While still alive, Marlborough had contributed to this awkwardness. It was definitely a principally Hanoverian army, but the British, particularly Marlborough, had been uncomfortable with, and not prepared to be seen as subordinate to, von Spörcken. The respite in winter quarters ought to have given Sackville ample time to prove his usefulness to Ferdinand. Instead, no sooner had the troops been settled into their billets than Sackville handed over command temporarily to Granby and went back to Britain.[83] There, he went through the motions of providing situational briefings to those in positions of authority. In fairness to Sackville though, Ferdinand took the opportunity to correspond with him in England, asking him to press for more subsidies of money and men, but particularly for light horse. Brought up under Frederick the Great, Ferdinand had been taught to appreciate the value which light cavalry brings in terms of scouting and intelligence gathering.

At that point it looked as if relations between Ferdinand and Sackville might be improving, especially as Sackville had been able to reassure Ferdinand that the government had agreed to support an increase in Hessian and Hanoverian light troops. In reality, though, the government was still anxious about the threat of a French invasion of England and, though the coastal raiding of France had been stopped, the troops released from this were being held back to protect Britain. Some individual replacements were made available, but no formed bodies were forthcoming. Pitt recognised that Hanoverian and Hessian manpower had now been virtually exhausted, but he might be prepared to underwrite recruitment in Brunswick. Sackville was able to help in one particular area though: as Lieutenant General of the Ordnance, he was able to procure 24 new and lighter field guns, those of Hanover becoming worn out and too heavy to be manoeuvrable.[84]

Having wintered in Britain, Sackville returned to Germany in March 1759.

In March 1759, Soubise was replaced by Broglie, who occupied Bergen, to the north of Frankfurt. Both French commanders fully grasped Ferdinand's

82 Mackesy, *The Coward of Minden*, p.30.
83 Mackesy, *The Coward of Minden*, p.42.
84 Mackesy, *The Coward of Minden*, p.43.

vulnerabilities, particularly his dependence on his resupply via his line of communications along the line of the River Weser. They planned to coordinate their own offensive to threaten this vital artery. The French plan was for Contades to re-cross the Rhine to seize Lippstadt and Münster, forcing Ferdinand back across the Weser onto Hanover. Meanwhile, Broglie would support his right flank, prepared for opportunities and recapturing ground given up in the autumn.

Ferdinand's aim was to hold the French and prevent their occupation of further German territories. With the challenge of defending between two converging armies, he had to seek to engage through small scale actions while avoiding becoming fixed and crushed by overwhelming enemy strength. He did so by skirmishing, by outpost actions and by raids conducted mainly by his cavalry.

An Austrian advance in March 1759 had threatened Prince Ferdinand's left flank but, by advancing rapidly in the direction of the River Fulda, he managed to neutralize this threat. Capitalising on this, he decided to strike further south still at Frankfurt, in order to deprive the French Armée du Main of its principal base.[85] Leaving the British contingent, as part of a corps under von Spörcken, he aimed to maintain the protective presence at Münster, thus preventing any threat to Hanover via Westphalia by the French Armée du Rhin.

By April 1759 Ferdinand's army was stirring from winter quarters, and each regiment marched off with two wagons for the sick and the regimental hospital stores, as well as two wagons for the regimental blankets. There is evidence an intensification of training, with live firing, as demonstrated by entries in orderly books: '9 Apr 1759. Lord George Sackville has ordered three barrels of powder…for each battalion, each regiment is to keep 18 rounds per man…and may make use of the remainder to practise live firings. The Welse Fusiliers have a field day tomorrow'.[86]

Ferdinand's bold southern move to strike the French Armée du Main was halted by Broglie in mid-April near Frankfurt, at Bergen.

Bergen

Bergen was a walled town, eminently suitable for defence, only four kilometres from Frankfurt. Sunken roads to both east and west added to its awkwardness, while a dense wood to the north and a boggy stream to the south would all hinder attempts to outflank it.[87] A small hill with a tower, the Friedberger Warte, just to the west provided an excellent viewpoint. Broglie ordered a dense artillery defence.

Ferdinand arrived early on 13 April. Thinking that he had caught Broglie before he had fully settled in he threw his army in piecemeal, rather than wait for his two flanking columns which were delayed by heavy going. This may

85 Szabo, *The Seven Years' War in Europe 1756-1763*, p.216.

86 Houlding, *Fit for Service: Training of the British Army, 1715-95*, p.362.

87 Battle summary from Savory, *His Britannic Majesty's Army in Germany*, pp.126-134.

have been a sign of his contempt for his opponents, but in this case it was not to work. His penny-packet approach in the face of a well-prepared artillery defence was doomed to fail. When his own slow-moving guns came up, they were employed as they arrived, but again were outgunned and the exchange was one-sided. Ferdinand then withdrew at midday, hoping to entice the French out into the open, but Broglie was not to fall for it. Instead, the gunners traded fire for the rest of the day, until Ferdinand elected to leave as evening fell. This may have been one of Ferdinand's lowest points, to the extent that Frederick was obliged to provide moral support and encouragement. Losing some 2,000 men, he was obliged to withdraw via Kassel to Münster where he re-joined Spörcken. Despite the failure of his venture, he was obliged to make a virtue of the outcome by concentrating his force along the line of the river Lippe between Soest and Werle. This he had done by June.

Despite the gravity of the situation, Major Richard Davenport, serving with the British 10th Dragoons, was experiencing social distractions:

> The dirty village and peasant's barn, which was my lot in Winter, is changed to a pleasant country place and a handsome, modern house, belonging to a chapter of canonesses, all of noble blood. Two of the four that live in the house with me are young and genteel and one of them as handsome as an angel. They are perfectly easy and well bred, without any affectation, speak French and love English country dances as well as any girls in England, which you will believe when I tell you that we have had three Balls a week ever since we came here… This was to have gone on at the same rate, but alas! This very afternoon as we were drinking tea and singing French songs under Pitt's new tent, there comes a scoundrel at full gallop, blowing a damned squeaking horn, and produces an order to march tomorrow morning.
>
> Adieu Nottuln! Adieu Madamoisells d'Ascheberg, de Chalis and van Galin! Adieu to the loves and graces that hover round the two former and to the Frowzy odour that exhales from every pore of the latter when she sweats in dancing.[88]

In Britain, meanwhile, fortunes were mixed. There was a continuing anxiety from the threat of a French invasion, slightly offset by success in Guadeloupe. Horatio Walpole, English antiquarian and man of letters corresponding with Sir Thomas Mann in Florence, wrote:

> Well! they tell us in good earnest that we are to be invaded; Mr. Pitt is as positive of it as of his own invasions. As the French affect an air of grandeur in all they do, "Mr. Pitt sent ten thousands, but they send fifty thousands." You will be inquisitive after our force—I can't tell you the particulars; I am only in town for to-day, but I hear of mighty preparations. Of one thing I am sure; they missed the moment when eight thousand men might have carried off England and set it down in the gardens of Versailles. There is great spirit in Motion; my Lord Orford is gone with his Norfolk militia to Portsmouth; every body is raising regiments

88 C.W. Frearson (ed.), *"To Mr. Davenport" being Letters of Major Richard davenport (1719-1760) to his brother during service in the 4th Troop of Horse Guards and 10th Dragoons, 1742-1760* (Society for Army Historical Research, Special Publication No.9, 1968), pp.68-70.

> or themselves—my Lord Shaftsbury, one of the new colonels of militia, is to be a brigadier-general. I shall not march my Twickenham militia for some private reasons; my farmer has got an ague, my printer has run away, my footboy is always drunk, and my gardener is a Scotchman, and I believe would give intelligence to the enemy. France has notified the Dutch that she intends to surprise us; and this makes us still more angry.[89]

Ferdinand's withdrawals had filled Walpole with gloom:

> Our part of the war in Germany seems at an end: Prince Ferdinand is retiring, and has all the advantage of that part of great generalship, a retreat. From America we expect the greatest things; our force there by land and sea is vast. I hope we shall not be to buy England back by restoring the North Indies! I will gladly give them all the hundred thousand acres that may fall to my share on the Ohio for my twenty acres here. Truly I don't like having them endangered for the limits of Virginia![90]

In anticipation of the invasion to come, the Militia had been mustering in England. It would appear that Walpole was in a minority:

> Well, I begin to expect you; you must not forget the first of August. If we do but look as well as we do at present, you will own Strawberry is still in its bloom. With English verdure, we have had an Italian summer, and
>
> Whatever sweets Sabaean springs disclose,
> Our Indian jasmin, and the Persian rose.
>
> I am forced to talk of Strawberry, lest I should weary you with what every body wearies me, the French and the militia. They, I mean the latter only, not the former, passed just by us yesterday, and though it was my own clan, I had not the curiosity to go and see them. The crowds in Hyde Park, when the King reviewed them, were unimaginable. My Lord Orford, their colonel, I hear, looked gloriously martial and genteel, and I believe it; his person and air have a noble wildness in them; the regiments, too, are very becoming, scarlet faced with black, buff waistcoats, and gold buttons. How knights of shires, who have never shot any thing but woodcocks, like this warfare, I don't know; but the towns through which they pass adore them; every where they are treated and regaled. The Prince of Wales followed them to Kingston, and gave fifty guineas among the private men.[91]

Meanwhile, the French had also combined. Contades had moved to his south-east to link up with the Armée du Main between April and June. Together, they advanced northwards, occupying one of Ferdinand's vital blocking points, Kassel. A further advance brought them within striking distance of

89 H. Walpole, *The Letters of Horace Walpole, (1749-59)*, Vol.II, Letter 320 To Sir Horace Mann. Arlington Street, June 22, 1759 <https://www.gutenberg.org/cache/epub/4609/pg4609.html> (accessed 24 February 19).

90 Walpole, *Letters*, Vol.II, Letter 322 To Sir Horace Mann. Strawberry Hill, July 8, 1759 <https://www.gutenberg.org/cache/epub/4610/pg4610.html> (accessed 24 February 2019).

91 Walpole, *Letters*, Vol.II, Letter 324 To George Montagu, Esq. Strawberry Hill, July 19, 1759 <https://www.gutenberg.org/cache/epub/4610/pg4610.html> (accessed 24 February 2019).

Ferdinand on the River Diemel. Forced further back still, Ferdinand was obliged to withdraw across the River Ems towards Osnabrück, which he reached on 8 July.

Back in England, Walpole continued his correspondence with Sir Horace Mann:

> If the French pursue their vivacity in Germany, they will send us more defenders; our eight thousand men there seem of very little use. Both sides seem in all parts weary of the war; at least are grown so cautious, that a battle will be as great a curiosity in a campaign as in the midst of peace.
>
> We have an evil that threatens us more nearly than the French. The heat of the weather has produced a contagious sore-throat in London. Mr. Yorke, the solicitor-general, has lost his wife, his daughter, and a servant. The young Lady Essex died of it in two days. Two servants are dead in Newcastle-house, and the Duke has left it; any body else would be pitied, but his terrors are sure of being a joke. My niece, Lady Waldegrave, has done her part for repairing this calamity, and is breeding.[92]

The French successfully maintained pressure on Ferdinand through a series of clashes between outposts. Fischer, scouting ahead, sent back information that, if the town of Melle could be masked, Minden could possibly be captured.[93] That, and a captured letter indicating that the fortress held large stocks of provisions, tempted Contades into giving Broglie free rein to attack. If the French could successfully capture Minden, and control its crossings over the River Weser, they would interpose themselves between Ferdinand and Hanover, blocking him off, with free rein to attack the capital.

Despite that the fortress of Minden had a reasonable garrison (a Hessian battalion and a variety of detachments from other units, amounting to about 1,500 men)[94] and that the British corps was in fair proximity, Broglie sent his younger brother, the Comte de Broglie, on ahead with a light force up to Bergkirchen on 9 July, following on himself but leaving a rearguard detachment under the Prince de Condé at Rehme in case he should be forced to withdraw. At about 5:00 a.m., French hussars drove in an outpost of German jägers supported by dragoons. A message sent to Minden's garrison commander, insisting on his surrender, was rebuffed as he had been ordered to hold it to the very end.

---

92 Walpole, *Letters*, Vol.II, Letter 326 To Sir Horace Mann. Strawberry Hill, August 1, 1759 <https://www.gutenberg.org/cache/epub/4610/pg4610.html> (accessed 24 February 2019.)

93 Claude P.V. Pajol, *Les Guerres sous Louis XV* (Paris: Firmin-Didot, 1891), Vol.4, pp.397-398. Translated by R. Couture.

94 'French Offensive in Western Germany' *Seven Years' War* <http://www.kronoskaf.com/syw/index.php?title=1759_-_French_offensive_in_Western_Germany> (accessed 15 January–31 October 2019).

7

Minden - The Ground

The battlefield of Minden lies north and west of the small town of the same name, which is situated on the west bank of the River Weser. The battleground was mainly heathland and stretched roughly nine kilometres east to west, by about six kilometres north to south.

Minden is a *Kreisstadt*, a county town. It lies 60 kilometres west of Hanover, 96 kilometres south of the port of Bremen, and 34 kilometres north-west of Hameln (Hamelin). Small towns with a connection to the battle are Petershagen, with its *schloss*, which lies to the north of Minden, and Bückeburg, also with a schloss, which lies east of the River Weser. Minden was founded in the year 800 by the Emperor Charlemagne. It became both a military bishopric and, as a member of the Hanseatic League, an important local trading centre. In 1648, it fell under the Elector of Brandenburg as a secular principality and was fortified by Frederick the Great.

Minden was a small walled town with classic star-shaped defences in the style of Vauban. Today, the glacis has been turned into green urban parkland, but its star shape can still be seen on maps and from the air. In addition to its cathedral, which dates from 953 (rebuilt in the thirteenth century), the town has many churches and a *Rathaus* (town hall) in gothic style.

The River Weser is a significant obstacle, only properly crossable by ferry or by bridge, although it might be forded at specific sites when the water level is low. There was one main fortified bridge and one ford at Minden itself, a further bridge to the north at Petershagen, with another, 25 kilometres further north still, at Stolzenau. At the time of the battle, two temporary additional bridges existed just to the south of Minden. These were erected by the French to facilitate the lateral movement of forces. The Weser frequently burst its eastern bank, giving rise to seasonal water-meadows on that side of the river.

Together, Minden and the Weser are key features in an important defile in a long, wooded ridge, the Wiehengebirge, which stretches east-west for 70 kilometres. The ridge rises steeply and is a considerable barrier to movement, but the gap, the Porta Westfalica or Gateway to Westphalia, permits straightforward passage to the north or south. With this dominating position, able to control road, river and inland waterway traffic, Minden had strategic significance.

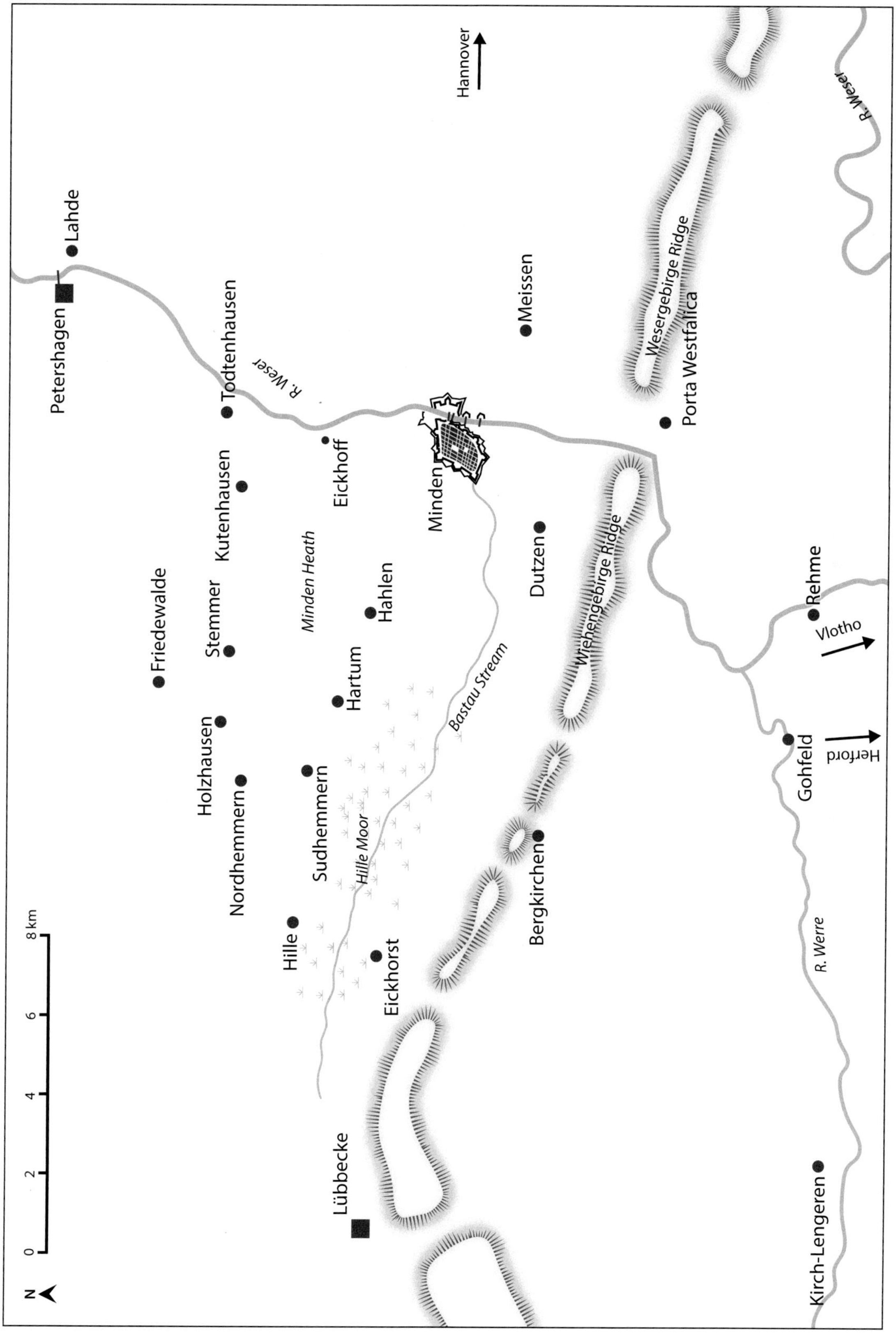

Minde, Gohfeld, and surrounding area. (Georeg Anderson, © Helion and Company 2021)

A pleasing, landscaped view of the Bastau (from the bridge on the Hohenstaufenring in Minden). In 1759, the steam would have been broader and the banks muddier, presenting a far more awkward obstacle. (Author's collection)

The terrain to the south of the ridge is hilly, the Weserbergland, while that to the north, including Minden Heath, is considered to be rather flat. However, as infantrymen know well, even seemingly flat terrain may have folds and undulations, and also that intervisibility may not be consistently good. Direct line of site when trees and crops are in full growth is not straightforward and, sometimes, it is only the glimpse of a church spire which suggests the location of a particular village.

A feature of the rural economy of the county was the frequency of windmills. Indeed, the county or Kreis of Minden-Lübbecke is known as the 'windmill county'. In flat country, such elevated positions would frequently have been sought by commanders. Contemporary maps show several windmills, some of which, or their replacements, still exist. These, and the many churches were undoubtedly used for observation.

Running parallel to the ridge and draining towards the Weser is the Bastau stream. The stream flows to the south edge of the fort at Minden, passing along the southern edge of the town. Today, the Bastau is a rather tame stream, but in the eighteenth century it posed a far more significant obstacle. Not only was the stream broader and deeper, with muddy banks, but it was surrounded by low-lying wet ground – the sinister Bastau bog, swamp or morass. In 1938, the Mittelland Canal was completed, and, while marring the battlefield, it has contributed to the drainage of the swamp.

Minden Heath was bounded by strings of small villages: westward from Minden, the villages of Hahlen, Hartum, Sudhemmern and Hille (during the battle, Prince Ferdinand's headquarters was at Hille, opposite Eickhorst which lay to the south of a causeway across the bog). To the north of Minden, and close to the west bank of the Weser, lay Kutenhausen and Todtenhausen; a similar chain of villages ran in a curve west then south from the Weser: Stemmer, Holzhausen, Nordhemmern. The villages were connected by a series of minor roads and tracks, readily passable to marching troops, artillery and wagons. The heath, with its relatively open nature, was considered to be good terrain for cavalry.

Of particular note, is the village of Todtenhausen, sometimes shown as Thornhausen or Thonhausen. The battle was sometimes known by the double titles of Minden and Thonhausen. Indeed, the centenary of the battle was commemorated by the erection of a German monument, at Eickhoff, half way between Minden and Todtenhausen. William Roy, Captain of Engineers and Assistant Quartermaster General of the British forces, surveyed the battlefield and left a remarkable record, 'Plan de la Bataille de Thonhausen près de Minden'.[1] This particularly detailed map, which is cartographically of very high quality, captured unit dispositions within immediate memory of the battle. It was recorded, engraved and published by 29 February 1760.

The companion battle of Gohfeld, which was directly linked to Minden as part of Prince Ferdinand's design, occurred on the same date. It took place 18 kilometres to the south, on the other side of the Wiehengebirge ridge and to the west of the River Weser.

The River Werre runs roughly parallel to the Wiehengebirge into the Weser from the west.

A pass links north and south of the Wiehengebirge between Lübbecke and Kirch-Lengeren. A lesser pass also exists in a saddle at Bergkirchen.

The old post road connects Herford and Minden, crossing the River Werre near Gohfeld by a bridge before running north-eastwards through the Minden Gap.

1 W. Roy, *Plan de la Bataille de Thonhausen près de Minden* and insert *Journal des Mouvements de l-Armee Allie de sa Majeste Britiannique, aux Ordres de S.A.S. Mgr le Duc Ferdinand de Brunswic depuis le 14 Juillet jusqu'au 2me Aout 1759* (Schley, 1760). Author's collection.

8

Broglie Captures the Fortress-Town

To the elderly German commander of Minden, *Generalleutnant* Christian Nicholaus Friedrich von Zastrow, common sense dictated that the French threat to his garrison would emerge on the left bank of the Weser, from the west. He had, however, destroyed most local crossings over the Weser, leaving a main bridge to the fortress, protected on the right bank by a hornwork. However, it was from this very direction that Broglie's younger brother, the Comte de Broglie, approached early on 9 July. At 9:00 a.m. Broglie wrote that he doubted that he could effectively storm the fort without great loss, but that he had an instinct that the governor's resolve might not be quite so firm as expressed and that indications provided clues that the garrison might withdraw during the coming night.[1] Carriages and wagons were in evidence but, being blocked by the river, Broglie was powerless to engage.

The Royal-Nassau Hussards, patrolling along the river and looking for a ford, persuaded a local farmer, Sander, originally from Ravensburg, to point out the whereabouts of a hidden punt in return for payment. After the battle, it is said that Sander was sentenced to death by hanging, which was later commuted to public shunning.[2] Some bold and enterprising Frenchmen managed to swim the Weser, creating a small foothold to the south of the fortress wall and ferrying back the punt. This allowed parties of 40 infantrymen to cross at a time.

Eventually some 300 Chasseurs de Fischer and Volontaires de l'Armée (regular soldiers volunteering for the duration of special, forward missions, under Stanislas Louis de La Noue Vieuxpont, Comte de Vair) were across and guided by the Baron de Closen (presumably an intrepid volunteer) around the fortress to the north side in a blocking movement in front of the

1 'French Offensive in Western Germany', *Seven Years' War* <http://www.kronoskaf.com/syw/index.php?title=1759_-_French_offensive_in_Western_Germany> (accessed 15 January–31 October 2019).

2 Anecdotal evidence, according to inhabitants of Todtenhausen.

Nienburg Gate, to prevent the garrison's escape.[3] Broglie's light troops then attacked the bridge while, in an admirable demonstration of combined-arms support, a few French guns were able to enfilade the hornwork and bridge with a few rounds of cannon fire.

The first French attack was repulsed but the second succeeded in driving the hornwork's defenders back into the town in such haste that they failed to haul up the drawbridge before a party of grenadiers of the Chasseurs de Fischer pursued them and managed to enter and secure the entrance to the fort. Two such groups gained entry from this unexpected direction, effectively to the rear of the defenders, and opened the fort to French cavalry which had crossed by a ford just south of the bridge. Although Zastrow's garrison had resisted for a period, by 9:00 p.m. the fort was in French hands. 1,200 prisoners were captured, along with ample munitions and supplies.

By this bold measure, the French had managed to interpose themselves between Ferdinand and Hanover, the capital which he was trying to protect. They had also secured a crossing over the river Weser, and the way to Hanover was now open.

Ferdinand now faced a dilemma. He was two days' march away from the important Nienburg magazine, but the French at Minden could potentially beat him to it in half the time. An alternative option would be to head in the opposite direction, to Münster, where he could be resupplied along the River Ems, but that too was at least two days' march distant. Against the advice of his secretary Westphalen, and contrary to his normal command style, Ferdinand held a council of war with his three contingent commanders, Imhoff, Spörcken and Sackville.[4] The two Germans had opposing views. Imhoff, the Brunswicker, thought that Nienburg would fall to the French before the allies could get there. Spörcken, the Hanoverian, was in favour of heading east to the River Weser, to protect Hanover.

Ferdinand then asked Sackville's opinion, probably the first time that he had done on any subject. Sackville felt at a disadvantage, not having been previously briefed on the full circumstances. On balance, said Sackville, he favoured Münster, as that would protect the most direct line of communications with Holland, and thence to Britain, plus Westphalia offered good winter quarters. However, as Ferdinand appeared to think that Münster would also fall to the French, Sackville, suggested that they should head for Nienburg, accepting that they would be likely to brought to battle in the process. Sackville's advice was equivocal and did not give Ferdinand the reassurance he seemed to need.[5] On further debate, Sackville stopped equivocating, and came out strongly in favour of Münster, with its communication with Britain. It appears that he may even have expressed a view that the British might be recalled if the communications with home were so easily surrendered.[6] It was at this point that Ferdinand's opinion

3 R. Waddington, *La Guerre de Sept Ans. Histoire Diplomatique et Militair* (Paris: Firmin-Didot et Cie, 1867), Vol.III, p.34.

4 Savory, *His Britannic Majesty's Army in Germany*, p.147.

5 Reid, *The Battle of Minden 1759*, pp.85-87.

6 Mackesy, *The Coward of Minden*, p.69.

of Sackville began to sour. The situation was not helped a week later, when Frederick wrote to Ferdinand that the British ministry had been concerned by Ferdinand's abandonment of his more direct communications with England. Frederick went on to point out that the British constitution made it as important to brief and maintain the confidence of ministers as it was to brief the King. This was because ministers could cultivate public opinion, and the people must not be allowed to believe that Prussia or Hanover would be prepared to sacrifice British interests.

As it was, Ferdinand elected to strike east to the Weser. On 12 July, a hard-riding party of German hussars and jägers encountered and dispersed a force of 600 French cavalry heading towards Nienburg. Two days later, on the 14th, Ferdinand reached Stolzenau on the Weser, effectively blocking off further French attempts on Nienburg. Also on the same day Bremen was occupied by *Generalmajor* Karl Heinrich von Dreves with four battalions. At least the main magazines on the lower Weser were now secure in German hands.[7]

The remainder of the combined French armies advanced towards and invested Münster, Lippstadt and Hameln. Contades was unable to come up to Minden as quickly as he might have wished, having difficulties with his own supplies, and was obliged to delay for several days in Herford, a town about 24 kilometres to the south-west of Minden. This can have been of scant comfort to Ferdinand, for whom the situation was now desperate, and, despite having numerically inferior forces, he felt obliged to 'fix' and hold the superior French forces by engaging them in combat. For all the delays experienced by Contades, the increase of French strength in and around Minden must have seemed inexorable to Ferdinand. He tried to distract and draw off a proportion of the French main body, by threatening its lines of communication back to Kassel, but, only able to spare small detachments, this had scant effect.

By 14 July, Contades' combined forces were in strength, in what must have seemed an imposing and impregnable position. His rear, to his south, was protected by the steep, wooded slopes of the Wiehengebirge feature. Further to his rear was his line of communications, stretching back through Gohfeld to Kassel. The largest part of his force occupied a triangle of the rising ground between the Wiehengebirge and the low-lying quagmire through which flowed the Bastau stream. Apart from crossings around Minden, the only other crossing of the Bastau lay 12 kilometres to the west, at a causeway which served the road between the villages of Hille and Eickhorst. The Bastau flowed eastwards into the Weser, itself a significant barrier, but Contades had access to, and could control, the main crossing point over the river at Minden. The fortified town of Minden jutted out to the north of Contades' positions, with picquets further north still, on the plain of Minden Heath.

The Duc de Broglie's corps, having captured the fortress, initially occupied it.

7 Hotham-Thompson, *Operations of the Allied Army under the Duke of Brunswick 1757-1762*, p.73.

For all the impregnability of Contades' positions, their very strength also restricted his own freedom of movement, and he was obliged to keep an eye on, and protect, his line of communications.

For Ferdinand to engage in combat, he would have to draw Contades out from the relative security of his positions by tempting him with a seemingly irresistible target. To do this would involve considerable risk. In doing so, he displayed 'a penetrating and uncommon genius in the art of war, and perhaps there is no instance of generalship so complete and finished as his manoeuvres on this occasion'.[8] He planned a series of moves designed simultaneously to threaten and tease Contades, unsettling him and, ultimately, baiting a trap for him.

On 16 July, Ferdinand moved to the River Weser, to the small town of Petershagen, which lies to the north of Minden. Facing south, his force had its left flank on the river. His headquarters was set up behind the left wing of his army, at Ovenstadt. He deployed an advanced guard, under the Erbprinz, ahead of the main body, along the edge of Petershagen wood.[9] This consisted of *Generalmajor* von Wangenheim's corps of 10 squadrons and eight battalions of Hanoverians, along with eight squadrons of Hessian dragoons and five battalions of grenadiers.

On the morning of the next day, 17 July, this vanguard drove in a French outpost of grenadiers and some horse which had been in a wood in front of the allied positions and then, on the instructions of the Erbprinz, advanced onto the Minden Heath. There they formed up, cavalry in front and infantry to the south of the line formed by the villages of Stemmer, Kutenhausen and Todtenhausen. This action caused those French troops encamped on the heathland to retire under the protection of the fortress artillery.[10]

Ferdinand ordered the remainder of his army to advance onto Minden Heath, in nine columns, while he himself rode forward to survey what he could of the French dispositions. His army marched southwards to form a line between the villages of Stemmer and the area behind the village of Todtenhausen. His first column was made up by the cavalry of his right wing; the second column comprised the heavy artillery of his right wing; the third and fourth columns were made by the infantry of the right wing; the centre, or fifth column was the heavy artillery of the centre; the sixth and seventh columns were the infantry of the left wing; the eighth was the heavy artillery of the left wing while the ninth was the cavalry of the left wing.

This show was maintained until about 4:00 p.m., when the main body retired back to its camp area, but it had its effect on Contades who, despite the apparent strength of his positions, ordered Broglie's corps over the Weser after dark, presumably to ensure that he had a secure foot on the other bank. Broglie's corps camped with its right flank on the village of Meißen and his left stretching back to the Weser. At the same time, the French main

8 H.N. Cole, *Minden, 1759* (London: Charles Knight & Co., 1972), p.7.

9 Hotham-Thompson, *Operations of the Allied Army under the Duke of Brunswick 1757-1762*, p.74.

10 Hotham-Thompson, *Operations of the Allied Army under the Duke of Brunswick 1757-1762*, p.74.

body adjusted, and refused, its left flank curling back up the slopes towards Uphausen.

With Ferdinand's army back in its original encampment, Wangenheim's corps similarly moved to its earlier positions to the north of Petershagen Wood. A 'grand guard' was maintained to the south of Todtenhausen, providing overwatch of Minden and the heath, supported by a battalion of grenadiers in Todtenhausen itself, while a detachment of Hanoverian hussars patrolled the area between Stemmer and Kutenhausen.

Ferdinand's next moves took place on 18 July, when 50 horse and 500 foot were sent to occupy Friedewalde. On the 19th, the villages of Stemmer and Holzhausen were picquetted and, during the night, a force of French hussars was attacked in the direction of Hille, with 40 prisoners taken. On the 20th, Ferdinand ordered openings to be cut in the Landwehr dyke between Holzhausen and Todtenhausen to 'facilitate the army's entry to the plain of Minden, by squadrons and grand divisions'.[11] On the 21st, cavalry patrols were used between Friedewalde and Holzhausen, while Nordhemmern, Holzhausen and Stemmer were picquetted by standing patrols of foot. At the western edge of the marsh a patrol was pushed out as far as Hille, where it could observe the causeway on the road to Eickhorst.

On 22 July, von Wangenheim adjusted his corps' dispositions. His cavalry now took the right flank, with heavy artillery on his left and conventional infantry in his centre, just to the right of his grenadiers. Petershagen was to be secured by Kielmansegg's Regiment, while the Schaumburg-Lippe-Bückeburg Regiment was to defend Petershagen windmill. Having completed these adjustments, Wangenheim's corps then made a show of advancing south to occupy positions somewhat isolated ahead of the main force, from just east of Stemmer through Todtenhausen to the Weser. At this stage Wangenheim's corps consisted of 18 squadrons of horse and dragoons (some 2,160), 15 battalions of foot (10,500, which included the converged battalion of British grenadiers, taken from the six British regiments of foot and commanded by Major John Maxwell of the 20th Foot), and a brigade of artillery. Wangenheim's force totalled some 12,700.

On 24 July, the allies completed a pontoon bridge over the Weser to the north of Minden near Petershagen, allowing two squadrons of Luckner's Hussars, the Hanoverian grenadier battalions Sydow and Wense, and about 200 Hanoverian jägers, all under *Oberst* Laffert, to be stationed on the opposite bank to watch for any northward movement by Broglie.[12] For the time being, they remained in the villages of Ilse and Windheim protecting the crossing.

Ferdinand detached the Erbprinz with about two brigades on 27 July.[13] He directed him towards Lübbecke in order to drive out any French forces

11 Hotham-Thompson, *Operations of the Allied Army under the Duke of Brunswick 1757-1762*, p.75.

12 Hotham-Thompson, *Operations of the Allied Army under the Duke of Brunswick 1757-1762*, p.75.

13 Hotham-Thompson, *Operations of the Allied Army under the Duke of Brunswick 1757-1762*, p.75.

there which Contades had intended would provide left flank protection of his main body and of his lines of communication with Gohfeld. To accomplish this, the Erbprinz was given eight squadrons of cavalry and six battalions of infantry (two Brunswick battalions and the Hanoverian Regiments Behr, Bock, Diepenbroik and Zastrow). The Erbprinz reached Lübbecke on 28 July and, having succeeded in driving out the French garrison there, then turned eastwards to cut or exert pressure on the French lines of communication.

In Contades' mind, there must have been competing pressures. This new threat to his rear was balanced by the fresh tempting bait provided when, on 29 July, Ferdinand left Wangenheim's corps in what must have seemed a rather exposed and isolated position at Todtenhausen while his main army moved from Petershagen south-westwards onto Minden Heath. Both factors must have mounted up in Contades mind, encouraging him to leave his protected positions and to venture out into open country to attack the Allied army.

Ferdinand issued his orders for his move on 29 July, at his headquarters near Petershagen early on the previous evening.[14] At 1:00 a.m. on the 29th, those elements necessary for an orderly move and the marking out of encampments (camp colour parties, the quartermaster general and quartermaster staffs) were to assemble by Schloss Himmelreich in Friedewalde and to move off at dawn.

The main body was roused at 3:00 a.m. on the 29th, fallen-in at 3:30 and marched off at 4:00 a.m. in three large columns. Prince Ferdinand personally headed the left column, with the heavy artillery under the *General-Feldzeugmeister* Wilhelm Friedrich Ernst zu Schaumburg-Lippe-Bückeburg, as Grand Master of the Artillery, in the centre column, while *General der Infanterie* von Spörcken commanded the right column.[15] Pack animals were to march level with, but on the right of, their own units. Only essential baggage was to accompany the army, any inessential baggage being sent back to Stolzenau and on to Nienburg. However, the vital bakery, sutler and infirmary wagons were to follow the regiments.

Ferdinand's march was designed to be highly visible to the French and was conducted with plenty of show, with bands playing and colours flying. The cavalry marched by quarter ranks while the foot marched in column in files of four. Ferdinand was insistent that the march was to be conducted in good order and that his generals were to pay particular attention to this.

It must have been an impressive sight and which would have made a considerable impact on the local civilian population. The 43 squadrons of cavalry, 28 battalions of foot, with their colours flying and the rattle of drumming, plus the artillery brigades and supply columns, amounted to over 25,000 men. Contades would have been informed of what was happening, and this was exactly what Ferdinand intended.

14 F.O.W.H. Westphalen, *Geschichte der Feldzüge des Herzogs Ferdinand von Braunschweig-Lüneberg* (Nachgelassenes Manuscript von Christian Heinrich Philipp, Edler von Westphalen) (Berlin: Mittler & Sohn, 1871), pp.420-422.

15 Hotham-Thompson, *Operations of the Allied Army Under the Duke of Brunswick 1757-1762*, p.76.

To maintain security and to prevent premature engagement by the enemy, patrols were out on the flanks. The guns were to be ready to be brought into action quickly and, to that end, no baggage was to be carried on the pieces.

To create further uncertainty in his enemy's mind, Ferdinand simultaneously directed Wangenheim to form his corps up under arms in front of Todtenhausen, near where Schaumburg-Lippe had sited batteries. When Ferdinand's main body had reached its intended encampments in an arc on the heath, von Wangenheim retired back to his own camp, but the Bückeburg Regiment and his heavy artillery remained in place out in front.

The furthest march of any of Ferdinand's units was 15 kilometres to Hille. The new camp lay in a long line between Hille and Friedewalde, behind the villages of Nordhemmern and Holzhausen. The rest of that day was spent building the new tent lines. At some point in the day, those elements detailed for picquet duty were assembled, their posts shown to them and orders given: cavalry picquets were stationed on the Hartum-Hahlen road and north of the wood, east of Hartum; British troops of the 37th Foot were to picquet Hartum; Hessians were in the wooded terrain between Hartum and Holzhausen; Hanoverians were at Sudhemmern; Brunswickers were at Stemmer. The brigades of British light artillery were put under the command of the 'General of the Day' in support of the picquets and were positioned at Hartum. Ferdinand established his own new headquarters at Hille, in which village were stationed the British 12th and 20th Regiments of Foot.[16]

Major Richard Davenport described the activities in cavalry vedettes: 'our outposts are within a hundred yards of the enemy's and the patrols of both armies pass one another at still less a distance. Their officers and ours bow to one another at a distance but are not allowed to go beyond their own vedettes, or to converse'.[17]

From Contades' perspective, the allied army was now quite spread out over a large area. Wangenheim's corps looked quite dislocated and isolated from Ferdinand's main body, and there was a further small 'penny packet' over the Weser by the northern pontoon bridge. This situation made more extreme still when, on 30 July, Ferdinand detached yet another force of 2,000 to hold Lübbecke when the Erbprinz turned from there to threaten Gohfeld to the south. On the other side, whilst Contades' and Broglie's troops were separated by the Weser, they were within a relatively straightforward march of one another by crossings which were in French hands and protected by the fortress of Minden, which was strongly garrisoned by artillery and four infantry battalions. Contades felt that he could direct some 8,000 men, under *Lieutenant-Général* the Duc de Brissac, to protect his own lines of communication and, specifically, prevent the Erbprinz from taking Gohfeld.

Now was the time for Contades to strike at the allies in their dispersed dispositions and before they could concentrate.

16 Please see colour section for map indicating the encampments of the two armies.

17 Frearson (ed.), *"To Mr. Davenport"*, p.71.

9

The Battle of Gohfeld

The engagement at Gohfeld was part of Prince Ferdinand's wider scheme of developing multiple simultaneous threats and temptations for Contades. The Gohfeld action was a mere 18 kilometres to the south of Minden Heath and took place at the same time as Ferdinand was luring the French out of their strong positions near Minden, so is directly linked in terms of Ferdinand's plan.[1]

The Erbprinz had been tasked with threatening the French line of communications which ran through the Minden gap and on, southwards. To do this he was given a force of eight squadrons, six battalions and 16 guns. He was directed to cross the Wiehengebirge ridge from Lübbecke, and then swing eastwards to carry out his mission.

He had reached Lübbecke on 28th July, where he had a skirmish with French hussars from the Bercheny and Turpin regiments, successfully driving them off. On the following day he reached Riemsloh, marrying up with *Generalmajor* Karl Heinrich von Dreves with his four battalions from Bremen, and *Hauptman* von Schlieffen of the Malachowski Hussars, assembling a force now 9,700 strong.[2]

The mission was already beginning to have the desired effect as Contades who, hearing of the skirmish at Lübbecke, started to detach troops to protect his rear. *Lieutenant-Général* the Duc de Brissac was sent south of the Wiehengebirge ridge to Bünde, about 10 kilometres west of Gohfeld, while the mounted Volontaires de Dauphiné were to liaise with him over the ridge, via the small saddle of Bergkirchen. De Brissac initially created defences near the River Else at Bünde, but was then ordered to move further east, specifically to defend the road south, along which ran the French line of communication.

On the 30th he successfully protected a resupply convoy driving from Herford to Minden. However, on the following day, the 31st, the Erbprinz and *Generalmajor* Dreves directly threatened the lines of communication between Minden and Paderborn and Kassel by establishing themselves between Kirchlengern and Quernheim. To counter this, that evening de

1 Please see colour section for map of the battle.

2 Savory, *His Britannic Majesty's Army in Germany*, pp.153-153.

Brissac moved directly onto the post road at Gohfeld, with the River Werre to his north, in order to guard the main bridge, the Gohfelder Werrebrücke.

The Erbprinz decided to strike him there the following morning, at almost the same time as the Battle at Minden was beginning. His plan was to envelop de Brissac and cut the road. He divided his force into three parts. In the centre was to be *Generalleutenant* von Kielmansegg, with four battalions, a squadron of dragoons and the bulk of the artillery, who was to advance along the northern bank of the River Werre and engage de Brissac frontally, to fix him. This would require him to negotiate a defile on his route, known as 'Haus Beck'. The right wing, under Dreves but led by the Erbprinz himself, with three battalions, four squadrons of dragoons and some jägers, and would cross to the south of the Werre, having earlier crossed the River Else at Kirchlengern to strike de Brissac's left flank. The third element, the left wing, under *Generalmajor* von Bock, with three battalions and four squadrons of dragoons, was to swing wider to the north of Kielmansegg, and reach out beyond the east of Gohfeld as a cut-off group preventing a French withdrawal to the east.[3]

At 3:00 a.m. on 1 August, the Erbprinz's force marched out from the camp at Kirchlengern. However, de Brissac had decided not to sit passively and wait. Leaving only two companies to guard the bridge, he had ordered the bulk of his force across the River Werre to attack the allies himself. He reckoned that the flat terrain there, an area later to become known as the 'bloody meadow', offered better going for his cavalry. As Kielmansegg's troops emerged from the defile at Haus Beck, and while not yet fully balanced, they came under attack. Without proper support, Kielmansegg's only mounted troops, a squadron of Hanoverian Breidenbach Dragoons, put in an attack, but was beaten back by the French. Then something of a stalemate developed and both sides settled down to bombard one another for the next couple of hours. Another charge by the French cavalry was repulsed by the Hanoverian infantry regiment of Alt Zastrow. Despite this, de Brissac was prepared to maintain his position to block the Erbprinz, preventing him from advancing towards the Minden Gap to debouch into the rear of Contades' forces during the Battle at Minden.

As the allies had come forward, de Brissac sensed that they had spread out, leaving their centre looking relatively thin and vulnerable. At 7:00 a.m., he ordered another cavalry charge, but the deployments required had been noticed by the Germans who had rapidly committed infantry reserves there. As a result, when the French attack went in it was subjected to heavy fire. Although it broke through the first allied line, it foundered on the hastily positioned-infantry reserve, which poured on intense musketry and inflicted serious loss. There then followed a lull in the firing.

While this was going on, the Erbrinz and Dreves, having crossed to the south of the Werre, had advanced all the way to the bridge, defended by only two French companies. As soon as de Brissac realised that his left flank had been turned, he abandoned the bridge and ordered a withdrawal northwards

3 Reid, *The Battle of Minden 1759*, p.90.

towards Bergkirchen, which nestled in a col on the Wiehengebirge and was a feasible crossing point of the otherwise steep ridge. However, as his party made its way north, pursued by the allied centre, it ran into, and was engaged by, the artillery of von Bock's allied left wing, the cut-off group. At this, de Brissac's corps effectively dissolved, with individuals making the difficult climb up the ridge or fleeing eastwards towards the Minden gap, just in time to meet the defeated remnants of Contades' army from Minden. Shortly afterwards, the Erbprinz, in pursuit occupied Bergkirchen. The allies captured five French cannon, 300 prisoners and much baggage. In the following years, 1,900 skeletal remains and many balls were found in the area of the 'bloody meadow'.

At Rehme, the local French commander directed any transport to turn away and return southwards to Vlotho. He also decided to destroy the Werre bridges at Rehme, thus effectively severing Contades' lifeline back to Herford.

The Erbprinz's reputation was now enhanced. On the French side, having been bested by a superior force, de Brissac did not suffer and he went on to become a *Maréchal de France*. Similarly, his subordinate Philippe-Henri de Ségur, who commanded the French infantry at Gohfeld, went on to become Secretary of War in the 1780s and also obtained his baton.

10

The Battle of Minden

So, on 31 July, Ferdinand's main army (approximately 18,000 strong) lay encamped along a rough line from one kilometre north-east of Hille to one kilometre south-west of Friedewalde, facing south-east and about 11 kilometres from the fortress of Minden, with picquets out to the front and along the border of the marshes north of the Bastau stream.[1]

The marsh was described as a 'morass' and was impassable. There was only one feasible crossing of the marshes, the causeway on the road between Eickhorst and Hille, so the French might attempt to use that, but Ferdinand had blocked this with a force of 500 men and two 6-pounder guns.

The now relatively detached force of Wangenheim, approximately 10,000 strong, occupied higher ground north of Todtenhausen, some seven kilometres north of Minden, with its left flank anchored on the bank of the River Weser and its right in the woods west of Heisterholz.

Meanwhile, the French army (in the order of 48,000 strong) occupied a strong position well-suited to defence and blocking the Minden Gap. The main force under Contades, about 35,000 strong, was encamped on the left bank of the Weser between the marshes of the Bastau stream and the steep Wiehengebirge ridge. The right flank of his camp was anchored near the Weser while his left lay south-west of the village of Dützen. Contades' headquarters was located on the slopes not far from Dützen, overlooking the river and the Minden Gap. Broglie's corps, approximately 13,000 strong, was encamped on the right bank of the Weser. Both elements could communicate and support each other via the bridges over the Weser which were themselves protected by the fortress town of Minden with its strong garrison.[2]

So, in all, there were some 76,000 troops gathered within a 10-kilometre radius.

The day before a battle is always tense. There is a strange mixture of time hanging heavy and, yet, plenty of important work to be done. Routine

1 Grossen Generalstabe, Kriegsgeschichtliche Abteilung II (ed.), *Die Kriege Friedrichs des Grossen, Dritter Teil: Der Siebenjahrige Krieg. 1756-1763. Plan 27* (Berlin: Mittler und Sohn, 1912).

2 Grossen Generalstabe, *Die Kriege Friedrichs des Grossen, Dritter Teil: Der Siebenjahrige Krieg. 1756-1763. Plan 27.*

administration and feeding must continue, while weapon preparation takes on a special significance. Ammunition is inspected and distributed. Personal equipment and boots are checked. In the days of horse and musket, edged weapons would have been sharpened on portable whetstones and flints would be replaced and then checked that they 'sparked' well. For the cavalry, in particular, there was even more to be done. The horses required feeding and watering, while tack, saddlery and horseshoes required checking and maintenance. Then would come that pregnant pause when, with tasks completed, soldiers could rest and contemplate the trial they were about to undergo. In a rural setting like Minden, there would be lanes to explore, orchards to scrump in and country folk to attempt to talk to and barter with. For the many of some form of religious persuasion, there would have been prayers while, for those of superstitious bent, there would have been personal lucky rituals.

Meanwhile, for commanders, there is plenty of planning and briefing to be completed. Both Ferdinand and Contades had finalised their plans. Ferdinand had assessed Contades' defensive arrangements as being extremely costly to assault, so had baited his trap; a subtle balance of coercion and enticement. Using the Erbprinz to threaten the French lines of communication to the south forced Contades to do something; by appearing to spread his army over a wide area, Ferdinand aimed to lure Contades to attempt to break out from his strong defensive positions and to roll up and defeat him in detail. Wangenheim's Corps of 10,000 men, in particular, was designed to look isolated and, therefore, a tempting target for destruction. He further assessed that those very defensive virtues of Contades' position would also make it difficult to break out from. If he could catch Contades mid-move and astride the obstacles, he would catch him at a disadvantage. For Ferdinand, everything hinged on early warning and then on a prompt and efficient concentration

Ferdinand directed that his officers were to familiarise themselves with the ground, ensuring that they knew the routes to be to be followed so that his whole army, currently rather dispersed, could concentrate its force quickly.[3] His generals were to 'reconnoitre all outlets to lead to the plain of Minden in order to render the ground familiar to them in case the army should march that way'.[4] In particular, they were to focus on the area between the windmill at Hahlen and Stemmer village where the army would concentrate and form up for battle. One vital task was to remove obstacles such as fences, and to prepare and cut openings (*débouchés*) in hedges along the planned routes from the encampment.

Ferdinand's plan was for his main force to advance from its spread-out encampments which were on the circumference of an arc around Minden. Having enticed the French out their own defensive positions, and by advancing as the French were emerging, he would converge and concentrate

3 Hotham-Thompson, *Operations of the Allied Army under the Duke of Brunswick 1757-1762*, p.76.

4 Cole, *Minden, 1759*, p.15.

his force, one of the key principles of war.[5] On orders, his main force would move out of their bivouacs and march rapidly towards the town of Minden, in eight converging columns.[6]

His first, and right flank, column was 24 squadrons of cavalry commanded by Sackville (14 squadrons were British: three squadrons of Bland's; two of Inniskillings; three of 'Blue Guards'; two of Howard's; two of Mordaunt's and two of Grey Horse with 10 Hanoverian squadrons (one of Horse Grenadiers; one of Garde du Corps; four of Breitenbach's Dragoons; two of Bremer and two of Veltheim) together with a battery of Saxe-Gotha artillery. The second column was composed of a brigade of German heavy artillery commanded by *Major* Hase, and the British heavy artillery commanded by Captain Forbes MacBean. The third column, von Spörcken's, is of particular interest, as it was made up of the famous six battalions of British foot, with two of Hanoverian Guards. When it shook out into battle lines, it would deploy with Major General Waldegrave's Brigade in the first line, with (from the right) the 12th, 37th and 23rd Foot. In the second line, Major General Kingsley's Brigade would be (from the right) 20th, 51st, 25th Foot, then the two battalions of Hanoverians.

The fourth column, the Prince of Anhalt's command but commanded by *Generalmajor* von Scheele, comprised six battalions of Hanoverian, Brunswick and Hessian Infantry. The fifth column was *Oberst* von Braun's brigade of Hanoverian heavy artillery. The sixth, was made up of six battalions of Hanoverian and Hessian infantry with a brigade of light artillery, and commanded by *Generalleutnant* von Wutginau. Seven Hanoverian and Hessian battalions of infantry with a brigade of heavy guns made up the seventh column under *Generalleutnant* von Imhoff. The eighth column, on the left wing, comprised 19 German cavalry squadrons (two of Hammerstein's; two of Prinz Wilhelm; two of Leib-Regiment; five of Holstein; two of Pruschenk; two of Miltiz and four of Finckenstein) under the command of *Generalleutnant* Herzog Georg Ludwig von Holstein.

Ferdinand's plan must have been clear in his own mind. However, some vital pieces of information, which would have been important to his subordinates, were absent from his orders. What effects did Ferdinand want from his troops? He omitted to mention that he believed that he had provided enough temptation to cause the French main effort to be directed against Wangenheim. The cavalry on the right wing would be led by a guide, Meyer, to the windmill near Hahlen village, which was to be held by picquets, but there was no elaboration on what he wanted it to do once there. Furthermore, unlike Contades, who briefed his officers in person, Ferdinand's orders were distributed in written form.[7]

Enforced rest would have been an important consideration for both sides after the midday meal. For the French, they were to be ready to move at last

5 J.F.C. Fuller's Principles of War, memorised by the author at Staff College, are: Selection and Maintenance of the Aim; Maintenance of Morale; Offensive Action; Security; Surprise; Concentration of Force; Economy of Effort; Flexibility; Cooperation; Administration.

6 See Appendices for detailed orders of battle in detail.

7 Mackesey, *The Coward of Minden*, pp.92-93.

light and their efforts would carry them through the night and into the next morning. For the allies, they were to be like a coiled spring in a trap, ready to march and concentrate as soon as the French commenced their own moves.

The area chosen by Ferdinand for the forthcoming battle was roughly triangular, with Petershagen to the north, Hille to the south-west, and Minden to the south. The Weser formed one side of the triangle, while the Bastau stream formed another. In its course, the Bastau meandered eastwards through marshy ground, its banks being gradual, easily overrun and boggy. At times five metres in width, it presented a significant obstacle to an eighteenth-century army. The field which lay at the centre of this triangle, however, provided attractive terrain for manoeuvre. Whilst sprinkled with small villages and farms, it was relatively flat and open and appeared to be particularly suitable for cavalry.

Ferdinand's scheme to coerce and entice Contades out of his defensive positions came at a time when the latter had been under considerable domestic pressure to take the offensive. He had been urged by his subordinate commanders to attack, but also, no less, by his own French War Minister, Belle-Isle, in Versailles.[8] So, when Ferdinand appeared to be making some naïve errors in his own dispositions, Contades, under pressure from his own side, took the opportunity to engage in what he thought could be a crushing victory.

Contades plan was that he would use Broglie's corps as his main effort, to attack frontally Wangenheim's dislocated corps at Todtenhausen in order to dominate the enemy's left flank.[9] The attack was to be rapid and intense in order to drive Wangenheim backwards, effectively cutting him off from the rest of the allies. Broglie had 18 squadrons of horse and 28 battalions of foot with supporting artillery. In addition, he would be further supported by two strong brigades of infantry under *Lieutenant-Général* the Chevalier Antoine de Nicolai, over which Broglie was to have operational control, and with 10 additional guns. Broglie's force, which was camped on the opposite side of the Weser, would cross the river and pass through Minden on its way towards Todtenhausen.[10]

As a distraction from the main attack by Broglie, a feint attack by four battalions, with cavalry and artillery support, was planned on the opposite flank, south-west of Hille. At the same time, and in concert with these movements, Contades' main body would cross the Bastau stream and manoeuvre onto Minden Heath to Broglie's left: 63 squadrons of cavalry supported by three further brigades of infantry and some 30 artillery pieces. Further left still, and effectively holding the ring along the line of villages north of the Bastau and the swamp, would be four brigades of infantry under

8 Savory, *His Britannic Majesty's Army in Germany*, p.160.

9 Baron de Jomini, *Traité des Grandes Opérations Militaires* (Paris: Magimel, 1811), Vol.III, pp.29-40, translated by Richard Couture.

10 Archives Départementales de l'Aube, Xavier, Prince, Archives de la guerre de Sept ans et correspondance familiale: le fonds du prince Xavier de Saxe, EE81 and EE82. Translated by Richard Couture.

the Comte de Guerchy, seconded by de Maugiron and, in their rear and in support, 13 Saxon battalions under the Comte de Lusace.

The French manoeuvres were to be conducted under the cover of darkness, with the beating of tattoo, the traditional drumming ceremony ordering troops to return to their nightly billets, to be the signal to muster and begin the advance.

Orders were given that bridges over the Bastau were to be constructed to facilitate the crossing by Contades' main force. The precise number of bridges is not known, but 18 is the commonly accepted figure. In the local area, it is known that timbers were purloined from local farms for the carpentry: for example, a farm two kilometres south-west of Haddenhausen, at Luttern, had its timbers removed as material for the French engineers.[11] There was also ample wood to be had from the forested slopes.

The bridges would have been of relatively rudimentary design. With a stream width of five metres it is likely that foot bridges were prefabricated and, at last light, carried down and launched. Those used by the cavalry, artillery, and supply wagons would have required small trestle supports and may have required some on-the-spot lashing. It is also quite possible that the approaches to the bridging sites, the banks, and parts of the marsh and were prepared for the masses of horses, men and wheels, by the laying of rubble and timber.

Therefore, the main attack was to be by Broglie, against Wangenheim, confident that his left flank was protected by the bulk of the rest of the army, and his right flank effectively close to the Weser. The whole French force would form a five-kilometre arc around Minden between the Bastau and the Weser. Because the terrain on his flanks was closer and more constrained, Contades put his huge mounted force under the Duc de FitzJames in what is often considered to be his centre. An alternative interpretation might be that the presence of such a heavy cavalry force was intended initially to fix Ferdinand, while de Broglie struck from the allied left as the French 'main effort', and then subsequently exploit any disintegration of the allied army.

The French surplus stores and baggage were sent back south-westwards to Gohfeld on the route guarded by de Brissac.

Contades' contingency plan, in the event of failure, was that the army would retire to its starting positions, with Broglie and the artillery of the Minden fortress covering the withdrawal.[12]

An odd little episode, which had the potential to charge subsequent events, occurred on the eve of battle, 31 July. Ferdinand's headquarters in Hille was visited by a local German civilian, one Jobst Heinrich Lohrmann.[13] His story was bizarre: that he was carrying a pair of ordinary soldier's shoes which he had been given by the French in Minden to take to de Brissac's headquarters

11 Friedrich Vormbaum, *Die Schlacht bei Minden 1759* (Minden: J.C.C. Bruns' Verlag, 1959), pp.101-102.

12 Archives Départementales de l'Aube, Xavier, Prince, Archives de la guerre de Sept ans et correspondance familiale: le fonds du prince Xavier de Saxe, EE81 and EE82. Translated by Richard Couture.

13 Vormbaum, *Die Schlacht bei Minden 1759*, pp.131-138.

in Gohfeld. The account went that he had been recommended by Minden's *Burgermeister* as a French-speaking former sailor and a dependable man who the French could rely upon. However, he had become suspicious of his task and, while on route, had decided to part company with his horse and cart at Porta Westfalica. He had made his way up onto the Weihengebirge, worked round the back of de Contades' camp, and headed west, crossing the swamp by the causeway between Eickhorst and Hille.

When the shoes were examined, there, hidden in one of the heels, was a message from Contades to de Brissac, advising him of the plan to attack the allies at Todtenhausen.[14] Was this a bluff by the French, intended to fix the allies for some other strike? Ferdinand's staff must have debated just how reliable this information was. Under most normal circumstances, an aide-de-camp could have carried the message safely between headquarters under escort. The road to Gohfeld was not far, some 14 kilometres, and was on Contades' lines of communication, so routinely used by the French. Indeed, had not their baggage been sent back on that very route? Was it assumed by the French that Lohrmann would break faith and deliver the shoes, with their secreted message, to the allies?

Whatever the final decision reached about the veracity of the message, Ferdinand was alerted that something was afoot. He issued further orders that his army was to be under arms at 1:00 a.m. So, at 6:00 p.m. on the eve of battle, Ferdinand issued orders for 'The men to gaiter and putt on their accoutrements, the horses to saddle, and the artillery horses to be harnessed tomorrow morning at one o'clock and be ready to form at a moments warning'.[15] Effectively this meant that by 1:00 a.m. the men were to be rested, but at short notice to move when ordered.

Anyone who has taken part in night operations, or passed time before an attack, will know the tension experienced by the allies. At last light the allied main body waited, probably rather uncomfortably, like a coiled spring, in its camp lines between Hille and Friedewalde. It was guarded by 200 cavalry and 1,600 infantry deployed forward on picquet duties under command of the Prince von Anhalt, the General Officer of the Day, and also by the force of Brunswick infantry, with two guns, covering the causeway over the swamp between Eickhorst and Hille. Prussian hussars from the Duke of Holstein's cavalry maintained communications with Wangenheim at Todtenhausen.

Ferdinand's password for the night 31 July/ 1 August was 'Albert and Augsburg'. He had instructed that every picquet post was to 'be very attentive, giving notice of the least motion they should observe'.[16] One can imagine the sentries peering into the gloom and being kept on their mettle by the rounds of officers and sergeants.

14 Cole, *Minden, 1759*, p.19.

15 'Neux' (pseud.), 'The Battle of Minden 1759', *Journal of the Society for Army Historical Research*, Vol.11, No.14, p.48. Order Book (The Royal Artillery Institution) which bears on the cover in ink the words 'Orders from July 19, 1759 to January 23, 1760'. Entry dated 31 July, 1759 and timed 'Past 6' written at 'Hille Camp'.

16 Cole, *Minden, 1759*, pp.22-23.

While the allies waited uneasily, the French were moving. In both Contades' and Broglie's camps, the drums beating 'tattoo' was the signal for regiments to form up and to prepare to move. The French engineers and work parties carried their prefabricated bridges down to the preselected bridging sites late in the evening, as the light was fading, so that Contades' force could cross in the dark. At 10:00 p.m., a sudden gale blew up and of such force that it drowned out the sound of Minden's church bells striking the hours. It also masked the sounds of the French activity: the sounds of large numbers of horses, the rumble of guns on the move, and of the clink and rattle of military equipment.

Broglie's Corps crossed the Weser at midnight, passing via two pontoon bridges at Neesen and Schweinbrücke, and by the town bridge.[17] It entered Minden by the Wesergate and its densely packed columns marched through the fortress, emerging by the Fishergate to the north-east of the town. It then made its way through the outskirts and, three kilometres out from Minden, formed left and right of the road through Wallfahrtsteich, ready to take on Wangenheim's isolated force which was dispersed in front of Todtenhausen. Over to the west of Minden, the regiments of Contades' main force streamed down the slopes from their encampments towards their assigned bridges over the Bastau, and on, over to erupt out in the direction of Minden Heath.

Attacking at night provides both advantages and challenges. The biggest advantage is surprise, but maintaining it through the sequencing of actions and coordination of all of one's forces is demanding. It is remarkably easy to miscalculate distances in the dark, as it is for bodies of men to become separated. It requires far greater control by its commanders and confidence by its soldiers than its daylight equivalent. However, the benefits available to the French commander, if he could ensure that Broglie's reinforced corps could launch a surprise attack on Wangenheim's corps, seemingly dislocated from the rest of the allied army, were compelling. The result of the night's work, having up to 48,000 men, horses and artillery debouched across significant obstacles and onto their start lines on Minden Heath, was a credit to French staffwork, preparation, organisation and discipline.

At about 1:00 a.m., two French deserters from the Brigade de Picardie who had been picked up by an outpost of the British 37th Foot in Hartum were bundled off to the allied General Officer of the Day, the Prince of Anhalt.[18] It is not now possible to discern the amount of pressure required, but they revealed what Ferdinand had anticipated, that the entire French army was manoeuvring. For some reason though, through inexplicably poor allied staffwork, it appears that two valuable hours of time were lost before Ferdinand was informed of this crucial information. As soon as he received the information from *Generalmajor* Johann Wilhelm von Reden, his Adjutant General, Ferdinand immediately sent an aide-de-camp with orders for his

17 Cole, *Minden, 1759*, pp.22-23.

18 Lees Knowles, *Minden and the Seven Years War – Primary Source Edition* (London: Simpkin, Marshall, Hamilton, Kent and Co. Ltd, 1914), p.20.

force to 'turn out accoutred' at best speed, to stand-to and to march to their planned positions, the ones previously identified and reconnoitred.[19]

Ferdinand himself mounted and, escorted only by a single orderly, rode off into the dark to confirm that his army was duly complying with his orders and closing the net on the French. The news that he had lost a valuable two hours through poor communication within his own chain of command must have weighed heavily on him, with the dire possibility that Contades had stolen a march on him.

He may have been slightly mollified to learn that the British 20th Foot had already formed up in under eight minutes and had marched off, leaving its camp and baggage in situ.[20] Indeed, seven of his columns had reacted promptly to their orders and had moved off. However, for some unaccountable reason, there was not yet any sign of the First Column of allied cavalry under Lord George Sackville on the army's right flank.

At this point the battle may best be considered in five broad stages: the shaping operations on the allied right wing south of Hille towards the causeway and in the villages bordering the Bastau; the action between Broglie and von Wangenheim between Minden and Todtenhausen; the significant engagement between the French horse under de FitzJames and de Poyanne and Spörcken's foot; the German completion of the destruction of the French centre; and lastly, the events associated with Sackville's cavalry force as it was withheld from the main engagement.

The Shaping Operations on the Allied Right

Shortly after 3:00 a.m. the French in the Eickhorst area commenced a bombardment of Hille with six guns which had been brought there during the night. Ferdinand had previously stationed a battalion of the Brunswick regiment of Imhoff, under *Oberstleutenant* Reinecke, with two 6-pounder guns at the northern end of the causeway.[21] Any French attempt to storm the causeway on a narrow front would have been difficult in the face of this force. Nevertheless, Ferdinand later sent word to direct that a further two field guns be sent to reinforce the Hille position.

Ferdinand's immediate priority was the security of the village of Hahlen where he intended to anchor his right flank. He rode quickly to Hartum, where he had stationed a picquet, and ordered it to advance the 2.5 kilometres to Hahlen, to seize it before the French. To his chagrin he learned that the French had beaten him to it, and that two battalions from the Brigade Champagne were already making inroads into the village. Riding to the line formed by the picquets, he ordered them to push on and, at all costs, to force the French out.

19 Cole, *Minden, 1759*, p.24.

20 Cole, *Minden, 1759*, p.24.

21 Grossen Generalstabe, Kriegsgeschichtliche Abteilung II (Ed.), *Die Kriege Friedrichs des Grossen, Dritter Teil: Der Siebenjahrige Krieg. 1756-1763. Plan 27* (Berlin: Mittler und Sohn, 1912).

'The conduct of Prince Ferdinand upon this occasion' wrote Colonel J. Durand from the allied headquarters in Minden on 3 August 1759 to the Earl of Holdernesse, 'can not be sufficiently admired, his readiness in forming the troops upon such short notice and his great coolness and attention to everything that happened during the action deserves the highest praises'.[22]

Fearing that von Spörcken's column could be threatened by the French seizure of Hahlen, Ferdinand found to his frustration that the Prince of Anhalt had indeed moved forward with the picquet from Hartum as ordered, but had unaccountably stopped short on the fringes of Hahlen.[23] This had allowed the French to flow into the village and occupy it. The Prince was ordered by Ferdinand to take the village at once and the allied infantry regained its momentum, attacking the village. The allied attack was put in in the nick of time, driving the enemy from the village before they could consolidate. The Brigade Champagne withdrew back down the approach road and the adjacent fields, firing some of the farm buildings and leaving behind some dead and wounded.

Having been focused on his right flank, and having become separated from his own headquarters, Ferdinand was unaware of what was happening to Wangenheim on his left. Indeed, Wangenheim had not bothered to send word to Ferdinand. The wind was still blowing vigorously away to the north-east, so the sound of cannon fire from Ferdinand's left may have been muffled. Accordingly, Ferdinand rode back onto the heath, sending an aide-de-camp on ahead to glean a battle picture from the area around Todtenhausen.

The Action Between Broglie and Wangenheim, Between Minden and Todtenhausen

As dawn broke, at about 4:30 a.m., it would have been possible to see smoke rising to the east around Todtenhausen, where Broglie's corps was in action against Wangenheim's. So, Ferdinand's army was now engaged simultaneously at three points: on the extreme rear-right flank at Hille; on the right, in and around Hahlen; and on the extreme left flank in the vicinity of Todtenhausen and Kutenhausen.

Wangenheim's force was engaged from first light by Broglie's strengthened corps between Kutenhausen and the River Weser. Wangenheim had returned to the positions it had occupied on the 29th. He had 18 squadrons on his right flank, stretching out towards Stemmer. His centre, around Kutenhausen, was composed of 15 battalions, while a brigade of Bückeburg artillery was on his left flank between Todtenhausen and the Weser.[24]

---

22 The National Archives of the United Kingdom (TNA). State Papers: 87: Secretaries of State: State Papers Foreign, Military Expeditions, Volume 29, 3 August 1759. Durand to Holdernesse, Colonel Durand had been sent as commissioner to confirm the strength of the allied army for which Britain was paying.

23 Mackesy, *The Coward of Minden*, p.98.

24 Grossen Generalstabe, *Die Kriege Friedrichs des Grossen, Dritter Teil: Der Siebenjahrige Krieg. 1756-1763. Plan 27.*

Broglie's corps, reinforced as the French main effort, comprised 22 squadrons and 22 battalions. Having crossed from the opposite side of the Weser and made its way through Minden during the night, this force had moved northwards from the fortress, using the Petershagen road as an axis of advance, in eight columns, in three lines. He had pushed his artillery well forward, along with the lead elements. The right flank of the first and second lines of infantry was on the bank of the river. Each line had cavalry on its left flank. Broglie had anticipated something of a set-piece battle. With his artillery pieces well forward, he intended that as soon as initial contact was made those guns would engage the positions known to have been occupied by the allies.[25]

Broglie's leading patrols bounced Wangenheim's forward outposts at about half an hour before dawn. The gale and the strong winds during the night had masked the sound of the French movement and, despite Ferdinand's orders and preparatory instructions, the sudden appearance of the enemy looming out of the half-light appears to have taken Wangenheim's outposts by surprise. After an initial exchange of fire, Wangenheim's picquets withdrew.

It fell to Broglie to destroy Wangenheim's corps, allowing the French to roll up Ferdinand's army from its flank, defeating it in detail. Yet, for some unaccountable reason, the forward French elements failed to press their advantage. Perhaps word of the initial success was not reported quickly enough to Broglie. At about 5:00 a.m., his artillery commenced a bombardment of what was assumed to be the allied positions. At this point, Broglie was opposed by only four German battalions whose withdrawing outposts had failed to give a general alarm.

The advantage lay with the French at this point, as the leading nine French infantry battalions in the first line were poised to deliver their attack. However, perhaps because it was not yet fully light or possibly because of early morning mist, Broglie hesitated in ordering the attack to be pressed home, preferring to err on the side of caution by awaiting the arrival of *Lieutenant-Général* Nicolai's brigades on his left flank.

Wangenheim's corps, meanwhile, after a dilatory start, was soon well aware of the proximity of the French and made up for lost time, turning out rapidly. The allied troops assembled with a sense of urgency and it now was not long before, having formed up, they were marching forward into their allocated deployment positions. The cavalry too was quickly mounted and ready. By the time it was fully light, the French could now see their opponents in full battle array. However, dawn also presented the French artillery, skilfully deployed well forward, with an attractive selection of targets. The French bombardment was intense and initially effective, so effective that the allied lines were ordered to kneel to reduce the target, an order that was considered degrading by the men of Major Maxwell's composite British

25 Broglie, L. de, and Vernier, J. (eds.), *Correspondance inédite de Victor-François, Duc de Broglie, Maréchal de France, avec le Prince Xavier de Saxe, Comte de Lusace, Lieutenant-Général, pour servir à l'histoire de la guerre de la Guerre de Sept Ans* (Paris: Albin Michel, 1903-1904), Vol.I, pp.36-48.

Grenadier Battalion, which felt it demeaning to bow to the enemy.[26] When the German artillery came into action with its own counter-battery fire, this eased the pressure on the allied infantry, which was able to return to its normal standing position, in time to open fire and halt the first French line of infantry.

Having previously paused to bring forward Nicolai's brigades on his left, Broglie now ordered them to attack von Wangenheim's centre, at Kutenhausen. However, the forward movement of the allied troops was assumed by Broglie to be a full counter-attack rather than the occupying of pre-planned positions. Accordingly, Broglie's confidence wavered, causing him to call off Nicolai's advance beyond his own first line, in order that together they could consolidate to repel what was assumed to be an allied offensive. Broglie's attack, the French main effort, had faltered.

The Significant Engagement Between the French Horse and Spörken's Foot

Meanwhile, back towards the allied right after 5:00 a.m., the action to clear the French from Hahlen had its effect. Additionally, the two British light brigades of artillery under Captains Duncan Drummond and Edward Foy went into action about 300 metres north-west of Hahlen, suppressing by their fire an enemy battery beyond the village, where they performed 'admirable service in the opening stages of the engagement'.[27] These two factors improved the opportunity for the infantry on Ferdinand's right wing to advance clear of the woods between Hartum and Hahlen with less hindrance from the enemy.

Simultaneously, the German columns in the centre, those commanded by von Scheele, Wutginau, Imhoff and Holstein, began their deployment. Just as the later historians have questioned Contades' positioning of his cavalry in the French centre, Holstein's were not dissimilarly disposed. The fact is that both Wangenheim's and Broglie's corps were thought to be about to bear the brunt of the action as the 'main effort', while both sides' cavalry was deployed from positions where they could sweep into the flanks of the battle around Todtenhausen.[28]

At about 7:00 a.m., Spörcken's column had made good progress and, having shaken out into line of battle, halted briefly just short of a belt of fir trees through which it then passed to get onto the heath. As it emerged from the band of trees, its right flank passed in front of Hartum and Hahlen. Those villages were covered by the guns of Drummond's and Foy's batteries which had been manoeuvring forwards, and also now by MacBean's heavy battery which came up to the left of Foy's. The leading line of von Spörcken's force was composed of the three battalions of Major General Waldegrave's Brigade: 12th Foot on the right; 37th Foot in the centre; and 23rd Foot on

26 Cole, *Minden, 1759*, p.46.

27 Cole, *Minden, 1759*, p.28.

28 Please see colour section for a map indicating the position of the two armies at this phase of the battle.

the left. In the second line was Kingsley's Brigade, with 20th Foot on the right, 51st Foot in the centre and 25th Foot. The two brigade lines were not exactly lined up from front to rear. On the left of Spörcken's division were two battalions of Hanoverian Guards.[29] In aligning the brigades, the presence of the Hanoverians may, to a certain extant, have caused 20th Foot to jut further out to the right beyond Waldegrave's Brigade in front. This had the effect of causing the 20th to pass in closer proximity to Hahlen when it advanced.[30]

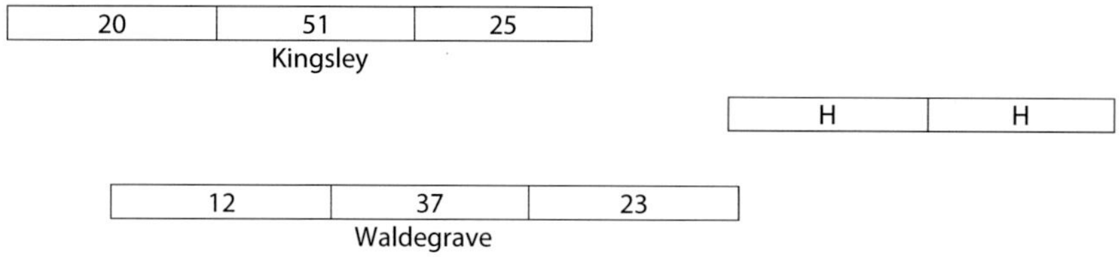

von Spörcken's Front

As the British and Hanoverian Guards battalions emerged from the strip of wood, and as the early morning mist cleared, at a range of just over 1,000 metres could be seen a large body of horse. This was the first line of FitzJames's cavalry. From the French perspective, the first three battalions of red-coated infantry would have been readily visible. All of the troops in Spörcken's division wore scarlet, the Hanoverians as well as the British. The red walls of men would have been punctuated by the twinkle of edged weapons: bayonets, sergeants' halberds and officers' spontoons. Each battalion bore a distinguishing facing colour, which was mirrored on the regimental flags: in Waldegrave's leading brigade, the facings were dark yellow (12th), pale yellow (37th) and dark blue (23rd).

Spörcken's force may have looked rather exposed, particularly as there was, as yet, no sign of whatever body of troops should have been between the British infantry and Hahlen – the planned area for Sackville's column. The first line of foot advanced, drums beating, for another 300 metres, halting in a slight dip which runs across the heath.

At this point, Ferdinand, who had watched Spörcken's division enter the belt of trees and then begin to deploy properly onto the open ground of the

29 J.W. Fortescue, The Hon., *A History of the British Army* (London, Macmillan, 1899), Vol. II, p.491. Note: Savory has one battalion of Hanoverian Guards in the first line, while Roy's map, with its superimposed leaves portraying different phases, shows both Guards battalions initially in the first line, but being outpaced and gradually joined by Hardenberg's battalion from the right of von Scheele's column. Kingsley believed that the attack was made by the British infantry, but sustained by the Hanoverians (Reid, *The Battle of Minden, 1759*, p.164). Arguably, this all goes to show the wisdom of the Duke of Wellington's remark after Waterloo, comparing a battle with a ball, in which no individual can recollect the order or the exact moment of events.

30 W. Roy, *Plan de la Bataille de Thonhausen près de Minden* and insert *Journal des Mouvements de l-Armee Allie de sa Majeste Britiannique, aux Ordres de S.A.S. Mgr le Duc Ferdinand de Brunswic depuis le 14 Juillet jusqu'au 2me Aout 1759* (Schley, 1760). Royal Collection K.Mil. RCIN 732200.

heath, sent one of his aides-de-camp, Graf Jakob von Taube, to Spörcken with instructions 'to advance with the regiments he had, with drums beating, and attack whatever he might encounter'. The message was passed by von Taube to Major General Kingsley in the second echelon.[31] So, instead of halting properly at that point and waiting for the signal, Waldegrave's Brigade merely paused to allow Kingsley's Brigade and the two Hanoverian battalions to emerge from the band of trees and begin to shake out, before the drums beat out again and the advance continued.[32]

Therein lies an important enduring lesson for all commanders and staff officers. It is vital that the message is clear to the recipients, and understood by them. In the heat of battle, when blood is up and the brain can be overwhelmed by sensory overload, it is quite possible for even clear and simple orders to be misunderstood. There is another important lesson about multinational alliances, in that communication is even more challenging. Subtleties and nuances may be lost on allies. There would have been those in both the British and German forces who spoke each other's language to some degree, but not necessarily with full comprehension. French may have been slightly more likely as a second language in both nations, but the possibility of misspeaking and then misunderstanding is not insignificant. The use of drums in armies was varied. They could be used to provide a cadence for actions such as marching and weapon handling, but they could also be used to transmit orders within units ('reveille', 'assembly', 'alarm' and 'tattoo' being examples) and, at higher level, within formations for the coordination of more than one unit.

The breaking out of drumming within Kingsley's Brigade, taken up by Waldegrave's in front and the Hanoverian Guards to the left, and then the recommencement of the advance of Spörcken's division, must have surprised Ferdinand. Despite the possibility that the whole division may only have been shifting to allow Kingsley's echelon to disentangle itself from the wood, to make sure, Ferdinand sent yet another aide-de-camp to stop the advance – in vain.

Spörcken's entire division was now on the advance, but slightly obliquely to its left. Possibly as a result of emerging from the wood or the dip in the ground, Spörcken's division was ahead of the rest of the allied army, edging across the face of von Scheele's Brigade of the Fourth Column and, because of the slight angle, the Hanoverian Guards were beginning to overlap in front of the Hanoverian regiment of Hardenberg.[33] As often happens after a storm, the day was clear and fine, albeit still windy, and the ensigns would have struggled with their colours out at full fly. Yet onward they marched to the drums of eight battalions.

Once started, the march of Spörcken's division gathered its own momentum and became inexorable. Prince Ferdinand later wrote, 'The infantry advanced

31 TNA, SP 87: Secretaries of State: State Papers Foreign, Military Expeditions, Volume 37/56, ff. 122, 123. Von Taube, statement (Paderborn, 12 February 1760).

32 Reid, *The Battle of Minden 1759*, p.101.

33 Grossen Generalstabe, *Die Kriege Friedrichs des Grossen, Dritter Teil: Der Siebenjahrige Krieg. 1756-1763. Plan 27.*

with a commanding and steady countenance. Their impetuosity was at the same time so great that the second line and the Brigade of Artillery in the centre could with difficulty follow them'.[34] MacBean's Heavy Brigade of Artillery, despite being drawn by teams of six horses per gun, was clearly struggling to keep up with the trudging infantry.

The first effective French fire was inflicted on the advancing infantry by the batteries of guns which had been brought up to the windmill north-east of the village of Hahlen and south-east of Maulbeerkamp. The French now had more than 60 guns; admittedly these were initially firing at long range but, as the battalions passed Hahlen, the range closed sufficiently for some guns to fire grapeshot. The two battalions on the right flank, the 12th and 20th Foot, suffered more than the others, but this was endured and the march continued, leaving small piles of casualties. Lieutenant Thomas Thompson of the 20th Foot wrote from the hospital in Minden on 18 August, 'I saw heads, legs and arms taken off every minute, my right hand file of men not more than a foot from me were all, by one ball, dashed to pieces and their blood flying all over me'.[35] It was the job of sergeants to redress the ranks and to maintain a solid wall of soldiers by ordering men from the rear ranks forward to fill any gaps.

Lieutenant Montgomery of the 12th Foot described the effect of the fire in a letter written to his home from Paderborn, just days after the battle:

> It was the most disagreeable march I ever had in my life, for we advanced through a most furious fire from an infernal battery of eighteen pounders, which was at first upon our front, but as we proceeded, bore upon our flank, and last upon our rear. It must be imagined that this cannonade would render the Regiments incapable of bearing the shock of unhurt troops drawn up long before on ground of their own choosing, but firmness and resolution will surmount any difficulty…
>
> At the beginning of the action I was almost knocked off my legs by my three right hand men, who were killed and drove against me by a cannon ball, the same also killed two men close to Ward, whose post was in the rear of my platoon, and in this place I will assure you that he behaved with the greatest bravery, which I suppose you will make known to his father and friends. Some time after I received from a spent ball just such a rap on my collar bone as I have frequently had from that most dreadful weapon, your crooked headed stick; it just welled and grew red enough enough to convince neighbours that I was not fibbing when I mentioned it. I got another of these also on one of my legs, which gave me about as much pain, as would a tap of Miss Mathews's fan. The last and greatest misfortune of all fell to the share of my poor old coat for a musket ball entered into the right skirt of it and made three holes. I had almost forgot to tell you that my spontoon was shot through a little below my hand: this disabled it, but a French one now does duty in its room.[36]

34 Cole, *Minden, 1759*, p.33.

35 Cole, *Minden, 1759*, p.35, quoting Colonel C. Field, *Echoes of Old Wars* (London: Herbert Jenkins, 1934).

36 National Army Museum (NAM) 1975-10-92. Lieutenant Hugh Montgomery to his Mother, dated Camp at Paderborn 9 August 1759.

An artillery duel commenced as MacBean's Brigade in its turn engaged from 200 metres north-east of the eastern end of the long strip wood to such effect that it succeeded in silencing the 18 French pieces which so menaced the right flank of Spörcken's division. This was achieved at the cost of only two guns put out of action.

At about this point in time, observing this unexpected and novel development, Contades sent word to Broglie on the right wing, to halt his own advance and to consolidate the position he had reached while FitzJames's cavalry dealt with this bizarre manoeuvre by the British and Hanoverians. Even at this stage he cannot have been completely confident, as he also issued a contingency order to Broglie to be prepared to cover any withdrawal if required.

For the French horse, it must have come as something of a surprise to observe unsupported infantry in line preparing to attack fresh, unbroken cavalry. Long used to forcing enemy infantry to receive and endure their mounted manoeuvring and charging, this must have felt like role-reversal

As it advanced, increasingly battered by artillery, and subsequently, as it came within range, by musketry from Guerchy's foot, Waldegrave's Brigade approached to 500 metres from FitzJames's cavalry. After initial bemusement at the sheer audacity of this manoeuvre, the French now recognised a splendid opportunity to destroy this upstart formation. The French cavalry would revert to its appropriate role of attacking. The command was given to 12 squadrons, under *Lieutenant Général* Charles, Marquis de Castries, to charge.

It would have been a magnificent sight, over a thousand horsemen in varied, gaudy uniforms. To achieve best effect, it was important that a cavalry charge was, at least initially, disciplined. Most manoeuvring was conducted at the trot to maintain control, building to a crescendo, to gallop only in the last moments. However, the temptation to spur on forward in a glorious abandonment of discipline must have been immense.

On the other side, discipline was also vital. It was important that infantry behaved as one and held its nerve.[37] For to break and run was to invite disaster as, rather than presenting a formidable wall of bayonets and lethal musketry, individual infantrymen fleeing would expose their heads and backs to enemy sabres and hooves. As FitzJames's cavalry began its charge, the order was given to the infantry to halt. Already loaded with powder and ball, the front rank knelt, and the remainder closed up to provide a locked phalanx. At such a tense moment, reassurance provided by the close presence of comrades acted to stiffen resolve. Similarly, the voices of sergeants provided control in the face of primal fear. The sergeants would have shouted that fire was to be held until the last possible moment, in order to make every shot count. The outcome emphasized the fighting powers of well-trained and well-disciplined infantry.

It was only when the first horses were within 30-40 metres of the front rank that the order was given to 'Fire!' At such short range, the effect of

37 Houlding, *Fit for Service*, p.351.

such a heavy volley must have been formidable, causing horses and riders to tumble. The volley would have sounded with a huge crash and, immediately, the view to the front would have been masked by gunsmoke. As the smoke cleared, a scene of carnage would have emerged, with dying and wounded mounts and riders sprawled on the ground. Distressed horses would have been whinnying, struggling and kicking with flailing hooves, a dreadful sight. Those untouched would, nevertheless, have found their way blocked by these appalling and terrifying obstacles, rendering them easy targets for a second infantry volley. At this, the charge was effectively ruined.

Ruined perhaps, but still with the capacity to kill. Such was the momentum of horseflesh that, on the right flank of the 12th Foot, tumbling horses and riders broke a path through the regiment. Lieutenant Montgomery wrote:

> When we got about a hundred yards from the enemy, a large body of French cavalry galloped boldly down upon us: these our men, by reserving their fire until they came within thirty yards, immediately ruined, but not without receiving some injury from them, for they rode down two companies on the right of our Regiment, wounded three officers, took one of them prisoner with our artillery lieutenant [an officer in command of two light guns organic to the battalion] and whipped off the tumbrells.[38]

Once any horsemen became separated from their fellows, and surrounded by enemy infantry, they immediately became vulnerable and few survived. Reins were grasped, and the riders bayonetted and dragged from their mounts. Those that could, turned off and away but even then were fired on as the infantry confirmed their destruction. It was at this point that the sergeants quickly restored order. Gaps in the line were closed and reloading ordered. Where necessary, the wounded were assisted to the rear of the line. During this brief respite, the two Hanoverian Guards battalions moved forward into line with Waldegrave's Brigade, and the regiment of Hardenberg likewise came into line with them, to their left.

FitzJames ordered his second echelon, under du Mesnil, forward: 22 squadrons of the Brigades du Roi, Bourgogne and Royal Étranger came on in a wave. Working their way over and around the obstacles presented by the ill-fated first line, they still managed to raise a charge. Again, the allied infantry held its fire until the enemy was about to crash home. Another tremendous volley cut down men and horses. Even then, those untouched emerged from the clouds of gunsmoke, only to be confronted by a solid wall of red which shot them at closer range. Where a few managed to penetrate the first allied line, they found themselves engaged by both Kingsley's Brigade and by the men in the rear rank of Waldegrave's who turned about to fire from behind. Lucky were the few who, having survived this double jeopardy, were able to gallop off to the flank to return to their own side.

Once again, the sergeants instilled order to the ranks. Reloading was vital, but so was the restoration of the line. Quickly now, and before the enemy

38 Cole, *Minden, 1759*, p.36, quoting Fortescue, *Following the Drum.*

could organise another charge, the drums started beating and the infantry resumed its offensive. The infantry advance placed Spörcken's division in an even more vulnerable position and its right flank became exposed to the Guerchy's infantry on the French left wing. Guerchy saw the opportunity presented and directed the eight battalions of the Brigades Condé and Aquitaine forward to engage. The threat of being outflanked in the age of the musket did two things, one physical and one psychological: firstly, it created a threat of being overwhelmed by the arithmetic of a greater number of barrels directed towards only a few; secondly, the threat presented to one's side, and even potentially eventually from one's rear is deeply disturbing. This was a dangerous moment for the allies, had not Waldegrave spotted the threat and ordered the 12th and 37th Foot to refuse their flank, by wheeling, thus presenting their front and the maximum number of muskets toward the advancing French.

A brief musketry battle between the opposing infantry ensued. For all the inaccuracy of the smoothbore musket, at close range and against massed targets it was a murderous weapon. Casualties were inflicted on both sides but gradually the attrition created by the rate of fire and the discipline of the British infantry told. Steadily at first, and then increasingly, Guerchy's foot melted away, dead, wounded or retreating.

However, rather like the curtains being opened on stage in a theatre, this withdrawal revealed a fresh, and greater, threat. Montgomery's account relates the advance from the enemy's reserve of a regiment of Grenadiers, 'as fine and terrible looking fellows as I ever saw. They stood us a tug, notwithstanding we beat them off to a distance, where they galled us much, they having rifled barrels, and our muskets would not reach them. To remedy this we advanced, they took the hint and ran away'.[39] Montgomery's description of an enemy equipped with rifled barrels is controversial. Rifles, whilst slower to load, would outrange and would be more accurate than the British smoothbore Long Land Pattern muskets.[40] After an initial exchange of fire, these grenadiers too were forced to withdraw. However, they did so with sufficient discipline to reform and re-engage beyond the effective range of the British muskets. To the British 12th and 37th Foot, the only appropriate solution was not to withdraw but to advance again into effective range, which they did, driving these grenadiers from the field. However, the cost of having successfully fought these serial engagements was revealed by a roll-call which showed that the 12th Foot could now only muster four officers and 13 files of unwounded men.

39 NAM 1975-10-92. Montgomery to his Mother.

40 This has been the subject of much debate, with few currently believing that the French army employed rifling at this stage in history. Indeed, the author was unable to find a single source reporting the French use of rifles in this period. As a result, and given the echelon of the French army being engaged, the author has assumed that the rifles must have belonged to Saxons. This theory is corroborated independently by Reid, *The Battle of Minden 1759*, p.107. Subsequent correspondence with the Militärhistorisches Museum der Bundeswehr has shown that, while not on general release, the Saxon Army had been experimenting with rifles for its cavalry (the 1745 Carbine – see U. Voller, *Deutsche Militärhandfeuerwaffen*, Heft 2), and that dismounted cavalrymen were used to form the grenadier companies of some of the Saxon units serving with the French.

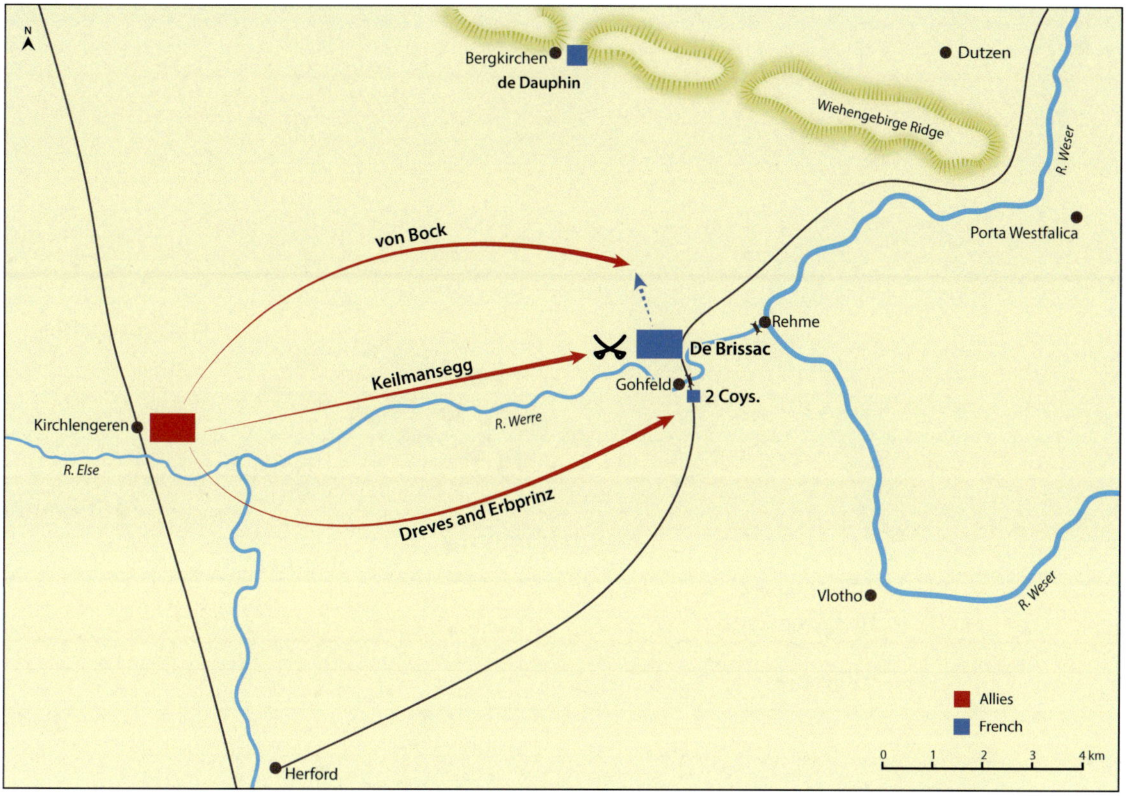

The action at Gohfeld, 1 August 1759, showing the advance of the three allied columns. (George Anderson © Helion and Company 2021)

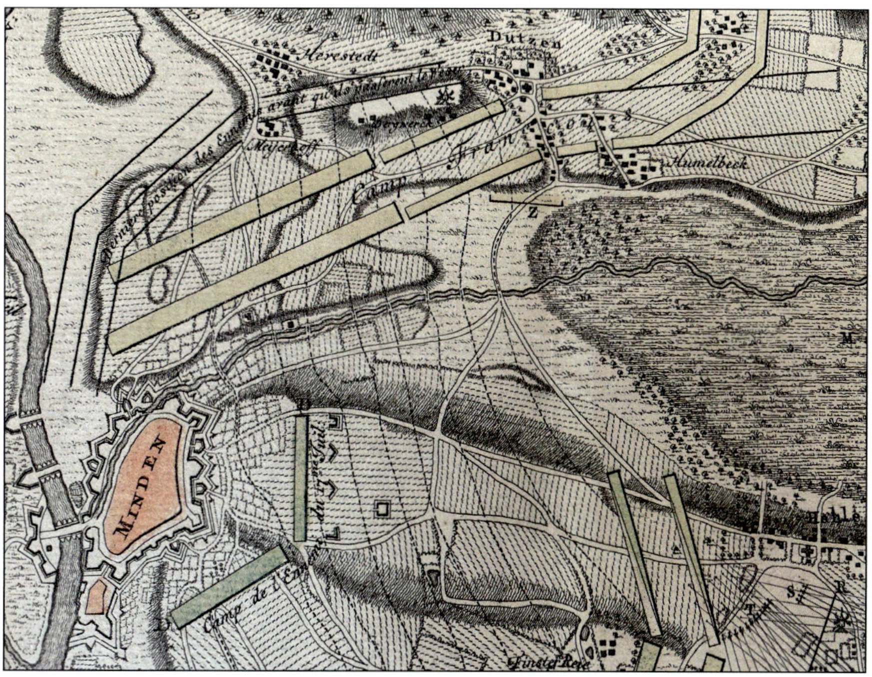

A section of the Roy map, showing the fortifications of Minden, some of the French encampments prior to the battle, and their improvised bridge sites over the Bastau stream. Roy was present at the battle, and the map was produced within only months of 1 August 1759. (Author's collection)

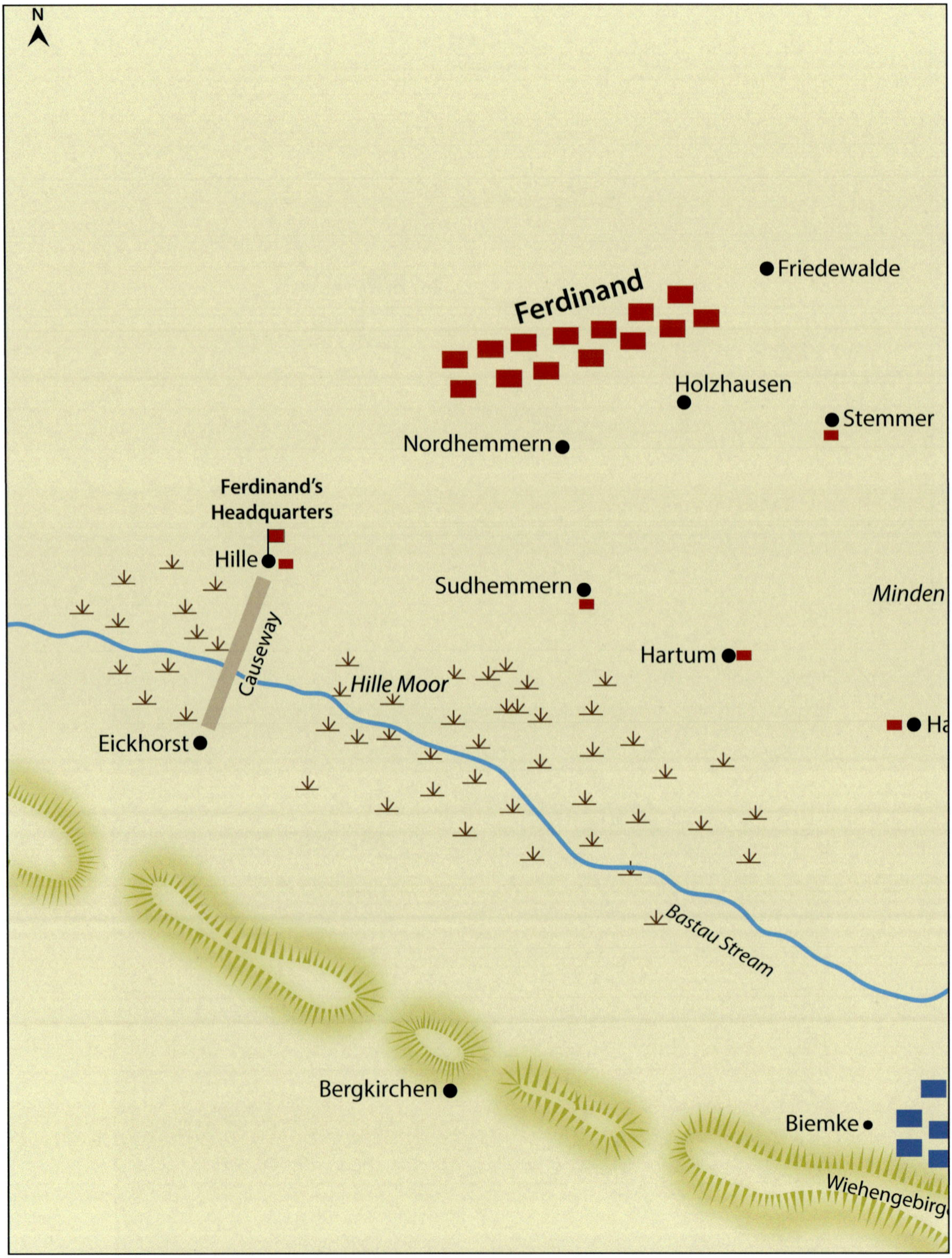

Pre-Battle encampments, as of the evening of 29 July 1759. The French were divided, with their main body (under Contades) protected behind (south) of the Bastau. The French also had a corps under Broglie on the east of the River Weser near Meissen. The allies were

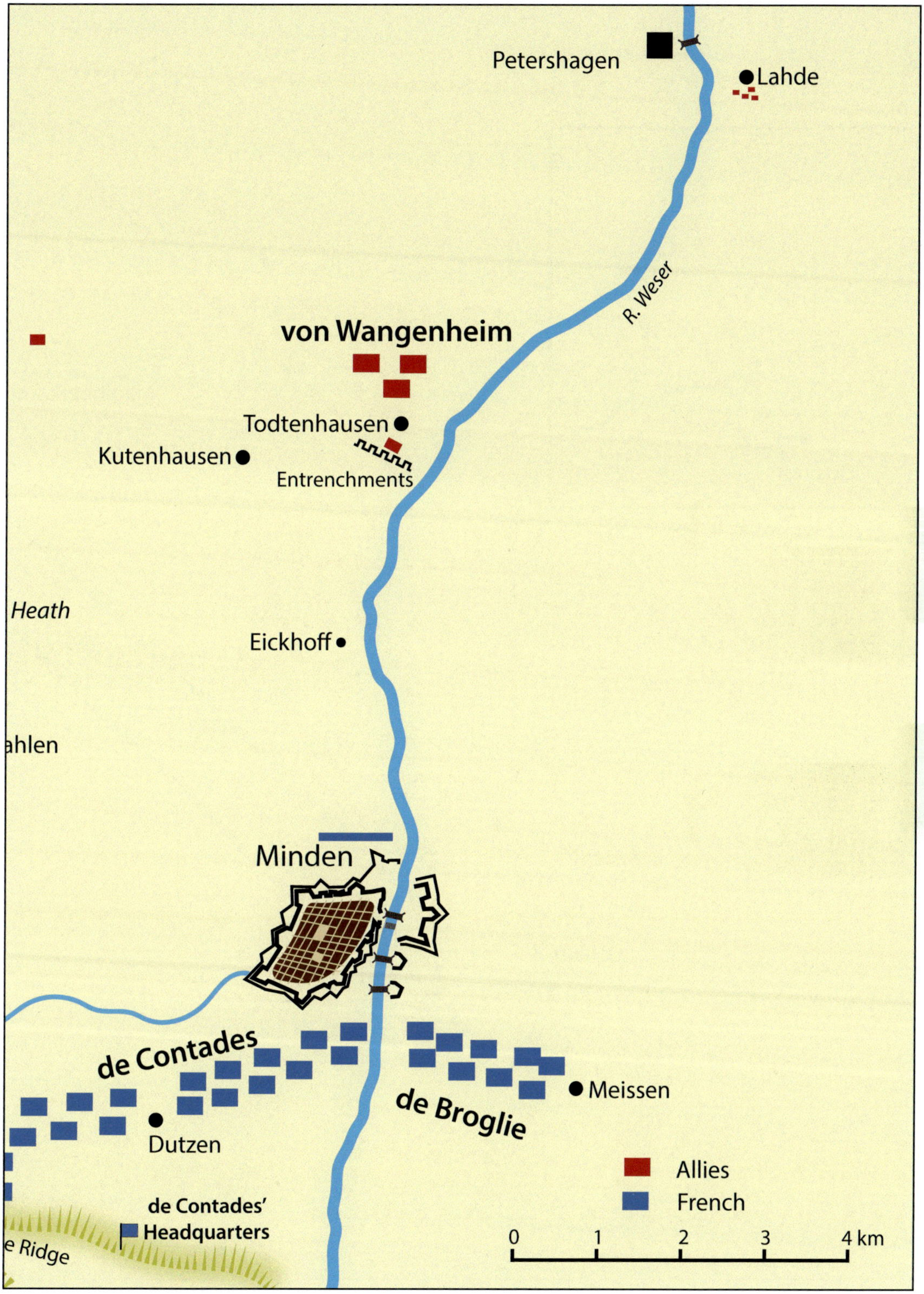

also divided, with a decoy force (under von Wangenheim) near Todtenhausen, and the main body in an encampment near Nordhemmern/Holzhausen. Prince Ferdinand, the allied commander had his headquarters at Hille.
(George Anderson © Helion and Company 2021)

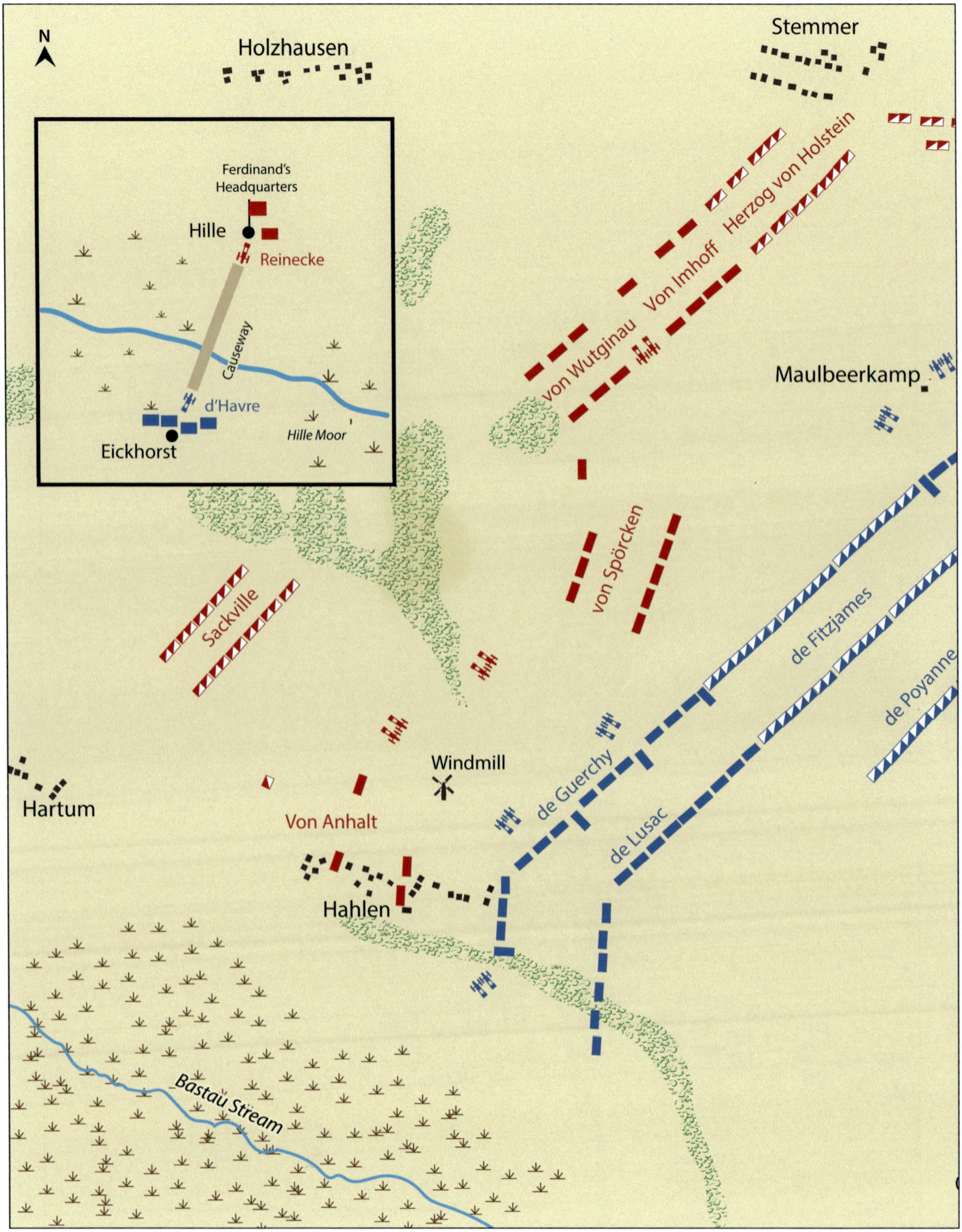

Battle of Minden, 1 August 1759. Situation at about 6.30 a.m. The French have crossed the Bastau and the allies have moved out of their bivouacs towards Minden Heath. The French right has attacked the area near Todtenhausen, while the left has begun to encroach on

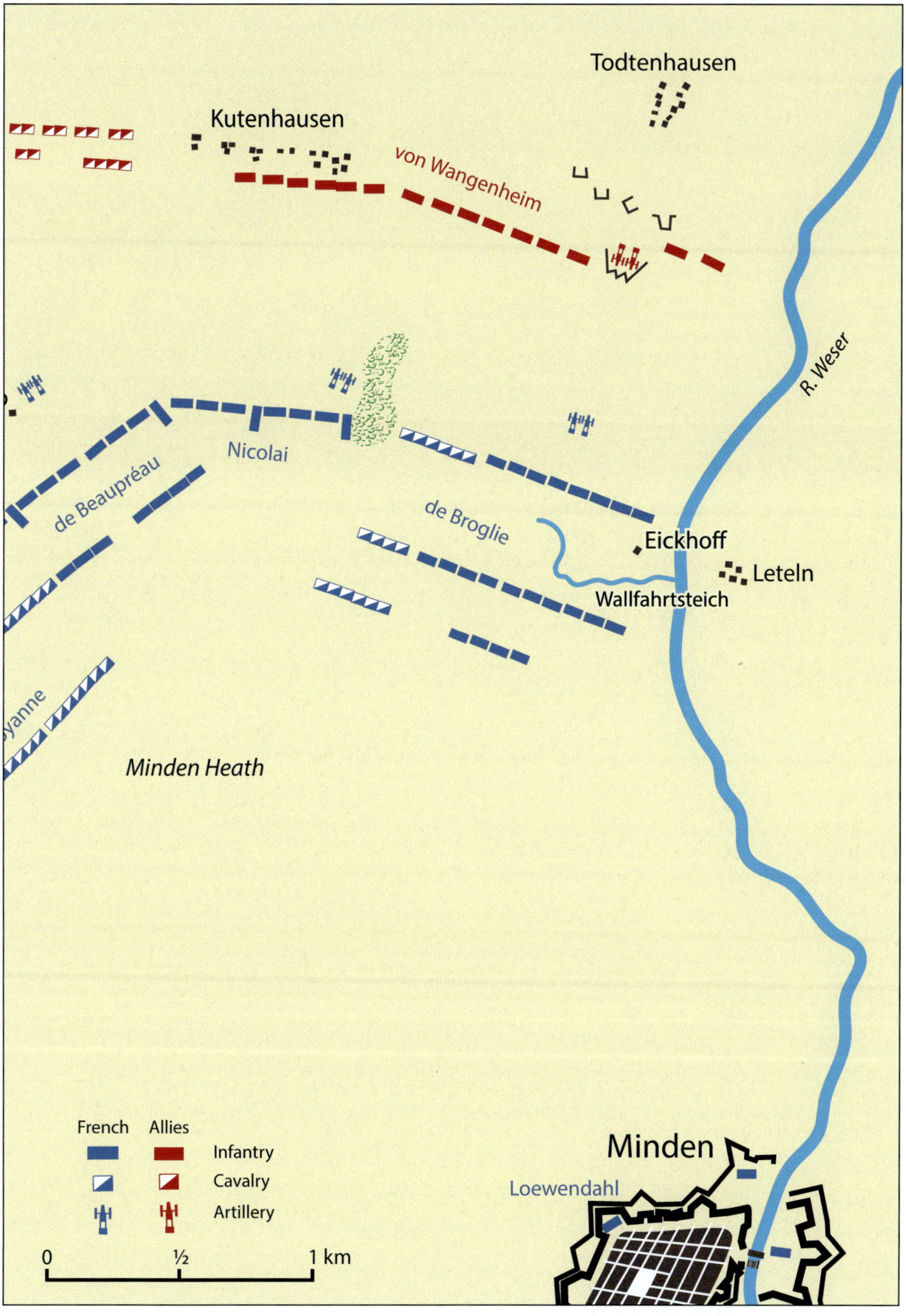

Hahlen. There is an attempt to distract the allies by an engagement across the Hille/Eickhorst causeway. Spörcken's column (including the British infantry) has got ahead of the rest of the allied line. (George Anderson © Helion and Company 2021)

Napier's 12th Foot, on the right flank of the leading brigade in Spörcken's column, continues its advance in the face of the French cavalry charges. By the battle's end, the regiment had suffered 56 percent casualties (5 officers and 93 soldiers killed, and 14 officers and 190 soldiers wounded). Despite the casualty rate, the 12th continued to fight resolutely. It is under attack by troopers of the Régiment du Roi, part of the

French second line of cavalry, while white-coated casualties of earlier French charges litter the ground of Minden Heath. (Patrice Courcelle © Helion and Company 2021)

British infantryman of Brudenell's 51st Foot. The 51st was a new regiment, raised only in 1756 and initially numbered as the 53rd. Sent to do garrison duty at Emden in the spring of 1758, it was the first British regiment to serve in Germany during the Seven Years War and at Minden fought in the centre of Kingsley's Brigade in the second line of Spörcken's column. (Patrice Courcelle © Helion and Company 2021)

Officer of the Hanoverian cavalry regiment of Hammerstein. Two squadrons strong, this regiment of heavy horse had served continually through the campaigns of 1757 and 1758, including the battles of Hastenbeck, Krefeld, and Bergen, before fighting at Minden in the first line of the Duke of Holstein's column on the left wing of the allied main body. (Patrice Courcelle © Helion and Company 2021)

French cavalryman of the Régiment Mestre-de-Camp Général. The post of Mestre-de-Camp Général was, by the time of the Seven Years War, a sinecure that could be purchased, and the post-holder was, ex-officio, colonel of the eponymous regiment. At the time of the Battle of Minden, the post-holder was *Lieutenant-Général* the Marquis de Castries. The iron-grey coat was a rare colour amongst French cavalry regiments, where white or blue coats predominated. Having previously fought at Hastenbeck and Krefeld, the two squadrons of the Régiment Mestre-de-Camp Général charged in the first line at Minden, where their casualties were so heavy that the regiment spent the remainder of the war in garrison and coastguard duty. (Patrice Courcelle © Helion and Company 2021)

French infantryman of the Régiment Champagne. With a history going back to the sixteenth century, the Régiment Champagne was one of the six 'vieux corps', the most senior regiments of the French line. Four battalions strong, the regiment had previously fought at Hastenbeck and Krefeld, and at Minden was posted on the far left of the French first line. Compared with those of other nations at the time, the uniform of French infantry regiments had a rather old-fashioned cut. (Patrice Courcelle © Helion and Company 2021)

Saxon infantryman of the Regiment Prinz Anton. After the Saxon army was taken prisoner en masse at Pirna in 1756, so many men escaped Prussian captivity that it was possible to re-form several regiments, and to re-equip them from Austrian stores. The Regiment Prinz Anton (previously Minckwitz) was one such unit, and had seen action at Lutterberg and Bergen prior to fighting at Minden in the second line of the French left wing. (Patrice Courcelle © Helion and Company 2021)

Yet again the sergeants would have pushed their men back into order around their colours. After another reload, there may have been the need to redistribute ammunition in order to be ready to face whatever the enemy would throw at them. The threat was resumed from this flank, this time by the battalions of Guerchy's division, and two brigades of Saxons in the French service.[41] Kingsley's horse was fatally wounded in four places and collapsed, trapping him while he was marched over twice by Saxon infantry.[42]

This time it was Spörcken who saw the threat and responded by half-turning to the right Kingsley's Brigade. So, these three battalions confronted a greatly superior enemy. Another infantry musketry battle followed and, despite the uneven numbers ranged against each other, the British infantry prevailed. Kingsley's Brigade eventually broke the enemy line through superior fire power and drove it off.

Lieutenant Thompson of the 20th Foot had already been hit by three musket balls, possibly at about the limit of their range, but was then more seriously hurt by another which burned 'like a red hot iron'.[43] Now at the limit of endurance and, having called for another officer to stand in for him, but none being available, he was permitted to fall out. The heath was strewn by the depressing debris of battle, the disfigured bodies of men and horses, discarded equipment, and the distressing cries and whimpering of the wounded. In places, wounded men had dragged themselves into the lee of dead horses to shelter from the fire. Thompson withdrew back across the heath but, even here, there was to be no respite as 'the balls came as thick as in front'. He met another soldier of his own regiment, limping back from a leg wound. Together they supported one another until the poor soldier's leg was taken off by a cannon ball, 'the wind from which fairly turned me around', Thompson wrote. His companion died shortly afterwards, so Thompson carried on, meeting another wounded officer, and the two supported one another until they encountered Lord Sackville's coach, with his personal surgeon in attendance. The surgeon was able to treat them and we owe it to him that Thompson was able to provide such graphic first-hand accounts.

Spörcken's was now severely bloodied and extremely vulnerable, having sacrificed its own depth, the second line having become committed forward. It was at this point that the enemy's cavalry reserve, 18 squadrons of the Gendarmerie de France and Carabiniers, under *Lieutenant-Général* de Poyanne, was ordered to inflict a third great cavalry charge.

Prince Ferdinand saw just how vulnerable his own force was at this potential tipping point. He had ridden the extent of his line, maintaining control, advising commanders and encouraging the men. One account reads, 'He animated the troops by his example, exposing his person like a young officer and, at the same time, putting in practice all the arts of a consummate general'.[44] Stationed as he was between Spörcken's and Scheele's formations,

41 Hotham-Thompson, *Operations of the Allied Army under the Duke of Brunswick 1757-1762*, p.81.

42 Mackesy, *The Coward of Minden*, p.124.

43 Cole, *Minden, 1759*, p.40.

44 Cole, *Minden, 1759*, p.39.

he promptly ordered the latter to bring forward five battalions of infantry (the sixth, Hardenberg, was already committed) to support Spörcken. He also directed the Hanoverian heavy artillery forward 'in order to assist the six English regiments who', he said, 'had behaved "like a brazen wall" but was doubtful would not be able to stand the next shock of the enemy', and it came into action quickly in between the two British Brigades of Light Artillery.[45] The Hanoverian artillery brigade included 30 heavy guns and howitzers, of British manufacture, under *Major* Hase.

A British artillery officer wrote 'we drew up our guns close to the six regiments and there waited undiscovered until the enemy came within pistol shot'. Things now became more chaotic. The 2,000 men of the elite of the French cavalry, the Gendarmes and Carabiniers, moved up to deliver the coup de grâce. Due to the shifted position of Spörcken's division, and the obstacles and detritus left by the previous two shattered charges, de Poyanne's own charge could not be frontal. Instead, it was aimed at breaking through thin crust of the Hardenberg Regiment and then enveloping Spörcken's division from its left flank. The same officer continued:

> When they were just going to gallop down, sword in hand, amongst the poor mangled regiments, we clapped our matches to our ten guns and gave them such a salute as they little expected, as they have since told us. Our balls had the desired effect for we mowed them down like standing corn. We fired quick, firing upon them for about twenty minutes during which time both armies stood in a kind of stagnation and never so much as fired one small arm…the French fell so very fast that the rest were so confused that they really confess that they did not know which way to fly for safety, but we paid no regard to their distress but as we had begun a good work we were determined to make an end of it and continued firing as long as we thought we could kill one man. This put the whole French army in confusion…[46]

After the battle, Contades wrote, 'As to the cannon, those of our enemy fired quicker, and did more execution than ours'.[47]

Despite the artillery fire, the might of de Poyanne's charge struck home to Spörcken's left: on the 23rd Foot, the Hanoverian Guards and regiment of Hardenberg. In places the line was punctured. The surviving enemy cavalry wheeled to deliver a second blow from the rear but found themselves trapped between the rear rank of Kingsley's Brigade, which had turned about to engage, and the now rapidly advancing battalions of *Generalleutenant* von Wutginau's Sixth Column. The two right flank battalions of Wutginau's Hanoverians and Hessians poured highly effective fire onto the cavalry at short range. 'The infantry gave such terrible fire that not even lions could have come on; such a number of them fell, both horses and men, that it made it difficult for those not touched to retire', wrote Lieutenant Thompson of the

---

45 Sir C. Firth (ed.), 'The Battle of Minden – 1 August 1759', *Journal of the Society for Army Historical Research*, Vol 7, No.28 (April 1928), pp.126-128. Letter by an artillery officer writing after the battle, from Franchenberg camp on 23 August.

46 Firth (ed.), 'The Battle of Minden – 1 August 1759', pp.126-128.

47 Blackmore, *Destructive and Formidable*, p.140.

20th Foot. The final French cavalry charge having been destroyed, 'Now was the time the English cavalry should have come up; every eye was looking with impatience.'[48]

Often in battle there are periods of lull. This was one such moment. The allied foot had withstood two cavalry charges, then the combined pressure of de Guerchy's infantry attack with the support of 32 guns, and finally the shock action of de Poyanne's charge. The line had wavered but had held – just.

After three unsuccessful cavalry charges, and much of its number lying dead and wounded around Spörcken's division, the French horse was in no position to rally to continue offensive action. After the battle, Contades wrote:

> I cannot help mentioning, what if I had not seen it, I should have thought incredible, that a single column of infantry penetrated and broke through three lines of cavalry. This column consisted principally of the English regiments, whose intrepid behaviour in this battle, it would be prudent to conceal from the troops designed to invade Great Britain from France, lest they should be intimidated by it.[49]

This was a new phenomenon, for the cavalry to have been beaten by infantry in line.

The moral effect of having been repelled now left the French vulnerable to rout. This would be the moment for the allied cavalry, particularly the fresh Anglo-Hanoverian horse, to exploit this opportunity to utterly destroy the enemy which could now be trapped against the Bastau. In the counter-attack, timing is everything. However, at this stage, unlike the infantry of Wutginau and Imhoff, and the brigade of Hanoverian artillery, the British cavalry was not to be seen.

The German Completion of the Destruction of the French Centre

Imhoff's column was exerting pressure on the French attempting to make a stand near Maulbeerkamp, and this action was supported by *Oberst* Braun's artillery which was also bringing its fire to bear on the enemy.

Contades' centre was now beyond repair. However, he still had eight battalions of infantry of *Lieutenant-Général* Beaupréau's corps in his first line, to the south of Maulbeerkamp.[50] Contades sent a rapid order for them to attack the left flank of the allied foot. They were to be supported by those survivors of the cavalry Brigade du Roi. This ad hoc formation pushed forward, re-treading the very ground which the earlier charges had covered. However, this took place at exactly the moment when Imhoff's column was also coming forward to join Wutginau's left flank and the momentum was in

48 Cole, *Minden,* 1759, p.40.

49 Blackmore, David, *Destructive and Formidable*, p.141.

50 Grossen Generalstabe, *Die Kriege Friedrichs des Grossen, Dritter Teil: Der Siebenjahrige Krieg. 1756-1763. Plan 27.*

favour of the allies. Four battalions of Imhoff's Hessians came forward at the double and put in a determined charge before Beaupréau's brigades could deploy fully, catching them on the hop and forcing them out of Maulbeerkamp at bayonet point. Worse was yet to come for Beaupréau's infantry, as the Duke of Holstein's Eighth Column of 19 squadrons of German cavalry had also now arrived from Stemmer, swirling round Maulbeerkamp and driving the French foot back onto its own supporting cavalry.[51] Despite the potential disruption to their own formation, the French horsemen of the Brigade du Roi managed to extricate themselves and, showing considerable determination even as much of their army was collapsing, put in their own spirited charge. They encountered, and were outnumbered by, the Hanoverian cavalry on the Duke of Holstein's left. Both bodies of horse converged and, on the French side, organisation broke down as command and control dissolved. The French charge had been defeated, but at a cost.

After the battle, Belle-Isle reflected on this phase in correspondence with de Castries:

> Can you provide me details of what happened to the cavalry in the unfortunate affair of the first of this month. I see that the cavalry charged courageously, but in detail and not in overwhelming strength; there would be too much to say in a letter, and I have no time. I cannot fathom how 60 squadrons in plain could not break and trample down 9 or 10 battalions, and yet in the same place, and a moment afterwards, a handful of enemy cavalry has cut down, broken and routed 4 of our infantry brigades, which comprised in number a third more combatants than the English battalions which repulsed our cavalry.[52]

Behind Beaupréau's first line, remained a further eight battalions of foot, the Anhalt and Auvergne brigades under *Lieutenant-Général* Claude Louis Comte de Saint-Germain and, as yet, uncommitted. Rather than continue the engagement with Imhoff's and Holstein's columns, they were to face a new threat, this time from Wangenheim.

When the British foot had emerged through the strip wood, shortly after 7:00 a.m., Contades had paused Broglie's advance, and this had resulted in something of a stand-off over to the east. For over three hours Broglie's and Wangenheim's respective corps had observed one another, Broglie's in the open and Wangenheim's in sturdy, prepared earthworks. Broglie was surprised by the ferocity of the fighting in the centre but, other than constant and heavy bombardment with artillery fire, desisted from any offensive action with his infantry.

Just as Saint-Germain's two brigades began to move forward towards the point where Beaupréau's division had been battered backwards by the Hessian infantry and Holstein's cavalry, the right wing of Wangenheim's corps started its own advance.

51 Cole, *Minden,* 1759, p.47.

52 Pajol, *Les Guerres sous Louis XV* , Vol.4, p.407, extract of a letter from Belle-Isle to Castries on the role of the French cavalry during this battle. Translated R. Couture.

The French centre was dissolving and, with that sense of alarm which sets in and communicates itself through the ranks of an army on the verge of defeat, the French army began to lose confidence and waver. Broglie had already been ordered to be prepared to cover any withdrawal. He was now formally directed to become the French rearguard and to withdraw himself too. While his corps had taken some casualties up until now, it was still in a relatively good state. His withdrawal was efficient and conducted in good order, facing about as needed to delay any pursuit.[53] As it was, leaving his earthworks, Wangenheim's advance was not pressed forward particularly aggressively, and some units only left their positions when ordered personally by Prince Ferdinand. Broglie was, therefore, allowed to retire southwards in relatively good order towards the town and fortress of Minden.

This withdrawal action was mirrored at the other end of the battlefield. *Lieutenant-Général* the Duc d'Havre's small diversionary force of four battalions and four guns was also retreating from the Eickhorst-Hille causeway. His attack had not progressed, largely due to Prince Ferdinand's prompt reinforcement of that flank on first hearing the initial bombardment. Ferdinand may have created the impression of a far more potent force than was actually present, so the French attack was not pushed home. Furthermore, d'Havre was tipped off that there was another body of allied troops, under *Generalmajor* Eitel von Gilsa, negotiating its way towards him along the lower slopes of the Wiehengebirge from Lübbecke.[54] Gilsa commanded three battalions of foot – Linstow (Hanoverian), Prince Karl (Hessian) and 1/Behr (Brunswick) and also some 300 British cavalry under Lieutenant Colonel Harvey of the Inniskilling Dragoons. News of this threat was the final straw for d'Havre. By 10:00 a.m., just as the French centre collapsed, his force began making its way back along to the south of the Bastau, back through Rothenuffeln, then Haddenhausen towards the French main pre-battle encampment between Dützen and the Weser.

Events Associated With Sackville's Cavalry

There had been several opportunities for Lord George Sackville's column of 24 squadrons of cavalry to intervene, to influence the course of the action and to exploit the outcome. Ferdinand's intention had been that Sackville would move in concert with the rest of his army, to the right of Spörcken's division. Several attack options would have been available for this large force of cavalry: either head-to-head or a flank attack on FitzJames's cavalry; an attack on the French guns and infantry around Hahlen; in concert with the German horse, to destroy Beaupréau's infantry brigades; to pursue and rout the remnants of the French centre. However, it was not to be, as there was no sign of Sackville's troopers.

It is worth examining the sequence of events in Sackville's 'no-show'. Sackville's column, in common with the entire allied army, had received

53 Hotham-Thompson, *Operations of the Allied Army under the Duke of Brunswick 1757-1762*, p.81.
54 Hotham-Thompson, *Operations of the Allied Army under the Duke of Brunswick 1757-1762*, p.82.

orders at 6:00 p.m. the previous evening to be at short notice to move, and prepared for action, by 1:00 a.m. This would have involved watering and feeding the mounts and men, and then resting. To be ready by 1:00 a.m., the order 'Boots and Saddles' would have been given at about midnight.

At about 4:45 a.m., one of Prince Ferdinand's aides-de-camp rode into the cavalry lines, where the men were prepared but still resting. He gave the order to the British brigade major, Major Stubbs, that the column was to move to the front along the routes pointed out by Prince Ferdinand in his orders the previous day. Major Stubbs passed this order on to all of the column's regimental commanders. By 5:30 a.m., the cavalry was formed up and mounted, ready to move, but only waiting for Lord George.

The column's second-in command, Lieutenant General John Manners, Marquis of Granby, had supervised the force's turning out and readiness to move. Aware of the orders, but also perhaps responding to the regimental commanders' impatience to be off, Granby rode quickly to Sackville's headquarters, a farm some three kilometres to the rear. He encountered Sackville who was on the point of mounting his charger but, on learning of what had happened, stated that he had not been informed of this development. He had complied with his instructions the previous evening on returning from inspecting his outposts. He had received the order to be prepared to move from 1:00 a.m., but that that would be normal procedure in proximity to the enemy.

Sackville mounted his charger and led his personal staff from his accommodation to the assembly area where his 24 squadrons awaited him: King's Dragoon Guards (Bland's Dragoons); the Inniskillings; The Royal Horse Guards (Blues); the Hanoverian Horse Grenadiers Breitenbach's Dragoons and Hanoverian Garde du Corps all were in the first line, under the command of Colonel John Mostyn and *Oberst* Max Breidenbach. The second line, commanded by Colonel Elliot and *Oberst* Bock, was made up of the 3rd Dragoon Guards (Howard's); 10th Dragoons (Mordaunt's); the 2nd Dragoons (Greys), and Bremer's and Veltheim's Hanoverian Horse. Colonel Preston, commanding the Greys, had been a kettle-drummer during Marlborough's campaigns and still wore a buff coat, the last time seen in action.[55]

Howard's	Mordaunt's	Greys	Bremer	Veltheim

Maj. Gen. Elliot — *Obst* Bock

Lt Gen the Marquis of Granby

Bland	Inniskillings	Blues	Gren zu Pferde	Breidenbach	Gd du Corps

Maj. Gen. Mostyn — *Obst* Breidenbach

Lt Gen Lord George Sackville

55 Cole, *Minden 1759*, p.24.

On arriving, Sackville immediately ordered the force to 'Walk, March!'. So the column set off at a somewhat desultory pace. En route, he was met, firstly by a guide, and then by one of Ferdinand's staff officers, a *Hauptman* von Malortie, who pointed out their planned dispositions.[56] Ahead of them was Minden Heath. At this stage, despite the apparent delay, Sackville's cavalry force arrived at this forming up point before von Spörcken's infantry had begun to deploy through the strip wood and also before the British heavy artillery had engaged. The cavalry then deployed into a first and second line and waited for further orders.

After 30 minutes, a *Hauptman* Wintzingerode, an infantry aide-de-camp on Prince Ferdinand's staff, rode up with orders that the cavalry was to advance. It was to move forward through the trees to its left, forming up behind Kingsley's Brigade in order to support the planned advance. For some reason, Sackville appears to have ignored this, or taken it merely to be a preparatory order, so the entire body of cavalry remained stationary. Another messenger arrived, this time Captain Edward Ligonier, the nephew of Field Marshal Ligonier, who had just ridden in haste from Prince Ferdinand's headquarters. He emphasised that it was vital that the order should be followed immediately by all of the cavalry.[57]

Sackville's response was to order the cavalry force to draw swords. To the recipients of this order, it was a clear statement of intent. Sackville's next move was to lead off the force to his right. At this, Ligonier pointed out that the aim of the order was to support the infantry and that the advance should, instead, be through the trees to the left. As this exchange was taking place, yet another horseman arrived from Prince Ferdinand, this time a Lieutenant Colonel Fitzroy who had been tasked by the Prince to instil some urgency. However, Fitzroy had stated that it was the British cavalry which was to move and Sackville's force was a mix of British and Hanoverian.

Sackville then revealed a pedantic streak. He insisted that the messengers clarify their orders and then he would obey. While both insisted that they had relayed the orders as stated, Fitzroy, who outranked Ligonier, emphasised that the French were in disarray and that there was a chance for the 'English' [sic] cavalry to earn distinction. Both staff officers had been alongside Ferdinand when they had witnessed the destruction wrought on the first French charge by Waldegrave's Brigade. The key point was that the infantry needed support, and urgently. Even if Sackville had only used the British part of his force, those 14 squadrons would have been invaluable in either bolstering the infantry or in exploiting any opportunity arising from the chaos of the broken French charge.

All this delay was of great concern to Ferdinand who, having already sent not one but two gallopers to bring up Sackville's horse, exclaimed to his staff in frustration, 'When is the cavalry coming?' and 'Good God! Is there no way of getting the cavalry to advance!'[58]

56 Reid, *The Battle of Minden 1759*, p.147.
57 Reid, *The Battle of Minden 1759*, p.150.
58 Cole, *Minden,* 1759, p.53.

With such a case put to him, Sackville realised that he needed to bring the cavalry forward, but insisted that he now needed a guide. Fitzroy said that he could do this. Just at this moment, the commanding officer of the 1st Dragoon Guards, Lieutenant Colonel Sloper, trotted over and interrupted Captain Ligonier with a heated outburst, 'For God's sake, Sir, repeat your orders to *that man* [Lord George Sackville] that he may not pretend not to understand them, for, it is half an hour ago that he received orders to advance, and he is still here!'[59]

Instead, Sackville, who had understood that Prince Ferdinand was out on the heath, through the belt of trees, and less than a kilometre away, decided to seek clarification from Ferdinand himself. Fitzroy led Sackville through the wood and then galloped promptly up to Prince Ferdinand to inform him that Sackville would report personally to him for direct orders. Meanwhile Sackville approached at a pace which was highly controlled. For Ferdinand, this was final. He instructed Fitzroy to return directly to the cavalry column, to seek out Sackville's second-in-command, Lord Granby, for him to advance with the second cavalry echelon, with the remark, 'At least he will obey me.'[60]

Fitzroy duly galloped back to the cavalry, passing Sackville en route. Finding Granby, he issued the order from Ferdinand. Granby opined that the order ought more properly be addressed to Sackville as his superior officer but Fitzroy insisted that the order was for him, Granby, and applied to the second line of cavalry. Granby quickly grasped the importance of the orders he had just received and rapidly set his second line in motion. However, his way was blocked by the first line, so he wheeled round the first and trotted forward to the wood, which he passed through. By now Sackville had seen the situation for himself and sent an officer back with instructions to bring the first line up. Trotting forward to Prince Ferdinand's view-point, without much apparent grace or embarrassment, Sackville demanded of the Prince what his orders meant.[61] Ferdinand's response, despite his inward agitation, showed considerable restraint and self-control, 'My Lord, the opportunity is now passed.'[62]

Turning back towards his column, Sackville saw Granby's line coming forward but ordered him to halt. He later claimed that this was to restore order and buy time so that he could deploy his first line alongside the second. However, he was directly countermanding Ferdinand's instructions to Granby of which he was, admittedly, unaware. At that stage of the battle, the cavalry could still have been of immense value, if only it had been made available forwards. After an unnecessary delay, Sackville's entire force of 24 squadrons formed up in a long line at about the start point of Spörcken's advance. However, the infantry had long gone and their backs could be seen in the distance. Rather than turn a victory into a decisive rout, Sackville's regiments had been kept pristine, to the immense frustration of their commanders.

59 Cole, *Minden,* 1759, p.53.
60 Mackesy, *The Coward of Minden*, p.135.
61 Reid, *The Battle of Minden 1759*, p.152.
62 Knowles, *Minden and the Seven Years' War*, p.30.

By 10:00 a.m. the Battle of Minden was effectively over. After the battle, when picking over the whys and wherefores, Ferdinand learned to his fury that his orders to the cavalry had indeed been delivered but that Sackville had, for whatever reason, dithered. The historian Savory delivered a damning verdict: 'Seldom, if ever, has there been in battle such disgraceful disobedience'.[63]

On the French side, Contades ordered a general withdrawal, but it was already being enacted without formal direction. The surviving French Horse of FitzJames' and de Poyanne's cavalry formations were already on their way rearward. Only Broglie's corps was relatively steadfast, covering the retreat of the others, withdrawing in good order and frequently turning about to face and present a front to the allies. Guerchy's and Lusace's foot were all fleeing back towards their crossing points over the Bastau. Likewise, Beaupréau's and Nicolai's infantry, which were heading directly back towards the fortress of Minden. The efforts of officers and sous-officiers would have been in vain as panic took hold and the retreat gathered a momentum all of its own. The scene would have been shambolic with loose horses, individual stragglers, and the field strewn with the depressing debris of a battle lost. 43 guns were abandoned by the French artillerymen and were captured by the victorious allies.

The allied gunners continued to lay down a steady fire on the retreating French, keeping pressure on what was now a fleeing mass. In particular, the British gunners near Hahlen fired mercilessly on their foes, ploughing cannon balls to great effect on any dense concentrations of the enemy. The gunners maintained their forward momentum, continuing to jockey forwards to engage the French rearguard. At the Bastau bridging points, while some French units crossed in good order the press from the rear forced others into wading, not always safely. The scene was 'all strewed with those who lay expiring from their wounds – a dismal sight'.[64]

By about 11:00 a.m., the bulk of Contades' army was back across the Bastau and moving up on the slopes of the Wiehengebirge. One artilleryman wrote that he, 'saw them make their escape up the hills like a flock of sheep and standing sometime amazed at not seeing our cavalry pursue them'.[65] Yet that was not to be. Neither the allied guns nor horsemen could reasonably manoeuvre on the swampy banks and surrounds of the Bastau. So, the gunners had to satisfy themselves with getting as close as they could to the marsh to fire their final rounds at the backs of the enemy before retiring back to re-join the rest of the allied army on the heath.

Having escaped across the Bastau to relative safety, the survivors of Contades' force made their way back to muster and call the regimental rolls in the area of Dützen. Contades summoned his senior officers to discuss their next moves. It might have initially seemed to the allies that, despite just having been defeated, the French were now back in their original strong positions. For Contades, however, not only had he been defeated, but now

63 Savory, *His Britannic Majesty's Army in Germany*, p.171.
64 Cole, *Minden,* 1759, p.56.
65 Cole, *Minden,* 1759, p.56.

the first stragglers were appearing, bringing news from the south, where the Erbprinz had soundly beaten and dispersed Brissac's force at Gohfeld. As a result of the engagement at Gohfeld, Contades was prevented from retreating in that direction and re-forming.

The precise whereabouts of the Erbprinz were unknown, but Contades had been planning to retreat through the Minden Gap towards Porta Westfalica and push his way down his own line of communications in the direction of Herford. As it was, this might have worked as the Erbprinz, at that stage unaware of the result of Minden, had moved his force off the French line of communications in a westerly direction up onto the Wiehengebirge ridge at Bergkirchen.[66] Instead, Broglie interrupted the deliberations, pointing out that if the Erbprinz was blocking the route across the Werre this option would be too risky. Instead, he pointed out that the French still possessed the main bridge, two pontoons and a ford over the Weser at Minden and that, if they were to use them to cross to the opposite bank, they could escape to the far side, out of reach of the allies. Supported by a majority in Contades' command group, this option was selected.

Broglie's corps, having retired in relatively good order, made its way back through the fortress of Minden, which still had a French garrison, on to the opposite side of the River Weser, crossing by the main town bridge and also by the two pontoons to the south.

The allied army paused for a period on the heath. Even successful forces often experience a post-battle lull as the enormity of their experience, and of their survival, begins to dawn on them. Then the imperative to reorganise takes over and the necessity to care for the wounded becomes obvious. Ferdinand issued orders that the entire army was to re-form and to march in column of route, a further two-and-a-half kilometres towards the fortress. The allies thus advanced and halted just short of the range of the guns on Minden's fortifications. To all intents and purposes the fort still presented an imposing and menacing view, protected as it was by a moat, glacis, ramparts and guns. No attempt was made to attack the fort directly. Instead, Ferdinand sent an officer and trumpeter to demand its surrender.[67] This was declined until the following day.

In its new positions, the allied army resumed the necessary tasks and administration after a battle. Most pressingly, the wounded were searched for and gathered for treatment.[68] They were carried by the drummers to have their shattered arms and legs amputated and their wounds dressed.[69] There were plenty of farms and villages in which the regimental surgeons could set up. Where possible, they would join together to support one another in their operations. With more than 1,000 casualties, the regimental surgeons and their mates would have worked flat out and the surgery would have

66 Savory, *His Britannic Majesty's Army in Germany*, p.172.

67 TNA, SP87/29, Durand to Holdernesse.

68 'Orders from July 19, 1759 to January 23, 1760, 'Neux' (pseud.), 'The Battle of Minden 1759', p.48.

69 Cantlie, *A History of the Army Medical Department*, p.124; as in modern combat, no doubt anyone available would lend a hand.

been of the most basic sort. The main field hospital had been established at Petershagen, but others were set up in Hille and, later, in Minden itself and there the most severely wounded would have been treated by more skilled surgeons. Each regiment was ordered to make a careful search of all the local farms, not just for allied wounded, but for the French as well. Infirmary wagons were used throughout the day, making the bone-jarring journey all the way to Petershagen.

A general hospital had been established by the allies in Bremen, and a more comfortable journey by barge carried those who needed onward evacuation there. For all the barbarity of field surgery, by the standards of the day much thought went into the management of the general hospital. Straw palliasses were preferred to domestic mattresses, which were awkward to clean, bed-linen being issued twice a week. Vinegar was used to wash the walls and floors, before fumigation with the smoke from damp gunpowder. On arrival, each patient was washed and provided with a clean shirt. Hands and faces were obliged to be washed every day, although feet were bathed only occasionally. Shaving was performed twice per week. In Bremen, dysentery cases were held in separate wards with separate latrines opening into the River Weser, an arrangement praised as admirable.[70]

On the battlefield, wounded horses were despatched if their injuries were more than slight. Equipment, weapons, ammunition and horse furniture were collected and sorted through for items still serviceable. The dead were collected, as many as 2,000 local peasants and townspeople being obliged to assist.[71] Burial was in large communal graves. In particular, the spot at Wallfahrtsteich, near Kutenhausen, where the Grenadiers de France and Grenadiers Royaux had been repulsed by Wangenheim's corps, was thick with dead and wounded. The bodies of slain horses were gathered into clumps and large bonfires built to cremate the bodies.

At some stage during the afternoon of 1 August, Ferdinand's headquarters issued orders for a service of thanksgiving to be held at 9:00 a.m. on the 2nd to 'return thanks to Almighty God for the victory of the day'. The orders for the evening's firing of the feu de joie, also on the 2nd, read:

> The brigades of heavy artillery are to take their respective posts on the wings, and, in front the three brigades of light artillery are to join those of the heavy brigade, and the regimental guns are to remain in the line. When the firing order is given it will be continued to three rounds, beginning upon the right, first the artillery and then the army. The order of firing to be as follows: 1st, the Regiment of Gotha's volley; 2nd, Captain Phillips' Brigade; 3rd, Major Hase's; 4th, Captain Drummond's Brigade; 5th, the Heavy and Light Artillery of the Centre Brigade; 6th, Captain Foy's Brigade; 7th, Lieutenant Colonel Huth's Brigade; 8th, Bückeburg's Brigade and Grenadiers. A volley then from the first line from right to left, followed by the second, from left to right; the cannon taken from the

70 Cantlie, *A History of the Army Medical Department*, p.126.

71 *The London Magazine, or, Gentleman's Monthly Intelligencer*, Vol XXIX, 1759, p.377.

> enemy to be placed in front with the centre Brigade of Heavy Artillery, and to fire with it.[72]

Meanwhile, wagons brought forward regimental tentage from the previous camp site so that new tent lines could be built in the new positions on the battlefield. Concurrent with the efforts by work parties to clear the field, cooks and sutlers prepared food for an evening meal. With the most urgent tasks completed, the allied army was able to settle down for its nightly routine in the field.

72 Cole, *Minden,* 1759, p.63.

11

The Butcher's Bill

The reality of combat is that, despite a commander's best intentions, the only certainty is that there will be casualties, as Contades found to his cost. Even the winning side will tend to have incurred casualties, as Ferdinand found to his.

A few days after the battle, one British officer wrote to his mother, 'I don't care who knows my sentiments when I say that my curiosity is satisfied and that I never wish to see a second slaughter of my fellow creatures'.[1]

For the French, their losses were heavy but hard to quantify exactly. The figures vary between 7,000 and 12,000.[2] It is possible that 7,086 were killed and wounded on the field, while a further 1,533 may have been found when the allies entered the town of Minden[3]. Many were lost by drowning during the retreat back across the Bastau and the morass, and even possibly in the Weser, but the numbers are impossible to confirm. Records of the 25th Foot show an estimate that some 4,000 were drowned, but that figure seems implausibly high.[4] However, the correspondence between Contades and Broglie after the battle suggests total French losses of between 10,000 and 11,000.

What is certain is that the French lost six generals and 438 other officers killed and wounded. Prince Camille was killed, while the Comte de Lutzelburg and the Marquis de Monti were both captured.[5] The French cavalry lost 28 percent of its strength. Poyanne's Gendarmes suffered particularly heavily with 358 killed and wounded from an effective strength of 778.[6]

Of the French infantry, the Régiment de Touraine suffered most heavily, losing 909 killed, wounded and prisoners from an effective strength of 1,230. In all, the French infantry and artillery lost about 5,000. The Saxons also

1 NAM 6807-142-13. Letter of an Officer Regarding the Battle of Minden.

2 Richard Waddington, *La Guerre de Sept Ans. Histoire Diplomatique et Militaire* (Paris: Firmin-Didot et Cie, 1867), Vol.III, p.70.

3 Hotham-Thompson, *Operations of the Allied Army*, p.88.

4 Cole, *Minden 1759*, p.58.

5 Hotham-Thompson, *Operations of the Allied Army*, p.82.

6 J-L.Vial, '1759 etat des officiers tués bataille de Minden'. E-mail (8 February 2019).

suffered heavily, their commander, the Comte de Lusace being wounded, with a loss of 33 percent of their strength.[7]

The allies captured 43 cannon, 10 pairs of colours and seven standards.

For the allies, the price of victory was almost 2,800 casualties, killed and wounded.[8] The British furnished almost half of that figure (variously 1,391 to 1,400).[9] Horace Walpole wrote, 'Two of our regiments are said to have suffered much, of which Napier's [12th Foot] most'.[10] Forty-two percent of the British infantry, less the converged grenadier battalion, became casualties: 16 officers and 330 other ranks were killed; while 63 officers and 961 other ranks were wounded; of 160 officers and 3,100 other ranks who went into battle on that morning.[11]

Despite Walpole's guess, it was actually the 20th Foot which experienced the highest casualty figures, with six officers and 80 other ranks killed and 11 officers and 224 other ranks wounded, just over half its strength (51 percent)[12]. The 20th had been on the right flank of Kingsley's Brigade, and had been closest to Hahlen. The other right-flank battalion, of Waldegrave's Brigade, was the 12th Foot, which also suffered heavily, with five officers and 93 other ranks killed or missing, and 14 officers and 190 other ranks wounded (actually a higher rate at 56 percent).[13]

In the Order of the Day, following the battle, the 20th Foot was actually taken out of the line, that because of its severe losses, it should cease to do duty, a measure to which the regiment refused to submit, resuming, at its own request, its place in the line.

The 23rd Foot sustained 35 killed and missing, and 172 wounded, while the 25th Foot lost 29 killed or missing and 126 wounded. The 37th Foot experienced 73 killed and 200 wounded, 54 percent of its strength. The 51st Foot 15 killed or missing, and 87 wounded.[14] The Hanoverian battalions in Spörcken's division lost 50 of all ranks between them.

Wangenheim's corps, which had been intended as the focus for the French main effort, lost approximately 500 casualties. Of the British converged grenadier battalion, Montgomery describes only one captain and one sergeant being killed.[15]

It is worth pondering the enormity of the equine casualties, the majority of which would have had to be destroyed.

---

7 'Battle of Minden', *Seven Years' War* <http://www.kronoskaf.com/syw/index.php?title=1759-08-01-Battle_of_Minden> (accessed 15 January–31 October 2019).

8 Westphalen, *Geschichte der Feldzüge des Herzogs Ferdinand*, pp.535-540, states 2,762. Hotham-Thompson, *Operations of the Allied Army*, p.82.

9 Westphalen, *Geschichte der Feldzüge des Herzogs Ferdinand*, pp.535-540, states 1,392.

10 Walpole, *Letters*, Letter 328 To George Montagu, Esq. Strawberry Hill, Aug. 9, 1759. <https://www.gutenberg.org/cache/epub/4610/pg4610.html> (accessed 24 February 2019).

11 Hotham-Thompson, *Operations of the Allied Army*, p.87 (Missing included by the author under killed).

12 Hotham-Thompson, *Operations of the Allied Army*, p.86.

13 Hotham-Thompson, *Operations of the Allied Army*, p.86.

14 Hotham-Thompson, *Operations of the Allied Army*, p.86.

15 Montgomery, *Letter to his Mother*, NAM 1975-10-92.

12

The Aftermath of Battle

Within the British contingent, there was puzzlement that the Anglo-Hanoverian cavalry under Sackville had not contributed to the victory, especially among the more senior cavalry officers. Feelings ran high, although Major General Kingsley, whose foot soldiers had endured so much, was initially more critical of Ferdinand than of Sackville. Lieutenant Colonel Sloper of the 1st Dragoon Guards was especially critical of Sackville, describing how Sackville had received his orders and that he had seemed confused. Captain Ligonier was briefly accused of having added to the confusion by bringing the wrong orders at a crucial moment. Tempers flared and had to be calmed by Captain Smith who reminded the gathered officers that no harm had been done.

Ferdinand experienced mixed feelings. Yes, he had just won a significant battle, but he felt badly let down by some of the commanders under him. His plan had been sound, and had been carefully communicated. Indeed, it had largely worked, but had come very close to becoming unhinged through the shortcomings of some of his subordinates. He was later critical of Sackville, but also of Anhalt, of Wangenheim and of Schaumburg-Lippe.

During the battle, Ferdinand had initially kept his irritation with Sackville under control, but as the opportunity to deal a catastrophic blow against the French had almost passed, he asked Fitzroy to carry an order to the Marquis of Granby, 'as I know he will obey me'. However, it would appear that Ferdinand had not been fully or accurately advised on the situation in the British cavalry. For example, he convinced himself that they had failed to saddle up early and that they had failed to complete their initial dispositions on time. Indeed, when Sackville joined the other allied senior officers at dinner on the evening of the 1st, Ferdinand is reported to have cried out, 'There is that man as much at his ease as if he had done marvels'.[1]

On the French side, Broglie's force reached the original camp site it had occupied up until the eve of battle by about midnight on the 1st. As it had passed through Minden, it gathered up the bulk of the garrison, some 2,500 foot, but left a skeleton force of 300 light infantry and, of course, the fortress

1 Mackesy, *The Coward of Minden*, p.145.

guns. Once Broglie's corps had crossed the River Weser, the pontoon bridges to the south of the town were destroyed by fire at about 3:00 a.m. on the morning of the 2nd. There was no rapid pursuit.

The French had previously established a hospital in the town which was now overflowing with some 1,533 wounded who would have had to be sheltered in whatever accommodation could be found.

For the allies, preparations would have commenced early on the 2nd in order to be ready for the parade and field service of thanksgiving for victory. Given its large scale, the service must have been notable, but it was reported that the cavalry of the right wing kept silent during the Te Deum. After the service, orders were issued for the celebration of victory, 'The Army is to be under arms at 6 o'clock this evening to fire a feu-de-joie'.[2] The service provided a brief respite from the normal duties and the additional work begun the previous afternoon of continuing to clear the battlefield. Within the lines of the British 12th Foot, the battalion's survivors had their spirits raised by the successful birth of a son to the sutler's wife. Lieutenant Montgomery reported that the battalion cheered the news and that the baby was immediately 'christened' Ferdinand.[3]

The allies, still out of cannon shot of the walls of Minden, maintained keen watch on the ramparts. The garrison commander, *Lieutenant-Colonel* Auguste Dagieu, also the commander of the Régiment d'Aquitaine, had successfully protected the withdrawal of Broglie's corps across the Weser, but was now faced by the challenge of treating and nursing a substantial number of wounded soldiers who outnumbered his much-shrunken garrison by five to one. He sent a trumpeter as envoy to Prince Ferdinand, offering to surrender the town and 'desiring that he would have the goodness to take care of the wounded he was obliged to leave behind at Minden', and also to save what private papers might be found in the baggage 'belonging to the principal officers' that had been taken.[4]

With respect to the captured baggage, Montgomery wrote of his friend, Captain Rainey, who was well: 'He is at present in advance of the Grenadiers plundering French baggage and taking prisoners. I would venture to give him forty ducats for his share of the prize money'.[5]

Ferdinand accepted Dagieu's offer of surrender and, by midday, marched a proportion of his force in to occupy the town. In doing so, in combination with those captured the previous day, he now had 10 enemy colours, seven regimental standards and 43 guns. Shortly after, he brought his own Headquarters from Hille into Minden, but not before issuing a special 'Order of the Day' which stated:

> [T]he greatest thanks be given to the whole army for their bravery and good behaviour yesterday, particularly to the British infantry, the two battalions

2 Hotham-Thompson, *Operations of the Allied Army under the Duke of Brunswick 1757-1762*, p.87.
3 Cole, *Minden, 1759*, p.60.
4 Cole, *Minden, 1759*, p.60.
5 NAM 1975-10-92, Montgomery to his Mother.

> of Hanoverian Guards and to all the cavalry on the Left wing; to General von Wangenheim's Corps, particularly the regiments of Holstein, the Hessian cavalry, the Hanoverian regiments and Hammerstein's and the same to all the Brigade of heavy artillery.
>
> His Serene Highness declares publicly that, next to God, he attributes the Glory of the day to the intrepidity and extraordinary good behaviour of these troops, which, he assures them, he will retain the strongest sense of, as long as he lives, and, if ever upon any occasion he may be able to serve these brave troops, or any of them in particular, it will give him the utmost pleasure…[6]

The Prince publicly thanked the Duke of Holstein, Spörcken, Imhoff and Urff. He stated that he was 'infinitely obliged to Major Generals Waldegrave and Kingsley for the great courage and good order in which they conducted their Brigades'. He was 'extremely obliged to the Graf von Bückeburg for all his care and trouble in the management of the artillery which was served with great effect'. Similarly, 'the commanding officers of the Brigades of Artillery, Colonel Braun, Lieutenant Colonel Huth, Major Hase and the three English Captains Phillips, Drummond and Foy' for the work of the British Artillery. It was unfortunate that he accidentally missed Captain MacBean, so he later tried to make amends by writing to him personally,[7] and he also sent gifts of a thousand crowns to Captain Phillips and five hundred each to Captains Drummond, Foy and MacBean to reward their efforts. The following members of his staff were also mentioned: The Duke of Richmond, Colonel Fitzroy, Colonel Watson, Captain Ligonier, Captain Wilson (aide de camp to Major General Waldegrave), Graf von Taube, *Hauptman* Malortie and Adjutants General Bülow, Derenthal and Estorff.

Of the British cavalry, he ordered that it should 'be declared to the Marquis of Granby that he was persuaded that if he had had the good fortune to have had him at the head of the cavalry on the right wing, his presence would have greatly contributed to make the decision of the day more complete and more brilliant'. He emphasised that he required and ordered the generals of the army that 'upon all occasions when orders are brought to them by his Aides-de-Camp, they be obeyed punctually and without delay'.[8]

The glaring omissions from Ferdinand's Special Order are Anhalt, Schaumburg-Lippe and Sackville, but especially the latter. That omission, coupled with the emphasis on immediate obedience by generals, made it sufficiently obvious to the army just what Ferdinand thought of Sackville's conduct. So rather than make a formal complaint to the British government at a time when the British would be celebrating a victory, Ferdinand made Sackville's position as head of the British contingent untenable. Mauvillon thought that Ferdinand's handling of Sackville was '*bewunderswürdig*' [worthy of wonder]![9]

6 *The London Magazine, or, Gentleman's Monthly Intelligencer*, Vol XXIX, 1759, p.388.
7 Knowles, *Minden and the Seven Years' War*, p.34.
8 *The London Magazine, or, Gentleman's Monthly Intelligencer.* Vol XXIX, 1759, p.388.
9 Mackesy, *The Coward of Minden*, p.146, quoting J. von Mauvillon, *Geschichte Ferdinands Herzog von Braunschweig-Lüneberg* (Leipzig: Dyk, 1794).

For Sackville, the Order came as a complete shock. Only that morning, he had written to John Stuart, 3rd Earl of Bute – the Prince of Wales's mentor who, subsequently became Prime Minister, and who negotiated the Treaty of Paris – appraising him of the victory and his happiness. Now he had to write again, stating that he was most miserable. Sackville wondered whether this was the result of personal hostility stemming from his own suggestion that the British contingent could be recalled on Ferdinand's abandonment of Westphalia. Whatever the case, he had been judged and damned with no opportunity to defend himself. Had the issue not been made public through its copying into the order book of every regiment in the allied army, another man might have lain low to let it blow over. However, soon it would be published and common knowledge in Britain.

Sackville tried to build his case, restating the facts as he saw them. He hoped that Ferdinand would cancel his order. Hotham was despatched to argue Sackville's case. Sackville next called for Granby, asking him to counter-sign Sackville's own version of events. Granby refused. Not only had he not been alongside Sackville when Ferdinand's orders were delivered, but Granby also had a very different recollection of how events had occurred, and he could not in all conscience sign Sackville's version. Furthermore, Granby refused Sackville's request to write separately to Ferdinand: he was not a particularly enthusiastic correspondent; he felt that his own written French was not up to the task; and, anyway, he thought that the British cavalry's advance on the heath had been too slow. Whilst not prepared to write, Granby was prepared to describe events in person to Ferdinand. In frustration, Sackville then attempted to pen an account for Granby's signature but, after another disagreement, Granby put an end to the attempt.

With no written support likely to be forthcoming from Granby, Sackville began his own version, 'The order it pleased your Serene Highness to issue today struck me like a thunderbolt. I feel it so much and see myself so deeply concerned by it that for my own peace I must take the liberty of relating the matter simply as it happened'.[10] He described the contradictory orders which had been the reason for his halts and for his personal visit to Ferdinand during the cavalry's detour through the wooded area.[11] He also stated that Granby was prepared to give Ferdinand his own testament in person. He finished by requesting that Ferdinand withdraw or recall his order. However, Sackville was not confident that Ferdinand would do any such thing, and certainly not admit to any personal failings of his own. He confirmed this view to Bute, which was borne out by Ferdinand's peremptory response which arrived as Sackville was in the process of writing to Bute. Ferdinand was galled to have to go over the same ground again. Having given Sackville the opportunity of dealing the death blow to the French, if he had only duly followed the orders issued to him, Ferdinand could not calmly reflect on the conduct of the British cavalry on the right of the army. Ferdinand further requested that Sackville should not press him for more detail nor ask again for a retraction of the order which he was convinced was accurate. He finished with, 'I have

10 Mackesy, *The Coward of Minden*, p.148.

11 Reid, *The Battle of Minden 1759*, p.152.

grounds for being ill satisfied with the non-execution of my orders. To what I should attribute it I do not know, and I suspend my judgement on it'.[12]

In fact, it was rough justice to refuse to hear Sackville's side of the story. Further, Ferdinand's complaint that Sackville had limited his purview of the battle to the cavalry column when he should have balanced his appreciation of the situation across the whole British force, thereby gleaning a better picture of how and when to commit his horse, was unfair: Ferdinand's own operational order had committed Sackville to the allied cavalry column, the first column of eight. To mix Sackville's administrative responsibility with this tactical command, retrospectively, caused Sackville to claim that he 'never knew anything so unfair, so unjust and I must say so wicked'.[13] Despite this, a perception grew among the staff that Sackville had wrongly mal-located himself with the cavalry.

Ferdinand's praise of Granby, at Sackville's expense, could hardly be taken lying down by the latter. Ferdinand recorded, 'Sackville who was insensible to the fine opportunity he had to gain glory, was offended by the observation I had made in favour of Lord Granby. He saw in it only, according to his way of thinking, an indirect censure of his own conduct'.[14] Yet, this is exactly how it appears more than two centuries later.

Ferdinand received and rebuffed Sackville's request on 3 August. Ferdinand was in the process of sending his British aides-de-camp, Ligonier, Fitzroy and Richmond, back to London with accounts of the victory. If Sackville were to attempt damage limitation to protect his reputation, he would have to act quickly.

Fitzroy had personally witnessed Sackville's conduct during the battle. Sackville wrote to him, describing the sequence of events as he saw them, how his orders had been contradictory, how Ligonier and Fitzroy had ridden to him (although he reversed the sequence of their arrival), how he had attended on Ferdinand, and he described his advance onto the heath. He wrote, 'The orders of yesterday you may believe affected me very sensibly. His Serene Highness has been pleased to judge, condemn, and censure me, without hearing me, in the most cruel and unprecedented manner', and continued, 'It is impossible to sit silent under such reproach, when I am conscious of having done the best that was in my power. For God's sake, let me see you before you go for England'.[15] The was a rather undignified tone of pleading by a senior officer. Fitzroy's response included, 'I hope your Lordship will think I did nothing but my duty as aide-de-camp in mentioning to his Serene Highness my orders being so much questioned by your Lordship'.[16]

Richmond had already been talking of a missed opportunity and of the effect the cavalry might have had. Sackville asked him to call in at his headquarters before departing for England, to no effect.[17] Richmond

12 Mackesy, *The Coward of Minden*, p.148.

13 Mackesy, *The Coward of Minden*, p.149.

14 Mackesy, *The Coward of Minden*, p.149.

15 Sackville, *Lord George Sackville's Vindication of Himself, in a Letter to Colonel Fitzroy*, (London: R.Stevens, 1759).

16 Quoted in Sackville, *Vindication*.

17 Mackesy, *The Coward of Minden*, p.150.

maintained through the rest of his life that he had waited for an hour and a half for the cavalry to come up, and that he had personally timed it on his watch.

It seemed that Ferdinand's personal staff was not for turning. If Sackville could not persuade them, and if Ferdinand's account could not be prevented from reaching England, at least Sackville could send some of his own staff with his own version of events. Captains Robert Keith and James Smith were both sent, Keith bearing Sackville's letter of resignation and also a private letter to Lord Holdernesse, the Secretary of State. First, though, Keith was to attend on Lord Bute to ask how and when to best deliver them:

> To deliver them instantly was my first thought; I am now advised if things are not misrepresented to the King etc. to delay them if practicable 'til the end of the campaign, nothing should make me stay longer after that, but I own I should be happy beyond expression if I could hereafter upon a future occasion make the Prince ashamed of this scandalous behaviour of his, and at the end of the campaign at least I might tell him freely my real opinion of his attempt upon my character.[18]

Meanwhile, on 4 August, the allied army marched off from Minden, through the Minden Gap towards Gohfeld.[19] At that stage, Sackville still commanded the second line, which would become the right-hand column. On the 5th, Ferdinand expressed his further displeasure about arrangements concerning the British light artillery. Colonel Hotham refuted the allegation, but it seemed that Ferdinand had expressed his 'sovereign disapproval' without a full grasp of the facts. However, the rebuke was allowed to stand. The situation deteriorated when Ferdinand suggested to Reden that perhaps Granby, rather than Sackville, ought to lead the second line. Sackville continued to attempt to build support and drafted a paper which explained his conduct during the battle. He was, however, unable to garner much support by potential co-signatories within the senior ranks of the cavalry.

Matters were coming to head. Ferdinand complained formally to George II, threatening to resign if Sackville were not removed. Whilst Ferdinand focused initially solely on Sackville's conduct during the battle, in parallel complaints to the Hanoverian Minister-in-Attendance on the King, and who could be certain to brief the King, Ferdinand complained that Sackville's attempt to coerce his subordinates was upsetting the harmony of the army. Although tempted to make a declaration to the army on the topic, Ferdinand was persuaded by the calming influence of Westphalen not to lower himself in this way.

News of the victory was brought to London by a German who had taken the most direct route, through enemy territory via the Hague, to England in a fishing vessel. That messenger reached London on 8 August and his news was a welcome relief to a nervous and tense London. The city erupted with

18 Mackesy, *The Coward of Minden*, p.151.

19 Hotham-Thompson, *Operations of the Allied Army under the Duke of Brunswick 1757-1762*, p.89.

a plethora of celebratory bonfires, and all the talk was of Granby rather than Sackville. Walpole wrote:

> Mr. Yorke has sent word that a Captain Ligonier is coming from Prince Ferdinand to tell us that his Serene Highness has beaten Monsieur Contades to such a degree, that every house in London is illuminated, every street has two bonfires, every bonfire has two hundred squibs, and the poor charming moon yonder, that never looked so well in her life, is not at all minded, but seems only staring out of a garret window at the frantic doings all over the town. We don't know a single particular, but we conclude that Prince Ferdinand received all his directions from my Lord Granby, who is the mob's hero.[20]

Corresponding with the Earl of Strafford, Walpole wrote:

> My dear Lord, Lord Granby has entirely defeated the French! The foreign gazettes, I suppose, will give this victory to Prince Ferdinand: but the mob of London, whom I have this minute left, and who must know best, assure me that it is all their own Marquis's doing. Mr. Yorke (Minister at the Hague) was the first to send this news, "to be laid with himself and all humility at his Majesty's feet", about eleven o'clock yesterday morning.[21]

On the 10th, Ligonier and Estorff brought Ferdinand's formal report and, as was usual, the bearers of good news were rewarded, Ligonier receiving a purse of £500 and a lieutenant colonelcy in the 1st Guards. Ligonier visited the Commander-in-Chief, his uncle and reported discretely on the Sackville affair. However, when Fitzroy and Richmond arrived a couple of days later, the story broke, Richmond being rather frank. As is often the case, popular opinion latched onto the scandal. Walpole wrote:

> Probably by this time you have seen the Duke of Richmond or Fitzroy—but lest you should not, I will tell you all I can learn, and a wonderful history it is. Admiral Byng was not more unpopular than Lord George Sackville. I should scruple repeating his story, if Betty [a celebrated fruiterer in St. James's Street] and the waiters at Arthur's did not talk of it publicly, and thrust Prince Ferdinand's orders into one's hand.
>
> You have heard, I suppose, of the violent animosities that have reigned for the whole campaign between him and Lord Granby—in which some other warm persons have been very warm too. In the heat of the battle, the Prince, finding thirty-six squadrons of French coming down upon our army, sent Ligonier to order our thirty-two squadrons, under Lord George to advance. During that transaction, the French appeared to waver; and Prince Ferdinand, willing, as it is supposed, to give the honour to the British horse of terminating the day, sent

20 Walpole, *Letters*, Vol.II, Letter 327 To Sir Horace Mann, Arlington Street, Aug. 8, 1759 <https://www.gutenberg.org/cache/epub/4610/pg4610.html> (accessed 24 February 2019).

21 Walpole, *Letters*, Vol.II, Letter 329 To the Earl of Strafford. Strawberry Hill, Thursday, 3 o'clock, Aug. 9, 1759 <https://www.gutenberg.org/cache/epub/4610/pg4610.html> (accessed 24 February 2019).

> Fitzroy to bid Lord George bring up only the British cavalry. Ligonier had but just delivered his message, when Fitzroy came with his. Lord George said, "This can't be so—would he have me break the line? Here is some mistake." Fitzroy replied, he had not argued upon the orders, but those were the orders. "Well!" said Lord George, "but I want a guide." Fitzroy said, he would be his guide. Lord George, "Where is the Prince?" Fitzroy, "I left him at the head of the left wing, I don't know where he is now." Lord George said he would go seek him, and have this explained. Smith then asked Fitzroy, to repeat the orders to him; which being done, Smith went and whispered to Lord George, who says he then bid Smith carry up the cavalry: Smith is come, and says he is ready to answer any body any question. Lord George says, Prince Ferdinand's behaviour to him has been most infamous, has asked leave to resign his command, and to come over, which is granted. Prince Ferdinand's behaviour is summed up in the enclosed extraordinary paper; which you will doubt as I did, but which is certainly genuine. I doubted, because, in the military, I thought direct disobedience of orders was punished with an immediate arrest, and because the last paragraph seemed to me very foolish. The going Out Of the way to compliment Lord Granby with what he would have done, seems to take off a little from the compliments paid to those that have done something; but, in short, Prince Ferdinand or Lord George, one of them, is most outrageously in the wrong, and the latter has much the least chance of being thought in the right.
>
> The particulars I tell you, I collect from the most accurate, authorities. I make no comments on Lord George, it would look like a little dirty court to you; and the best compliment I can make you, is to think, as I do, that you will be the last man to enjoy this revenge.
>
> Adieu![22]

The King was jubilant about the victory which had preserved Hanover. He promptly bestowed the Order of the Garter and £20,000 on Ferdinand. Sackville was not similarly lauded. The Prince of Wales was cynical about the criticism of the British commander, suggesting it was 'pretty pert for a little German prince to make public any fault he finds with the English commander, without first waiting for instructions from the King on so delicate a matter'.[23] Sackville had managed to fall out with Bute several months previously, so when Keith appeared carrying Sackville's letter of resignation, Bute did not delay in passing it to Pitt. Pitt's focus, as ever, was on the national interest rather than on supposed friendship while Newcastle, never the boldest at defending anything likely to prove unpopular, kept a low profile away from London in Sussex. Pitt stated to Bute; 'I have the satisfaction to acquaint your Lordship that the King has given leave to Lord George Sackville to return to England. This mode of returning, your Lordship will perceive, is a very considerable softening of his misfortune'. However, he was ambiguous with regard to his own interaction with Sackville, 'As I have already, so I shall

22 Walpole, *Letters*, Vol.II, Letter 330. To the Hon. H.S. Conway. Arlington Street, Aug. 14, 1759<https://www.gutenberg.org/cache/epub/4610/pg4610.html> (accessed 24 February 2019)

23 Mackesy, *The Coward of Minden*, p.154.

continue to give him, as a most unhappy man, all the offices of humanity, which our first, sacred object, my dear Lord, the public good, will allow'.[24]

The King's instructions to relieve Sackville of command were en route at exactly the same time as Ferdinand's call for Sackville's recall.[25] When they arrived on 21August, Sackville was stunned. He may perhaps have anticipated Bute's transmission of his letter of resignation, but he certainly had not believed that it would be accepted. In an act of desperation, he appealed to Ferdinand to explain how he had failed so badly as to deserve such treatment, 'a thousand times worse than death'. Ferdinand rebuffed the request, claiming to be uninvolved in the process about which Sackville was complaining. He did admit to having written to the King about Sackville's subsequent disruption of the morale of the army, but that could not have arrived before Sackville's recall had been issued by the King.

Sackville's only recourse was to slip discretely away from the army, which he did accompanied by the chaplain John Hotman, Lloyd and Sutherland, but already the campfire rumour was that he had been sacked in disgrace. One Greys farrier recorded in his journal, 'He was disgracefully dismissed from our army, his sword broke over his head, and sent by a strong guard through the whole front line and straight off to England'.[26] Some officers were more measured, observing that only a clear gathering of the facts would explain why the cavalry had not been committed to battle. Sackville steered away from the Hague, where Sir Joseph Yorke, son of Lord Hardwicke and well-versed in political manoeuvrings, had been advised of both sides of the story. He had prior knowledge of Sackville, both having served together on Cumberland's staff. He disliked him. He opined to his brother, Lord Royston, that Sackville seemed to be out to prove himself a better general than Contades who was, in turn, better than Ferdinand.[27]

As resilient armies do, the British contingent carried on, with Granby now in command. Yorke opined that a relieved Britain's effusive gratitude would outweigh any previous concerns about Ferdinand. By October, Granby had been sent the Order of the Garter by the King with which to invest Ferdinand while close to French encampments.[28] Rising to the occasion, Granby even stretched to make a speech in French: 'Among so many princes and sovereigns who have thought themselves honoured by the Garter, only Gustavus Adolphus and your Highness have received it at the head of an army'.[29]

A sober review of the effect of Minden revealed that, whilst a valuable victory, it was not completely decisive. Although the French were on the retreat, Ferdinand's pursuit had been leisurely. The French, although shaken and reduced, had got away and would attempt to threaten Hanover anew. In the bigger picture, though, Minden had bought the alliance breathing space

24 Mackesy, *The Coward of Minden*, p.155.
25 Savory, *His Britannic Majesty's Army in Germany*, p.474.
26 Mackesy, *The Coward of Minden*, p.156.
27 Mackesy, *The Coward of Minden*, p.158.
28 Archenholz, *Prussia and the Seven Years War 1756-1763*, p.192.
29 Mackesy, *The Coward of Minden*, p.156.

which would allow Ferdinand to drip-feed reinforcements to Frederick who had just suffered a catastrophic reversal at Kunersdorf, losing 42 percent of his army of almost 50,000, 178 guns and 26 colours.[30] By the year's end, Ferdinand, who was ever in awe of Frederick, had transferred some 12,000 reinforcements, including the Erbprinz, to Frederick.[31]

For the British government, the nub of the difficulty of the Sackville affair was that to defend Sackville would necessarily be to discredit Prince Ferdinand. In the end, the national interest took precedence and it was vital to support the commander of the allied army. Granby was warned to punctiliously obey Ferdinand. If only Ferdinand could confront and defeat Contades again, or perhaps separate him from his supply base in Frankfurt, the alliance would be the better for it. There was even concern that, as a result of Kunersdorf, the French threat to Hanover might be eclipsed by a fresh threat from Austria and Russia.

Walpole reflected on Sackville's woes:

> Truly I don't know whether one is to be rejoicing or lamenting! Every good heart is a bonfire for Prince Ferdinand's success, and a funeral pile for the King of Prussia's defeat [Kunersdorf].
>
> The mob, to comfort themselves under these mishaps, and for the disappointment of a complete victory, that might have been more compleater, are new grinding their teeth and nails, to tear Lord George to pieces the instant he lands. If he finds more powerful friends than poor Admiral Byng, assure yourself he has ten thousand times the number of personal enemies; I was going to say real, but Mr. Byng's were real enough, with no reason to be personal. I don't talk of the event itself, for I suppose all Europe knows just as much as we know here. I suspend my opinion till Lord George speaks himself—but I pity his father, who has been so unhappy in his sons, who loved this so much, and who had such fair prospects for him. Lord George's fall is prodigious; nobody stood higher, nobody has more ambition or more sense.[32]

When Sackville arrived back in London on 7 September, the public outcry had not died down. The press was overwhelmingly critical. This was the voice of the mob which had clamoured for the blood of Admiral Byng who had been shot for the loss of Minorca. A few pamphlets, very much a minority, were produced, calling for reason, but some of them had been so incompetently produced to be more of an embarrassment to Sackville, who felt forced to publicly eschew them. The majority of those published were against Sackville, some of them so extreme as to be ridiculous, such as those which claimed that he had been bribed with French gold (similar charges had been levelled against Byng). Even more extreme was that a common link was that both were sodomites, 'It has been said of the admiral, that he was addicted to a certain vice which seems incompatible with a military character; and it is

30 Szabo, *The Seven Years War in Europe 1756-1763*, p.238.

31 Savory, *His Britannic Majesty's Army in Germany*, pp.190-191.

32 Walpole, *Letters*, Vol.II, Letter 331 To Sir Horace Mann, Strawberry Hill, Aug. 29, 1759 <https://www.gutenberg.org/cache/epub/4610/pg4610.html> (accessed 24 February 2019).

well known that the gentleman to whom we are now comparing him, has been so much traduced by the vulgar upon the same head'.[33] There were calls for the death penalty.

Eventually some more reflective reviews began to emerge. The pre-existing rancour between Ferdinand and Sackville started to be exposed, the *London Magazine* drawing on the disagreement when the allies' eastward retreat had cut the British communications with Emden.[34] Another source put forward the view that, after Bergen, Ferdinand had become timorous and insecure, which had triggered a hyper-sensitivity to Sackville's criticisms.

Sackville wrote a statement, *His Lordship's Apology*, in which he refuted Ferdinand's allegations: he was not late; his orders had been ambiguous: the advance onto the heath had been prompt; Fitzroy had caused some of the misunderstanding with Ferdinand.[35] Sackville believed that he could clear his name by trial by court-martial, but was now also becoming sanguine that an exposure of some truths might be unpalatable to ministers. On reaching England, Sackville asked Bute for his support and sent him a draft of his application for trial by court-martial. Bute, nervous of swimming against a popular tide, was reticent and sat on his hands. Sackville was beginning to see not just that the opinion of the mob was swaying even his potential allies, but also that it was inevitable that ministers would feel obliged to stand by Ferdinand. Newcastle, in particular, often timorous, was anxious to retain Ferdinand's services. Pitt had a far stronger character, but he had previous form in his denunciation of Byng. For Pitt, political pragmatism would be all important. Sackville wrote to Pitt, enclosing a copy of his request for a court-martial. Pitt's response reflected a painful combination of inexperience in military matters along with the layman's perplexity at Sackville's conduct. Pitt hedged his bets, all the while maintaining his friendship yet beginning to distance himself, telling Newcastle that he would remain impartial yet remaining loyal to Ferdinand.

Realising that if the King were to dismiss him from the Army, his situation would become tougher as he could no longer rely on trial by court-martial, Sackville promptly wrote to the Secretary of State:

> I am conscious of neither neglect nor disobedience of orders , as I am certain I did my duty to the utmost of my ability, and as I am persuaded that the Prince himself would have found that he had no just cause of complaint against me had he condescended to have enquired into my conduct before he had expressed his disapprobriation [sic] of it from the partial representation of others; I therefore most humbly request that I may at least have a public opportunity given me of attempting to justify myself to His Majesty and to my country by a Court Martial being appointed, that if I am guilty, I may suffer such punishment as I may have deserved, and if innocent that I may stand acquitted in the opinion of the world,

33 Mackesy, *The Coward of Minden*, p.160.

34 *The London Magazine, or, Gentleman's Monthly Intelligencer*, Vol.XXIX, 1759, p.405.

35 Reid, *The Battle of Minden 1759*, p.151.

> but it is really too severe to have been censured unheard, to have been condemned before I was tried, and to be informed neither of my crime nor of my accusers.[36]

The government was riding high on recent relative military successes, and to rake over Minden risked diminishing the victory. Further, Sackville's case against Ferdinand was a zero-sum debate: if Sackville were to successfully defend his conduct, Ferdinand, the Government's much-needed hero, would find his position untenable. Sackville's insistence that he should have his day in court could be embarrassing so the King and his ministers, who would have preferred him simply to fade away, opted to delay: during the campaigning season, the necessary witnesses were indispensable in Germany.

Walpole developed the story:

> Lord George Sackville, the hero of all conversation, if one can be so for not being a hero, is arrived. He immediately applied for a court-martial, but was told it was impossible now, as the officers necessary are in Germany. This was in writing from Lord Holderness—but Lord Ligonier in words was more squab—"If he wanted a court-martial, he might go seek it in Germany." All that could be taken from him is his regiment, above two thousand pounds a-year: commander in Germany at ten pounds a-day, between three and four thousand pounds: lieutenant-general of the ordnance, one thousand five hundred pounds: a fort, three hundred pounds. He remains with a patent place in Ireland, of one thousand two hundred pounds, and about two thousand pounds a-year of his own and wife's. With his parts and ambition, it cannot end here; he calls himself ruined, but when the Parliament meets, he will probably attempt some sort of revenge.
>
> I cannot help shifting at the great objects of our letters. We never converse on a less topic than a kingdom. We are a kind of citizens of the world, and battles and revolutions are the common incidents of our neighbourhood. But that is and must be the case of distant correspondences: Kings and Empresses that we never saw are the only persons we can be acquainted with in common. We can have no more familiarity than the Daily Advertiser would have if it wrote to the Florentine Gazette. Adieu! My compliments to any monarch that lives within five hundred miles of you.[37]

Meanwhile an increasingly irascible George II would seal his support for Ferdinand and exercise his royal prerogative in dismissing Sackville from the Army. The Secretary at War, Lord Barrington, was tasked with telling Sackville of his dismissal and offered the options of a letter or verbally. Sackville opted for the letter, which stated, 'I have received His Majesty's command to let you know, that he has no further occasion for your services as Lieut.-General, and Colonel of Dragoon Guards; I am concerned that I have no better occasion to assure your lordship, that I am, My Lord, your Lordship's most humble and obedient servant'.[38]

---

36 Mackesy, *The Coward of Minden*, p.164.

37 Walpole, *Letters*, Vol.II, Letter 332 To Sir Horace Mann, Arlington Street, Sept. 13, 1759 <https://www.gutenberg.org/cache/epub/4610/pg4610.html> (accessed 24 February 2019).

38 Mackesy, *The Coward of Minden*, p.166.

Walpole, writing again to the Earl of Strafford, noted, 'Lord George is come, has asked for a court-martial, was put off; and is turned out of every thing. Waldegrave has his Regiment, for what he did; and Lord Granby the Ordnance—for what he would have done'.[39]

Sackville's determination to be heard at court-martial was a high-risk decision. He had had influence but no matter how many allies he could gather to speak in his favour, the weight of those opposing him was likely to be overwhelming, and the public was baying for blood. He could have dropped quietly out of sight, admittedly with a greatly reduced income, but instead he stood firm in his demand. Interestingly, he was not universally condemned, with some public figures expressing their friendship and others prepared to wait to hear the facts.

Realistically, though, it was hardly likely that the decision would be in favour of Sackville over Ferdinand. In addition, the affair was not taking place in a vacuum. There were political opportunities and threats, as others built their careers and reputations, possibly at Sackville's expense. Sackville's best hope was to rely on credible witnesses from Germany, but one of those, Major General Granville Elliot, had died there on 10 October. He was hopeful that the punctilious Colonel Charles Hotham would bring copies of all the relevant orders. Hotham's family had long been friends of the Sackvilles, but Hotham was an able and rising officer, who would not wish to jeopardise his ties with those placed over him in Germany.

After a brief reconsideration of the validity of trying a former officer by court martial, and for offences committed outwith the King's realms, the law officers decided that the case could be heard, but on what charge? Sackville had not been charged so, extraordinarily, was being asked to suggest a charge. Sackville assumed that Ferdinand must have informed the King of his displeasure with Sackville's conduct in order for the King to dismiss him. Accordingly, he asked to be, 'legally prosecuted for whatever crime I may have been thought guilty of'.[40] He felt that the case against him was nebulous. His alternative to a trial was to organise some form of public-relations exercise.

At this stage in the war, France was gearing up for the conquest of Hanover and Hesse, to compensate for defeat at Quebec and the loss of Canada. Also, after Frederick's defeat at Kunersdorf, he had compounded his own woes by a precipitately launching an attack on the Austrians under *Generalfeldmarschall* von Daun, resulting in the surrender of 12,000 of his men at Maxen in November.[41] While the allies may not have sought a high-profile case with the potential to threaten Ferdinand's reputation the alternative, Sackville's own public relations exercise, could be even more damaging. So, it was agreed that, on 26 January 1760, a warrant would be issued, 'that the said Lord George Sackville hath disobeyed the orders of

39 Walpole, *Letters*, Vol.II, Letter 333 To the Earl of Strafford. Arlington Street, Sept. 13, 1759 <https://www.gutenberg.org/cache/epub/4610/pg4610.html> (accessed 24 February 2019).

40 Mackesy, *The Coward of Minden*, p.173.

41 Szabo, *The Seven Years' War in Europe 1756-1763*, p.251.

Prince Ferdinand of Brunswick, which charge we have thought fit should be enquired into by a general court martial'.[42]

All of this meant that Sackville had effectively arranged to be charged with a capital offence, that of disobedience. Many in senior positions were amazed by Sackville's determination to face trial as, when the full account emerged and if it showed him in a bad light, the effect would be catastrophic. The mood against him was stoked by Ferdinand's own account, which was published in the English press in February. Naturally, it was written from Ferdinand's perspective, at the expense of Sackville's reputation, but it bolstered national pride. Granby's own account arrived at about the same time and reinforced Ferdinand's position. Granby was openly critical of Ferdinand's German subordinate generals, although he was more reticent about Sackville.

42 Mackesy, *The Coward of Minden*, p.174.

13

Sackville's Court Martial

Courts martial were unique affairs, almost more focused on honour than on law. For a general, they required 13 senior officers, and it would be a rare thing indeed for any to possess a detailed knowledge of law. The Judge-Advocate was both prosecutor and the panel's director on law and process. The accused was permitted 'friends of the court', who could counsel him, but he was responsible for conducting his own defence.

Sackville was advised by a tough and able Scot, Alexander Wedderburn, one of Bute's circle. Wedderburn was convinced of Sackville's case. His basic aim was for Sackville to be acquitted. His further aim was for a glorious triumph. Wedderburn coached the accused. He advised him to focus on the orders he had received, on the true reason for the cavalry halts on the heath, and their short duration. Sackville was permitted 14 witnesses, not an ungenerous amount. The court was convened on 29 February 1760, with Sackville being formally arrested for disobedience the day before, although he was not put in confinement. The House of Commons provided another opportunity for Sackville to back down, offering the court martial of a former soldier as a breach of privilege, but he refused, his brother-in-law confirming to the House that the trial was exactly what Lord George sought.

The Prosecution

Sackville's trial began on Friday 29 February 1760 at Horse Guards. The Deputy Judge-Advocate General, Charles Gould, opened proceedings and administered the oath. Sackville was permitted, but declined, to object to any members of the court with the sole exception of General William Belford from whom Sackville had taken over as Lieutenant-General of the Ordnance, which had rankled.[1] Once again the question was posed as to whether Sackville, now as a civilian, could still be subject to court martial. After a week of adjournment, it was decided that there were no grounds to doubt the jurisdiction of the court martial. The court reconvened with Sir

1 Reid, *The Battle of Minden 1759*, p.170.

Charles Howard as President. The charge was read and the prosecution's case unmasked: neglect of orders to prepare to move; Sackville's late arrival at the head of the cavalry; disobedience to orders transmitted by Winzingerode, Ligonier and Fitzroy; and the halts during the march onto the heath.

The Germans from Ferdinand's staff who had been called as witnesses were surprised and became resentful of what they perceived to be the leeway permitted to Sackville, under the British system, to question witnesses.

During Fitzroy's questioning, he observed that when Ferdinand had sent him to hasten the cavalry, he had added 'to Lord Granby, for I know he will obey me'.[2] One particular debate which developed was whether, in Fitzroy's opinion, if the infantry had been broken without cavalry to the rear in support, then the whole would have been lost. Sackville objected to this line of questioning, observing that the main question was whether he had obeyed or disobeyed Prince Ferdinand's orders. As the case developed, Lord Barrington, who was observing the trial on Newcastle's behalf, wrote that it had been proved that Sackville had arrived late at his post. As the case proceeded, Barrington was impressed by the statements of the witnesses and became convinced that the case for the prosecution was strong.

A key witness would be Lieutenant Colonel Sloper of the 1st Dragoon Guards, who had been putting about his own account of the affair. He had clearly heard the orders brought by Winzingerode, relayed in both English and German. Sackville had asked for clarification and Winzingerode had insisted that they meant a move to the left, which had wasted 25 minutes in not obeying. Sloper was noted to be particularly antagonistic towards Sackville. One possible underlying reason might have been that, in the year before, Sackville had objected to a nephew of General Humphry Bland, the regimental colonel, being given a vacant troop in his regiment on the grounds of age and inexperience, an appointment which Sloper had supported. Another reason could have been that Sloper was close to Lieutenant General Mordaunt, of whom Sackville had been heavily critical during the inquiry into the Rochefort expedition.

When Sloper was called as a witness on the third day, it was obvious that he was sticking to his story. Winzingerode had passed the instruction to move to the left. When Sackville had appeared puzzled, he had intervened to confirm the intent but that there had been a long delay until Ligonier had arrived with orders to advance towards the left. Sloper had intervened and, during the trial offered that he had said: 'For God's sake, Sir, repeat your orders to that man, that he may not pretend not to have understood them, for it is near half an hour ago that he received orders to advance, and yet we are still here, but you see the condition he is in'.[3] When asked by the Judge-Advocate to clarify the last point, Sloper replied:

> My opinion is that my Lord George Sackville was alarmed to a very great degree. When his Lordship ordered me to advance, he seemed in utmost confusion. The original orders were to the left; Captain Ligonier's orders were to the left. The

---

2 Cole, *Minden 1759*, p.53.

3 *The London Magazine, or, Gentleman's Monthly Intelligencer*, Vol XXX, 1760, p.181.

> cavalry afterwards made a move to the left, and the order his Lordship had given me, was to move with the regiment straight forwards.[4]

So there it was: Sloper had effectively accused Sackville of cowardice. Wedderburn's advice had been to belittle such an allegation and then somehow have it expunged. However, in an age when a gentleman's honour was everything, Sackville struggled to restrain himself and attempted to refute the accusation, but the court insisted that he restrict himself to cross-examining Sloper. During the cross-examination, Sloper was openly insolent towards Lord George and was rebuked by Lord Albemarle. However, despite the clearly biased nature of Sloper's evidence, the mere hint of cowardice began to stick.

On day four, Sloper was recalled and continued to be contemptuous of Sackville. While the court prevented him from developing his theme, the damage done by Sloper was beginning to take effect. To the public observer, the doubt sown was beginning to tarnish Sackville's reputation.

Three more witnesses were called: Derenthal, to demonstrate Ferdinand's impatience; Lieutenant Colonel Pitt, of the 10th Dragoons, who described the slow pace of the cavalry's march across the heath; and Granby, who thought the cavalry's advance had been to too slow and with too many halts. Granby voiced the opinion that, had the cavalry advanced at the trot on receiving the orders from Winzingerode, it would have arrived 15-20 minutes earlier, yet still unblown and in a good condition, in time to attack the enemy and do much execution. However, compared to Sloper's overt attack on Sackville, Granby's restraint from overtly criticising him actually did more damage.

Fifty-six years after Minden, the Duke of Wellington described how difficult it was to recall exactly what had happened to whom, and where, and in what sequence at the Battle of Waterloo. Sackville attempted to get his lawyers to review exactly what Granby had thought happened as the second line of allied horse had halted at the fir wood, to enable the first line to come up into one single line and then, once again, to allow the two regiments on the extreme right to catch up and come into line. It could be argued that the fact that Sackville was seeking clarification rather than making a certain assertion may show that his evidence was more realistic than those witnesses were so completely convinced that their version of events was infallible.

In all, the evidence for the prosecution had taken six days. By this stage, spectators could not imagine how Sackville could defend himself after such an impressive body of evidence. The Government was concerned that Sackville could be too critical of Ferdinand. It was beginning to look as if it would be easy for Sackville to disprove that the cavalry had not been saddled by 1:00 a.m. as ordered. In fact, it was later decided not to include this in Ferdinand's account and Derenthal began to advise Ferdinand that he may have been misadvised by false reports.

---

4 Quoted in Anon., *The Trial of the Right Honourable Lord George Sackville at a Court-Martial held at the Horse-Guards, February 29, 1760, for an enquiry into his conduct, being charged h Disobedience of Orders, while commanded the British Horse in Germany* (London: W.Owen, 1760), p.38.

When the court reopened three days later, it was mobbed by the public, anxious to see how this would play out. Sackville had kept his peace in the intervening period since the battle, anxious to make an appropriate and dignified impact. Again, anticipating Wellington's views by half a century, Sackville opined that any single witness could only have seen a part of the whole. Lord George thanked the King for granting him a court martial and emphasised that he was a willing defendant, anxious to prove his innocence.

Sackville's defence took nine days in total. In order to disprove the charge of disobedience, he maintained that the court only required to confirm the orders which he had received and to consider whether those orders could be obeyed. It was important to understand the situation as it was understood at the time, and not viewed in retrospect knowing what the court now knew.

Sackville's point was that he was unable to see the infantry engagement as it was hidden by the woodland and that the cavalry had been ordered to wait until the village of Hahlen had been cleared. The instructions he received had been brought by junior officers with only a partial understanding of the whole picture.[5] The risk, from his perspective, was that if he had acted in haste, and acted wrongly, he could jeopardise the entire allied army's operation.

Sackville then listed the instructions which he had complied with: within the constraints of his duties from being General of the Day, he had reconnoitred the routes onto the heath; his cavalry had been saddled by 1:00 a.m.; whilst Ferdinand's orders to march had been delayed, he (Sackville) had marched with his troops immediately. Sackville was of the view that these aspects had been included simply to swell the charge sheet.

However, Sackville then went on to criticise Ferdinand: if it were indeed true that a battle was expected imminently, any normal Commander-in-Chief would issue a plan for the battle itself; the aspect of being saddled by 1:00 a.m. had happened so frequently in the previous two weeks that it was no clear indication of the immediacy of battle;[6] when, as General of the Day, Sackville had reported on the state of the picquets, Ferdinand had made no comment to indicate that he expected a battle on the morrow; it was not only Sackville who was taken by surprise, but rather the whole army which should have been placed in a higher state of readiness; those criticising his approach march as being slow were in no position to judge, otherwise why would the rear of the column be obliged to hurry to keep up?[7]

The Judge-Advocate was quick to deny that the questions over compliance with the pre-battle orders had been added simply to swell the charges. Sackville then invited the court to review why those aspects had been covered in such detail. This forced the Judge-Advocate eventually to withdraw them.

Moving onto the orders borne by Winzingerode, during the 30 minutes or so, when Sackville and his cavalry were penned in near Hartum, vulnerable to enemy artillery fire, awaiting word that Hahlen had been cleared, had he (Sackville) not ordered the British artillery forward on his own initiative?

5 Reid, *The Battle of Minden 1759*, p.149.
6 Reid, *The Battle of Minden 1759*, p.146.
7 *The London Magazine*, 1760, pp.171-183.

When Winzingerode had said that the cavalry was to form one line and advance 'to sustain the infantry', had he not begun immediately to comply?[8]

As to the precise wording of the orders themselves, while the prosecution had only produced one witness (Winzingerode himself), he could produce five and, as for Sloper, his word could not be believed – 'In what manner his evidence was given I need not remind the court'.[9] Besides, apart from Sloper's poor behaviour in court, Sackville's five witnesses would demolish and disprove his evidence. To reinforce his point, Sackville reminded the court that Sloper was unable to recall the name of any officer whom he saw in Sackville's company, other than a *Hauptman* Hugo, and that only by being reminded by Winzingerode.

Turning to Winzingerode's exact words, Sackville was polite about Winzingerode and his honesty – no doubt he genuinely believed that he said to move to the left (although he could not now be entirely certain, unlike Sloper who was absolutely certain), but his five witnesses were adamant that the instruction was to advance to the front. Next, Winzingerode had stated that Ferdinand had expressed his frustration that the cavalry had not yet appeared, effectively that Sackville had caused the delay. In fact, Sackville opined, it showed that Ferdinand desperately wished that he had cavalry in a position where he had failed to order it. Furthermore, Winzingerode only learned of Ferdinand's anxiety as he was on his return journey, having delivered his orders, when he encountered Ligonier. Winzingerode had ridden at the gallop, so how was it possible that a large body of cavalry (24 squadrons in all) could beat Winzingerode back to the Prince? Not only had Sloper exaggerated the length of time between Winzingerode's order and that of Ligonier, but he had varied by some 15 minutes his account of the delay.

Then there was a fundamental challenge. Was he to follow the instruction brought by Ligonier, which he had done, immediately, or was he to follow the order borne by Fitzroy, which was at variance with it?[10] If Ligonier had mentioned to move to the left, which he believed he had done, perhaps that part of the order had been muffled, and not been heard, because of the noise of the drums. Fitzroy's order made no sense at all, as it required the British component only to move to the left.[11] Movement to the left was different from previous instructions and, if the cavalry was needed quickly, the British element was actually some 800 metres further away than the Hanoverian cavalry. Furthermore, when the French had such a preponderance of cavalry, it made no sense to divide his own force in proximity to the enemy.

The two orders had been delivered almost simultaneously, and had been assumed by bystanders to have the same meaning, yet they were different and neither messenger would back down. While both officers believed the truth of their own account, but neither had heard the other deliver his message, it was impossible to prove what they imagined had been said. A further factor was that verbal messages delivered by junior officers were prone to error:

8 Anon, *The Trial of the Right Honourable Lord George Sackville*, pp.286-313.
9 Mackesy, *The Coward of Minden*, p.195.
10 Reid, *The Battle of Minden 1759*, p.151.
11 Reid, *The Battle of Minden 1759*, p.111.

> The distinctness or indistinctness of two young aides-de-camp might have decided the fate of an army… Entrusted with such a command as I bore… I determined to act upon more certain grounds, having already experienced too much confusion of the orders sent by aides-de-camp.[12]

If Sackville had hesitated, it was over that variance and, given that Ferdinand was only a few hundred metres distant he had approached him in person for clarification. As Sackville rode towards Ferdinand, he was accompanied by Fitzroy who insisted that his version was the correct one. On the way, Sackville discovered that the woodland opened sooner than he had expected and, in the face of Fitzroy's persistence, decided that it might indeed be possible to bring up the British cavalry, so he sent Captain Smith to summon them while he rode on to the Prince.

The last item concerned the slow pace across the heath, and the frequent halts. He was to form his squadrons in a single line to advance to sustain the infantry. In his view, every halt made was necessary. If Ferdinand had ordered a rapid pursuit, he should have used whatever cavalry came to hand. As far as Sackville knew, the battle was raging and he had to ensure that his cavalry was under control and in good order to be ready for any contingency. Manoeuvring such a large body of cavalry was a matter of judgement and, in Sackville's opinion cavalry was more valuable in the attack if it was kept fresh and under tight control than if it rushed.

This was an aspect of cavalry command about which the court was keen to learn more. Lieutenant General James Cholmondeley observed that he had seen cavalry moving so quickly that 'they could not move at all afterwards'.[13] Taking the contrary view, Sloper was of the opinion that even if his regiment had been forced to gallop in the approach, it would still arrive 'fit to defeat any three French Squadrons'.[14] Lieutenant Colonel Pitt of the 10th Dragoons was quizzed on the pace of Sackville's advance and pointed out that Lord George was always very slow whenever he marched at the head of a line of cavalry, not just at Minden.

Sackville could therefore justify his pace on the grounds of control and keeping his mounts fresh for action. There had also been a lack of clarity in subsequent instructions about exactly which portion of the line Granby was to bring forward, the whole line or simply the British element. Ferdinand's order to sustain the infantry had not been specific about which infantry. Sackville had indeed closed up behind the eight battalions of infantry which he could see. He had, therefore, complied with his orders.

Sackville concluded by returning to the issue of how accurate the accounts of the battle and his actions could be. There was tremendous variety in people's memory of time, not only between the witnesses for the prosecution and the defence, but significant discrepancy within the prosecution. Additionally,

12 Anon, *The Trial of the Right Honourable Lord George Sackville*, pp.286-313.

13 Mackesy, *The Coward of Minden*, p.198.

14 Mackesy, *The Coward of Minden*, p.198. In fact, in a curious twist of fate, at Warburg in 1760, Sloper's regiment was put to the test after a long trot and was overthrown.

someone such as Fitzroy's idea of the time could hardly be trusted as he was not carrying a watch, nor did he consult anyone as to the time.

The Defence

Sackville initially called five witnesses for the defence: Colonel Hotham (who had already been called by the prosecution); Captain Richard Lloyd (one of his aides-de-camp); Captain John Smith (of the 3rd Guards); Lieutenant Bissett (of the 51st Foot); Lieutenant James Sutherland (the camp quartermaster).[15]

Each one of the five witnesses was asked the key question about Sackville's demeanour on the day, in order to counter Sloper's allegation of cowardice. To a man they defended Lord George, being consistent that he appeared absolutely normal, with Captain Smith adding a dramatic flourish, 'I believe that Lord George would have gone to his death that day had it been necessary'.[16]

Gradually, the tide of public opinion began to turn. Sackville had laid out his case clearly and elegantly. He had refrained from direct criticism of Ferdinand, albeit that allegations of unreadiness and lack of clarity in orders reflect badly on any commander. The Germans were less impressed, thinking that the court had allowed him too much leeway, and the King himself was determined to prevent any further criticism of the Prince.

Two gunners were the next witnesses, Captains Griffith-Williams and Forbes MacBean. As scientific professionals, their evidence was undramatic but competent. Williams was particularly familiar with the long wood on the cavalry's flank having studied the mapping and having scouted it. Both demonstrated that the woods to the flank and the front had undergrowth which would not permit the cavalry to move in anything greater than four abreast (in other words, certainly not in line).[17] Both reinforced the opinion that Sackville had directed them in a positive way, despite the otherwise confused situation.

When Sackville then turned to consider each element of the charge, he called on Hotham who confirmed the assumption that Winzingerode had conveyed the order that the cavalry should form a single line as a third line to sustain the infantry, and advance. Hotham confirmed that Sackville had asked Winzingerode to repeat his orders and would have assumed that advancing meant moving forwards. Hotham had not seen Winzingerode speaking to *Hauptman* Hugo, nor had he seen or heard any exchange between Sackville and Sloper.

Another witness was the Hanoverian aide de camp, *Hauptman* Hugo. He agreed that he took Wintzingerode's instruction to mean to advance to the front. Although there was some discrepancy about the precise time lapse between Wintzingerode's leaving and Fitzroy's arrival, the average was about seven and a half minutes. Neither Hugo, nor the three subsequent witnesses,

15 Mackesy, *The Coward of Minden*, p.200.

16 Quoted in Anon., *The Trial of the Right Honourable Lord George Sackville*, p.105.

17 Reid, *The Battle of Minden 1759*, pp.170-182.

Bisset, Lloyd nor Broome (Sackville's ordnance aide) observed any signs of fear from Lord George. Of this group, Bisset admitted that he had taken an unauthorised look through the wood to the left but had not reported it to Sackville as he believed that Sackville's priority would be the enemy to the front.

There then followed a curious episode where Sackville was hasty to defend Bisset against assumed criticism by Lieutenant General Cholmondeley, creating more friction than illumination. However, the upshot was that the court decided to change from the process agreed at the outset, whereby Sackville would work through the charge, item by item. He was asked, and agreed, to fully examine each witness.

Now something critical happened, something which appeared to demolish Sloper's story. Sloper had alleged that he had been at the right-hand of the 1st Dragoon Guards and that he had heard Winzingerode deliver his instructions to Sackville. When examined, Captain John Smith, who had not heard Winzingerode as he had been on the right of the line, loading his pistols, had ridden back and heard Sackville directing Hugo to get the Hanoverian regiment of Saxe-Gotha moved from his front.[18] Yet when Ligonier had passed his orders to Sackville, the latter had been at the head of the right squadron of the next regiment along, the Inniskillings, whereupon Sackville had drawn his sword and ordered the line to march.

At that point, Sloper had inquired of Smith whether he thought the line was about to charge. When Smith had answered in the affirmative, Sloper had become concerned that his regiment was carrying its picket poles, rather than having abandoned them, which would prevent it charging. Sloper had asked Smith to ride to warn Sackville, and to beg him to stop for one minute. Sackville had refused to halt, telling Smith to relay that Sloper's regiment should drop its poles on the move as he would not stop the line. Instead, Sloper had actually ordered a stop, saying that his regiment could achieve the whole action more quickly that way.

Smith's evidence did several things: it showed that Sloper was nowhere near Sackville when Ligonier had delivered his orders (and this was confirmed by the other witnesses, not least Lieutenant Whiteford, carrying the guidon in the right squadron of the Inniskillings); it showed that Sloper's regiment was not properly made ready to charge at the right moment in the presence of the enemy; and it showed that Sloper's criticism of Lord George for causing delay could perhaps equally be levelled at himself for having his regiment improperly prepared for battle.

The general opinion of the witnesses for the defence was that it had been difficult to overhear the conversation between Sackville, Ligonier and Fitzroy but that Sackville had insisted on clarification. In the end, Fitzroy having been the more forceful, Sackville had asked him to confirm exactly where he thought he should go. One witness, Lloyd, was very clear that the route Sackville had wanted to follow would have put him in touch with the infantry

18 Mackesy, *The Coward of Minden*, p.207.

and that the cavalry would have been in time to influence the battle had not Fitzroy intervened.

Having been against Sackville at the beginning of the trial, public opinion was now swinging in his favour. Walpole picked up on this and reported in his correspondence with Horace Mann in Florence, 'The colour of it is more favourable for him than it looked at first. Prince Ferdinand's narrative has proved to set out with a heap of lies'.[19]

A New Court Convened

However, the authority of the court expired on a technicality due to the expiry of the Annual Mutiny Act on 25 March 1760. A new court would have to be convened. This would allow the prosecution, now armed with a full knowledge of the case for the defence, to re-examine its witnesses and to call new ones. Instead, an offer was made, to accept on oath the previous evidence, with the glaring exception of Sloper's as it had been seriously challenged, causing the Judge-Advocate to call for new evidence.

Lord George was taken aback by this and struggled to understand whether this was proper. He was unsure the extent to which the Judge-Advocate would pursue the quest for fresh evidence or whether he would have the right of reply. In the end, Sackville's evidence was completed on Saturday 29 March 1760. Newcastle, aligned against Sackville, still hoped for a satisfactory result but with less confidence than at the beginning. Thomas Grey, the poet, wrote of Lord George, 'People wonder at (and some there are that celebrate) his dexterity, his easy elocution, and unembarrassed manner'.[20]

The remainder of the conduct of the court became a bone of contention – Sackville wished to be able to hear the additional evidence prior to his final address, so that he could deal with any fresh points. He also clashed with the Judge-Advocate who he characterised as neither a soldier, not a lawyer, so unfit to pronounce in either sphere.

Sackville attempted to sum up. He had been diligent and had attempted to obey his orders. However, with Winzingerode, Ligonier and then Fitzroy, he had received three versions. Had he stuck to his original course, until diverted by Fitzroy, with the benefit of hindsight it now looked probable that the cavalry would have shared full part in a resounding victory along with the infantry. He asked the court to acquit him on the charge of disobedience.

The Judge-Advocate now called five witnesses to prove that Sloper had definitely heard Ligonier deliver the orders to Sackville. However, none of those provided clarity, the only exception being a very junior officer, Cornet Erle, of Sloper's own regiment, although he had not been able to overhear Ligonier and Sackville, nor Sackville's orders to Sloper. On the final day of the trial, 3 April 1760, Lieutenant Colonel Johnston of the Blues was called. Whilst he asserted that Ligonier had ridden past him on his way to the 1st

19 Walpole, *Letters*, Vol.III, Letter 17 To Sir Horace Mann, March 26, 1760. <https://www.gutenberg.org/cache/epub/4773/pg4773.html> (accessed 24 February 2019).

20 Mackesy, *The Coward of Minden*, p.213.

Dragoon Guards, the right squadron of which was five squadrons away from his own regiment.

In the Judge-Advocate's final speech, he opened with a strong defence of Sloper. Any criticism of Sloper's evidence could be weighed equally against the witnesses for the defence, he asserted. It was clear that Ligonier had passed the orders on to Sackville in front of the 1st Dragoon Guards, and that Sloper was able to hear them clearly. Sloper had been uninfluenced by Ferdinand's censure of Sackville as Sloper had already aired his criticism clearly, and before Ferdinand's censure had been made public.

The Judge-Advocate then withdrew the accusation that Sackville had arrived late at his post with the cavalry. However, once Winzingerode had delivered his orders, if only Sackville had acted immediately upon them, there would have been no dispute about the precise wording of the instructions brought by Ligonier and then Fitzroy. Sloper and Granby's evidence that Winzingerode's orders were that the cavalry was to move through the trees to the left (although the Judge-Advocate conveniently omitted to mention that Granby had not actually heard the conversation between Winzingerode and Lord George) trumped the evidence given by Bisset, Hotham and Hugo.

The impediments to the cavalry's movement were the guns passing on its left and the regiment of Saxe-Gotha. The guns on the left could have been ordered to halt immediately. To the front, the Saxe-Gotha regiment could have been moved in two minutes, although the defence had maintained that that act would have taken at least five minutes. As it was, it took far too long after Ligonier's arrival for Sackville to get the Saxe-Gotha regiment cleared and to generate movement. Anyway, regardless of whether Ligonier had instructed that Sackville should move to the left, or Fitzroy's insistence that it should be to the front, Sackville had dithered indecisively for at least a quarter of an hour.

The Judge-Advocate's final point related to the pace of the advance once on the heath, which had been far too slow. Clearly, that was a matter for the court's judgement but, if it had been delayed for no obvious reason, then Sackville had breached his orders:

> If any of the orders brought by Captain Winzingerode, Captain Ligonier or Colonel Fitzroy appear not to have been obeyed, with all the expedition which under the several circumstances now before you in evidence shall appear to have been practicable; or if any blameable delay was afterwards made in the march…I submit you shall be under the disagreeable necessity of finding his Lordship guilty….In your judgement you will have regard to the degree of the offence, with respect to the proportion and motive for the delay.[21]

By this last sentence, the Judge-Advocate was setting the bar for guilt extremely low. By introducing the option of subjective opinion, the situation was no longer black or white: did Sackville obey or disobey his orders? There

21 Mackesy, *The Coward of Minden*, p.220.

was now a whole range of grey shades which made it harder for Sackville to escape some sort of negative interpretation of his actions on the day of battle.

Normally the Judge-Advocate's address would have been final. However, in the very unusual circumstances of the trial, new evidence had been heard after Sackville's last statement, and he thought he would also be allowed to provide some final comments. In fact, this had been not been formally confirmed and remained ambiguous. Sackville was permitted to make another statement, but only after more friction with Lieutenant General Cholmondeley, with whom Sackville had previously clashed in court. Sackville restricted himself to comment on the fresh evidence: while it would have been obvious if a general had received orders at the extremity of either end of the line, it would be hard to be certain of the exact spot anywhere else. Most of the witnesses had not seen or heard the orders passed, nor where they were given out. Four witnesses knew that it had happened somewhere to the front of the main body but only two, Ligonier and Sloper, thought that it was at the end of the line, to the right of the 1st Dragoon Guards. Sackville then asked the court to consider the methods of the Judge-Advocate as being more akin to those of a prosecutor than an impartial judge. He concluded that he did not stand to gain by lying, he thanked the court for its patience and put reliance on its honour, 'If I am guilty, let me be declared so: if I am not guilty, let the court shew by their sentence that they will with pleasure protect the innocent'.[22]

While the opinion of the public audience swayed, in some cases depending on who had spoken last, elements of the establishment were briefing the King that the Judge-Advocate had produced a masterly performance. However, as no soldier, the Judge-Advocate was very much an arm-chair general, for whom there was no friction, nor fog of war. Orders, no matter how ambiguous, were to be obeyed unhesitatingly until their ultimate and successful conclusion. The generals on the court, however, were soldiers well-versed in the realities of war.

The sentence would require Royal approval. Sackville could only be sentenced to death if two-thirds of the court found him guilty. The Judge-Advocate would gather the verdict, starting with the most junior member. Those who found him guilty would pass sentence, but those who found him not guilty could impose some mitigation.

To an extent, the officers of the court had little room for manoeuvre. Sackville could hardly be acquitted as this would embarrass both the King, who had dismissed Sackville, and the allied Prince, Ferdinand who had won the victory. The King had something of a track record in this: Admiral Byng had been shot after Minorca despite his court unanimously recommending mercy. Under this King, the relations with the German allies were of the greatest importance. Many in London assumed that the sentence would be death. The King claimed not to know the result but arranged for Granby to punish the witnesses for the defence by removing them from the staff

22 Quoted in Anon., *The Trial of the Right Honourable Lord George Sackville*, p.342.

and returned to their regiments.[23] In this way, Ferdinand would not have to encounter them.

Lord George Sackville was pronounced guilty, the King confirming the sentence on 16 April. However, the court was able to make its own decision on the punishment. The Judge-Advocate informed Lord George by letter, that he had been found guilty of having disobeyed Prince Ferdinand of Brunswick and that he was adjudged unfit to serve his Majesty in any military capacity whatsoever.[24]

It was the oddest punishment. Many, including Newcastle, thought it far too lenient, virtually an acquittal. It was the least the court could do to protect the King's reputation and that of Ferdinand, to whom a copy of the sentence was sent with minimum delay. However, in an age where a gentleman's honour was everything, the punishment would be hard to endure.[25]

Sackville's name was erased from the Privy Council and the Irish Privy Council in Dublin. The King was determined to maximise the impact of the sentence and ordered it to be published in Army Orders, to be written into the Order Book of every regiment in the British Army and, unheard of except at executions and floggings, to be read out on parade.

The *London Gazette* announced:

> It is his Majesty's pleasure that the above sentence be given out in public orders; that officers being convinced that neither high birth nor great employment can shelter offences of such a nature, and that, seeing they are subject to censures much worse than death to a man who had any sense of honour, they may avoid the fatal consequences arising from disobedience of orders.[26]

23 Mackesy, *The Coward of Minden*, p.223.
24 *The London Magazine, or, Gentleman's Monthly Intelligencer*, Vol XXX, 1760, pp.183-184.
25 Guy, *Oeconomy and Discipline*, p.21.
26 Mackesy, *The Coward of Minden*, p.226.

14

The Strategic Aftermath

After the victory at Minden, and because their supply lines from Paderborn had been severed, the French were forced to venture into areas where supplies could not be assured. They retreated initially to Kassel, then south and west towards Frankfurt, before falling into a passive lull for the rest of the year and were not to attempt to repeat the venture towards Hanover for the remainder of the war. The allied army advanced into Hesse, recapturing Kassel, Marburg and Münster, and recovering all the territories lost in the course of the campaign.

In central Europe Frederick was – incredibly, despite his losses at Kunersdorf and Maxen – still in the field. Ferdinand was required to send Frederick some 12,000 reinforcements to make good the latter's losses, so his own army lost its mass, and thereby some of its momentum. Both the French and the allies went into winter quarters having run out of energy. Contades was relieved of his command and replaced by Broglie.

1759 had been a remarkable year for Britain, an *Annus Mirabilis*. Although on the continent her ally Prussia struggled through 1759, having to deal simultaneously with multiple threats from Austria, Russia and Sweden and suffering some significant reverses, the allied army had seen off the threat to Hanover. The new French chief minister, the Duc de Choiseul, believed that Britain might be sufficiently distracted by a counter-blow at the homeland: if Britain could be forced to defend everywhere, France might be able to concentrate sufficient force to strike a blow across the Channel. However, the French concentration was destroyed by Boscawen who anticipated the fleet from Toulon, defeating it at Lagos. To compound French misery, Wolfe stormed the heights of Abraham outside Quebec and destroyed the French garrison in a couple of minutes of volley fire while, at sea, Hawke smashed the French Brest fleet in November in Quiberon Bay.

Walpole, as ever the observer and acerbic commentator, wrote:

> You have seen the French epigram on Madame Pompadour, and fifty vile translations of it. Here IS Mine—
>
> "O yes! here are flat-bottom boats to be sold,
> And soldiers to let-rather hungry than bold:
> Here are ministers richly deserving to swing,

> And commanders whose recompense should be a string.
> O France! still your fate you may lay at Pitt's door;
> You were saved by a Maid, and undone by a *****."[1]

In the east, French supply difficulties were certainly serious. An example might be d'Ache's failed attempt to relieve Pondicherry in August 1759. Departing from Mauritius, he was intercepted and attacked immediately. Although in possession of a significant superiority, D'Ache appears to have been daunted by the risk of defeat. Determined to protect his fleet at all costs, he limited himself to dropping some supplies at Pondicherry and then withdrew.

Turning to Pitt himself, his fortunes reversed in 1759 with a series of victories which enabled him to portray himself as the representative of Britain's fate. Breaking the stupor of reaction into which Britain had fallen in 1756, when French invasion had seemed inevitable, Pitt was insistent that Britain should maintain its course, retaining the initiative not only in Germany, but particularly in Canada.[2] Pitt's acceptance of the inevitable need for support in Germany is an indication of his ability to see the bigger picture in spite of his personal preferences.

Pitt held an unusual amount of power among the political elite. He was extremely popular with the citizens of the Britain as well. In any case, it is Pitt who proposed, along with several of his supporters, that North America be the primary objective. Though he mistrusted the Prussians, Pitt wanted to pay Frederick the Great and his army to wage the continental war with France, freeing Britain's navy and army to do battle with France on the oceans and in the colonies.

When Pitt joined the ministry, the strategy changed drastically. Pitt pushed for permanent control once an area or objective was taken. Thus, it became state policy to pressure France in all corners of the globe, not just on the Canadian frontier. As a result, the fighting was not left to frontiersmen and colonists, but the professional military was directly involved. It became clear that new expenses came with the expansion of the military's role in a global war.

Canada itself proved to be a far more resilient opponent. The new British garrison almost lost Quebec when the harsh Canadian Winter sealed it off from the sea and allowed the French army to isolate and invest it.[3] The end of winter came just in time for the British fleet to break the ice and bring much-needed relief to the beleaguered and hard-pressed garrison. British naval superiority having been restored, both at sea and on inland waterways, Britain was able to get a stranglehold, advance on Montreal and take effective control of Canada in 1760.

---

1 Walpole, *Letters*, Vol.II, Letter 335 To George Montagu, Esq. Strawberry Hill, Saturday, October 11, 1759 <https://www.gutenberg.org/cache/epub/4610/pg4610.html> (accessed 24 February 2019).

2 Black, 'Pitt the Elder', p.41.

3 Anderson, *Crucible of War*, p.392.

Britain was now able to exploit her success. Coote routed the French and their Indian allies at the Wandiwash in January 1760, de Bussy being captured and the remaining French coastal positions, with the exception of Pondicherry, being seized. Pondicherry's isolated, stubborn garrison clung on, encouraged only by the hope of relief from the sea but d'Ache never appeared, having been ordered to defend Mauritius because of a rumour that Pitt intended to capture it, a credible threat made realistic by Britain's maritime capability. Beleaguered Pondicherry was compelled to surrender through starvation, thus ending the war between Britain and France in India.[4]

In late June 1760, Broglie's Army attempted to reinvade Hesse, the Comte de Saint-Germain being ordered to leave Dortmund with his Armée du bas-Rhin to effect a junction. The Erbprinz attempted to prevent this but was surprised by a reverse at Corbach on 10 July, while the French managed to bring together the armies of Broglie and Saint-Germain. During the retreat from the engagement, the British foot provided a rearguard but was pressed so hard that the Erbprinz had to intervene personally, by leading two squadrons of the 1st and 3rd Dragoons Guards. The 1st Dragoon Guards lost 66 of the 90 men who charged.

Some six days later, the Erbprinz attempted to destroy an important French field bakery at Marburg. A robust French resistance prevented this but the 15th Light Dragoons, recently arrived from Britain, distinguished itself in a long-running brigade action at Emsdorf.

Broglie manoeuvred to block the allies from Paderborn and Lippstadt. The Erbprinz recognised that a French corps had become relatively isolated at Warburg and, seizing the opportunity, recommended that Ferdinand engage it frontally while he sought to strike at its flank. In a stiff fight on 27 July, the British cavalry redeemed its reputation from Minden, led by Granby and trotting with increasing urgency some eight kilometres to reach the battle. During the advance on a swelteringly hot day, Granby lost both his hat and his wig. His head reportedly 'shone like a beacon', thus bringing into the English language the expression 'to go bald-headed at something'. While the killed and wounded figures were not dissimilar for both sides (1,200 Allies as against 1,600 French), the French lost a further 2,000 as prisoners and 12 guns. Ferdinand effectively now had free access to Westphalia.

In 1760 the Austro-Russians planned to make a three-pronged attack on Berlin. Despite Frederick winning a victory at Liegnitz, Berlin was momentarily captured on the 9 October. Frederick won another victory at Torgau on 3 November, but heavy losses on both sides led to a temporary suspension of conflict. In Western Germany, despite several battles, the French did not manage to make any significant progress in Hanover.

The new King George III, crowned in October 1760, was no great admirer of Pitt, seeing him as arrogant and abusive, yet he permitted his continuance in office. Early in his reign, George fostered a public view of himself as 'English', having actually been born in England. He expressed

4 Baugh, *Global Seven Years War*, pp.479 and 483.

relative disinterest in governing Hanover, although a lukewarm affection for Hanover did not necessarily mean antipathy to the German war.[5]

1761 saw the various opponents totally exhausted in Europe. Frederick entrenched his army in a strong position at Bunzelwitz where the Austro-Russians did not dare to attack it. Meanwhile the French occupied Brunswick and Wolfenbüttel. On 8 July, once again the French Armies of the Upper and Lower Rhine effected a junction, this time at Soest. Together they amounted to some 100,000 men, with the hope that their strength would force Ferdinand to abandon Lippstadt. Ferdinand, with some 60,000, refused to be intimidated and held firm. At Vellinghausen on 15/16 July, Broglie and Soubise agreed to a coordinated attack, but Broglie launched his prematurely while Soubise seemed content to remain relatively uncommitted and allow Broglie to flounder. Henceforth they became bitter enemies, while Ferdinand's reputation as a dangerous opponent, even when outnumbered, was confirmed.

In America, with Canada now conquered, Great Britain turned its attention towards Dominica which fell in June.

Pitt's determination as a war leader did not transfer well to the give-and-take required in peace negotiations. In 1761 both his colleagues and the French recipients of his correspondence thought his letters undiplomatic. Even his friend Hardwicke speculated, after reading one of Pitt's drafts in cabinet on 14 August 1761, that nations might be 'writ' into perpetuating a war.[6]

Pitt's success in the Commons, his verbose, hubristic, antagonistic style, did not mark him out for success as a diplomat. He had no training or experience in diplomacy and his wariness of the Bourbons was found room for expression in his confident, intolerant manner. In fairness, he appears to have tried to moderate his forcefulness during negotiations and, had the French been more willing to compromise, there would have been a better chance of success. France, however, was enabled to continue the war because she had garnered new support in the form of Spain. The consequence of this was that, through failure of discussions with France, a fresh threat arose, that of a Spanish war. Pitt urged the Cabinet to declare war on Spain in September 1761 believing that procrastination could only damage Britain's situation. Pitt was virtually isolated and his war-weary colleagues, anxious about the expense of another war, and hopeful that Spain would not actually act against Britain, opposed him. Instead, believing that Britain had insufficient cause to attack Spain, they pushed for a formal request that Spain might provide a guarantee of her peaceful intentions. They feared that an attack on Spain would simply have a counter-productive outcome, that of forcing France and Spain into each other's arms. Pitt, however, could not agree to this and refused to accept the Cabinet decision. Thus it was over Spain rather than France that Pitt finally broke with the Cabinet in October 1761. In fact, he had been willing to settle with France if a satisfactory agreement could be reached. It might be said that Pitt had delayed too long but previous experience in the Wars of the Spanish and Austrian Successions had shown that even with

5 Arnold-Baker, *Companion to British History*, p.1009.

6 Black, 'Pitt the Elder', p.42.

lengthy bargaining, peace was elusive. Indeed, even without Pitt's pugnacious temperament, the Cabinet pacifists found the Bourbons difficult to deal with and that they could not straightforwardly agree among themselves. Pitt's reputation fell and he was castigated in the summer of 1761.[7] However, his self-belief, that only he could be trusted to protect the nation's interests had been confirmed in his own eyes.

The Earl of Bute was now a favourite of the new King, and yet rather than rely on him to negotiate an early peace, contributing to animosity between them, George allowed Pitt to continue in office and attempt, unsuccessfully, to agree peace terms. However, it was to be the imposition of Bute as Prime Minister by the King, and Bute's relationship with the Bourbons, but also Pitt's stubborn idiosyncrasies which created a policy discontinuity and ultimately tipped the balance in Pitt's departure.

Pitt's last Cabinet meeting was on 2 October 1761. When his opponents reiterated their stance that Pitt's desired pre-emptive attack on Spain would be premature and only serve to drive the Bourbons together, Pitt made his valedictory address.

On 5 January 1762, the death of the Tsarina Elizabeth saved Prussia, since her successor Tsar Peter III, an admirer of Frederick, broke his alliance with Austria, mediated a truce between Prussia and Sweden, and even supplied some 18,000 men to Frederick, his new ally. This eased the pressure on Frederick, so that he now had the luxury of being able to finish his war on the winning side and of playing Britain differently. Deprived of her Russian partner, Austria became quiescent.

In the West, the French were pushed back across the Rhine. In the Americas, the British conquered Martinique and Cuba.

Pitt resigned because he believed the policy to be wrong. He was later justified when war with Spain did indeed break out that winter, in January 1762, confirming Clausewitz's view that war has its own dynamic. What was unacceptable to Pitt's fellow Cabinet members was his arrogant approach to the business of government. At that time, with the absence of a party whipping system, government was achieved through cooperation combined with Royal direction. Pitt struggled with the concept that he might need to accede to, or at least accommodate, the views of colleagues with whom he did not agree. Pitt stood out almost as a war-monger at a time when the majority were war-weary, and there is a lesson here about internal relationships. For all his sense of honour and drive, Pitt was never easy to work alongside, whether in or out of power.[8] The war with Spain presented an opportunity, that of a combined force launched against both French and Spanish colonies in the Caribbean and Philippines. Interestingly, even an 'on the ropes' France kept an eye on the extent of British distraction and seized the opportunity to retake Newfoundland by mid-September. After capturing Manila, the British found that Spain abandoned the Philippines in order to concentrate on Portugal which had joined the war on Britain's side. The attempted Franco-Spanish conquest of Portugal was resisted by the latter, assisted by a British force.

---

7 Baugh, *Global Seven Years War*, pp.551-554.

8 Simms, *Three Victories*, pp.482-483.

Pitt's resignation, against the backdrop of the continued war, triggered an acrimonious debate over the nation's interests and objectives. By 1762 Bute insisted in severing relations with Frederick of Prussia and sought to return to a compromise with France. Paradoxically, George III was more closely aligned with the 'Patriotic' position, spurning a family custom of involvement in German matters. Pitt had advocated close relations with Prussia and, at a time of increasing British isolationism, he found himself out on a limb and an irritation to the Government.[9] On 12 May 1762 he reminded the House of Commons that previous great English and British rulers had employed intervention on the Continent:

> When I give my advice to the House I consider myself as giving advice to the crown…The Continental Plan is the only plan otherwise all Europe will be interdicted by these haughty oppressions of the House of Bourbon from receiving you whom they affect to treat as an overgrown pirate from their ports. Increase of power must be continued with increase of commerce or both will dwindle. The best the speediest issue, is to continue your full forces on the Continent this year…this will bring you a speedy, a sober and a well understood and permanent peace…I am convinced this country can raise 12, 13, 14 or even 15 million this year… The only question is whether grievous and permanent as that tax must be, it is not to be preferred to the perpetual dishonour of the nation, the aggrandizement of the enemy, the desertion of your allies, all of which tend to an inglorious and precarious peace… Think of your greatness in every part of the world…The moment you withdraw your troops there are 140,000 French to be employed in the Low Countries.[10]

Meanwhile, the war in Germany continued. On 24 June 1762, at Wilhelmstahl, Ferdinand took the initiative and, with an inferior allied force of 40,000, attacked and forced the retreat of a superior French force of 70,000. However, on 30 August, the Erbprinz was wounded in an unsuccessful action at Nauheim. Ferdinand continued to exert pressure on the French despite, yet again, being outnumbered. He sought to recapture Kassel, but both he and Soubise converged on 21 September at Amöneburg, where a stiff but even engagement was fought, principally by mutual bombardment. British involvement included three regiments of Foot Guards, along with converged grenadiers, highlanders and two regiments of horse. Ferdinand effectively halted the French advance and was able to concentrate on his siege of Kassel, which surrendered to him on 1 November.

Bute's ministry actually successfully negotiated favourable terms for Britain in 1762, retaining Canada, Cape Breton, Newfoundland, the Ohio Valley, and the lands east of the Mississippi, while being in a position to dominate India. France was obliged to renounce her claim on New France, receiving in return, two islands off Newfoundland. She was allowed to retain an unfortified Pondicherry. Belle Isle was exchanged for Minorca, Goree for Senegal. The Caribbean was effectively divided between Britain and France.

9 Simms, *Three Victories*, pp.489-493.

10 Black, 'Pitt the Elder', p.45.

Britain returned Cuba and the Philippines to Spain in return for Florida. Spain withdrew from Portugal.

Early in 1763, all belligerents made peace. The treaties of Paris and Hubertusburg made an end of the conflict which left the political map of Europe essentially unchanged, but saw Prussia remarkably survive multiple threats and allowed Britain to eliminate its most important competitor for the domination of the seas.

Yet to Pitt those terms were simply not good enough. He insisted that the ministry had failed to secure better terms and also that there was a continuing risk of a Bourbon *revanche*. However, quite how the latter could ever be fully prevented was not evident. Pitt's persistent opposition to the terms promoted his popular reputation as the protector of the national interest. Pitt was heavily critical of allowing France to retain a share of the Newfoundland fisheries, which could form the basis for a fresh Atlantic challenge. That, and retaining Guadeloupe and Martinique, might provide the means for France to recover and to become, once again, a threat to Britain's security and trade. The paradox of victory was that the price of Britain's absolute security was the complete insecurity of her enemies.[11]

The Seven Years War may have been the last gasp of old Europe, but it was certainly conducted with spirit and for important ends. The immediate outcome of the Seven Years War was Britain's high point in the eighteenth century and Pitt's supporters attributed the success to his policies, and these differed from the policies and feats of earlier governments.[12] The French were decisively defeated at sea, and in North America and India. Success in the latter two, and elsewhere was, it was claimed, due to the commitment of resources in Germany. From 1758 this had included troops on the ground and it led to wider success.

The post-war period of British domestic affairs was turbulent. The Government was close to bankruptcy and 1763 saw Bute's resignation.

At the outbreak of the Seven Years War all of the belligerents brought their economies to the brink of ruin. The war fostered major developments in global perspectives, not just the era of imperialism, but also that hegemonic powers recognised that the economy was a more powerful instrument of hegemony than territory. Significantly, the economic chaos resulting from the war had far-reaching consequences.

Britain's superior economic resources had allowed her to subsidize Prussia to the tune of £670,000 per annum along with other North German armies which fell under Prussia. The subsidy, arranged in April 1758, enabled Frederick of Prussia to continue his struggle to dominate Central Europe. Such an agreement was not a novelty for Britain, having underwritten Austria during the 1740-1748 war. However, while the arrangements of the War of the Austrian Succession were fragile, Pitt's strategy in the Seven Years War was far more durable. This protected and preserved Hanover as the rest

11 Simms, *Three Victories*, p.512.

12 Black, 'Pitt the Elder', pp.35-51.

of Europe became enmeshed in a stalemate, while Britain was able to focus on defeating France overseas.[13]

By the war's end, Britain's debt had significantly increased to £132.6 million, almost double the previous amount.[14] Britain's sources of income, including tax, were not sufficient to cover the cost of the war. The annual tax revenue increased only slowly while annual military expenditures increased rapidly. In effect, the total annual tax requirement was doubled by annual military expenditures. Therefore, the additional funds (approximately £58 million) had to be borrowed.

It was not long before prominent citizens were discussing the reasons for entering the war with France and questioning its necessity.

The rupture with Frederick was fundamentally due to a lack of common interests. This latter had been papered over by the results of diplomacy in 1756. From about 1710 onwards, Prussia had actually been preoccupied with France and Western Europe. Now, instead, Frederick had become much more enthusiastic about an alliance with Russia. When he had finally effected it by 1764, Frederick did not want that relationship to become thinned or skewed by involving Britain. Nor did he want further unnecessary conflict with the Bourbons, which would be made more likely through an alliance with the British.[15]

On the other hand, Pitt, now the Earl of Chatham, had actually wished that the Prusso-Russian realignment of 1762 might provide Britain with another opportunity, so Bute's failure to seize that opportunity, compounding his over-generous peace terms with France, was further evidence of Bute's dilatory approach to the national interest.

The Paris Peace Treaty of 1763 was one of the key factors in Britain's ranking in the eighteenth century. Britain was now the world's pre-eminent colonial power: she was dominant in Canada, North America, India and the West Indies. Anderson describes the Peace of Paris as a 'phenomenal diplomatic coup for Britain'. In contrast, his view of the Peace of Hubertusburg conducted between the Hohenzollerns, the Habsburgs and the Elector of Saxony is that, apart from changing perceptions of Prussia, 'six years of heroic expenditure and savage bloodshed had accomplished precisely nothing'.[16]

By the war's end, a fresh European balance of power had been established. French and Austrian power had declined while a strong Prussia was now very clearly a great Continental power. However, as Clausewitz wrote, 'In war the result is never final'.[17]

13 P. Kennedy, *The Rise and Fall of Great Powers* (London: Harper Collins, 1989), p.146.
14 J. Brewer, *The Sinews of Power* (Abingdon: Routledge, 1989), p.30.
15 Simms, *Three Victories*, pp.546-548.
16 Anderson, *Crucible of War*, p.506.
17 Clausewitz, *On War*, p.80.

15

Reviewing the Seven Years War and the Battle

Having followed the strategic context through to the return of peace, the aim of this chapter is to reflect on aspects of the Seven Years War and the Battle of Minden.

Reflections on the Seven Years War

Perhaps the first and most valuable lesson is to identify vital national interests, to attempt to arrange them in relative order of importance and then to set priorities. Britain and France shared general 'core' interests: maintaining or increasing their security, power and influence in Europe. More specifically Britain sought to preserve the 'Liberties of Europe', to balance power in Europe and to prevent France from having any outlet to the sea, including the 'Dutch Barrier'. She used alliances, sea power and trade as instruments, although the latter two almost became ends in themselves. The Atlanticist versus the Continental position is central to the debate of this period and shows that the dichotomy faced since William III continued through the Seven Years War. The point may be that this was not some zero-sum calculation, that Britain actually did not have a choice, and that she had to maintain both interests. Even Pitt, in spite of his earlier antipathy to the Continental option came to recognise this. Protecting Hanover was a transient wild-card necessity created by the peculiarities of Britain's royal interests. Balancing power in Europe was an act short of war, yet assuming bipolarity and opposing predominating powers – in Europe at that time probably Bourbon, almost certainly France – was of moderately high risk. Protecting the 'Liberties of Europe' implied a willingness to act, to go to war.

The roots of war frequently lie in the outcomes of previous conflicts. This was certainly the case in the Seven Years War where the War of the Austrian Succession had created simmering resentments, but also left a residue of concentration on the Low Countries in British policy.

Should Britain exert her maritime power, or should she rely on the Army, with the Navy in a defensive role?[1] Such debate was particularly concerned with whether Britain should become embroiled in Frederick the Great's affairs, which were strictly of no real relevance to Britain and which only came about after Britain was already involved in her fight with France in the colonies. Direct European intervention appeared to have little to recommend it to Britain. It was understood that tactical victories were achievable but that decisive strategic victory was impossible. France could always achieve numerical superiority on the Continent such that defeat there was almost ultimately inevitable. On the other hand, it was suggested that the justification for sending troops to Hanover was that Britain could prevent France from focusing on flexing her maritime muscle by supporting Frederick in what was effectively a military diversion. Of course, Britain was actually bound, through alliance, to assist him. Clearly there was an inconsistency. One view might have refuted the necessity to protect Frederick regardless of alliance obligations, or whether he was the Protestant Hero; even if Britain were politically obliged to support Frederick, Britain should not be held to do so in any particular way. Further, Britain had other options available than just to send land forces. Instead, and as Frederick himself actually suggested, Britain could much more strenuously attack the French along their own coast, and in the West and East Indies, if her resources and energy were not being expended in Germany. It would be preferable to employ Britain's singular strength at sea than to squander it in Germany where conclusive results would be far more elusive. Not only could a clearer decision be achieved in this war, but future conflicts could also be avoided by putting future colonial quarrels beyond the reach of possibility, for it could profoundly eliminate France as a potential maritime rival. In Britain it was generally understood that while France and Continental powers, without naval vessels, could march their armies hither and thither, Britain could remain immune. Further, having captured French colonies or wrecked her trade, France's economy had been written down to such an extent that she was unable to afford sufficient land power to terrorise Europe. This latter view was understood, and even confirmed, by some French writers. Richmond quotes from M. de Flestay who wrote in 1759 that

> [T]he English, by their sovereignty at sea, increase their own wealth and prevent France from making use of hers; the war demonstrating how with her wealth she assists the continental armies, who put it out of the power of France to use against the English the resources which might otherwise have been the case.[2]

In both the Seven Years War itself, and also with the prospect of peace, British foreign policy was concerned with strategy and with alliance politics. Britain required a stable Europe. Allying herself with an aggressive power could be counter-productive. Also, alliances wax and wane and it is

1 Richmond, *National Policy*, pp.45-47, and quoting from *Considerations of the Present German War* (London: 1760) and *A Full and Candid Answer to the Pamphlet Entitled 'Considerations of the Present German War'* (London: 1760).

2 Richmond, *National Policy*, p.311.

important to recognise both false or over-optimistic impressions of shared interests, but also when interests have started to diverge. Natural strains occur in an alliance where partners have mutually exclusive objectives or different regional priorities. Apart from habit, in such cases, it may actually be counter-productive to maintain an alliance artificially. In the Seven Years War, coordination of allied operations was tentative and both the British and the Germans had the ability to surprise each other.

It was, however, recognized that there were finite limits to the amounts of money or manpower that Britain could raise. Even Frederick recognised that Britain's purse was not bottomless.[3] In a sort of balancing act, it was necessary to retain some of the pool of labour in agricultural and manufacturing tasks in order to sustain the nation, rendering that manpower unavailable for military service.[4] Likewise, purchasing foreign mercenaries would only accumulate debts and ruin the economy. The economy featured prominently in the deliberations, along with the need to continue 'steady-state' running of necessary normal functions. Countries must maintain an appropriate balance between the teeth and the tail: between the front line and all those other logistic, commercial and support functions which sustain the martial effort, maintain the nation and pay for both. Within that equation lies an enduring issue, that of the proper balance of the employment of manpower. In the Seven Years War, the British government was well aware of this quandary.

The subjective nature of war makes it a gamble.[5] It seldom consists of a single short blow. The probability of real life replaces the extreme and absolute required by theory.[6] In the Seven Years War, and at Minden, as ever, the enemy got a 'vote', and there were unintended consequences. Even victors have setbacks and when forces clash there will some a degree of attrition somewhere. The Seven Years War highlights the danger of making assumptions about fading powers. In theory France had the weaker navy and colonial forces. Yet she showed that any power by definition has the capacity to inflict damage, even when ageing or fatally wounded.

Wars and battles seldom develop thematically towards an elegant end pre-determined by historians. Instead, as Clausewitz observed, they are fuelled by a complex brew of huge forces with the added ingredients of passion, friction, chance, ambition and inadequacy, and leadership, both for good or ill.

The French Performance

General Observations

It could be said that for too long the standard British version of the French performance during the Minden campaign has been dismissive. However,

3 D. Fraser, *Frederick the Great* (London: Allen Lane, 2000), p.447.
4 Duffy, *The Military Experience in the Age of Reason*, p.93.
5 Clausewitz, *On War*, p.85.
6 Clausewitz, *On War*, pp.79-80.

the initial French seizure of Minden by Fischer's intrepid raiders was inspired, showing considerable élan and initiative.

Similarly, the staffwork and preparation involved in getting Broglie's corps across the Weser at the same time as launching a series of bridges across the Bastau and getting Contades' army across it in the dark are to be admired.

Conventional wisdom would have it that in the horse and musket era, the infantry would deploy in the centre with artillery and cavalry on the wings. However, Minden is not the only battle of the period in which the French put their cavalry in a relatively central position. At the Battle of Bergen in April 1759, Broglie's right wing infantry was anchored in the town, while his cavalry was deployed in flat ground towards his centre. Broglie successfully resisted Ferdinand's attempts to take the town. This suggests that French commanders studied the ground and were prepared to adjust their deployments to put their troops where they were best suited to exploit their strengths.

The Comte de Lusace reflected on the campaign:

> I do not enter debate on what caused the loss of the battle. I stick to the facts, as I have seen them in the part where I have fought, and as officers exempt of any partisanship, servants of the state, and friends of truth have told me, to record them in the places where they were…
>
> I do not know exactly how long the siege of Lippstadt would have lasted, but I know that with the oat magazines which we had in Minden, the ovens established there, the flour transported there, and the foraging which we could have done on the right of the Weser, and even if the Erbprinz of Brunswick would have interrupted our communication with Herworden [Herford] which could have lasted beyond the end of the expedition of M. d'Armentières on Lippstadt, we could easily have endured this for eight days, and it is unlikely that Lippstadt would have held longer.
>
> Nor do I examine if it would not have been better (assuming that the concern about the corps of the Erbprinz and our communications was the reason which determined the Maréchal to give battle) to immediately form a corps decidedly superior to the forces of the Erbprinz's march towards Cooweldt, to drive him back with losses on the right of Prince Ferdinand, and dissuade him from harassing our convoys.
>
> Finally, I do not enter into the discussion of the possibility, or impossibility, of success of the attack which the Duc de Broglie was charged with making on the entrenchments of Todenhausen and the left of the camp of M. de Wangenheim. On this I only have difficulty to conceive that one could attribute to a General who has won two battles, and who is generally renowned as too virtuous a citizen to sacrifice national glory, the baseness of a particular interest, that one can refuse to believe that he sanely judged what he had seen with his own eyes, and I positively know that the various reports which the Duc de Broglie had made, and made himself to the Maréchal, were done only after he had personally reconnoitred from the curtain, on the higher ground on which he established himself with his cannon, the entrenchments of Todenhausen, and the camp of M. de Wangenheim.
>
> I consider the battle only in the part where it really occurred, that is to say, the ground where the troops charged, fought in the open and, in a word, manoeuvred.

I leave aside the cannonade which was exchanged between the Duc de Broglie and Wangenheim, who reciprocally contained themselves, and I examine only what I think should have been done before the engagement, and then during the engagement, to achieve the success which we were seeking, and avoid the misfortune which has happened to us.

I believe we only have ourselves to blame for letting the wood extending across our front mask all the manoeuvres which would please Prince Ferdinand to have executed from the right to his left, while by making ourselves master of the edge of this wood on the side of the enemy, and by occupying instead of the village of Hahlen the one of Harthum, where the cannon established at the same place where the enemy placed his own against our left, would have sufficiently defended ourselves against the attempts that the enemy would have wanted to make on our left flank on the side of Rothenussen. By this I mean we would have clearly seen the dispositions of the enemy, and we could have made our own under the cover of the wood, to oppose him at the places where we would see fit, as he has been able to do himself by using the very same wood against our centre of cavalry, devoid of infantry.

The only objection that I can make to myself about the necessity of occupying the outer edge of this wood, which masked our front, is that the terrain beyond it might not have been as favourable to to our cavalry, but in the supposition that according to the disposition of the Maréchal de Contades, the Duc de Broglie had pushed M. de Wangenheim back on the left of Prince Ferdinand, should not this same cavalry have debouched towards Stemmer to follow the success of the Duc de Broglie? While on the heath, where it was posted with its nose against the wood, it could be useful only in the event of the retreat of M. de Wangenheim towards Hahlen, which could hardly be imagined, or in the case of the enemy debouching from the wood against our centre, which is what happened, but which we certainly had not predicted.

Another advantage we would have gained by first making ourselves master of this wood which was between the enemy and us is that this covered position would have moved the brigades Picardie and Belsunce under the command of the Chevalier de Nicolaï, on the hedges of the village of Codenhausen, where they would had distracted the attention of M. de Wangenheim, and eased the difficulty which prevented the Duc de Broglie from attacking on the main effort. Considering the passage of the cavalry through this wood, its ease was demonstrated by what the enemy cavalry was able to execute against the Brigades of Rouergue and Touraine. In short, the original battle plan had been to push M. de Wangenheim back onto Prince Ferdinand, while cutting off, if possible, the enemy from the Weser, and it seems that if we had made ourselves masters of the wood, as I have just explained, we could actually have driven Prince Ferdinand onto M. de Wangenheim, while dislocating him from the corps that the Erbprinz of Brunswick had under his command.[7]

7 Archives Départementales de l'Aube, Xavier, Prince, Archives de la guerre de Sept ans et correspondance familiale: le fonds du prince Xavier de Saxe, EE81 and EE82. Translated by Richard Couture.

The great Franco-Swiss military thinker, Henri Antoine Baron de Jomini, assessed the French defeat some 60 years later:

> Tempelhof [G.F. von Tempelhof, who wrote *Geschichte des Sieben-Jahrigen Krieges*] thinks that this battle is one on the most remarkable and of the most interesting of the art. The dispositions which preceded the action, and those which took place during the combat itself deserve, according to him, to be recorded for posterity. Duke Ferdinand shows himself as an accomplished general there, who understands the profoundest complexities of the art of war. His manoeuvres to bring the enemy to a point of his own choosing are unquestionably masterpieces; nothing proves more the solidity of his maxims, than the daring concept of weakening himself in order to be stronger. The subdivision of his army (already outnumbered) into several corps; that of the Erbprinz in the vicinity of Gohfeld; the one of General Gilsa at Lübbecke; and the one of von Wangenheim near Tonhausen, had in fact all the appearances of a fault, and presented the French generals so many opportunities that they simply could not resist engaging them.
>
> One ought not to blame the Maréchal de Contades for having fought the battle, but rather for not having known the character and the talents of his adversary, and not guessing that there was a hidden reason behind the Duke's faulty dispositions. We have already said, and one simply cannot repeat it often enough, the first virtue of a General is to know well the passions, the talents and the maxims of his opponent, if he wants to penetrate his most secret designs and grasp the real goal of his operations, and of his movements.
>
> The order of battle of the French Army was basically defective. It was doubtless consecrated by usage to place the cavalry in the plain, and the infantry on broken ground; but this usage must be subordinated to the important maxim of never breaking a line of infantry, and certainly of not breaking it up with a cavalry corps, which has no solidity *per se*. The cavalry, in an attack, must be on the two wings, on only one wing, or behind the infantry: in these different situations it must restrict itself to completing what the infantry has started, that is to break a shaken troop already in disorder, or to charge to gain time and re-establish the situation. If the French Generals had remembered the battle of Höchstädt or of Blenheim, they would not have committed the same fault which had lost those battles for their predecessors.
>
> The plan to overwhelm von Wangenheim's Corps was sound, but the means used were pitiful. It is not with a cannonade that one forces a general to abandon his post, especially when he knows the effect. Cannonades are akin to paying compliments, to which both parties respond, and they are almost all as insignificant as the one of Minden. One is always forced to use infantry when it comes to the question of striking a decisive blow.
>
> It necessarily follows that the latter must get involved with all possible promptness, charging the enemy as soon as it is formed, not losing time with musketry fire: why should it loiter for two to three hours, on parade, to serve as a target for the enemy artillery?
>
> It has been proven by experience that artillery fire is always less important in a battle than one thinks. However, a distinction must be made between the physical and moral effects. It is common practice to precede a battle with a lively cannonade, with the intention of destroying enemy artillery, and to reduce the

danger to advancing infantry, but this is highly erroneous. Tempelhof cites several examples where batteries of 20 to 30 pieces have bombarded his own over several hours, without destroying pieces, nor men, nor horses, and without having the infantry line harmed in any manner. One might try to justify common practice with arguments about the construction of artillery pieces, and from the way one fires in combat, but experience must suffice, and it is certain that if the hundredth part of cannonballs directed against batteries in the combats of the last war, had hit a cannon, there would not have remained a single piece of artillery of any party.

The outcome of the battle depended on the success of the attack on von Wangenheim's Corps; the Maréchal de Contades knew this only too well, and he should have set his line to be enabled to take such a direction as to vigorously support the Duc de Broglie's Division, holding his left refused, and thus gradually committing his army as he observed the progress of the main attack. This disposition of the Maréchal would also have given him the advantage of marching more easily: he only had to march by line and by the right.

Thus, the most essential faults were:

a. The slowness of the Duc de Broglie. Von Wangenheim's Corps had, in fact, been surprised, but Broglie's poor pace gave von Wangenheim time to form himself in front of the village;
b. The length of time it took to deploy the columns, which lasted from sunrise till after 7:00a.m., consequently a full four hours, after which the infantry was still not in order.

On the other hand, the conduct of Duke Ferdinand, the sagacity of his manoeuvres, and the energy with which he decided to attack the French cavalry with his infantry, deserve the greatest praise.

We have seen the long instructions of the Maréchal de Contades to his generals, explaining to them all the detail of the composition, march and formation of the columns. We have seen these columns, despite the fact that they had been nine in number, and composed of two brigades or of three at the most, took four hours to form their line which, even then, was not completed; some being too close, others leaving too considerable intervals: nevertheless, the distances are much easier to respect when they are not too extended.

How would Guibert [Jacques Antoine Hippolyte, Comte de Guibert, who wrote *Défense du Système de Guerre Moderne* (Neuchâtel, 1779) in defence of Frederick the Great's tactics] have managed it, with his four columns of five to six brigades, having to estimate the space required visually?

It seems that this judicious author had used his system to assess the conduct of Duke Ferdinand who, indeed, managed to form his eight columns. But where does one find, in military annals, a second battle of Minden, an army which starts out with eight routes to reach where it will form a frontage, and an enemy who places itself exactly at the débouché of these marches. It would require, for this, a combination of circumstances which would never be repeated.

A battlefield similar to the one of Minden would be absolutely necessary, constrained between the marsh and the Weser, to allow the Duke to combine his deployment in advance and use such a system; which would never happen to him twice.

The affair of Minden offers two additional events which are worth some observations: the useless cannonade of the Duc de Broglie, which was contrary to the Maréchal's instructions, and on the other side, Lord Sackville's disobedience. These two incidents give rise to many interesting questions which only governments can resolve.[8]

Contades

Contades reflected on his plan to Belle-Isle after the battle:

> I have received this morning, before leaving Lutternberge [Lutterberg], the letter that you honoured me by writing on the 7th, after having received the courier who informed you of the unfortunate events of the 1st. I think as you do, and can hardly begin to believe that the King's Army has been beaten; I feel all the misfortune and am pierced by the most intense pain, which I continue to bear in order that the service of the King does not suffer from it. The plan that I made to attack Prince Ferdinand, and that I had the honour to send you, answers to an extent all the questions which you asked me about what happened on the 1st. I will, however, follow the order of your letter and answer them.
>
> I had formulated the plan to attack the enemy, certain as I was, that Prince Ferdinand had weakened himself by 12,000 or 15,000 men. All of the army, put into action on the night of the 31st to the 1st, was in battle at daybreak. My order was that the attack would begin half an hour before the day; that the signal would be given by the attack of the right, and that, the first shots having been fired by this right, the centre and the left would march forward to attack. According to the intelligence that I had gathered of the enemy dispositions, and which the Duc de Broglie, charged with the attack of the right, had himself taken the day before, I had made my dispositions in consequence. On the actual day of the action, the Duc de Broglie did not judge that it was possible to attack, being supported by the 16 battalions under the command of the Chevalier de Nicolaï, who was to his left and to which I added a further two infantry brigades of the second line and one cavalry brigade.
>
> I have related to you what had happened: it transpired that the enemy was not attacked on his left, while I was attacked on mine and at the same time in the centre; where I was broken through, having put my main forces to the right; it is true that the enemy had only eight or ten battalions, the greatest part English, in this part, who were in battle [line] and not in column. Despite being harassed by our cannon from the right and left, they determined themselves to attack our line of cavalry, whose totality was gathered in the centre in two lines, composed of 61 squadrons. The first line, seeing this infantry, determined to attack it across a mown [*rasé*] heath, and charged it at full speed; there were regiments which entered into the infantry line, who, without breaking, made a prodigious fire. Our cavalry fell back as fast as it had charged; the second line made the same manoeuvre with as little success; the Gendarmerie and the Carabiniers had the same fate. There were afterwards a few squadrons which rallied and who made new charges, equally unsuccessful. As I have already had the honour to explain,

8 Baron de Jomini, *Traité des Grandes Opérations Militaires*, 2nd ed. (Paris: Magimel, 1811), Vol. 3, pp.47-56. Translated by R. Couture.

eight or ten battalions, on a short heath, defeated 61 French squadrons: if I had not seen it, I would not believe it!

The Grenadiers de France have lost a lot of cannon: I had grouped them with the reserve of M. Broglie to attack the enemy left; the Touraine and Rouergue brigades supported their left to the right of our cavalry. At the moment when M. de Beaupréau made them march forward to support a battery which he wanted to establish to take the English infantry in flank, these two brigades were attacked by the enemy cavalry and defeated. The du Roi Cavalry Brigade, which I had allocated to support them, pushed back the enemy cavalry and freed a lot of prisoners who had been taken, including MM. De Beaupréau and de Séchelles.

The Picardie Brigade was at the right of the first line, having to its right the Grenadiers de France; the Belsunce one at the left of Picardie, then Touraine and Rouergue. They were the four brigades which were to attack the enemy left in conjunction with the Duc de Broglie; Champagne, le Roi, Condé and Aquitaine were on the left, resting their right on the cavalry. The two Brigades of Condé and Aquitaine have been charged and lost much. The Auvergne and Anhalt Brigades were in the second line behind Picardie and Belsunce. The Navarre Brigade supported a battery that we had on the road crossing the marsh, and this battery had the enemy right flank in sight. It was not possible for me to continue to hold the position that I had at Minden before the action, even though the greatest part of the infantry had not fought, the 61 squadrons being in no condition to render any service and being necessary for this position. The enemy followed it with some cannon and forced it to retire, separated my right from my left and obliged me to opt for retreat.

M. d'Armentières, being at Lippstadt, was too far away from the little Bega (?) river to trouble the Erbprinz, and I had no bridges on this river, because the officer who was in charge of heavy baggage had burned them. I would have had difficulty crossing this river, finding a corps of 15,000 men in front of me and a victorious army behind.[9]

Belle-Isle responded:

It is not without reason, M. le Maréchal, that I brought today to the Council the two letters of the 2nd and 3rd with which you have honoured me; because, even though the King had read them, even before me, on the day when your courier arrived, he has also read your account from one end to the other; but he had not read the order which you had provided the day before, containing your dispositions: they are the complete proof of the truth of your account; because, with the people with whom you are dealing, one must perpetually be on one's guard, the countless supporters that M. Broglie amasses by all kind of writings and a continual effort to spread them would not fail to say that one can put whatever one wants in the report made after the fact; but they cannot assert the same thing against the order that you had given the day before to all your general officers, containing the general disposition for the attack of the army, in which order it is expressly and very clearly stated everything

9 Pajol, *Les Guerres sous Louis XV*, Vol.4, pp.416-418; letter of M. Contades to the Maréchal de Belle-Isle on his plan for the battle (from Kassel on 11 August 1). Translated by R. Couture.

that M. Broglie must do, and, notably that the attack he was to make must be aggressive and fast. Therefore, it is absolutely certain that he had very precise orders to attack promptly, and that he failed to do so. You will see by the letter which he has sent to me by courier, which he dispatched to me from Oldendorf on the 3rd, the way in which he describes the affair. I expressly send you the very exact copy, in which I have underlined the excerpt which I related to you in my preceding letter which I believe, however, to have forgotten to put in with the bundle. I have been extremely surprised, and I am not the only one, that you have allowed M. Broglie to send a courier here; the King himself, in full council, has said that it was against regulations of having the General alone who should send couriers, the more so because this courier has brought several other letters which are certainly much different from those he wrote to me; copies of these letters have been made, which are now spread among the houses of Paris and Versailles, and they assert that it was M. Broglie who saved, who covered and facilitated the retreat of the army, and that he provided the rearguard. This is common knowledge in coffeehouses; there have even been placards made, and as all this is done without the knowledge of the authors, who are nonetheless not unknown, but who cannot be proven, it results in a popular clamour against us. I am not spared, and one says there that the prejudice that I keep against M. Broglie, because of what happened in Bohemia and Prague, is the reason I prevented him from becoming Maréchal de France and from commanding the army; and from there one continues in a manner you may imagine most insolent.

All this has thus reached such a point that I considered that I must speak of this in particular with the Lord Dauphin, because the Comte de Broglie writes directly to Madame the Dauphine. This Princess, otherwise full of the most respectable qualities, believes herself obliged to him because he has been able to persuade her that he had made wonders at Dresden in the service of her father. The King believes everything he reports on his brother [the Duc de Broglie]; she acts accordingly with the Dauphin, in very good faith but without seeing the wrongdoings that result from this by authorizing and accrediting a cabal that she does not know, because she would certainly otherwise not do it.

Therefore, I have read your letters to the Council, the report and the order of the day before, which contains the dispositions that the King had not read. I had the orders of 31st July read to the Lord Dauphin in particular, and to the Maréchal d'Estrées, to M. de Soubise and to M. de Choiseul; your plans received a general approval, and the Maréchal d'Estrées said, with the frankness that you know of him, that he would have been greatly honoured to have made similar dispositions. I will not reproduce here the speech that I made to the King after this reading; I spoke a good half hour with all the force, the unction and the tenderness, I dare use this term, that I have for the King. I think that I have not omitted anything and I can tell you that I have touched the entire Council, whose members embraced me when we left.

I have implored the King to decide that I would not be the judge of a question where the public could be [???] of having two Maréchaux de France in the Council. It was completely natural to charge the Maréchal d'Estrées, who is the senior, to see all this by himself; that it was difficult at Versailles to go deeper into the conduct and the intrigues concerning the main fact, that it weighed entirely against M. Broglie, who had been ordered to attack and had done nothing, resulting in the loss of the battle.

The subject on which I have been most insistent is the impossibility that anyone could nowadays command an army yet tolerate gossip, writings, intrigues and cabals; that the General should be the absolute master of all those subordinate to him in his Army, but also that he should be assured of the entire confidence of the King and of the support of all his authority. It is on this subject where I dare say that I have not omitted anything and where I made an impression.

The Maréchal d'Estrées took up this topic, after me, on cabals and intrigues, of which he too has been a victim, and M. de Soubise, who is perhaps the one man in the Kingdom who has the most to complain about regarding M. Broglie, as you can easily figure out, did not contradict him; but as it would not be appropriate in any manner, particularly where the dignity of the Generalate is concerned, it appears that the King could appoint a member of his Council as Maréchal de France, to go and investigate the reasons the Duc de Broglie gives for not attacking as if judging a trial and, there is a second motive, which is equally true and in a certain way necessary, which is to discuss with you the plan for the rest of the campaign and the subsequent locations of our troops in their next winter-quarters. This equally important and urgent subject requires thorough discussion, the more so as we must yet build the sea-borne project, which still exists, and which would weaken your Army by at least 24 battalions, when you have ended the campaign.

The plan that you had submitted for winter-quarters is unlikely to remain unchanged, unless through a successful second battle which would repair the damage made to affairs of state the loss of the one of the 1st August. Therefore, it is equally natural and necessary that a man of the trade, instructed in the secrets of the state and of the King's will, take to the field to discuss the matter with you. If I could have left the huge task, and the minor details, of which I am charged for three weeks, I would have willingly taken this commission on myself; but you can feel that, notwithstanding this decisive obstacle, the opinion of MM. Broglie [that is, both the Duc and the Comte] would have created among the public about my attitude towards them is an additional motive for not taking charge of it personally; but the Maréchal d'Estrées, who, in the public eye would be above suspicion, will not consequently give any pretext. Therefore, it will be said, as it is in fact, that the King sends the Maréchal d'Estrées to discuss with you and support you in the planning of operations for all the rest of the campaign, which would be too long and almost impossible to do in writing. This will satisfy the courts of Vienna and of Russia and will produce, I believe, a very great good, in that he will have instructions to relate to the whole army the esteem and the confidence that the King has in you, and he will also be able to advise better than anybody else against the intrigues and cabals of the writers. I estimate that he will remain at most seven or eight days with you, after which he will return here to report to the King on the state of the Army and on what you will have agreed together.

Here is, Sir Maréchal, what I have been very pleased to inform you in advance, and I beg you to keep this for yourself, until I inform you, by the first courier that I will dispatch, the stance that the King has taken, which you could then announce as you see fit.

I believe, Sir Maréchal, that I could not render a greater service to the King, to you and to me, than by behaving as I have done and by taking the position which

> I have tried to summarize for you: firstly, for the King, as he must be the master in all his Kingdom, but mainly of his Armies and of his military staff, and that must have the justifiable confidence to order or criticize his forces as he sees fit; secondly, for you Sir Maréchal, because the esteem and the confidence that the King has in your person will be expressed with more authenticity, notwithstanding the misfortune that you have just experienced; that your authority will be more respected, and that the Duc de Broglie will know the uselessness of his intrigues and will be, at least, more circumspect, otherwise, one would crack down on him. But as it does not show outside, it will be easier for him to behave with the respect and subordination which he owes you, and it is of your wisdom, of your prudence and of your love for the King and the good of the state, to ignore outwardly all that I have just told you and to really act as if it did not exist [*si cela n'était pas*]; thirdly, for me, because I have shown the crux of my soul by not demanding an inquiry against M. Broglie and the punishment which would have to follow. He is a good soldier; there are not many to choose from; the King needs him; but he must at the same time be kept in his place, until one could send him off alone. I even have to resist any idea that he might have remained inactive, on the 1st of August, to make your attack fail; such an act would be too black and too criminal, and I cannot believe him capable of it. Anyway, I must stay silent on this subject, and any time the King would employ him in particular, I will do my best [*je me mettrai par dessus la tête*] to help him with all my means and all my forces to make him succeed, because I only want the good, and, after the misfortunes that I have experienced [his son had been mortally wounded at the Battle of Krefeld in 1758], I have devoted myself to the King and to his affairs without any other particular view, whatever they might be. I dare to flatter myself that the King is persuaded of it, and you too.[10]

Broglie

Frederick II had a view on Broglie's performance, overhead and reported by a Monsieur d'Alembert who, 'has heard the King of Prussia saying that, at the battle of Minden, if M. Broglie had attacked the enemy and supported M. Contades, Prince Ferdinand would have been beaten. Broglie having had somebody ask of M. d'Alembert if it were true that he had heard this said by the King of Prussia, he had answered, yes.'[11]

Broglie reported to Belle-Isle on 5 August:

> I have not had the honour to write to you, Sir Maréchal, on the day of the first of this month, and I had not even considered to do so, believing that it is solely for the General to report to the Minister of His Majesty what happens in the Army. However, the Maréchal de Contades has had the honour of informing me this morning that he had reported this affair regarding me, and has thus placed me in a situation with the indispensable obligation to inform you of how I conducted myself.

---

10 Pajol, *Les Guerres sous Louis XV*, Vol.4, pp.420-424 Letter of the Maréchal de Belle-Isle to the Maréchal de Contades discussing the battle (from Versailles on 12 August). Translated by R. Couture.

11 Pajol, *Les Guerres sous Louis XV*, Vol.4, p.407. Translated by R. Couture.

You have been able to see, from the instructions which M. Contades had made the day before and to be followed during the battle, that I was entrusted with 22 battalions and 18 cavalry squadrons to attack the corps of M. de Wangenheim, which one estimated to equate to 10,000 to 12,000 men, and who had an entrenchment in front of his left, and that this attack should begin the affair. When the Maréchal read these instructions on the eve of the action in front of all General officers, I stated that I could start this attack only when the corps of M.de Nicolay, who was on my left, could march as far north as me on the village of Todtenhausen to cover my left flank, to prevent the enemy cavalry emerging from the gap which is near this village, and to attack what would be there. This is a fact to which the Prince de Condé and the General officers who were with the Maréchal can be witnesses. The Chevalier de Nicolay came to my billet when we left the Maréchal; I repeated the same thing to him, and we agreed.

To meet the Maréchal's intent, I made my reserve leave its camp at the prescribed hour. As we emerged from the town, the Grenadiers de France and Royaux took the lead. These troops arrived first, despite starting from much farther away, and they were in position before daybreak. I took advantage of a rather large ravine to place the infantry there, so that it was not visible to the enemy who, at daybreak, deployed his patrols and sentinels on a small ridge where he had sited them for several days.

I waited some time for news from M. de Nicolay. I approached the location where I thought he could be and found him near a house which we had christened the 'Red House'; M. de Saint-Germain joined him there. I explained my orders to them, telling them that I could not attack unless he did the same against the hedges of the village of Todtenhausen, and that I would march forward simultaneously and would attack the entrenchment which was at the head of the farmstead of Todtenhausen. He informed me that he could not do this, while his left flank was not covered by some cavalry, and that he would arrange this, effectively putting the brigades of Picardie and Belsunce on the move. I ordered M. de Saint-Auban, who commanded the artillery which was under my orders, to take position on the ridge where the enemy patrols were, and where it would find itself advantageously situated to defeat the redoubt to their left. The artillery marched there. The two lines of my infantry, each composed of nine battalions, also advanced to support it, and I ordered a few picquets to charge the sentinels and patrols. I went forward and, as I arrived there, I discovered the enemy in two battle lines with one in front of the hedges joining the village of Todtenhausen to the farmstead of Todtenhausen, and the other being behind the hedges. The first line was marching forward quite rapidly when I saw it; it had on its right a cavalry column which I could not see the rear of and which was building up to a gallop; their front was much wider than mine, and they were coming on aggressively.

This caused me come back promptly to my cavalry, to form it into two lines to my left, in order to be able to receive the enemy which I thought would charge me in the flank. The guns then started to fire on the redoubt and on the front of the enemy line, and they responded with a very lively, and much superior, fire. Shortly afterwards, the Brigades of Picardie and Belsunce came up as far as I was. I informed the Chevalier de Nicolay of the disposition of the enemy which seemed to me, as well as to the Chevalier Du Muy who was with me, to be in such force and in such a superior position to prevent me from attacking them successfully on my own. The Chevalier Du Muy will not refuse to certify the truth of what I have just said.

M. de Roquémont, an officer of the General Staff, then arrived on behalf of the Maréchal to ask me when I would attack. I pointed out the enemy positions and charged him to report to the Maréchal, to whom I had already sent M. de Kéralier, aide-major general, to inform him of this, to receive his orders and to inform me of what plan he had to support the left flank of M. de Nicolay without any direct order. And I begged M. de Roquémont to tell the Maréchal that, as soon as M. de Nicolay could march on the hedges of Todtenhausen, I would attack the redoubt and the lines which were to my front. I made him note that my right, being extremely close to this redoubt, and much closer than the infantry of M. de Nicolay was to Todtenhausen, that he (*Nicolay*) would have to start marching before me in order to arrive simultaneously on our objectives. He answered that he would report verbatim what I had just said to M. de Nicolay to then be able to carry his answer to the Maréchal. However, as the Chevalier de Nicolay had many troops under command, he was unable to pick him out so returned to tell me. I then decided to go find the Maréchal myself with M. de Roquémont and left at the gallop with him. I was joined on my way by M. de Nicolay. We searched for the Maréchal without success for some 15 minutes, and, not finding him, decided to return to our Divisions and to jointly attack the enemy left, and we departed. We were recalled, I believe, by M. de Roquémont who told us that the Maréchal was close by and pointed him out on the heath, where we joined him. I described to him what I had seen, to which I added that he had been able to see by the letter from M. de Rozen, a Colonel detached with 200 Horse to our outpost on the right bank of the Weser, which I had passed to him the day before, that towards evening he (*Rozen*) had observed the camp of M. de Wangenheim considerably reinforced. I asked the Maréchal for his orders, and assured him that within six minutes of my return to the right, the Grenadiers de France would have commenced its assault on the redoubt.

Just as the Maréchal was about to issue me my orders, he remarked that the enemy which had just begin a bombardment on the left, had started to debouch onto the heath and, to cap it all, the red infantry was advancing excessively fast and forming. The Comte de Noailles told him that this attack looked serious, and perhaps he ought first to see if it was successful before thinking about the other. Almost simultaneously, he saw the cavalry of the left go to charge this infantry, penetrating it, and then being repulsed. He then told me to concentrate only on containing the enemy opposite me until he saw how this would turn out, and, in the event of the affair going wrong, to enable the retreat of the army to the best of my ability.

I returned to my Division. I could see that the various attacks had been unsuccessful; and, when the Picardie and Belsunce Brigades began to retire, and having received the Maréchal's order through two different aides-de-camp to do the same, the entire reserve retired in two lines, protecting the retreat of Picardie and Belsunce. The enemy then debouched in six columns and climbed the curtain wall (*rideau*) from which they bombarded the reserve with great intensity and with three heavy pieces up as far as the hedges of Minden. It stopped twenty times between the battlefield and that point, moving along the hedges only once the Army had recrossed back over the stream. Then, seeing that the troops were useless in this position and that they would be heavily mauled by the cannonade of the enemy who was beginning to make them suffer, I had them withdraw back into the town and had a few pieces of heavy artillery directed on a cavalier to dissuade the enemy from approaching. I was then summoned by the Maréchal. I joined him on a knoll between the gorge of the Weser and Minden. There he informed me that the Duc de Brissac had been attacked and pushed back by the Erbprinz, with 12,000 men, a few hours ago, near Konfeld [Gohfeld], and he told me that I must march there immediately, through the gorge of the Weser, to try to open the passage for us to retire on Herford. M.de Montchenu and the aide-de-camp of M. de Brissac, who had just arrived assured us that the Erbprinz with his Corps was beyond the Bega [?], on which there was now only the bridge, the one at Rehme being destroyed.

I took the liberty of representing to the Maréchal that, if the Erbprinz was with a corps of 12,000 men behind the Bega, it would be impossible to force him because there were only the two bridges of Rehme and Konfeld [Gohfeld?] over which we could cross and that, one being destroyed and the other guarded, one ought not to flatter oneself that one could succeed. I begged him to consider that if the entire Army, hindered by a prodigious number of carriages and in a great disorder, entered into the gorge where it would certainly be followed by the enemy army which continued to cannonade it, the attack on Konfeld would fail, and the entire army would be destroyed with no survivors. He agreed about the risks of this plan and honoured me by asking me if I could suggest alternative options. I answered him that the situation in which we found ourselves was challenging and that all options presented risks, but that it seemed to me that there would be much less inconvenience recrossing to the opposite side of the Weser. That there were three bridges and some fords which the cavalry could use, while the infantry and the heavier baggage used the bridges. Once we reached the Hameln valley, which is rather narrow, we could block the enemy with infantry alone and guarantee a successful retreat. The Maréchal canvassed opinions, sounding out all of those General officers present, I think, the Prince de Condé, d'Anlesy, the Duc de Fitzjames, the Comte de Noailles, du Mesnil, de Vogüé, the Duc de Laval, de Saint-Chamans, de Castries and de Monteynard, and a few others whose names I don't recall. With the exception of M. de Castries and M. de Monteynard, all of the others agreed that we should recross the Weser, and the Maréchal ordered it. I am not unconscious of drawing attention to oneself by offering advice in challenging situations where all of the options are risky; but I believe in offering a truthful opinion, regardless of the consequences for me. The Maréchal has once again today publicly agreed that, with the report then available to us that the Erbprinz was at Konfeld with 12,000 men, and the army of Prince Ferdinand within short cannon range, at that stage bombarding and looking as it was about to march against us, there was no other option than to take this plan.

This is, Sir Maréchal, the accurate account of my conduct. I am convinced that in the report the Maréchal de Contades has made to you of the action of the first of this month, he did not seek to blame me for the reasons which led me to alter the attack and to request orders from him regarding the situational changes from those determined the day before, and that he simply told you that it [the attack] had not been done. I am even persuaded that I have no need for self-justification towards him; but, as I hear that there are others who approach him who, in all likelihood without his participation, are commenting on this, I felt that I had to clarify the situation. The Maréchal de Contades has seen this letter, and I begged him to allow that I would have the honour to send it to you through a courier so that it surely and promptly reaches you, and that you could inform the King of the truth.

I cannot sufficiently praise the resolve that all of the troops which were with me, particularly the Grenadiers de France, displayed during the liveliest cannonade that I have ever experienced in my life. Despite being placed out of direct sight of the enemy and being covered by the curtain, they suffered heavily from the cannon directed at our batteries which they were there to support, being well within range of both the redoubt and the enemy line. They lost there two Colonels, who deserve our sympathy. The Piémont and Waldner Brigades also suffered heavily.

I have the honour to send you attached, Sir Maréchal, the copy of a letter which I wrote on the second of this month to the Maréchal de Contades, by which you will see that I envisage that the best option to take was to recross the Weser above Hameln to get closer and to protect Paderborn. You will also see from it the grounds on which I based this advice. I have the honour to inform you of it only to show that I do not neglect any means to assist the Maréchal de Contades and to support him in such a critical situation as the one in which we now find ourselves.

I have the honour to be, etc.[12]

Belle-Isle replied to Broglie from Versailles on 12 August:

The Maréchal de Contades has sent me a copy of the orders that he issued the day before at his Headquarters, containing the complete plan, very precise and very instructive, for the General officers who commanded the various Divisions and who should lead the columns. I see in it that everything was very clear and that, as you agree, you were entrusted with the first and main attack, which required to be executed most promptly and most rapidly for the reasons explained within. I see from the account which the Maréchal de Contades has sent me, for your part, everything was limited to a very lively cannonade which has lasted around three hours; and, from his letter of the 2nd that, on the first representation that you made to him that the enemy seemed much stronger than had been believed the day before, he had ordered M. de Nicolaï to act in concert and even to join you for this attack, which he considered to be decisive, and that, for even greater insurance of success, he had grouped two additional Brigades from the second line to these reinforcements, and that finally that he ordered you to attack, but that rather than do this you came to look for him, which had already consumed much time before reaching him. He refrains from making any form of complaint but sticks to a simple description of facts. I must believe what the General of the King's Army reports, whose account accompanied by the orders issued the previous day, is an authentic and public item. You do not deny these capital facts in your letter. You are so highly experienced [éclairé] in war that one has to doubt your reasons; I can thus only be afflicted.

12 Broglie and Vernier (eds.), *Correspondance inédite*, Vol.I, pp.36-48 Letter of the Duc de Broglie to the Maréchal de Belle-Isle on 5 August. Translated by R. Couture.

The intervening text is not present in Pajol's work but it may be assumed that he comments on Broglie's letter which did not follow the official 'route', as can be seen from the next paragraph:

> Your letter has been read there from one end to the other (on the King's advice); it would have been preferable for it to come via the official channel of the General of the Army. The arrival of your courier caused quite a stir, which drew attention to it. This would have been avoidable if it had reached me in the normal way. I must repeat that the Maréchal de Contades has not made any sort of complaint, and I note with approval, from his daily communications, that he has continued to select you in preference for command of the vanguard or rearguard, whichever is the most interesting, believing that he could not entrust it to safer hands.[13]

Broglie communicated with Prince Xaver two years later on 22 April 1761:

> MM. the Marshals d'Estrées, Contades and de Soubise have conspired against me: only jealousy could unite them on such apparent good terms and make them forget, I daresay, the great obligations they had towards me…
>
> M. the Marshal d'Estrées cannot have forgotten that it was I who, in presence of MM. The Marquis de La Salle, de Lucé and de Peyre, prevented him from following the advice of the War Council and from retiring, without attacking Cumberland [at Hastenbeck in 1757]; that it was I who, the same day, sent him M. de Béville, my aide-de-camp, both out of friendship to him and for the wider benefit, to tip him off that the enemy was retiring, and inspire him to march against them and bring them to battle.
>
> M. the Marshal de Soubise is also well aware of all the services which I have performed for him. He certainly recalls my conduct in the two campaigns [1757 Rossbach, 1758 in Western Germany, but no mention at that stage of Vellinghausen in 1761] which I conducted with him. I couldn't prevent his defeat at Rossbach; but he could not disagree that it was down to me to save the remainder of the Army he commanded; and I performed similar feats two or three times in the campaign of 1758. I have correspondence from him which is evidence of the gratitude that he must have felt, and which he said that he would remember all his life…
>
> It is said that M. Contades is up to his old tricks involving me in the affair of Minden. One only needs to consider the plan which Price Ferdinand had set to destroy them, to be able to prove the truth of what I have expressed in front of any impartial man. I can say in all confidence that on that day I saved the Army, by my conduct during the action and by the advice which I gave afterwards, in the presence of the Comte de Noailles and of all the General officers, to cross over the Weser and retire using the right bank of the river. And if one had been willing to re-cross it later above Hameln, as I had proposed to him in writing the day after the battle, we could have held onto the Paderborn country and Hesse, and undo the damage that day had caused.[14]

---

13 Pajol, *Les Guerres sous Louis XV*, Vol.4, pp.419-420, letter of the Maréchal de Belle-Isle to the Duc de Broglie discussing the battle (from Versailles on 12 August. Translated by R. Couture.

14 Broglie and Vernier (eds.), *Correspondance inédite*, Vol.I, pp.28-30, Letter of the Duc de Broglie to the Baron de Thiers 22 April 1761. Translated by R. Couture.

Napoleon was dismissive, not only of Broglie's performance, but also of his motivation:

> M. Contades debouches onto the plain at daybreak. M. Broglie commands the avant-garde, destined to be the decisive attack of the village. The success of the day depends on him: his indecision, his slowness, make him fail. He pretends that the order given on the eve is impossible to execute, the enemy having reinforced itself: he engages in a light cannonade, goes to the Maréchal; hours go by, giving Prince Ferdinand the time to reinforce his left, which would have been crushed. This General was guilty; he was ill-disposed and envious of his chief'.[15]

Pajol quotes from an unknown source, D.G. (possibly a French officer from the centre-right?), who offers the three main causes for the loss of the battle:

> The first, on the failure to carry out the orders given to the right to attack; this is the principal cause from which all others resulted, and on which I will not go into detail. I will only report what I observed, and which will serve as evidence of the things that Prince Ferdinand has told our prisoners since then. One can remember once again the position of the detached Corps of the enemy; the King's one [army] had passed the stream and had formed up for battle on the far side, before daybreak, without the enemy having been alerted. The first news they had of our movements came only from the deception attack of Navarre on our left; as Prince Ferdinand was waking up, and his army was taking arms, he sensed that the first important thing to do was to march with all his Army to his left. This march was made within the sight of the entire left and of the centre of the King's Army; the enemy ignored all other objectives, to fulfil that one, and it is only after realizing that the Corps on the left was only being cannonaded and that no deployment had been made for an assault against it that we saw again the same columns, who had marched from the right to the left, march back from left to right and debouche to attack our centre. One easily appreciates from the evidence of the enemy movement just how much their left mattered to them, as it was the first objective which they took care of and that it was only after making sure of the security of our right that they thought to change their dispositions.
>
> The second fault didn't decide the outcome of the battle, but resulted in two infantry Brigades being torn to pieces. The centre of the line was to extend itself towards the stream where the left of the Army was intended to rest. One changed the general disposition and brought 2 B[rigades] of the centre forward in order to reach the far side of a heath which separated them. What was intended? One supposes that the two Brigades were to prevent the enemy from debouching; but as they would have been vulnerable to early attack by coming out of the main line, from which they could not be supported, they would have in all likelihood been lost. Anyway, they had no time to reach their destination; the enemy cavalry having debouched onto the heath, and, M. de Nicolaï, having made a movement to his right to link with the corps of M. Broglie. M. de Beaupréau, who was on his left and who commanded the 2 B[rigades], ordered them to separate to link with

15 Napoléon Bonaparte, *Précis des Guerres de Frédéric* (Paris: Hachette, 1872), Vol.III, p.286, quoted in Pajol, *Les Guerres Sous Louis XV*, Vol.4, pp.406-407. Translated by R. Couture.

him [*de se rompre pour se lier à lui*]. This movement was executed in such close proximity to the enemy cavalry that it was able to reach the gaps between our brigades before they had reformed. Being in transition at that time, all defence on their part was impossible; so they were all cut into pieces, with the exception of 2 B. of the left, which our right hand cavalry brigade saved by advancing, but which disrupted the first charge of cavalry by the focus that this brigade of the right had to have on the English column which occupied the ground opposite.

The third main fault of that day came from the Commandant of the left wing. The enemy's manoeuvres had secured his positions; we witnessed their entire Army march to its left, so that ours could only mask it. If that were carried to a logical conclusion we could have outflanked his line of cavalry, and this was proposed on many occasions; but a few shots in front of the left prevented the necessary movement which, I believe, would have been effective, because, if one had been willing to bring two or three Brigades into the woods in front of the cavalry line, they would have flanked the whole heath and no troop would ever have debouched there. If this had happened the enemy would have had no other choice, if they were to challenge us, than to re-march to its right to attack our left in force, which he would not have been able to do without entirely unpicking [*se découdre entièrement*] himself. One believes that he would not have dared to risk it; because, if he had done so, all the contingent redeployment would probably have given enough time for the Duc de Broglie to execute the orders which he had received.[16]

The Allied Performance

Ferdinand

Ferdinand was hailed in allied public opinion as the hero of the hour. His plan to draw the French out of Minden was a fine balance of temptation (the seemingly isolated elements in the arc around Minden Heath) and threat (to Contades' lines of communication), but the plan was elaborate and relied on a rapid response. His estimate that marching his own force together onto the heath from its camp locations in an arc would both close the net and concentrate his force was sophisticated, while his time appreciation that he could achieve this faster than the French could cross the Bastau was bold. He was clearly a commander of some intellect.

However, he was also quite private. This had the effect of rendering his communications rather terse. In alliance operations, particularly where they are multi-lingual, it is important that the commander's intent is made very clear, and that confirmation is sought that the orders' recipients understand their place in the scheme and understand the orders themselves. He seems not to have taken his key subordinate commanders, on whom he placed so much reliance, into his confidence.

When the French began their movements on the night of 31 July/1 August, Anhalt appeared to underestimate the important significance of the

16 Pajol, *Les Guerres sous Louis XV*, Vol.4, pp.413-415. Analysis of the main causes of the French defeat (from D. G) Translated R. Couture.

appearance of the French deserters, allowing the French to steal a march on him by pre-empting the allied shaping operation in Hahlen. Equally, Wangenheim seems to have been taken by surprise on the allied left.

In similar vein, Ferdinand's headquarters' staff work and communications were vague and unclear. When the order to form up and march was passed, not all of the subordinate commands fully understood what was expected of them. Examples would include the British artillery, which was not at all clear on what it was to do.[17] Similarly, Spörcken's column launched itself into its advance prematurely. The words of the order recalled by the messenger, von Taube, were not the same as Ferdinand recalled.[18]

At the tipping point, as the enemy was on the point of collapsing, if Ferdinand appreciated it, he did not fully exploit it. Despite the damage caused to the French in the attritional parts of the battle, Ferdinand was unable to maximise his advantage. Had he chosen, he could still have used Sackville's cavalry to exploit the situation. As it was, the surviving French were able to withdraw back across the Bastau.

Ferdinand's deliberate omission of some subordinates from his Special Order of the Day of 2 August, and his arrangements for the removal of Sackville, arguably showed evidence of vindictiveness.

British Musketry

The common assumption that British musketry was superior to that of its peers and rivals bears examination. John William O'Sullivan, the Jacobite Adjutant General, wrote of his Government opponents in 1746, 'There are no troops in the world but what they overcome in firing, if you don't go in Sword in hand, or the bayonet among them'.[19] Contemporary commentators describe the destructive power of British musketry. Minden and its almost contemporary peer battle, Quebec, both fall into this bracket, Fortescue describing the musketry at Quebec as 'the most perfect volley ever fired on a battlefield'.[20]

Given that the musket itself was inaccurate beyond about 50-80m, the aim of tactics and skill-at-arms was basically to get the troops to a situation where they could lay down as heavy a fire as possible at close range, and to reload as quickly as possible. The British would often add closing with the enemy rapidly, with fixed bayonets.[21]

Stuart Reid ascribes this superiority to three factors: the use of the platoon firing system, creating a continuous rolling barrage of fire within a grand division, repeated about four times along a battalion's front; a shortage of training facilities for complete battalions and above meant that greater effort was put into basic weapon handling and platoon firing than Continental armies; and the edge provided by the equipment. Whilst French muskets may have had better quality control, the heavier British musket ball and

17 Mackesy, *The Coward of Minden*, pp.108 and 231.

18 Mackesy, *The Coward of Minden*, pp.111 and 231.

19 Stuart Reid, *King George's Army 1740-93* (Oxford: Osprey, 1995), Vol.I, p.17.

20 Fortescue, quoted in Blackmore, *Destructive & Formidable*, p.1.

21 Blackmore, *Destructive & Formidable*, p.137.

the consistency of British powder (using saltpetre imported from Bengal) produced a greater practical effect.[22]

There were plenty of drill books produced officially and by enthusiasts. The most consistently applied was Humphrey Bland's *Treatise of Military Discipline*, first produced in 1727, but so popular that it went through nine editions until 1762. However, there was no single centralised system of interpreting them. Similarly, there was no centralised teaching of officers until the foundation of the Royal Military College in 1801. While this may sound like a disadvantage, in reality it meant that each regiment thought about its trade and developed a system which worked for it. This meant that, rather than being rigid automata, the British infantrymen were tough, practical and adaptable.

Bland's system of dividing a battalion into grand divisions and then into platoons, meant that, at any one time, between four and five platoons were actively firing, while the remainder were at varying stages of the loading sequence. Not only did this produce constant fire, but the distribution of firings meant that no part of the Battalion was ever vulnerable for long. Also, the system familiarized the soldier with the need for fire discipline, despite the sound of firing to the left and right.

Bland was confident that a well-trained unit using his system would withstand hostile cavalry:

> If Foot could be brought to know their own Strength, the Danger which they apprehend from Horse would soon vanish; since the fire of one Platoon, given in due Time, is significant to break any Squadron...one battalion of well-disciplined Foot may despise the Attacks of a whole Line of Horse.[23]

Corporal Todd describes that volley fire and, indeed, rank firings, while seldom featuring in regulations, were practised.[24] This shows that, in reality, units could adapt their system of firing to deal with different tactical situations.

The great risks for any army were that fire discipline would break down and that the majority would fire off their shot too early, and at too great a range to be effective, or that after a volley too many men were not loaded for far too long. After a wild and chaotic experience at Dettingen in 1743, much effort went into training. In particular, great care was put into loading drills, at which the British excelled.[25] With the smoothbore musket, it was important to wad and ram the ball home hard with the iron ramrod, in order that the powder was tightly compressed to maximize the power of the shot. The use of the more durable metal ramrod, which had superseded the old wooden one, also contributed to a higher rate of fire.

---

22 Reid, *King George's Army*, Vol.I, p.23.

23 Bland, quoted in Blackmore, *Destructive & Formidable*, p.101.

24 A Cormack and A. Jones (eds.), *The Journal of Corporal William Todd 1745-1762* (Stroud: Sutton for the Army Records Society, 2001), p.63.

25 Mackesy, *The Coward of Minden*, p.26.

French writings of the period give some clues as to the opposition's relative failings.[26] The most important was inexperienced troops firing too early, and at too great a range. It was understood that wasting the first shot was a serious mistake as, compared to subsequent shots which may have had to be loaded in haste, the first shot could be carefully and methodically loaded, ensuring that all was correct. The French had fired their first shots at long range at both Dettingen and at Fontenoy (about 80 metres in the latter case).

Lieutenant Thompson describes being under French fire at Minden:

> All the time their left wing was pelting us with small arms, cannon and grape shot, and we were not suffered to fire, but stood tamely looking on whilst they at their leisure picked us off as you would small birds on a barn door. I cannot compare it to anything as their shot came full and thick, and had one quarter of them taken place [i.e. hit the target] there could not have been a man left.[27]

Another problem was what has become known as 'tap-loading':[28] in order to load quickly, after the first shot, soldiers of all nations had a tendency to cut corners by not using the ramrod, relying simply on a tap of the weapon's butt on the ground to cause the charge and ball to fall towards the breech. Failing to compress the ball onto the powder charge reduced the power of the shot and, in extreme cases, might cause the ball to jam within, or even burst, the barrel.

The French noted that the British foot would advance through French fire, holding their own until the last moment, then discharge their pieces at closer range. If this was quickly followed by an aggressive bayonet charge, the defending troops would usually flee in terror. La Fausille noted that Britain's allies often preferred to rely on firepower alone, but that the British combination of a volley and a bayonet charge caused them (the British) to suffer fewer casualties in the end. Also, as soon as a regiment had broken an enemy, it paused to reorganise, a vital part of which would be a careful and deliberate load (any man who had merely tap-loaded previously would be required to ram his charge and ball fully home), thus effectively restarting the whole process.

Bland also recognised that tap-loading occurred – it was a response to human nature.[29] He pointed out the reasons why it should be avoided, including that the paper of the cartridge might fall within the barrel between the touchhole and the powder, preventing ignition and causing a lengthy stoppage. Despite all this, there is evidence that the British Army thought about, and weighed up, the pros and cons of ramming and tap-loading. Omitting to use the ramrod could cut the time for the loading sequence almost by half. At extremely close range, the benefit of achieving a higher rate of fire, might give one side the advantage.[30]

---

26 La Fausille, quoted in Blackmore, *Destructive & Formidable*, p.104.
27 Reid, *The Battle of Minden, 1759*, p.104.
28 Duffy, *The Military Experience in the Age of Reason*, p.210.
29 Blackmore, *Destructive & Formidable*, p.105.
30 Blackmore, *Destructive & Formidable*, p.105.

There were some shortcomings in the system of Platoon firing, as Bland acknowledged. It was complicated. Dividing the unit into even-sized firings sometimes disrupted the normal chain of command, although this drawback could be surmounted by frequent training. The real challenge, especially in peacetime, was to ensure that sufficient of the unit was in one place to be able to make practice worthwhile and realistic.

New regulations produced in 1748 simplified the system, reducing the firings to three and formally linking platoons and grand divisions. In 1756, new regulations reduced the distances between files, giving each man 0.6m rather than 0.75m). Close Order (one pace = 0.75m) was introduced for both manoeuvring as well as for firing, which reduced the time needed to transition from one to the other. Bland also introduced 'locking', which improved the use of space between the centre and rear ranks. Regardless of the merits or demerits of Bland's system, the intense focus on training had its effect on the field.

Sackville himself, originally an infantryman, had also thought about musketry and appears to have encouraged the British contingent in Germany to evolve away from the complex sequence of platoon firings, which required detailed numbering off before combat, favouring the much simpler system of larger fire units (usually by company) which would fire alternately.[31]

In reality, after the first shot, most armies' fire discipline appears to have dissolved, with every man firing at his best personal speed, or *billebaude*. Furthermore, despite all the parade ground rehearsal, it appears that both the British and French foot would kneel or crouch forward to present a smaller target. However, when the enemy did so too, the British would learn to hold their fire until the opposition rose again, evidence of coolness under fire.[32]

At Minden, Contades thought that the French foot fired more rapidly than the British, but at greater range:

> Our musquetry, indeed, fired faster and oftener, being discharged sooner, and at a great distance; but the enemy reserved their fire till they discharged it in our teeth; by which means they did thrice the execution; and then rushing in with their bayonets, prevented our troops from giving any more.[33]

This is a clear demonstration of the effectiveness of British doctrine and practice, and a frank acknowledgement of its superiority.

Ensuring that every man had sufficient powder and ball to sustain a fight was clearly a growing concern. In the following year, Corporal Todd of the 12th Foot recorded in his diary that, after practising their 'firing motions', his regiment made up additional cartridges so that each soldier had sixty rounds ready on his person, with reserve stocks held in the tumbrils.[34] At Klosterkamp, the fire of the British foot was 'so rapid and deadly that three

31 Mackesy, *The Coward of Minden*, p.46.
32 Colonel Russel, quoted in Blackmore, *Destructive & Formidable*, p.106.
33 Contades, quoted in Blackmore, *Destructive & Formidable*, p.140.
34 Cormack and Jones (eds.), *The Journal of Corporal William Todd 1745-1762*, p.141.

French brigades were almost wiped out of existence'.[35] However, this came at the expense of the allies virtually running out of ammunition in a battle which lasted about five hours.

By the war's end, most units were practising the simpler method of alternate firing by companies. Bland's concern, that portions of the battalion would be vulnerable during the load phase, had been rendered less important due to the speed of loading achieved through well-rehearsed drills with the metal ramrod.

In addition to dry drills, live firing, at a mark, was popular training. In peacetime, a battalion would receive a powder allowance for 31,000 to 60,000 rounds per year.[36] In wartime, the allowance rose and was appreciated. The 15th Foot managed to fire three days per week in 1757: 'Every man has fired about 84 rounds, and now load and fire Ball with as much coolness and alacrity in all the different fireings as ever you saw them fire blank powder, hitherto without the smallest accident'.[37] The soldiers themselves valued good shooting and Captain James Stewart's Company Order Book of the 42nd Highlanders makes mention of soldiers practising informally on roving 'marks' and shooting at farmers' fences.[38]

The study of musketry requires a final, crucial ingredient, that of the fighting soldier himself. There is consistent evidence of the stubborn resilience of the typical British infantryman. Even in cases where the British Army may have been defeated, the soldiers themselves, standing with their mates, refused to be beaten. Of the 12th Foot, and of its 507 officers and men who marched onto Minden Heath, 320 were killed, wounded or missing, and yet the regiment refused to give up.

Sackville

It is clear that Sackville underperformed, but was he a coward? No – a pedant perhaps, concerned for his comfort rather than his safety, but not a coward. He appears to have been diligent in his duties. He had a good prior record in war: in the War of the Austrian Succession, at Fontenoy, while in command of the 28th Foot which he led in a bold attack, he was wounded, captured and presented to Louis XV in person; he had played his part in suppressing the Jacobite rebellion; and he had participated in the early days of the British amphibious raids on the French coastline along with Marlborough until boredom had set in and they had managed to get themselves sent to Germany.

Ferdinand and Sackville had a poor relationship, particularly since the debate of 10th July, when the latter had advocated falling back onto Münster, to the extent that Ferdinand appears actually to have disliked Sackville. After the battle, Ferdinand was convinced that Sackville had been disobedient.

The trial had failed to demonstrate any motive for disobedience. No-one, other than Sloper, had seen any sign of physical fear. In fact, Sackville's intended course of action on receipt of the orders brought by Winzingerode

35 Fortescue, quoted in Blackmore, *Destructive & Formidable*, p.141.

36 Stuart Reid, *British Redcoat 1740-1793* (Oxford: Osprey, 1996), p.23.

37 Reid, *British Redcoat*, p.23.

38 Reid, *British Redcoat*, p.23.

was to advance his cavalry through enemy artillery fire, not off to the left behind the allied foot. When directed off to the left, he had queried this and sought clarification.

The allied commanders had been instructed to become familiar with their approach routes onto the heath. Sackville had partially achieved this but had been hindered by his duties as General Officer of the Day.

Despite Ferdinand's intentions, the allies had been taken by surprise. Sackville actually knew little of Ferdinand's plans, other than that he was put in charge of one column of cavalry which convention would place on a flank of the battle line. The enemy's pre-emptive seizure of Hahlen spoiled his approach to his forming up point and he was waiting for the allied picquets to clear the village. At that stage, it would have been sensible to have sent scouts forward and to the flanks. In which case he could have been kept informed of the infantry's progress on his left and on the thickness and going through the woods.

Once cleared he would be able to proceed down the lanes of woodland towards the windmill, then turn at the wood's end onto the heath. He would not have expected to be told to disrupt his formation so that he could make a messy transit through the wood on his left. Winzingerode had admitted that he was not fully aware of the enemy's dispositions. Within a relatively short space of time, Sackville had received three sets of contradictory instructions: to advance; to split his cavalry force in the face of stronger enemy numbers; and to extract his cavalry from the allied army's line in order to march through a wood into the centre-rear of that army. It is entirely reasonable that the sensory and cognitive overload which Sackville experienced would have confused him. Having had contradictory instructions delivered second-hand, it may not have been unreasonable to approach Ferdinand personally to confirm his orders at source. As soon as he appreciated the situation, his immediate sending of Captain Smith back to the main body is evidence of his intention and willingness to comply.

The subsequent slow advance appears to reflect a desire to obey Ferdinand's orders and, at the same time, to maintain control over a large formation. While Granby might have been a more natural cavalryman, had a better *coup d'œil*, and conducted the action *con brio*, Sackville, previously an infantryman, was going by the book. The situation may have required the former rather than the latter. In previous and subsequent wars, the British cavalry had sometimes become carried away and lost control. In a different tactical setting, Sackville's control might have saved the day. If Sackville failed, it was that he did not recognise the needs of the moment.

From the alliance's point of view, however, it was necessary to sacrifice Sackville in order to preserve Britain's relationship with Ferdinand.

16

A Guide to Visiting the Battlefield

The battlefield is well worth visiting. Minden itself is a quaint town. Despite some patches of rather poor and ugly post-Second World War civic planning, there are many beautiful buildings and curiosities. In 1759 Minden was a fortified town, and even today a look at a modern street-plan gives an impression of that by the star-shaped glacis, which has now been levelled and converted to civic gardens, criss-crossed by cycle paths

There has been some modern encroachment on to the battlefield. Development has spilled over the former town boundaries and the battlefield has seen random building which threatens an unobscured view. Additionally, the completion of the Mittelland Canal in 1938 altered the southern part of the ground, including draining much of the marshy going around the Bastau stream, which was a factor in the planning. On a plus point, for the modern battlefield visitor, the canal gives a clear idea of the northern edge of what was considered difficult terrain.

This tour is intended to provide a selection of possible stands which may be added or dropped depending on priorities and the time available.

The tour is probably best conducted by car/minibus or bicycle. Some of the roads used are narrow or really intended for agricultural use. Common sense about safety, parking, damage to crops and respect for the locals should, of course, be applied.

Stand One – Village of Hahlen – Old Church near the junction of Hahlerdorfstrasse and Schulstrasse

We are now in the village of Hahlen. It has grown since 1759, and become more sprawling. This church, however, existed at the time of the battle and was at the heart of the village. The area between Hahlen and the next village to the west, Hartum, was picqueted by the Hessians.

Ferdinand's plan involved his force leaving its encampments and moving towards the town of Minden in eight columns. As they did so, they would become more concentrated, because the quadrant formed by their start

Hahlen church. The church is tucked behind a Balkan restaurant. It should be possible to park in Alte Schulstrasse. (Author's Collection)

positions would shrink as they moved towards the town. In a sense this was the reason for his concern about time, because Ferdinand had lured the French out of their secure positions by the bait of his dispersed encampments. If the French could get sufficient force out of Minden, across the Bastau stream and onto Minden Heath, they had the chance to defeat him in detail. If, on the other hand, he could concentrate his army in time, he could catch a large portion of the French, perhaps off balance, as they were emerging. His right flank was to be anchored by the village of Hahlen.

There are still many timber-framed farm buildings in the village, some dating from the second half of the eighteenth-century. A few bear inscriptions from the period on their beams, including commemoration that a quarter of the village was destroyed by fire as the French withdrew.

Stand Two – Windmill on the west edge of the village of Hartum (north of Mindenerstrasse)

A windmill existed at the time of the battle. Ferdinand's' plan was for the right flank of his advancing army to be protected by the village of Hahlen (2.5 kilometres to the east), the village you have just been in. Hartum was picqueted by the British, and Hessians were picqueting the ground to the north towards Holzhausen.

Ferdinand's headquarters was actually in Hille, two villages to the west, so he would have come through here to see what was going on in Hahlen.

Hartum windmill. The windmill lies towards the Western end of Hartum. It should be possible to park on the main road (Mindenerstrasse), but be wary of traffic which can be busy for a minor road. If traffic becomes too much of an irritation, you have the option of cutting your script short here and resuming it in the quieter environment of the next stand. (Author's Collection)

He ordered the advance picquets from here to advance and occupy Hahlen. Having just observed them move off, he learned that the French had narrowly beaten him to it, and that two battalions of the Brigade Champagne (and there's a great name for any formation!) had already taken it. So he pressed forward to the advancing picquet line and ordered them to drive out the French at all costs.

Stand Three – Eastern wall of the church in Sudhemmern

You are now in the village of Sudhemmern. Sudhemmern was picqueted by Hanoverians. It lies at the southern end of the quadrant encamped by Ferdinand's army. This church also predates the battle and, as a curiosity, if you go to the eastern wall, you will see what is reputed to be a French cannonball embedded under the eaves.

However, if you imagine the range and trajectory of, say, an 8-pounder cannonball, it would have to have been fired from about one kilometre away. That would put the French gunners midway between here and Hartum, and that does not conform to accounts of where the French reached. However, it is rather a fun curiosity and confirms that the Germans do have a sense of humour.

More importantly, one has to admire the French planning which went into getting both Broglie's and Contades' forces assembled and across obstacles in the dark, and then towards their planned positions with an element of surprise.

The church in Sudhemmern. It should be possible to park at the Western end of the church. (Author's Collection)

The east wall of Sudhemmern church, showing the 'French cannonball'. (Author's Collection)

Drive through the villages of Nordhemmern and Holzhausen

I have described Ferdinand's encampment as being like a big quadrant. The villages of Nordhemmern and Holzhausen were typical of the areas in which Ferdinand's main camp lay. In fact, the camp lay slightly to the north of these villages, on the other side of a stream which ran down through these villages, draining into the moor between Sudhemmern and Ferdinand's headquarters in Hille.

Nordhemmern church, which was in existence at the time of the battle. (Author's collection)

The road between Nordhemmern and Holzhausen, looking south-east. In the distance, faintly, you can see the Wiehengebirge feature (the Minden Ridge) with the 'Minden Gap' (12.5 kilometres distant) through which flows the significant obstacle of the River Weser. From here, the town of Minden is about nine kilometres away, so slightly left of the gap. (Author's Collection)

Village of Holzhausen, looking to the north-west (the building in the centre of the picture is a working historical smithy). The allied foot would have been encamped in a long quadrant just beyond the village and would have advanced towards the camera. (Author's Collection)

Drive through the small settlement of Im Tannen, passing the Garden Centre of Netzeband

The settlement with the two tall trees is variously named. On maps from the time of the battlefield, it is called Netzeband, and the settlement includes a garden nursery called Netzeband. On modern maps it is now also called 'Im Tannen' ('in the pine trees'). Accounts of the advance of the British Foot describe it pausing briefly before a line of pine or fir trees before continuing the advance.

Minden Heath, looking to the north-west. This picture is taken from the same spot as the following one. Author's collection.

Stand Four – Crossroads (junction of Muhlenfeld and agricultural track)

Minden Heath. Junction between Muhlenfeld and agricultural track, looking south-east. Muhlenfeld is the long road running away into the distance. The village of Hahlen lies at the end of the road, to the south. This road provides a good impression of the alignment of the British line. The track running off to the left (to the east) provides a good approximation of the axis of the British advance. (Author's Collection)

You are now at the junction of Muhlenfeld, the road which runs south to Hahlen, and a track running at right angles to the east. If you look to the north-west, at a distance of about 800 metres is a small settlement. It is centred on a garden nursery called Netzeband, and you may see the glasshouses reflecting light. As noted above, Netzeband features on contemporary maps but the settlement is called 'Im Tannen' now.

Ferdinand's main body was generally formed up and prepared for action by about 5:00 a.m. Clearing the enemy from Hahlen allowed his right flank to move forward, which it did under fire support from British light artillery. At the same time, on his left flank, his column of German cavalry was formed up just to the south of the village of Stemmer, and in a good position to cooperate with the cavalry on von Wangenheim's right flank near Kutenhausen.

Shortly before 7:00 a.m. von Spörcken's column had shaken out into battle lines and had temporarily halted at a belt of fir trees, and then passed through the wood onto the open country of Minden Heath. By the author's reckoning the settlement of Im Tannen is where the pine wood was. So you are standing where the British infantry passed just over 250 years ago. Stand and look east down the track. Muhlenfeld gives a good approximation of the line of the 3rd column, von Spörcken's, with its six British battalions and the Hanoverian Guards. The track to your front provides a reasonable impression of the axis of advance. The column was supported by Captain Foy's artillery battery from just over your right shoulder, between Hartum and Hahlen.

Minden Heath, looking south-west (the view from the junction), in the direction of Sudhemmern. Sackville's cavalry was delayed in this area. (Author's Collection)

Walk to Stand Five – 'French Cemetery' (Franzosen Friedhof) to the north-west of junction between Sieben Bauern and An der Spandau

Follow the agricultural track to the east. This gives a very good idea of the axis of advance of the British Foot. Use the cemetery, even though it has no direct connection with the battle, to talk about the next phases of the battle.

This short walk provides an impression of the axis of advance of the British foot. This cemetery, known as the 'French Cemetery' actually dates from the First World War, as there was a prisoner of war camp adjacent. However, it is not uncommon for burial sites to be re-used, so it is perfectly possible that it was used for mass graves after Minden.

The interior of the French Cemetery. (Author's Collection)

Walk to Stand Six – Memorial Stone

A further walk towards the road junction between Zähringerallee and Stiftsallee brings you to the site of the former Cold War British Army barracks, Kingsley Barracks. This memorial stone can be found under the trees at the roadside.

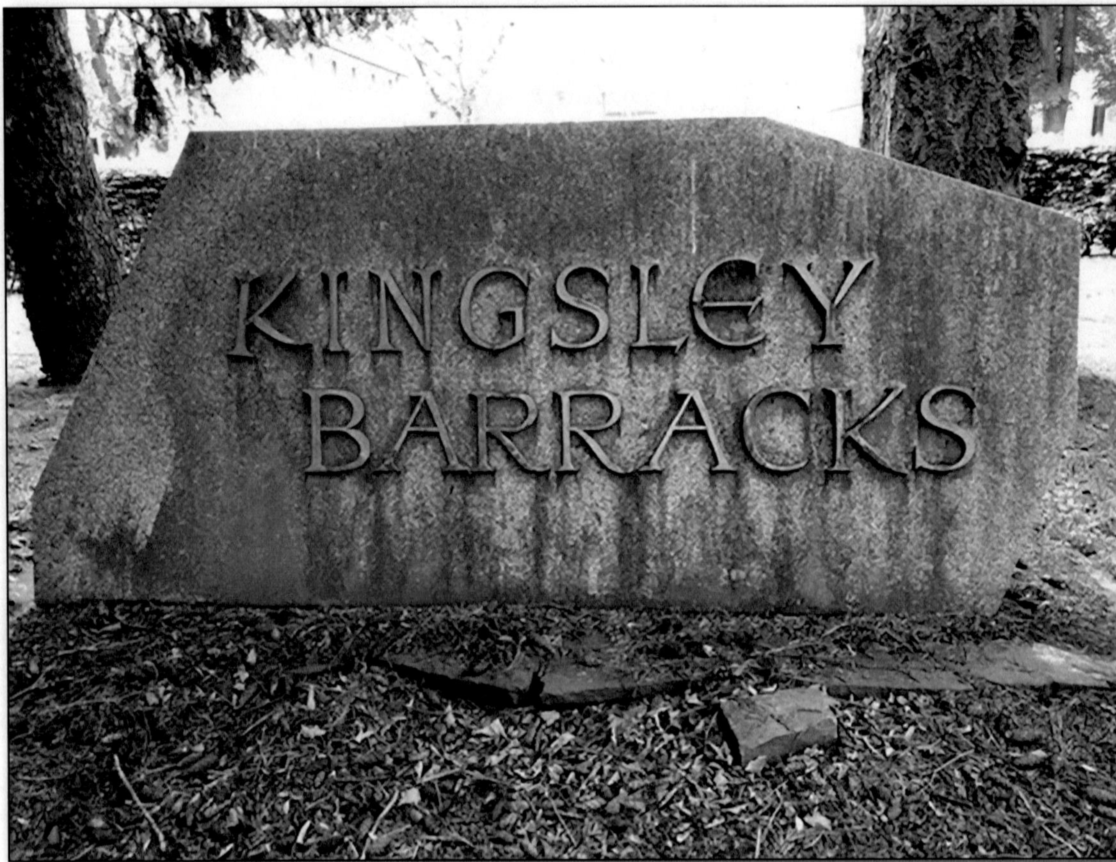

Kingsley Barracks memorial stone. (Author's Collection)

Stand Seven – Small Private Graveyard to the Southern edge of the Civic Cemetery 'Friedhof Minderheide'.

Enter the civic cemetery by the main gate on Petershager Weg (be aware that the cemetery is still in use and that caring for family graves is a popular pursuit in Germany, so there are likely to be people around as you visit. Respect required). Go towards the southern edge of the cemetery, and just beyond its border you will find a small fenced-off private graveyard. I would recommend viewing it from the civic side, rather than tramping onto private land.

This is the family graveyard of some local landowners, the Bohme family. At the end of the Second World War, the family believed that British soldiers from the 1759 battle had been interred here. Sadly, by the 1980s, a younger generation had inherited the farm and that oral tradition had been lost. However, it may be pleasing to think that in this pleasant, peaceful spot, may lie redcoats from Lancashire, Suffolk, Wales or the Scottish borders.

The Bohme family graveyard which local memory had as a burial site for British soldiers. (Author's Collection)

Stand Eight – The Windmill between Stemmer and Maulbeerkamp (to the east of Stemmer Landstrasse)

The windmill between Stemmer and Maulbeerkamp. Whilst not the original, it gives a good impression of the sort of building used for observation. The collapse of the French centre occurred near here. (Author's Collection)

This is the windmill between Stemmer and Maulbeerkamp. Whilst not the original, it gives a good impression of the sort of building used for observation. The collapse of the French centre occurred near here.

The reader will recall that Contades had eight battalions of Infantry uncommitted in front of Maulbeerkamp. Orders were given for them to attack von Spörcken's left flank. Just as the French were forming line to advance, the four lead battalions of von Imhoff's Hessians came up at the double and put in a spirited charge, driving them from this area.

This was exploited by the arrival of the Duke of Holstein's cavalry from Ferdinand's left at Stemmer, just to the north. The forward squadrons of Prussian hussars swept around here and into the French infantry, which was still in chaos after the Hessian bayonet charge, driving them backwards.

Todtenhausen – Looking Southwards

Von Wangenheim's force had pre-prepared positions at about this spot which it occupied when Broglie's corps attempted to advance up the road. Despite any gun positions having been evened out by cultivation, a local farmer, Herr Gieseking, reports that in dry conditions variations in colour can be observed in the ground when the vegetation is short. Five French cuirasses were discovered in a sandpit nearby and musket balls continue to turn up.

Todtenhausen – looking south along Thorenfeld. (Author's Collection)

Stand Nine – The Battle of Minden Monument (Denkmal), which stands on the East side of Todtenhauserstrasse, opposite a pub/restaurant (Baier's)

The monument (Denkmal) to the Battle of Minden. It was unveiled at the centenary of the battle. This site was chosen because Eickhof was the scene of significant engagement by German forces under von Wangenheim. (Author's Collection)

This monument was constructed for the 100th anniversary of the battle. That it is here, rather than on Minden Heath, sometimes baffles British visitors. The answer lies in the site of German involvement. The plaques, now rather worn, show the key German commanders. British military representatives were invited to the unveiling, and also to the 150th anniversary, shortly before the First World War.

The restaurant directly opposite the monument, now called Baier's, used to belong to the Lohrmann family. Lohrmann was the 'Spy' of Minden.

Wallfahrtsteich. Broglie's force would have crossed this ditch during its advance on the morning of 1 August. After the battle, the ditch was described as being filled with French dead. Traces of the stream have been lost through development, but the line of the ditch is still evident. It lies approximately 500 metres south of the monument. (Author's Collection)

The Lohrmann Pub. This restaurant lies directly opposite the monument. It used to belong to the Lohrmann family. Lohrmann was the 'spy' of Minden. (Author's Collection)

Gohfeld

Gohfeld. The River Werre, from the south bank. De Brissac encamped here on the eve of the battle, protecting the bridge which carried the post road. He crossed the river on the morning of 1 August to engage the allies, leaving two companies to guard the bridge. (Author's collection)

The Blutwiese ('Bloody Meadow'), looking north-west, from de Brissac's point of view. The River Werre lies behind the viewer. (Author's Collection)

Memorial, which lies across the Borstelstrasse from the Bloody Meadow. (Author's Collection)

Optional Additional Stands

Mindener Museum, Ritterstrasse

The civic museum has a good collection of relics related to the battle, some battlefield finds and a fine diorama made with 'flats'. However, in 2019 the battle collection was temporarily closed to the public. It would be worth checking whether this has reopened.

Minden, Preussen Museum. Simeonsplatz, to the west of Portastrasse

Site of a Prussian barracks from 1829. Closed for renovation as of 2016, but the forecourt could perhaps be used as a briefing spot to give the introductory talk, especially if linked to the Bastau, which runs along the northern edge of the parade ground (now the museum car park).

Minden, Preussen Museum. (Author's Collection)

View of the River Weser, from the right bank

This option allows for a view of the Weser from the direction of approach of Broglie on 9 July 1759. It was roughly here that soldiers of Fischer's corps swam across to collect a punt which ferried troops onto the far bank. Two bridges can be seen: the more substantial distant bridge follows the route of the main town bridge, which was protected by a hornwork. The nearer, pedestrian, footbridge lies between the sites of two additional temporary bridges later put in by the French.

The River Weser, from the right (east) bank. (Author's Collection)

French artillery platform, covering the extreme left flank of Contades' encampment

To the south of the village of Biemke, as it ascends towards the Wiehengebirge ridge. The platform is in the back garden of 167 Unterm Berge.

French artillery platform, 167 Unterm Berge, Biemke. (Author's Collection)

Minden, Rampenloch

Small lane off to the east of Königswall in Minden. Had been functioning continuously as a 'red light' district since the middle ages, and certainly at the time of the battle, and advertised on the 250th anniversary of the Battle of Minden as, '250 Years Rampenloch'! Rather seedy, but contemporary. Sadly, the town authorities have decided to tear it down and, despite a spirited resistance by the town's history enthusiasts, that plan looks likely to proceed.

Minden, Rampenloch. (Author's Collection)

Schloss Petershagen
At the north-east corner of the town of Petershagen. Prince Ferdinand was encamped on Petershagen Heath in July.

Schloss Bückeburg
Roughly 10 kilometres east of Minden in the small town of Bückeburg. Very anglophilic family (the Schaumburg-Lippe family, descended from the commander of the allied artillery). Has a good restaurant, and hosts reenactments.

The Westphalian Mill Route
Of peripheral interest to the battle, but a pleasant diversion, is a collection of cycle paths, designed to allow tourists to connect the various mills (both wind- and water-), which feature in the county of Minden-Lübbecke.

Eating and Drinking
Restaurant Böhmerwald, Minden. Large mock gothic villa near the junction of Königswall and Königstrasse. Was a Prussian artillery officers' casino. Serves Bohemian (Czech) and German food. Recommended.

Schwedenschenke. A timbered building off the old market in Minden, opposite the Martini-kirche. Was a pub (it was called the 'Swedish Pub' because it was used by Swedish soldiery in the 30 Years War). May no longer be functioning as a pub. If not, there are plenty of other bars nearby. Also in the area is 'The English Shop', run by a German Napoleonic reenactor lady.

Epilogue

Celebrating Minden

Minden continues to be celebrated on its anniversary (1 August) every year, both at the monument at Todtenhausen and wherever the 'Minden' regiments of the British Army are stationed.

Minden was awarded as a 'battle honour' and is used on regimental colours and drums. The Minden regiments have undergone amalgamations, sometimes multiple unions. Despite that, the following units will celebrate the anniversary:

12 (Minden) Battery, 12 Regiment Royal Artillery.
32 (Minden) Battery, 16 Regiment Royal Artillery.
The Royal Regiment of Scotland (specifically the Royal Scots Borderers), as successors to the 25th Foot, wears red roses.
1st Battalion, the Royal Anglian Regiment, as successor to the 12th Foot, wears red and yellow roses.
The Royal Regiment of Fusiliers, as successor to the 20th Regiment of Foot, wears red and yellow roses.
The Royal Welsh, successor to the 23rd Regiment of Foot.
The Princess of Wales's Regiment, successor to the 37th Regiment of Foot, wears a red rose.
3rd and 5th Battalions, The Rifles, successors to the 51st Regiment of Foot, wear a white rose.
Headquarters Company, 3rd Battalion, The Royal Anglian Regiment commemorates the 12th Regiment of Foot.
The North Saskatchewan Regiment of the Canadian Army, affiliated with The Rifles, wears a white rose.

A common feature of the commemorations is the distribution and wearing of roses, which may be used to decorate headdress, drums and the Regimental colours. The colour of the roses varies with the unit, but the most commonly used are red, yellow and white.

It is thought that the use of roses dates from the battle itself. Various theories include British soldiers plucking roses on the approach march to the battle, or that after the battle they decorated their hats and drums in celebration.

In the Royal Regiment of Fusiliers Officers' Mess, the anniversary is celebrated by a dinner. After the Loyal Toast, those officers present who have not previously attended a Minden dinner are presented with, and required to eat, a rose washed down with champagne.

One charming ritual faithfully followed is that a mystery donor sends red roses each year to the British Consulate in Chicago. Every year they arrive, accompanied by quality stationery marked 'In Memoriam'. The tradition appears to have begun in the 1950s at the Consulate in Kansas, before moving to Chicago in the 1960s. It continued unbroken until 2001 and 2002, when it is assumed that the mystery donor may have died. However, the tradition resumed, possibly through the directions left in a will. Consular staff attempted to investigate who the mystery donor was, but were told by the delivering florist that the sender was X.T. Atkins with an address of 1759 Albion.[1]

The centenary of the battle was marked by the erection of the monument, designed by the architect Moelle, at Todtenhausen. The 150th anniversary was also marked, rather poignantly with invited guests from the British regiments just five years before the outbreak of the First World War. The organiser was *Generalmajor* von Beck, commander of the 26. Infanterie-Brigade. The commemorations involved a religious service at the monument, followed by a march-past and lunch. Red roses were sent to the hotels in which the visiting British officers were staying, so that they could wear them to the ceremony.

The 20th Foot used an old German hymn, the Lammas Day Hymn, adapted to quick time as a march-past. This became adapted as The Minden March, during which the drummers would give out a Minden Yell.

Various unofficial commemorative medals were struck in silver, brass and copper. Many show representations of soldiers or Prince Ferdinand.

Two poems in English feature the battle: Rudyard Kipling's (1865-1936) 'The Men that Fought at Minden' and Erasmus Darwin's (1731-1802) 'Death of Eliza at the Battle of Minden'. An English folk song, The Lowlands of Holland, dating from the time of the Seven Years War, has a verse, 'My love across the ocean, wears a scarlet coat so fair, with a musket at his shoulder and roses in his hair'.

Sadly, the recipe for Minden Pudding is now almost impossible to find but, anecdotally, it is reported to be cannonball-shaped.

One pub, The Battle of Minden, still exists in Portsmouth in the South of England, while a garland dance side, Minden Rose based in Hampshire, continues to commemorate the battle. Yorkshire has adopted the anniversary of the battle as 'Yorkshire Day'.

1 Thomas (or Tommy) Atkins is a popular nickname for the generic British soldier. The Duke of Wellington is known to have used it in correspondence, but it may have been used as early as 1743.

Appendix I

Timelines

The aim of these timelines is to provide a relative and comparative sequence of events up to the Battle of Minden, and then a comparison between Minden and Gohfeld. Whilst not comprehensive, they are intended to convey the sequence and relationship of events in different areas of operation.

Synchronisation Matrix: Events Leading up to Minden

Date	Operations involving Ferdinand's Western Flank	Operations involving Ferdinand's Southern Flank	Solely British Operations
9 Jul 55	Ambush at Monongahela – French victory.		
8 Sep 55	Combat of Lake George – British victory.		
20 May 56	Battle of Minorca – French naval victory.		
28 Aug 56	Frederick invades Saxony.		
1 Oct 56	Battle of Lobositz – Prussian victory.		
12 Mar 57	Prussians evacuate Wesel.		
14 Mar 57			Cumberland arrives on R Elbe.
	French cross R Rhine.		
24 Mar 57	French occupy Münster.		
3 May 57			Cumberland in Bielefeld.
6 May 57		Battle of Prague – Prussian victory.	
	Estrées ordered to drive Cumberland across R Weser.		
12 Jun 57			Cumberland in defence at Teutoburger Wald.
13 Jun 57	Engagement at Teutoburger Wald.		
18 Jun 57		Battle of Kolin – Austrian victory.	
	Allies send garrison to Minden		Cumberland occupies Obenberg near Hameln.
23 Jun 57		Battle of Plassey – British victory.	
25 Jul 57	French begin attack on Obenberg.		
26 Jul 57	French win Battle of Hastenbeck by default.		
3 Aug 57	Estrées replaced by Richelieu.		
11 Aug 57			King George II orders Cumberland to seek terms.

Date	Operations involving Ferdinand's Western Flank	Operations involving Ferdinand's Southern Flank	Solely British Operations
8 Sep 57	Convention of Kloster Zeven – Hanover & Westphalia abandoned to French.		
	Berlin briefly occupied by Austrians.		
Sep 57			British attempt raid on Rochefort: inconclusive failure.
5 Nov 57	Battle of Rossbach – Prussian victory.		
	Ferdinand appointed allied commander.		
23 Nov 57	Ferdinand arrives Hamburg to take command.		
5 Dec 57	Battle of Leuthen – Prussian victory.		
13 Dec 57	Ferdinand advances south, but blocked on R Aller.		
24 Dec 57	Ferdinand orders withdrawal.		
Feb 58	Ferdinand ready to attempt break-out. Richelieu replaced by Clermont.		
18 Feb 58	Ferdinand pins French on R Aller and advances to Verden.		
	French evacuate Bremen. St Germain withdraws via Münster. Ferdinand able to create supply line Bremen-Nienburg.		
23 Feb 58	The Storming of the Hoya crossing by Erbprinz. Allied victory.		
15 Mar 58	Minden surrenders to allies. In 6 weeks, Hanover & Westphalia cleared of French. Ferdinand's HQ at Münster.		
		Broglie ordered to abandon Kassel.	British occupy Emden, initially RN then 51st Foot.
Apr 58			British units warned for operations. British Naval force captures French Fort St Louis in Senegal and returns with gold, silver and gum arabic.
Mid-May 58	Ferdinand coordinates actions with British amphibious raids. He will cross Rhine to get between French and R Meuse.		13,000 British troops encamped Isle of White. Marlborough appointed to command, Sackville as 2iC.
30 May 58			Embarked amphibious force sets sail: Howe to transport amphibious force; Anson & Hawke to cruise off Brest to prevent interference.
2 Jun 58			Initial British appearance off French coast, but 72 hours of storms give French time to react.
3 Jun 58	Ferdinand crosses Rhine via Holland. Clermont orders his Army to concentrate near Wesel should withdrawal across R Meuse be required.		
Jun 58			Amphibious force lands near Cancale, 15 kilometres east of St Malo.

Date	Operations involving Ferdinand's Western Flank	Operations involving Ferdinand's Southern Flank	Solely British Operations
7 Jun 58		Belle-Isle attempts to coordinate operations of Clermont and Soubise.	Amphibious force advances to St Malo. French vessels burned. After several days, the force returns to Cancale and is re-embarked.
20 Jun 58			Britain considers how to raise forces to support Ferdinand. Pitt concedes that elements of amphibious force could be used to reinforce Ferdinand. Marlborough and Sackville oust the nominated commander (Bligh) who is moved to the amphibious force.
23/24 Jun 58	Clermont fights defensive battle at Krefeld and is defeated by Ferdinand. Clermont withdraws to Köln.	Belle-Isle orders Soubise into Hesse to threaten Hannover.	
8 Jul 58	Battle of Carillon (Ticonderoga) – French victory		
8 Jul 58	French withdrawal exposes Austrian Netherlands. Clermont is replaced by Contades. Erbprinz occupies Roermond.		
9 Jul 58	Contades ordered to re-occupy Köln.	Soubise begins his advance into Hesse with 32 Sqns and 39 Bns (of which, Broglie's advance guard is 12 Sqns and 14 Bns) concentrated at Friedberg. He is opposed by Isenburg with 2 Sqns, 2 Bns, 5 Hessians Sqns and 3 militia Bns.	
16 Jul 58		Isenburg abandons Marburg.	
23 Jul 58	Ferdinand attempts to mount spoiling attack, planning to capture Allrath NE of Köln and inviting French attack.	Isenburg abandons Kassel and withdraws north. Engagement at Sanderhausen NE of Kassel, a disaster for Isenburg.	
24 Jul 58	Contades reaches Allrath before Ferdinand while the latter is unbalanced astride the bridge. However, Contades decides to wait for his full force. Night falls and Ferdinand breaks contact after dark. He assumes that the French will expect him to withdraw north. Instead he moves west.		
25 Jul 58	Ferdinand advances towards Roermond to threaten Contades' communications. However this is too subtle for Contades, who is initially unaware and then moves north to trap Ferdinand.	Soubise luxuriates in Kassel for 3 weeks, resorting only to raids on Göttingen, Münden and Warburg, while Hanover is vulnerable. Hanover is abandoned, the Govt. moving to Stade on the Elbe, to Ferdinand's distress.	
26 Jul 58	Fall of Louisbourg to the British.		
30 Jul 58	Contades sends Chevert to capture pontoon bridge at Rees, 17.7 kilometres from Wesel. Contades simultaneously attempts to block Ferdinand at Dulken, 18 kilometres SE of Krefeld in a 4.8km-wide corridor between R Meuse and lakes.		

Date	Operations involving Ferdinand's Western Flank	Operations involving Ferdinand's Southern Flank	Solely British Operations
3 Aug 58	Contades decides to withdraw rather than fight an attritional battle. Ferdinand attempts to 'amuse' Contades with Holstein-Gottorp's cavalry while he makes a break for Rees, but adverse weather slows him down. Chevert reaches Rees first.		
4 Aug 58	Marlborough disembarks at Emden.		Bligh sails to Cherbourg.
5 Aug 58	Warned of Chevert's approach, Imhoff leaves 500 to hold the bridge then takes 5 Sqns and 6 Bns to defend high ground at Mehr. Chevert gathers 2000 reinforcements to add to his 5000. He attempts to fix Imhoff while his grenadiers and light troops hook round to seize the bridge, but they become sucked into the main engagement. Chevert's militia-heavy force panics and retreats allowing Imhoff to save the bridge.		
7 Aug 58		Soubise advances north to threaten Hanover.	Bligh's lead elements attempt to land 8 kilometres west of Cherbourg at St Marais.
8 Aug 58			Remainder of force lands and works inland to Cherbourg, which is abandoned by the French. Cherbourg sacked.
10 Aug 58	All of Ferdinand's force is safely across the Rhine and able to focus on the threat to Hanover. After several days he makes a rendezvous with the British.		
15 Aug 58			Cherbourg harbour ruined.
16 Aug 58			Amphibious force re-embarked. Britain declares a victory, albeit dubious.
19 Aug 58	French Army has crossed R Rhine and takes up positions at Wesel.		
25 Aug 58	Battle of Zorndorf – 'Draw' between Prussia and Russia.		
3 Sep 58			Amphibious force returns to St Malo, this time to the West, but blocked by R Rance and defences. Opt to withdraw to attempt elsewhere. Storm threatens ships, so evacuation is planned from St Cast, 24 kilometres further west.
7 Sep 58		Soubise continues north to threaten Hanover.	Bligh orders vanguard to set out
8 Sep 58			The main body sets out but the French have assembled 12 battalions and are heading for R Arguenon.
10 Sep 58			While camped at Matignan, Bligh learns that the French have 30,000 men camped 4 miles away.

Date	Operations involving Ferdinand's Western Flank	Operations involving Ferdinand's Southern Flank	Solely British Operations
11 Sep 58			Disaster at St Cast signals the end of 'buccaneering'.
12 Sep 58		Fischer on the outskirts of Hanover.	
16 Sep 58	Contades moves east along R Lippe to Hann.	Ferdinand detaches Oberg, who is ordered to Paderborn. Soubise withdraws.	
26 Sep 58		Oberg on outskirts of Kassel. Soubise makes night march to protect Kassel and digs-in.	
28 Sep 58	Contades detaches 20,000 troops under Chevert to support Soubise.		
7 Oct 58	As Contades moves east along R Lippe, Ferdinand shadows him and reaches Münster.		
9 Oct 58		Oberg, learning of Chevert, elects to dig-in at Lutterberg, near Kassel.	
10 Oct 58		Battle of Lutterberg – French victory.	
12 Oct 58	Ferdinand moves west, seeking to engage Contades before Chevert can re-join.	Chevert begins to return towards Contades.	
14 Oct 58	Battle of Hochkirch – Austrian victory.		
17 Oct 58	Ferdinand reaches Lippstadt.		
18 Oct 58	Erbprinz pushes on to Soest and Werl, but is endangered by Contades' converging forces, and withdraws. Contades threatens Münster.		
31 Oct 58	Ferdinand protects Münster, and is re-joined by Oberg's remnants.		
Winter 58	Contades retires back across R Rhine for winter quarters between Wesel and Düsseldorf, to regenerate his force (~66,000).	Soubise evacs Hesse for Winter quarters south of R Lahn. His force is at less than half strength at ~21,000. Soubise replaced by Broglie, and is recalled to command the invasion force for Britain.	
31 Dec 58		Broglie's army forcibly occupies Frankfurt am Main as its firm base.	British Naval expedition captures Island of Gorée, a French trading post, in Africa, affecting French commerce.
Jan 59			British Naval force fails to capture Martinique.
22 Mar 59		Ferdinand leaves Münster for Fulda.	
31 Mar 59	The French become aware of Ferdinand's arrival in Fulda, but are uncertain whether he will strike SE against the Imperials, SW against Broglie or west against Contades.		
		Ferdinand forms junction with Isenburg at Fulda (totalling ~ 24,000) to prepare for descent on Frankfurt.	
9 Apr 59		Ferdinand orders march on Frankfurt.	
11 Apr 59		As Ferdinand reaches Büdingen, his intention of attacking Broglie becomes clear. Broglie elects to defend at Bergen, 4 kilometres from Frankfurt.	
13 Apr 59	Ferdinand withdraws towards Westphalia to prep for Contades' likely attack.	Battle of Bergen – French victory.	

Date	Operations involving Ferdinand's Western Flank	Operations involving Ferdinand's Southern Flank	Solely British Operations
25 Apr 59		Contades adopts Belle-Isle's plan and visits Frankfurt. He strips Broglie of 10,000 troops to reinforce his main army.	
May 59	Contades' army crosses R Rhine upstream near Bonn.		British Naval force captures Island of Guadeloupe.
31 May 59	Contades' army concentrates at Marburg. In response, Ferdinand leaves 9,000 at Münster, but crosses south of R Lippe between Dortmund and Lippstadt.	Broglie's corps concentrates at Friedberg, north of Frankfurt.	
Jun 59		Broglie occupies Kassel and Münden.	British Naval force captures island of Marie-Galante.
18-23 Jun 59		Broglie occupies Paderborn, then Detmold.	
1 July 59	Attempt on Lippstadt - allied victory.		
8 Jul 59	Ferdinand reaches Osnabrück, 55 kilometres to the west of Minden.	The French reach Herford, 25 kilometres SW of Minden.	
9 Jul 59		Broglie arrives near Minden. The garrison is summoned to surrender.	

Synchronisation Matrix, Minden and Gohfeld

Date	Time	Minden	Gohfeld
8 Jul		After considerable manoeuvring, the French reach Herford and the allies Osnabrück, rendering the French closer to Minden than the allies. Realising this, Ferdinand sends Erbprinz with 12 sqn and 15 bn to secure Minden before the French. Ferdinand decides that Nienburg must become his army's principal magazine.	
9 Jul		Broglie, with Fischer's corps under command, arrives opposite Minden while Erbprinz is still 30 kilometres away. Zastrow is summoned to surrender, but refuses.	
10 Jul	early	Fischer's troops swim the Weser to capture a punt, which is used to ferry 300 volunteers over. Broglie begins bombardment of the east end of the main town bridge over R Weser. Fischer storms the gate.	
	9:00 p.m.	Minden is in French hands.	
11 Jul		Estorff, on a forced march with 400 cavalry and 400 dragoons, disperses a French force 8 kilometres from Nienburg.	
14 Jul		The French army is concentrated in and around Minden. Ferdinand sends the Erbprinz to Petershagen (12 kilometres north of Minden), to cover Nienburg. Erbprinz discovers that the French have vacated Minden Heath and occupied strong defensive positions between the Bastau and Wiehengebirge ridge.	
16 Jul		Ferdinand marches to Petershagen, 12 kilometres to the north of Minden.	
17 Jul		Erbprinz drives in French outposts. Ferdinand makes a demonstration onto Minden Heath.	
18-21 Jul		Ferdinand sends detachments westwards to picquet the villages on Minden Heath.	
26/27 Jul	Engagement at Fort Carillon (Ticonderoga) – British victory		
27 Jul		Erbprinz leaves Petershagen with 10 sqn, 7 bn, 16 guns.	

Date	Time	Minden	Gohfeld
28 Jul		Erbprinz reaches Lübbecke, encounters French hussars, and drives them off.	When Contades learns of the Erbprinz at Lübbecke, he sends Brissac to Bunde to protect his line of communication.
29 Jul		Allies march into camp at Hille. Gilsa deploys to cover the Hille-Eickhorst causeway. Generals ordered to recce routes onto the heath. Sackville appointed General of the Day.	Erbprinz reaches Riemsloh, where he is joined by Dreves and Schlieffen (force now enlarged to 9,700 men).
30 Jul		Ferdinand detaches 2,000 troops to hold Lübbecke. Sackville relieves Imhoff in command of the Picquets of the allied army.	Brissac ordered to shift east to protect the main Herford-Minden road.
31 Jul		Sackville conducts his own recce. The French put two pontoons across the R. Weser to the south of Minden's bridge, to facilitate movement between the banks. Lohrmann visits Ferdinand's HQ.	Erbprinz and Dreves establish themselves between Kirchlengern and Quernheim. Brissac's Corps occupies position at Gohfeld, with R Werre to its front, to protect the Gohfelder Werrebrücke.
	5:00 p.m.	Anhalt relieves Sackville.	
	6:00 p.m.	Ferdinand issues his orders for his army to be under arms by 1.00 a.m. Contades issues his orders. Sackville reports to allied HQ.	
	dusk	A severe wind blows up from the west, masking sound. Broglie's corps to cross the R. Weser, pass through Minden and, reinforced by eight grenadier bns, to advance to attack Todtenhausen at sunrise.	
		The French approach Hahlen with two bns of light troops.	
1 Aug	0:00 a.m.	The bulk of Contades' army has crossed the Bastau	
	1:00 a.m.	The time for the allied army to be ready to march. French deserters captured in Hartum.	
	3:00 a.m.	Ferdinand awakened and informed, belatedly, that the French have broken out. French commence bombardment of Hille. Ferdinand orders Anhalt to gather the picquets to secure Hahlen.	Erbprinz leaves Kirchlengern to begin attack.
		On his way to Hahlen, Ferdinand is informed that the French are already in occupation.	Brissac moves north of R. Werre.
	4:00 a.m.	The allied army begins to fall-in in its encampment.	Keilmansegg emerges from the defile of Beck and is engaged by French.
	4:30 a.m.	Sunrise. The time for Broglie to launch his attack on von Wangenheim at Todtenhausen.	
	5:00 a.m.	Broglie's artillery opens its bombardment. Spörcken's column is making good progress through its 'debouchers', outstripping Scheele's column to its left.	Both sides settle in to a 2-hour bombardment.
	5-6:00 a.m.	Ferdinand sends his Adjutant General to alert von Wangenheim, then sees smoke rising from the direction of Broglie's initial barrage at Todtenhausen. Ferdinand hears firing from his rear right as d'Havre occupies Eickhorst. He orders two guns to support the defence of Hille, and recalls Gilsa from Lübbecke. Sackville is 'waked' by firing to the right of the allied army. By 5.30 a.m., Sackville's cavalry is mounted and formed, but awaiting Lord George.	
		Ferdinand energises the allied army. Broglie finds his guns overmatched by the artillery on the allied left. Rather than assaulting, he awaits reinforcement by Nicolai's two brigades.	French cavalry charge repulsed by Alt Zastrow, with heavy losses.

Date	Time	Minden	Gohfeld
	6:00 a.m.	Broglie's reinforced corps advances but personal reconnaissance reveals 9 Hanoverian bns and a substantial body of cavalry advancing to threaten him. Fearing a counter-attack, he orders a pause while he confers with Contades. The allied artillery leaves its encampments.	
	7:00 a.m.	Spörcken's column comes under enemy artillery fire. Foy's artillery responds.	Second French cavalry charge founders on allied infantry reserve.
		Two French cavalry charges on Spörcken's column. Broglie ordered to halt, consolidate and be prepared to cover the French army withdrawal.	Erbprinz and Dreves appear at the Gohfelder Werrebrücke, to the rear of de Brissac.
		Two French infantry brigades engaged on Spörcken's right flank. Wutginau's column moves up, as does Imhoff's. Third French cavalry charge. Contades orders Beaupreau's infantry forward from his centre. Holstein's cavalry overwhelms the Brigade du Roi. Wangenheim's corps pushes forward on the allied left.	Brissac orders his force to move north but is again engaged, this time by von Bock.
	10:00 a.m.	Main French offensive actions are over. Contades orders a general withdrawal, covered by Broglie's corps. Foy's and MacBean's artillery continue to pound the retreating French.	Brissac's force dissolves.
	11:00 a.m.	The main French army is back across the Bastau.	
		Immediate post battle drills by the allies. Roll-call, collection and treatment of the wounded, redistribution of ammunition. The allied army is ordered to advance to just outwith cannon range of Minden. Ferdinand calls upon the garrison to surrender. Field Hospital established in Petershagen. Orders issued for a thanksgiving service the following day.	Erbprinz occupies Bergkirchen on the Wiehengebirge ridge.
		While Broglie holds Minden, Contades's Army crosses to the right (east) bank of the Weser by pontoon. Broglie crosses the Weser, destroying the stone bridge behind him.	French commander at Rehme orders the destruction of remaining bridges over R. Werre.
2 Aug	dawn	Contades and Broglie retreat southwards for Frankfurt.	
	9:00 a.m.	Allied service of thanksgiving.	
	mid-morning	*Lt Col* Auguste Dagieu offers to surrender Minden. Ferdinand issues his 'Order of the Day'.	Erbprinz crosses the R. Weser to pursue the French army as it retreats towards Kassel.
	12:00 a.m.	The allies occupy Minden.	
	6:00 p.m.	Allied 'Feu-de-Joie'.	

Appendix II

Order of Battle for the Battle of Minden

The Orders of Battle provided are a product of synthesising the best available sources, but may as a result vary from each individual source in specific details.

French
(48,250 all ranks), formations listed from the right

Broglie's Corps (2,640 cavalry, 22 battalions), 22 pieces of artillery after battalions and before closing bracket

Infantry
Brigade Piémont (6 battalions)
  Régiment Piémont (4)
  Régiment Dauphine (2)
Brigade Royal Bavière (4 battalions)
  Régiment Royal Bavière
  Régiment Royal Deux-Ponts
Brigade Waldner (4 battalions)
  Régiment Waldner
  Régiment Planta
Brigade Grenadiers (8 battalions)
  Grenadiers de France (4)
  Grenadiers Royaux de Modène (2)
Grenadiers Royaux de Chantilly (2)

Cavalry
Brigade Commissaire-Général (6 squadrons)
  Régiment Commissaire-Général (2)
  Régiment Lameth (2)
  Régiment Des Salles (2)
Brigade Penthièvre (4 squadrons)
  Régiment Penthièvre (2)

Régiment Toustain (2)
Brigade Royal Allemand (6 squadrons)
Régiment Royal Allemand (2)
Régiment Nassau-Sarrebruck (2)
Régiment Wurttemburg (2)
Detached troops across the Weser (11 squadrons)
Dragons d'Apchon (4)
Volontaires de Schomberg (3)
Royal-Nassau Hussards (4)

The Right Wing (25 Battalions, each theoretically of 500 all ranks, ~12,000 all ranks)
Right of Infantry First Line under *Lieutenant-Général* Chevalier de Nicolai
Brigade Belsunce (4 battalions)
Régiment Belsunce (4)
Brigade Picardie (5 battalions)
Régiment Picardie (4)
Régiment Lamarche (1)

Left of Infantry First Line under *Lieutenant-Général* Beaupreau
Brigade Rouergue (4 battalions)
Régiment Rouergue (2)
Régiment Lamarche (1)
Régiment Tournasis (1)
Brigade Touraine (4 battalions)
Régiment Touraine (2)
Régiment Aumont (2)

Infantry Second Line under *Lieutenant-Général* St Germain
Brigade Auvergne (4 battalions)
Régiment Auvergne (4)
Brigade Anhalt (4 battalions)
Régiment Anhalt (2)
Régiment St Germain (1)
Régiment Bergh (1)

The Centre (63 Squadrons, each of 120 horses, a force of ~ 7,560 all ranks)
Cavalry First Line under *Lieutenant-Général* Duc de FitzJames
Brigade Colonel-General under *Lieutenant-Général* Marquis de Castries (9 squadrons)
Régiment Colonel-General (3)
Régiment Marcieux (2)
Régiment Vogüé (2)
Régiment Condé (2)
Brigade Royal-Cravates (6 Squadrons)
Régiment Royal-Cravates (2)
Régiment Talleyrand (2)
Régiment Surgère (2)

Brigade Mestre-de-Camp Général (8 Squadrons)
Régiment Mestre-de-Camp Général (2)
Régiment Poly (2)
Régiment D'Espinchal (2)
Régiment Fumel (2)

Cavalry Second Line under *Lieutenant-Général* du Mesnil
Brigade le Roi (8 squadrons)
Régiment le Roi (2)
Régiment Henrichemont (2)
Régiment Moustiers (2)
Régiment Noé (2)
Brigade Bourgogne (6 squadrons)
Régiment Bourgogne (2)
Régiment Raugrave (2)
Régiment Archaic (2)
Brigade Royal Étranger (8 squadrons)
Régiment Royal Étranger (2)
Régiment Balincourt (2)
Régiment Noailles (2)
Régiment Crussol (2)

Cavalry Third Line under *Lieutenant-Général* Marquis de Poyanne
Gendarmerie de France (8 squadrons)
Carabiniers (10 squadrons)

The Left Wing (16 French battalions, about 8,000 all ranks, plus 6,500 Saxons, a combined force of ~14,500 all ranks).

Infantry First Line under *Lieutenant-Général* de Guerchy
Brigade Condé (4 battalions)
Régiment Condé (2)
Régiment Enghein (2)
Brigade Aquitaine (4 battalions)
Régiment Aquitaine (2)
Régiment Vastan (2)
Brigade du Roi (4 battalions)
Régiment du Roi (4)
Brigade Champagne (4 battalions)
Régiment Champagne (4)

Infantry Second Line under the Comte de Lusace[1]
Second Saxon Brigade
Regt. Kurprinzessin (2)
Regt. Prinz Sachsen-Gotha (1)

1 Only 13 battalions present of the 14 listed here.

Regt. Prinz Anton (1)
Regt. Graf Brühl (1)
Fusiliers Regt. Rochow (1)
First Saxon Brigade
Regt. Fürst Lubomirsky (1)
Regt. Prinz Clemens (1)
Regt. Prinz Joseph (1)
Regt. Prinz Friedrich August (2)
Regt. Prinz Xaver (2)
Regt. Prinz Karl Maximilian (1)

Minden Garrison under *Maréchal-de-Camp* Bisson
Brigade Lowendahl (4 battalions)
Régiment Lowendahl (2)
Régiment Bouillon (2)

Force at Eickhorst under *Lieutenant-Général* the Duc d'Havré
Régiment Navarre (4 battalions)
Volontaires de Dauphiné (300 infantry)
Volontaires de Hallet (600 infantry and cavalry)
Volontaires de Muret (150 infantry)

Artillery
The French army had 162 guns, including the 22 with Broglie, manned by 2,000 gunners.

Allied (37,420 all ranks), formations listed from the right
No 1 Column 24 squadrons under Lieutenant General Lord George Sackville
First Line
Brigade of Major General John Mostyn (8 squadrons)
Royal Horse Guards (The Blues) (British – 3)
1st King's Dragoon Guards (Bland's) (British – 3)
6th Inniskilling Dragoons (British – 2)
Brigade of *Oberst* Karl Breitenbach (6 squadrons)
Grenadiere zu Pferde (Hanoverian – 1)
Max Breitenbach Dragoner (Hanoverian – 4)
Garde du Corps (Hanoverian – 1)

Second Line under Lieutenant General the Marquis of Granby
Brigade of Major General Granville Elliot (6 squadrons)
    3rd Dragoon Guards (Howard's) (British – 2)
    10th Dragoons (Mordaunt's) (British – 2)
    2nd Dragoons (the Greys) (British – 2)
Brigade of *Oberst* Bock (4 squadrons)
    Regiment Bremer (Hanoverian – 2)
    Regiment Veltheim (Hanoverian – 2)

No 2 Column 28 guns under *Major* Hase, escorted by one battalion
Hanoverian Heavy Artillery under *Major* Hase (sixteen 12-pdrs, four 3-pdrs, two howitzers)
British Heavy Artillery under Captain McBean (6 guns)
Regiment Saxe-Gotha (Hanoverian – 1)

No 3 Column 8 battalions under *General der Infanterie* von Spörcken
Brigade of Major General Waldegrave (3 battalions, 1st line)
    12th Foot (Napier's) (British – 1)
    37th Foot (Stewart's) (British – 1)
    23rd Foot (Huske's; Royal Welch Fusiliers) (British – 1)
Brigade of Major General Kingsley (5 battalions, 2nd line)
    20th Foot (Kingsley's) (British – 1)
    51st Root (Brudenell's) (British – 1)
    25th Foot (Home's) (British – 1)
    Garde zu Fuss (Hanoverian – 2)[2]

No 4 Column 6 battalions under *Generalmajor* von Scheele, in place of *Generalleutnant* Prinz von Anhalt who was commanding the advanced picquets and the force around Hahlen
Brigade of *Generalmajor* von Scheele (3 battalions, 1st line)
    Regiment Hardenberg (Hanoverian – 1)
    Regiment Reden (Hanoverian – 1)
    Regiment Scheele (Hanoverian – 1)
Brigade of *Generalmajor* Wissembach (3 battalions, 2nd line)
    Regiment Stolzenberg (Hanoverian – 1)
    Regiment Brunck (Hanoverian – 1)
    Regiment Erbprinz Friedrich (Hessian – 1)

No 5 Column 37 guns under *Oberst* Braun
Hanoverian Heavy Artillery under *Oberst* Braun (two 10-pounders, twelve 6-pounders, two 3-pounders, three howitzers)
British Light Artillery under Captains Drummond, Foy and Phillips (18 guns)

2 Grenadier companies detached as headquarters guard.

No 6 Column 6 battalions and 10 guns under *Generalleutnant* von Wutginau
Brigade of *Generalmajor* von Toll (3 battalions, 1st line)
Regiment Wangenheim (Hanoverian – 1)
Leibgarde zu Fuss (Hessian– 1)
Regiment Toll (Hessian– 1)
Brigade of *Generalmajor* von Bischhausen (3 battalions, 2nd line)
Regiment Prinz von Anhalt (Hessian– 1)
Regiment Bischhausen (Hessian– 1)
Regiment Mansbach (Hessian– 1)
Buckeburg Light Artillery (ten 6-pounders)

No 7 Column seven battalions under *Generalleutnant* von Imhoff
Brigade of *Generalmajor* von Einsiedel (4 battalions, 1st line)
Regiment Gilsa (Hessian– 1)
Regiment Prinz Wilhelm (Hessian– 1)
Leib-Grenadiere (Hessian – 1)
2/Regiment Behr (Brunswick – 1)
Brigade of *Generalmajor* von Behr (3 battalions, 2nd line)
Leib-Regiment (Hessian – 1)
Regiment Imhoff (Brunswick – 2)

No 8 Column 19 squadrons under *Generalleutnant* the Duke of Holstein
Brigade of *Oberst* Stein (11 squadrons, 1st line)
Regiment Hammerstein (Hanoverian – 2)
Regiment Prinz Wilhelm (Hessian – 2)
Lieb-Regiment (Hessian – 2)
Dragoner Regiment Holstein-Gottorp Nr.9 (Prussian – 5)
Brigade of *Generalleutnant* von Urff (8 squadrons, 2nd line)
Regiment Pruschenk (Hessian – 2)
Regiment Miltitz (Hessian – 2)
Dragoner Regiment Finckenstein Nr.10 (Prussian – 4)

Wangenheim's Corps
Cavalry
Brigade of *Generalmajor* Reden (4 squadrons, 1st line)
Leib-Regiment (Hanoverian – 2)
Regiment Heise (Hanoverian – 2)
Brigade of *Generalmajor* Grothausen (6 squadrons, 1st line)
Regiment Hodenberg (Hanoverian – 2)
Regiment Reden (Hanoverian – 2)
Regiment Grothausen (Hanoverian – 2)
Brigade of *Generalmajor* Hanstein (8 squadrons, 2nd line)
Leib-Dragoner (Hessian – 4)
Dragoner Regiment Prinz Friedrich (Hessian – 4)
Husaren Regiment Ruesch Nr.5 (Prussian – 1)

Infantry
First Line (7 battalions)
- Grenadier Battalion Maxwell (British – 1)
- Grenadier Battalion Donop (Hessian – 1)
- Grenadier Battalion Schlottheim (Hessian – 1)
- Grenadier Battalion Stammer (Brunswick – 1)
- Grenadier Battalion Wittorff (Brunswick – 1)
- Grenadier Battalion Wersabe (Hanoverian – 1)

Second Line (8 battalions)
- Regiment Spörcken (Hanoverian – 1)
- Regiment Jung-Zastrow (Hanoverian – 1)
- Regiment Halberstadt (Hanoverian – 1)
- Regiment Schulenburg (Hanoverian – 1)
- Regiment Oberg (Hanoverian – 1)
- Regiment Laffert (Hanoverian – 1)
- Regiment Schiether (Hanoverian – 1)

Reserve (at Petershagen; 1 battalion)
- Regiment Kielmansegg (Hanoverian – 1)

Artillery under Graf Schaumberg-Lippe (41 guns escorted by 1 battalion)
Hessian Artillery under *Oberstleutnant* Huth (sixteen 12-pdrs, six 3-pdrs and three howitzers)
Bückeburg Artillery (six 6-pdrs and ten 3-pdrs)
Regiment Bückeburg (Schaumberg-Lippe – 1)

Detached Force under *Oberst* Laffert on the eastern bank of the River Weser
- Luckner-Husaren (Hanoverian – 2 squadrons)
- Grenadier Battalion Sydow (Hanoverian – 1 battalion)
- Grenadier Battalion Wense (Hanoverian – 1 battalion)
- Freytag Jäger (Hanoverian, 50 mounted and 150 foot)

Appendix III

Order of Battle for the Action at Gohfeld

French under Jean-Paul Timoléon, Duc de Brissac.

Infantry under the Comte de Segur
- Grenadiers Royaux de le Camus (2 bns)
- Grenadiers Royaux de Narbonne (2 bns)
- Volontaires de Flandre Infantry (8 coys, 340 men)
- Volontaires du Hainaut Infantry (8 coys, 340 men)
- Volontaires Étrangers (17 coys, 750 men)

Cavalry under the Comte Turpin de Crissé
- Hussards de Turpin (6 sqns)
- Hussards de Bercheny (6 sqns)
- Volontaires de Flandre Dragoons (8 coys. 310 men)
- Volontaires du Hainaut Dragoons (8 coys, 310 men)
- Volontaires Étrangers Dragoons (8 coys, 310 men)

Artillery several guns, including five 4-pdrs

The French baggage was in Rehme, to the east of Gohfeld.

Allies under the Erbprinz of Brunswick, deployments as from the right

Right Column under *Generalmajor* Dreves (3 battalions, 4 squadrons, 200 Jäger)

Regiment vacant ex-Diepenbroick (Hanoverian – 1 bn)
Leib-Regiment (Brunswick – 2 bns)
Bock Dragoner (Hanoverian – 4 sqns)
Freytag Jägers (200 men)

Centre Column under *Generalleutnant* Graf von Kilmansegg (4 battalions, 1 squadron, 16 guns)

Regiment Alt Zastrow (Hanoverian – 1 bn)
Regiment Behr (Hanoverian – 1 bn)
Regiment Bock (Hanoverian – 1 bn)
Regiment Kanitz (Hessian – 1 bn)
Georg Carl Breidenbach Dragoner (Hanoverian – 1 bn)
Hanoverian Artillery (six 12-pounders, ten others)

Left Column under *Generalmajor* Bock (3 battalions, 4 squadrons)

Regiment Block (Hanoverian – 1 bn)
Regiment Dreves (Hanoverian – 1 bn)
2/Regiment Zastrow (Brunswick – 1 bn)
Busche Dragoner (Hanoverian – 4 sqns)

Light Troops

Hessian Jäger (400 men)
Husaren Regiment Malachowski Nr.7 (Prussian – 1 sqn)
Freikorps von Trümbach (Prussian – 1 bn; detached to Herford)

Appendix IV

Uniform Details

The following charts are intended to provide an impression of the colours of the uniforms worn. They may not be totally comprehensive and, in some cases are 'averages' of opinions and sources. Some generalisations are possible: in most cases, although not all, the colours of facings (collars, lapels, cuffs and turnbacks) and saddlecloth are consistent. Most wore a black tricorne hat, with some form of coloured lacing. Most regiments of heavy horse wore some form of buff waistcoat or vest and pale yellow leather breeches: kid, buff, chamois. For the foot, whilst the French are described as wearing white gaiters in the main, Saxon regiments wore black. Allied German units mainly wore black gaiters, although not exclusively; the British appeared to wear black, brown or grey gaiters on campaign. The reality would probably be that white would degrade very quickly, and may have been replaced by a more practical colour. Regimental lace trims are so varied and complex that they cannot easily be shown here.

Key: A.green = Apple Green; Br.red = Brick Red; Cochin = Cochineal; D. = Dark; Fr.blue = French Blue; Go.green = Gosling Green; Gr.grn = Grass Green; GW = Grey White; Li. = Light; R.blue = Royal Blue; R.green = Russian Green; TB = turnbacks.

French and Saxon Uniforms

Broglie's Corps, Mounted Troops

Regiment	Hat Lace	Coat	Collar	Cuffs	Lapels	TB	Waistcoat	Buttons	Saddlecloth
Comm-Gén	gold	GW	n/a	black	black	GW	buff	brass	red
Lameth	silver	GW	n/a	red	red	red	buff	pewter	blue
Des Salles	silver	GW	n/a	red	red	red	buff	pewter	blue
Penthièvre	silver	GW	n/a	red	red	red	buff	pewter	blue
Toustain	silver	GW	n/a	red	red	red	buff	pewter	blue
R Allemand	bearskin	blue	n/a	red	n/a	n/a	crimson	red	blue
Nassau-Sarrebruck	gold	r.blue	n/a	straw	straw	straw	buff	brass	blue
Wurttemburg	bearskin	GW	n/a	red	red	red	buff	pewter	blue
Apschon	silver	red	red	sky	n/a	red	red	white	red
Schomberg	helmet	green	n/a	red	red	red	buff	pewter	green
R Nassau Hus.	mirliton	blue	buff	buff	n/a	n/a	n/a	pewter	red

Broglie's Corps, Infantry

Regiment	Hat Lace	Coat	Collar	Cuffs	Lapels	TB	Waistcoat	Buttons	Breeches
Piémont	gold	GW	n/a	black	n/a	n/a	GW	brass	white
Dauphine	gold	white	blue	blue	n/a	n/a	blue	brass	white
R Deux-Ponts	silver	blue	n/a	red	red	white	white	pewter	white
Royal Bavière	silver	blue	black	black	black	white	blue	white	blue
Waldner	silver	red	n/a	blue	red	n/a	blue	pewter	blue
Planta	silver	red	n/a	blue	n/a	n/a	blue	pewter	white
Gren de France	bearskin	blue	scarlet	blue	scarlet	scarlet	blue	silver	blue
Gren Royaux	silver	GW	blue	GW	n/a	GW	GW	pewter	GW
Artillerie	gold	blue	red	red	n/a	n/a	red	brass	red

Right Wing Foot

Regiment	Hat Lace	Coat	Collar	Cuffs	Lapels	TB	Waistcoat	Buttons	Breeches
Rougergue	gold	GW	red	red	n/a	n/a	red	brass	GW
Lamarche	gold	GW	red	red	n/a	GW	red	brass	GW
Tournasis	gold	GW	n/a	red	n/a	n/a	GW	brass	GW
Touraine	silver	GW	blue	blue	n/a	n/a	blue	pewter	GW
Aumont	gold	GW	GW	GW	n/a	n/a	red	brass	GW
Belsunce	gold	white	violet	violet	n/a	n/a	white	brass	white
Picardie	gold	white	white	white	n/a	n/a	red	yellow	white
Auvergne	silver	GW	violet	violet	n/a	n/a	GW	pewter	GW
Anhalt	silver	blue	yellow	yellow	yellow	yellow	yellow	pewter	yellow
St Germain	gold	blue	yellow	yellow	n/a	yellow	blue	yellow	blue
Bergh	gold	blue	n/a	red	red	red	white	yellow	white
Artillerie	gold	blue	red	red	n/a	n/a	red	brass	red

Cavalry Centre

Regiment	Hat Lace	Coat	Collar	Cuffs	Lapels	TB	Waistcoat	Buttons	Saddlecloth
Col-Général	gold	red	n/a	black	black	red	buff	brass	red
Marcieux	silver	GW	GW	red	red	red	buff	pewter	blue
Vogüé	silver	GW	n/a	red	red	red	buff	pewter	blue
Condé	silver	GW	n/a	red	red	red	buff	pewter	buff
R-Cravattes	silver	blue	n/a	red	red	red	buff	pewter	blue
Talleyrand	silver	GW	n/a	red	red	red	buff	pewter	blue
Surgère	silver	GW	red	red	red	red	buff	brass	blue
Mestre de Camp	gold	grey	n/a	black	black	grey	buff	brass	red
Poly	silver	GW	n/a	red	red	red	buff	pewter	blue
D'Espinchal	gold	GW	n/a	red	red	red	buff	pewter	blue
Fumel	silver	GW	n/a	red	red	red	buff	pewter	blue
du Roi	silver	blue	n/a	red	red	red	buff	pewter	blue
Henrichemont	silver	GW	n/a	red	red	red	buff	pewter	blue
Moustiers	silver	GW	n/a	red	red	red	buff	pewter	blue
Noé	silver	GW	n/a	red	red	red	buff	pewter	blue
Bourgogne	silver	blue	n/a	red	red	red	buff	pewter	blue
Raugrave	bearskin	blue	n/a	yellow	yellow	yellow	yellow	pewter	blue
Archaic	silver	GW	n/a	red	red	red	buff	pewter	blue
Royal Étranger	silver	blue	n/a	red	red	red	buff	pewter	blue
Balaincourt	silver	GW	n/a	red	red	red	buff	pewter	blue
Noailles	silver	red	n/a	red	red	red	buff	pewter	blue

Crussol	silver	GW	n/a	red	red	red	buff	pewter	blue
Gendarmerie	silver	scarlet	scarlet	scarlet	n/a	n/a	buff	silver	red
Carabiniers	silver	blue	n/a	red	red	red	buff	pewter	blue

Left Wing Foot

Regiment	Hat Lace	Coat	Collar	Cuffs	Lapels	TB	Waistcoat	Buttons	Breeches
Condé	gold	GW	n/a	red	n/a	n/a	red	brass	GW
Enghein	silver	GW	n/a	red	n/a	n/a	GW	pewter	GW
Aquitaine	gold	GW	n/a	blue	n/a	n/a	blue	brass	GW
Vastan	gold	GW	black	GW	n/a	n/a	GW	brass	GW
Roi	gold	GW	n/a	blue	n/a	n/a	blue	brass	blue
Champagne	gold	white	white	white	n/a	n/a	red	yellow	white
Pr. Karl Max.	white	white	R.green	R.green	n/a	R.green	R.green	silver	white
Pr. Xaver	white	white	Li.blue	Li.blue	n/a	Li.blue	Li.blue	brass	white
Pr. Fr. August	white	white	yellow	yellow	n/a	yellow	yellow	brass	white
Pr. Josef	white	white	Cochin	Cochin	n/a	Cochin	Cochin	brass	white
Pr. Clemens	white	white	Fr.blue	Fr.blue	n/a	Fr.blue	Fr.blue	brass	white
Lubomirski	white	white	yellow	yellow	n/a	yellow	yellow	silver	white
Rochow	white	D.green	D.red	D.red	n/a	D.red	D.red	brass	white
Graf Bruhl	white	white	poppy	poppy	poppy	poppy	poppy	brass	white
Pr. Anton	white	white	Fr.blue	Fr.blue	n/a	Fr.blue	Fr.blue	silver	white
Pr. Sach-Gotha	white	white	Li.blue	Li.blue	n/a	Li.blue	Li.blue	silver	white
Kurprinzessin	white	white	Li.blue	Li.blue	Li.blue	Li.blue	Li.blue	silver	white
Artillerie	gold	blue	red	red	n/a	n/a	red	brass	red

Other Units

Regiment	Hat Lace	Coat	Collar	Cuffs	Lapels	TB	Waistcoat	Buttons	Breeches
Lowendahl	gold	blue	white	white	n/a	blue	blue	brass	blue
Bouillon	silver	white	black	black	black	white	white	pewter	white
Navarre	gold	white	n/a	white	white	n/a	red	brass	white
Vol de Hallet	white	red	chamois	chamois	chamois	n/a	chamois	pewter	chamois
Vol Dauphiné	gold	blue	red	red	red	n/a	white	brass	white
Vol de Muret	gold	white	n/a	blue	n/a	n/a	blue	brass	white

Allied Uniforms

No 1 Column

Regiment	Hat Lace	Coat	Collar	Cuffs	Lapels	TB	Waistcoat	Buttons	Saddlecloth
RHG (Blues)	yellow	blue	n/a	red	red	red	red	brass	red
1st Dr Gds	gold	red	n/a	blue	blue	blue	yellow	yellow	red
6th Dragoons	silver	red	n/a	yellow	n/a	yellow	yellow	white	yellow
Gren zu Pferde	mitre	red	n/a	black	black	red	straw	brass	red
Breitenbach	silver	white	n/a	Li.blue	Li.blue	blue	buff	white	Li.blue
Gd du Corps	silver	red	blue	blue	n/a	blue	straw	pewter	crimson
3rd Dg Gds	gold	red	n/a	white	white	white	white	yellow	white
10th Dragoons	silver	red	n/a	D.yellow	n/a	D.yellow	D.yellow	white	D.yellow
2nd Dragoons	gren cap	red	red	blue	n/a	blue	blue	white	blue
Bremer	white	white	n/a	A.green	n/a	Green	straw	pewter	A.green
Veltheim	white	white	n/a	blue	n/a	blue	blue	pewter	blue

No 2 Column

Regiment	Hat Lace	Coat	Collar	Cuffs	Lapels	TB	Waistcoat	Buttons	Breeches
Hann. Arty.	gold	L.blue	n/a	red	red	red	red	pewter	straw
Br. Arty	gold	blue	n/a	scarlet	scarlet	scarlet	blue	yellow	blue
Saxe-Gotha	white	red	n/a	D.green	D.green	D.green	white	pewter	straw

No 3 Column

Regiment	Hat Lace	Coat	Collar	Cuffs	Lapels	TB	Waistcoat	Buttons	Breeches
12th	white	Br.red	n/a	yellow	yellow	yellow	Br.red	pewter	Br.red
37th	white	Br.red	n/a	yellow	yellow	yellow	Br.red	pewter	Br.red
23rd	white	Br.red	n/a	blue	blue	blue	Br.red	pewter	Br.red
20th	white	Br.red	n/a	Li.yellow	Li.yellow	Li.yellow	Br.red	pewter	Br.red
51st	white	Br.red	n/a	Go.green	Go.green	Go.green	Br.red	pewter	Br.red
25th	white	Br.red	n/a	D.yellow	D.yellow	D.yellow	Br.red	pewter	Br.red
Gd zu Fuss	yellow	red	n/a	red	blue	blue	blue	brass	straw

No 4 Column

Regiment	Hat Lace	Coat	Collar	Cuffs	Lapels	TB	Waistcoat	Buttons	Breeches
Hardenberg	white	red	n/a	orange	orange	orange	orange	pewter	straw
Reden	white	red	n/a	black	black	black	white	pewter	straw
Scheele	white	red	n/a	straw	straw	straw	straw	pewter	straw
Stolzemberg	white	red	n/a	black	black	black	straw	pewter	straw
Brunck	white	red	n/a	Gr.grn	Gr.grn	Gr.grn	Gr.grn	pewter	straw
Erbprinz Frdk	white	D.blue	yellow	yellow	yellow	yellow	yellow	white	yellow

No 5 Column

Regiment	Hat Lace	Coat	Collar	Cuffs	Lapels	TB	Waistcoat	Buttons	Breeches
Hann. Arty.	gold	Li.blue	n/a	red	red	red	red	pewter	straw
Br Arty.	gold	blue	n/a	scarlet	scarlet	scarlet	blue	yellow	blue

No 6 Column

Regiment	Hat Lace	Coat	Collar	Cuffs	Lapels	TB	Waistcoat	Buttons	Breeches
Wangenheim	white	red	n/a	straw	straw	straw	straw	pewter	straw
Leibgarde	white	D.blue	red	red	red	red	Li.yellow	pewter	white
Toll	white	D.blue	orange	orange	orange	red	white	brass	white
Anhalt	white	D.blue	red	red	red	red	white	white	white
Bischhausen	white	D.blue	n/a	straw	straw	red	straw	yellow	white
Mansbach	white	D.blue	n/a	white	white	red	white	yellow	white
Buckeburg Arty.	unlaced	D.blue	D.blue	black	n/a	red	buff	pewter	D.blue

No 7 Column

Regiment	Hat Lace	Coat	Collar	Cuffs	Lapels	TB	Waistcoat	Buttons	Breeches
Gilsa	white	D.blue	n/a	red	red	red	straw	pewter	white
Pr. Wilhelm	white	D.blue	blood	blood	blood	blood	white	white	white
Leib-Gren.	gren cap	D.blue	Li.red	Li.red	Li.red	Li.red	straw	white	white
Behr	white	D.blue	red	red	red	red	white	pewter	white
Lieb-Regt.	white	D.blue	red	red	n/a	red	yellow	white	white
Imhoff	white	D.blue	white	white	white	white	white	brass	white

No 8 Column

Regiment	Hat Lace	Coat	Collar	Cuffs	Lapels	TB	Waistcoat	Buttons	Saddlecloth
Hammerstein	yellow	white	n/a	D.Green	n/a	D.Green	straw	brass	D.Green
Prinz Wilhem	white	white	blue	blue	blue	blue	white	brass	blue
Lieb-Regt.	yellow	white	red	red	red	red	white	brass	red
Holstein-Gottorp	unlaced	cobalt	cobalt	blue	n/a	cobalt	straw	white	blue
Pruschenk	yellow	white	sky	sky	sky	sky	white	brass	sky
Miltiz	yellow	white	green	green	green	green	white	brass	green
Finckenstein	unlaced	cobalt	orange	orange	n/a	orange	buff	white	orange

Wangenheim's Corps, Cavalry

Regiment	Hat Lace	Coat	Collar	Cuffs	Lapels	TB	Waistcoat	Buttons	Saddlecloth
Leib-Regt.	white	white	n/a	yellow	n/a	yellow	straw	pewter	yellow
Heise	yellow	white	n/a	orange	n/a	orange	straw	brass	orange
Hodenberg	white	white	n/a	scarlet	n/a	scarlet	straw	pewter	scarlet
Reden	yellow	white	n/a	D.blue	n/a	D.blue	straw	brass	D.Blue
Grothausen	yellow	white	n/a	crimson	n/a	crimson	straw	brass	crimson
Lieb-Drag	yellow	sky	red	red	red	red	blue	yellow	red
Pz Frdk Drag	white	sky	yellow	yellow	yellow	yellow	yellow	pewter	yellow
Ruesch	mirliton	black	black	black	n/a	n/a	n/a	white	black
Luckner	mirliton	D.green	D.green	D.green	n/a	D.green	brass	D.green	D.green

Wangenheim's Corps, Infantry

Regiment	Hat Lace	Coat	Collar	Cuffs	Lapels	TB	Waistcoat	Buttons	Breeches
Spörcken	white	red	n/a	straw	straw	straw	straw	brass	white
Jung-Zastrow	white	red	n/a	D.green	D.green	D.green	D.green	pewter	straw
Halberstadt	white	red	n/a	gold	gold	gold	gold	pewter	straw
Schulenburg	white	red	n/a	black	black	yellow	yellow	pewter	straw
Oberg	yellow	red	n/a	yellow	yellow	yellow	yellow	brass	straw
Laffert	white	red	n/a	gold	gold	gold	gold	pewter	straw
Schiether	yellow	red	n/a	D.green	D.green	D.green	D.green	brass	straw
Kielmansegg	white	red	n/a	Gr.grn	Gr.grn	Gr.grn	Gr.grn	pewter	straw
Freytag Jäger	unlaced	D.green	n/a	D.green	D.green	D.green	D.green	pewter	D.green
Buckeburg	white	blue	red	red	n/a	red	white	pewter	white
Hesse Arty.	white	D.blue	crimson	crimson	crimson	crimson	straw	pewter	straw
Buckeburg Arty.	unlaced	D.blue	D.blue	black	n/a	red	buff	pewter	D.blue

The companies making up the combined grenadier battalions in Wangenheim's corps wore the uniforms of their parent regiments. British and Hanoverian grenadiers wore a cloth 'mitre' cap; Hessian and Brunswick grenadiers wore a cap with a metallic front in the Prussian style.

Appendix V

Contades' Orders for the Battle of Minden

Text from Baron de Jomini, *Traité des Grandes Opérations Militaires* (Paris: Magimel, Paris, 1811), Vol.III, pp. 29-40, translated from the French by Richard Couture. Jomini mentions that he suppressed certain sections and that his version had previously been translated into German and that he had re-translated it back into French.

The reserve, under the command of the Duc de Broglie, is to form the right wing of the army; it will march frontally on the village of Tonhausen [sic], and will attack, simultaneously, the camp of the Prince of Bevern on the road to Petershagen. This attack will have to be executed rapidly and with great intensity, to drive back the Prince with all possible promptness and to cut off his retreat onto the army, in order to sow panic and confusion.

To ensure the success of this operation, the reserve will be reinforced by the Grenadiers de France and the Grenadiers Royaux; it will receive six pieces of cannon and four howitzers in addition to its ordinary artillery. The Duc de Broglie will arrange the assembly of the artillery, and will transmit the necessary orders to the grenadier regiments. One will employ all means for the success of this attack, which must make us masters of the left flank of the enemy, and on which all the success of this day depends.

The '*retraite*' will replace the '*générale*'. As soon as it has been beaten, the reserve will leave its camp, cross on the bridge and via the city, which it will leave by the gate leading to the grenadier camp; its heavy baggage will be moved to Rehme, where that of the army is, crossing the Weser on the farther pontoon bridge, in order to not impede the march of troops.

The terrain where the army must form, being thickish and constrained on the wings, its order of battle cannot conform to accepted usage. I thus place in the centre of the first line the cavalry brigades of Colonel-Genéral, Cravates and Mestre-de-Camp, under the command of the Duc de Fitz-James, of the *Lieutenant-Généraux* Vogue and Castries and of the *Maréchaux-de-Camp* Lutzelbourg, St Chamand, Villebonne and Courmainville. The four infantry brigades of Picardie, Belsunce, Touraine and Rouergue, under the *Lieutenant-Généraux* Nicolaï, Beaupréau, and the *Maréchaux-de-Camp*

Planta and Monty, will form the right wing of the first line, and will have 34 heavy calibre pieces. The left wing of this line will be composed of the four infantry brigades Condé, Aquitaine, le Roi and Champagne, under *Lieutenant-Général* de Guerchy, and the *Maréchaux-de-Camp* Duc de Laval and Maugiron; it will be provided with 30 positional artillery pieces. The Chevalier de Pelletier is to site all this artillery on the front of both wings, so that it covers the cavalry by a crossfire in the centre: he will give the necessary orders to this effect to the artillery brigadiers.

The first battalion of each brigade will be formed in column, the others will march in battle formation. The Auvergne Brigade, placed on the left of the infantry of the right wing, will form in reverse order, so that its first battalion will be formed in column, supporting the Colonel-Général Cavalry Brigade; the Condé Infantry Brigade, posted on the right of the left wing, will be formed as the others, that is to say that the first battalion would be formed in column, supporting Mestre-de-Camp Cavalerie.

The second line will march in the same order as the first: the infantry brigades Auvergne and Anhalt, under *Lieutenant-Général* de St Germain and the *Maréchaux-de-Camp* Leyden and Glaubitz will have the right. The cavalry brigades du Roi, Bourgogne and Royal-Étranger, under *Lieutenant-Généraux* Dumesnil, Andlau, and the *Maréchaux-de-Camp* Orlick and Galfeld, will occupy the centre; the left will be composed of the Saxon brigades, under the command of the Marquis [sic] de Lusace.

This second line being much less strong than the first, and having nevertheless to occupy the same frontage, the battalions from which it is formed will spread out much more than customary. The reserve, composed of the Gendarmerie and of the Carabiniers, under *Lieutenant-Général* Poyanne and the *Maréchaux-de-Camp* Bellefond and Bissy, will place itself in a third line behind the centre of the cavalry.

The Navarre and Lowendahl brigades will have special tasks.

The army thus formed will take its first position; the left behind the village of Hahlen, will rest on the marsh; the right will extend itself behind the red houses on the plain of Minden; it will extend up to the wood; the lines will march at a distance of 400 paces; the corps of the Duc de Broglie will rest its right to the steep banks of the Weser, making a front towards Tonhausen; its left will link with the right of the army, the infantry will be in the first line, and the cavalry in the second. This division, along with the Grenadiers-Royaux and de France, will follow exclusively the orders of the Duc de Broglie.

While these troops will attack Tonhausen and the camp of Petershagen, the army will deploy and march in battle formations to the enemy. In the event of delay, the infantry and cavalry brigades are to continue their movement in column on a front of battalion and squadron, maintaining the necessary distances to form.

The first battalion of each brigade, which must remain in column, will keep this order during the march and during the battle; the infantry brigades will be preceded by 100 labourers, with the necessary carts of tools.

As the right of the enemy is located at Hille, and the left behind Holzhausen, the focus will be directed to its left flank. If the attack of the Duc de Broglie succeeds, he will then have to seek to reach this flank, in order to turn it. The other manoeuvres of the army will depend on the enemy reaction. The *Maréchal* Contades will give, in all cases, orders adapted to the circumstances.

The Navarre Brigade, the Volontaires de Hainaut, Dauphiné and Muret, under the command of the *Lieutenant-Général* Duc d'Avré, will make a feint attack on the dyke leading across the marsh towards Hille.

The artillery park is to furnish them with a supplement of four pieces of eight to this effect. The Duc d'Avré is to direct an intense fire upon the enemy redoubt over the dyke; but he is to cross the marsh only in the event of the army penetrating up to the vicinity of Hille, and if he can effect a junction with it. Until then, he must restrict himself to harassing the enemy, to prevent him from resting his right on the marsh. This corps will have to, if needed, cover the retreat of the army by holding the dyke, and defending the passage. It will also have to be careful to crown the heights behind with infantry and light troops, to stand up against those parties that the enemy could detach from Lubeke [sic]; this precaution is important.

The Duc d'Avré is to be aware that the Duc de Brissac occupies Goosfeld [sic, Gohfeld] with a division, to observe the Erbprinz. He will have to communicate with this division through the vale of Bergkirchen, and will employ for this service the cavalry of the Volontaires de Dauphiné who know the terrain and the roads. The posts at Kolhof and Hartenhausen will be maintained because they overlook [*éclairent*] the vicinity of the marsh.

The Lowendahl Brigade, under the *Maréchal-de-Camp* de Bisson, will enter Minden as soon as the '*retraite*' has been beaten; it is to occupy the ramparts and the three bridgeheads. The major part of the heavy artillery is to be placed on the cavaliers in order to cover, if needed, the army's withdrawal. One will also place a few pieces in the works which cover the stone bridge, in order to defend the approaches to the bridgeheads against attempts by light troops who infest the left bank of the Weser.

The '*retraite*' which will take the place of the '*générale*', as we have said, will be beaten at the ordinary hour.

The army will immediately take arms in front of the camp, and will march in eight columns. The first, under the Comte de Guerchy, will be composed of the infantry brigades of Champagne and du Roi; it will leave the wood located near Amelbeck to the left, will pass the Barthe on the leftmost bridge, near the marsh, and will march march up to the last hedgerows in front of Hahlen, where it will remain in column until daybreak. The army will then form, the left resting against the aforementioned hedgerows, and the right taking its direction towards the red houses located on the plain. Eight pieces of heavy calibre will be grouped with these two brigades in the evening, and will remain to their fore during the battle. M. de Ste-Ville, *Aide-Major-Général-des-Logis*, will lead this division.

The second column will consist of the brigades of Aquitaine and Condé, under the command of M. de Maugiron. It will be led by the *Aide-Major-des-Logis* Baudouin, who will indicate the bridge where it must cross the Barthe, the place where it will remain in column behind the height, to wait for daybreak, and the area where it must form afterwards. This column will have six pieces of heavy artillery.

The third column is composed of the two Saxon brigades, under the command of the Comte de Lusace; the *Aide-Major-des-Logis* Montant will conduct them and will designate the location where they will have to remain in column behind the height, waiting for daybreak, to then form the second line of the first column, at a distance of 400 paces.

The fourth column will include the cavalry brigades of Mestre-de-Camp, Cravates and Royal-Étranger, under the command of the Duc de Fitzjames. They will be led by the *Aide-Major-des-Logis* Angers, who will assign them the place where they will have to wait for daybreak. When they form, the Mestre-de-Camp Brigade will rest on Condé Infantry Brigade; the Cravates will align its right towards the red houses; and the one of Royal-Étranger will place itself in the second line of Mestre-de-Camp, at a distance of 400 paces.

The fifth will consist of the cavalry brigades Colonel-Général, le Roi and Bourgogne, under the command of *Lieutenant-Général* Dumesnil; it will be led by *Aide-Major-des-Logis* Dumay, who will indicate the place where it will remain to wait for daybreak. As soon day breaks, the Colonel-Général Brigade will form the first line, resting on the one of Cravates, and taking its direction towards the red houses; the brigades du Roi and Bourgogne will form the second line behind those of Cravates and Colonel-Général.

The sixth column, under *Lieutenant-Général* Beaupréau, will be composed of the infantry brigades Touraine and Rouergue. They will cross the Barthe on the bridge indicated by *Aide-Major-des-Logis* Germain, and will advance to the redoubt in front of Picardie, and will await daybreak there to form at the right of the Colonel-Général Brigade. This division will take eight positional guns which will remain to its front during the battle.

The seventh column, under the command of *Lieutenant-Général* de Saint-Germain, will consist of the brigades Auvergne and Anhalt. The first of these brigades will cross the bridge shown by M. d'Ouné, of the État-Major, and will march, up to the camp of the second, in the gardens in front of the city. The Anhalt Brigade will place itself second to those of Picardie and Belsunce.

The eighth column, under the Chevalier Nicolaï, consists of the brigades of Picardie and Belsunce. It will direct its march towards the red houses, and will remain there till daybreak; it will then form, extending its right up to the wood, and taking the direction from the left of the reserve under the command of the Duc de Broglie. The *Aide-Major-des-Logis* Grandpré will lead this column; the artillery park will send eight pieces of cannon, in the evening, which are to remain with these brigades during the action.

The Corps of the Duc de Broglie will form the ninth column. The Gendarmes and the Grenadiers [sic, more probably the Carabiniers are meant] will mount and will remain in front of their camp, until they receive the order to place themselves in the third line behind the centre.

One has thrown nineteen bridges over the stream which flows in front of the camp from the marsh into the Weser, in order to facilitate the withdrawal of the army, should that be necessary. If this misfortune should happen, the centre and the left would retire across these bridges to the present camp. The right and the reserve would retire towards the city, would occupy the hedgerows and the gardens which surround it, and would site artillery in front of their positions to contain the enemy, in conjunction with the town's artillery.

Appendix VI

Account of the Comte de Lusace

The Comte de Lusace, *Relation of the Battle of Minden, with Military Reflections on what has Preceded and Followed the day of the 1st of August*, a manuscript. Archives Départementales de l'Aube, Xavier, Prince, Archives de la guerre de Sept ans et correspondance familiale: le fonds du prince Xavier de Saxe, EE81 and EE82. Translated by Richard Couture. Lusace, Prinz Xaver of Saxony, was the Dauphine's brother and commanded the Saxon troops in the French service.

In the month of May, the allied army assumed the general defence of everything it had held during the winter, and its winter-quarters were distributed from the Ems to the Fulda: as strange as this scattered distribution appeared, at least it forced the French army not to advance on any single point without appropriate dispositions. It became very spread out. Prince Ferdinand was confident of stopping the *Maréchal* de Contades for a time at Münster or Lippstadt, which he had resolved to defend, if he marched by the Lower Rhine: on the other hand, if the alternative force under the Duc de Broglie attempted to penetrate into Hesse, Prince Ferdinand had kept some options either to support and reinforce the camp of Fritzlar, which de Wangenheim occupied with 10,000 to 12,000 men, or to withdraw this force onto the centre of his dispositions along the Lippe. He would be able to successively delay the march of the French on the Weser at Kassel and at Münden.

One has some difficulty conceiving how Prince Ferdinand could take the decision to abandon so many garrisons in places vulnerable to being besieged, effectively depriving himself of available fighting manpower by using his infantry in this way: but one ceases to wonder when thinking about the agreement made from court to court to immediately exchange prisoners taken by both sides. Based on this convention, and on the 4,500 men that the Prince had returned in advance of the remaining French prisoners of the winter campaign of 57 to 58; it was clear that the enemy garrisons, after having defended the besieged places for a set period of time, would be returned as prisoners of war the day after the surrender of the place, and would join the same day the forces of the allied army according to the terms of the convention, up to the number of the troops of the Most Christian King which had been given back in advance. This convention was advantageous to us in a way, since we could usefully distribute these prisoners inside the kingdom, but it was certainly also costly for us in Germany until we would be even with the enemy. Reflecting on the nature of the convention of exchange explains the measures taken by Prince Ferdinand at the beginning of this campaign.

The *Maréchal* de Contades' assembly of the army under his command on the Lahn, and its gathering at the camp of Gielsen [sic, Giessen] on the 31st of the month of May, had been executed with the greatest precision. The speed with which the Duc de Broglie had made the force at Fritzlar withdraw, had captured Kassel, and then maintained the pressure on the enemy to prevent him rallying at Münden, coupled with the *Maréchal* de Contades' advance by Marburg, Franckenberg, and Corbach to reach the defile of Stadtberg and pass the Diemel, had all disrupted plans of the Prince de Bevern, who had not anticipated us acting with such pace and coordination.

It seemed that our swiftness prevented this Prince from disputing the passage of the gorges of Stadtberg, the only really challenging part of the whole plan, which however was accomplished with the enemy being either insufficiently assembled, or too surprised, to oppose it. The Duc de Broglie, passing the Diemel and the gorges of Kleineberg, was able to advance with his reserve on the left flank of the enemy army, which had concentrated at Buren, with the exception of the sole corps, opposed at Dulmen by the reserve of M. d'Armentières.

From this moment on, the only obstacles which could hinder the progress of the French Army came from logistics. It became necessary to wait for twelve days encamped at Merhoff while our requirements were met by the attention and efforts of M. de Ceyre, Purveyor General. Thereupon, we made for Paderborn, which we reached on 24th June. Meanwhile, the enemy by withdrawing his posts along the Lippe had abandoned Lippstadt to its own forces. It seemed that we would have little difficulty cornering the enemy at the mouth of the Weser, or the Elbe, providing that we advanced against him with the prudence which, until then, had served us so well.

If only the love of glory and the pleasure of defeating the King's enemies had driven us, rather than the value of a campaign by which we should have made ourselves masters of their country and of their fate without battle, there is no doubt that by marching on the night of 29th June from our camp of Lipsprinck [sic, Lippspringe] on Stuckenbrock, the *Maréchal* de Contades could easily have forced Prince Ferdinand to fight in a disadvantageous situation. The latter would have had to make his retreat through the defiles of Bielefeld, or march towards Münster, placing himself between the reserve of M. d'Armentières and the army of the *Maréchal* in front of which he would have retired. But if the French army had come off worst on that day, fighting within sight of Paderborn and its magazines, it would have lost not only the battle but also all the achievements of the campaign in a single day.

It seemed preferable safely and progressively to continue in the aim which we had set ourselves, to corner Prince Ferdinand. This Prince only sought to postpone the moment by a wise defence which left him, however, the liberty to benefit from our errors if we put aside the principles of prudence which we had followed until then, and made mistakes directly in front of him.

At the approach of the Reserve under the Duc de Broglie, the enemy evacuated Bielefeld which the army came to occupy, the reserve still covering its right flank, and worrying the left of the enemy, as it had constantly done since the camp of Mehrhof. As soon as the Duc de Broglie was master of the gorge of Engeren [sic, probably Enger], Prince Ferdinand broke his camp at Dyssen [sic, Dissen] and moved towards Osnabrück, to draw us as far away as possible from the Weser by forcing us to worry about the marches which he could make against the reserve of the Marquis d'Armentières who had moved closer to Münster to lay siege to it.

It is clear that without the capture of Minden, the Hanoverian general would not have left his camp of Osnabrück as promptly as he did. However, as soon he saw against his hope that this door into the Electorate of Hanover was open to the French Army his priority had to be to march himself diligently to the Weser to contain us at Minden as long as the sieges of Münster and Lippstadt, which he now abandoned to their own forces, would last.

The small particular advantages that various enemy detachments had had over our own raised the courage and the confidence of the allies. Prince Ferdinand, fearing that after the surrender of Münster, which ought to be imminent, the totality, or at least the largest part, of the reserve of the Marquis d'Armentières would march to our left to threaten the right of his camp of Petershagen, tried to prevent this misfortune by surprising us in our camp of Minden, which at the first position may not had enough depth [*assez de fond*] and could very easily be turned by our left: but the new dispositions that the *Maréchal* de Contades ordered the army to take, by deploying it in battle to receive the enemy, and in which it was encamped until 31 July, had been reconnoitred by Prince Ferdinand. He considered that he could not reap the benefit of the surprise he had planned, and after some cannonade in front of Todenhausen [sic, Todtenhausen] on our right, and a few demonstrations on our left, which made us spend the day of the 17th [July] in order of battle, he took back on the same day the road to his camp between Petershagen and Meyseling [sic, probably Messlingen], keeping an advanced corps of light troops, supported by three battalions and a few squadrons of regular cavalry to reconnoitre the right of our camp, and to take post on the bank of the Weser from Todenhausen to Codenhausen [sic, Kutenhausen].

It was in this new situation that the two armies remained from the 17th to the 27th of July. Prince Ferdinand wanted to try to expel us from this position, which he may have considered as unassailable because of the necessity where he would have been in attacking, to have no communication between his left and his right, separated from each other by the marshes of Dützen, had a corps of his right march to Lübbecke: on the day following this movement, the *Maréchal* detached the Marquis de Guerchy from the left towards the same location. The enemy having retired during the night, M. de Guerchy returned the same day to the line. We learned on the following day that a corps of 4,000 men had marched from Vechte [sic, Vechta] on Osnabrück, and had dislodged the Volontaires de Clermont who had suffered many losses, but making the nicest retreat and the most vigorous defence under the orders of M. de Commeyras their Commandant. The city and the magazines of Osnabrück being in the hands of the enemy, we had no spare troops on their right to reconnoitre the various movements which they could perform in this area to hinder our communications with Herworden [sic, probably Herford], from which we got our convoys via Cooweldt [sic, Gohfeld] on the small Wehre [sic, Werre] river.

If after the surrender of Münster, M. d'Armentières, reinforcing the troops who made the blockade of Lippstadt with an infantry brigade, had marched from Warendorpp [sic, Warendorf] on Dyssen [sic, Dissen] and Lubbecke [sic, Lübbecke], this march would undoubtedly have forced Prince Ferdinand to change position himself, to retire on Niembourg [sic, Nienburg] and Bremen, as his previous arrangements sufficiently indicated. It would have been a very natural continuation of the project that we attributed to him to defend Westphalia foot by foot and to draw us away as long as he could from the Electorate of Hanover. However the *Maréchal* de Contades instead of having M. d'Armentières take the road of Lübbecke, had sent this General with his reserve to lay siege to Lippstadt. From that moment on, Prince Ferdinand could hope to turn our left, and to induce us to some false undertakings for the protection of our convoys. With this in sight after having covered the post of Todtenhausen with a good redoubt and having secured the camp of M. de Wangenheim at Codenhausen to his left, he advanced and extended his right from Nordhemmer [sic, Nordhemmern] to Hille encamping in two lines between these two villages. He put a few battalions in front of Hille and a redoubt to cover the débouché of a dam which runs from Hille to Eichhoff, a village behind our left some 10 kilometres distant from Minden by Rothenussden to Hattenhaysen, Humelberg and Dützen. With this new position of Prince Ferdinand, our own having not changed, the Hanoverian general was able to detach the Erbprinz of Brunswick to intercept and hinder our communication with Herworden by Cooweldt [sic, Gohfeld] and the Wehre [sic, Werre].

On the 30th the Hereditary Prince having appeared around Neüenkirchen, the Duc de Brissac who had been detached on the same day with 3,000 to 4,000 men and five pieces of cannon of the park to reconnoitre the movements of this Prince, and secure the communication, had an engagement with him, where the advantage remained with the French troops; the Hereditary Prince retired towards Lubbecke, and the Duc de Brissac remained on the Wehre to continue to monitor the Prince's fresh attempts.

It is in these circumstances that the *Maréchal*, keen to secure the communication with Herworden by a glorious feat, decided to give battle to Prince Ferdinand, and to seize the moment when the Hereditary Prince was separated from the allied army, with the corps under his command. As soon as the *Maréchal* had taken this decision, he assembled the general officers to inform them of his plan, according to which the same day of the 31st, the cannon shot of the '*retraite*' serving as '*générale*', the army and the reserve would take arms to march to the enemy and to fight them the next day 1st August. The army should march in eight columns and be in order of battle at daybreak on the curtain of Hahlen. The reserve of the Duc de Broglie, to which the Corps of the Grenadiers de France and Royaux was assigned for the day of the affair, formed a separated ninth column charged in particular with the attack on the entrenchments of Todtenhausen, and on the camp of Codenhausen which it should push with the utmost vivacity back to the left of the camp of Prince Ferdinand who, unable to come to help against this attack, because of the presence of the army in front of which he would have had to manoeuvre while marching from his right to his left, would be unable to avoid abandoning the battlefield to us, with losses all the more considerable as he was cut from the corps which was in front of his right under the command of the Hereditary Prince. The Duc d'Havré detached the same day with the Navarre Brigade, some cavalry, and five or six pieces of cannon of the park, had taken position at Eichhoff from where he should make a false attack at daybreak, vivaciously cannonading the village of Hille, and the redoubt which covered the dam on the side of the enemy, to draw all their attention on that side, and favour the real attack on our right. A secondary task of the Duc d'Havré was to prevent the passage of the dam of Eichhoff, so that the enemy would not be able by penetrating through these parts, fall on our left flank, and cut our retreat by establishing themselves in the gorges, which would have been easy if they had been master of the passage of the dam, and thus of the heights against which our camp was nestling.

Such were the dispositions with which the *Maréchal* wanted to fight the enemy on the following day, 1st August. Any military man looking at this arrangement as a masterpiece of common sense and of military prudence, would assume that M. de Wangenheim would be surprised in his camp, that the measures which Prince Ferdinand had taken since several days to secure this left would be surmountable, or that this Prince being unwarned of the great project of the *Maréchal* had not reinforced on the eve of the battle the camp of Codenhausen. However, according to the report that the Comte de Rosen made to the Duc de Broglie on the evening of the 31st, from the post where he was detached on the right bank of the Weser on the left flank of M. de Wangenheim, he explained to the general of the reserve that the camp seemed to increase considerably The Duc de Broglie immediately sent this important report to the *Maréchal* who, however, did not change anything in the immutable order by which he intended to fight. I do not enter debate on what caused the loss of the battle. I stick to the facts, as I have seen them in the part where I have fought, and as officers exempt of any partisanship, servants of the state, and friends of truth have told me, to record them in the places where they were. The reflections which I add are an account which I make to myself, for my own instruction and for my friends. I write truth for myself firstly; and then for them: I do not pretend to praise, nor to blame anyone.

At four o'clock in the morning, the troops of the reserve of the Duc de Broglie had entirely passed to the left bank of the Weser, and were ranked in order of battle in two lines, the infantry with the Grenadiers de France and Royaux forming the head, first, and the cavalry second. The Duc de Broglie's intent, as he communicated it to the officers of the reserve, was to start by breaking down with cannon the ridge of the entrenchments of Todenhausen, to ease the storming of the same entrenchment and then form on the left of M. de Wangenheim, as he had been particularly charged, on the left of Prince Ferdinand. To start to achieve these various goals and judge the state of the enemy the Duc de Broglie, after having chased and driven back the sentinels and small outposts which the enemy had on a curtain between them and the advanced posts of our right, personally went to reconnoitre this curtain, where he immediately had his cannon established to raze the top [*écrêter*] of the entrenchments, as he had decided. This general noted the troops of M. de Wangenheim in order of battle, and a cavalry column which a wood prevented him from seeing in depth, which came to form to the right of the entrenchment, assessed with a glance all the difficulties which would impede the success of an attack by force in this part. The Duc de Broglie sent to the *Maréchal* to give him an account of the situation. Meanwhile he advanced his cannon to the curtain from which he constantly fired upon the entrenchments of M. de Wangenheim, whose superior fire now became a new obstacle to the attacking force. This fire from the entrenchments of Todenhausen was deadly for the Corps of the Grenadiers de France and Royaux, which had attempted to advance up to the foot of the curtain, where the cannon were established in order to be able to support them. There were, I have been told, many messengers between the Maréchal, and the Duc de Broglie in regard to the execution, and to the impossibility, of the attack on Todtenhausen. One has even assured me that the Duc de Broglie went in person to give an account to the *Maréchal* on the state of things on the right, and that on this last account which had been done at the moment where the enemy started to attack our left and our centre, the *Maréchal* had ordered the Duc de Broglie to content himself with holding firm where he was, to contain M. de Wangenheim, and cover in case of misfortune the troops of the right in their retreat. Anyway, things effectively remained in this manner, from the beginning of the affair. The troops of the reserve had not a single musket shot to fire, and they endured a continuous cannonade from the entrenchments of Todenhausen for more than three hours, where some deserters claimed that there were 50 heavy pieces. During the retreat I spoke to soldiers of the Grenadiers de France, who I asked if there were any means by which, instead of remaining exposed so cruelly to cannon, they could have attacked the work covering the enemies, and stormed it at the point of the bayonet? Here is their answer: 'Sir, if we had surprised the enemy by attacking him unexpectedly at night, and if we had carried screens to cover the holes which they had made around their entrenchments, we may have succeeded, because at night everything can succeed when people are surprised, but when we saw them during the day, from where we were, we thought that we could not carry the position since they had so many cannon, and because they were prepared for us in such a good position; if one had insisted, we would have advanced on it, but we would all have been killed, and we would still have gained nothing more.'

Were they wrong or right? Was their perspective correct? I cannot say, because I was not on the right wing but, in speaking with me, they had no other intent than to tell me the truth. They told me what they had perceived without any self-interest, and as such their testimony is worthier to me than any other.

Regarding the army, the eight columns which composed it after marching during the night found themselves between four and five o'clock in the morning on the plateau of Hahlen, the brigades of Picardie and Belsunce to the right followed by those of Rouergue and Touraine towards the centre, where a dense heath favourable to the movements of the cavalry had determined to place this arm. The brigades of Aquitaine, Condé, du Roi, and Champagne, in the order where they are listed, formed the left of the first line which leaned against the village of Hahlen, which was occupied by the Champagne Brigade. The Saxons formed the second line from the village of Hahlen up to the Condé Brigade inclusively, leaving great intervals between battalions to give the impression that we would occupy all this ground. The Gendarmerie and the Carabiniers came out on that very morning at daybreak to go from their camp near the village of Osterhall in front of the town which was in front of our camp, and they waited in reserve behind the rest of the cavalry for the moment to charge.

It was only around seven o'clock that the enemy, that we had sought to fight on his left, debouched with two column heads from a small wood extending from our left and beyond up to Codenhausen. Even though this wood was not very deep, it prevented us from properly assessing the number of enemy appearing in this area, and from which one could see only the head at the edge of the wood, near the villages of Hartum and Rotthenusden, from where they established batteries of cannon which livelily fired upon the Champagne Brigade at the village of Hahlen, and on the Brigade du Roi, whose left held to the right of the same village. The artillery of the park which was to our left, and the one of the regiments of the first line replied with the greatest vivacity to the fire of the batteries of Hartum and Rothenussden.

On this demonstration of the enemy, which the Compte de Guerchy probably assumed to be the main attack, he ordered the Comte de Lusace [the author of this account] to successively retire the right in order be able to double with his left brigade, the Champagne in the village of Hahlen, and with his right brigade the Du Roi Brigade, which was to the right of the same village.

In the very moment when this happened on the left, a corps of English and Hanoverian infantry debouched from the same wood, and formed along its edge, from which it marched with much speed and pride towards the French cavalry, which was in order of battle on the heath. This cavalry, onto which the Gendarmerie and the Carabiniers joined themselves, did not hesitate to charge this infantry, which received it with as much order as intrepidity, and despite the successive charges that it had to withstand from the multitude of squadrons which were vis-à-vis, it stuck to its direction, and continued to advance on the heath, the column that it then formed always increasing from the troops debouching from the wood. Several squadrons which, inspired by the presence of their commanders and, above all, by the dazzling example of the Prince de Condé, penetrated the ranks of this infantry with the greatest valour, but these successes were never enough to break it, and after having withstood these various assaults and having repelled the cavalry through the considerable losses that it had inflicted on it, forced it to retire from the centre, on the left, to seek protection from the fire of the infantry, which had continued to follow it, attacking at the same time as this cavalry which was now retiring in front of it.

I have been told that during the various charges of the French cavalry towards the enemy infantry, the *Maréchal* had the Brigades of Rouergue and Touraine march to the hedges of the village of Stemmer, already occupied by the enemy, and that this movement of two brigades having been done while the progress of the English infantry had started to drive our squadrons back from the centre to the left, a few enemy squadrons which covered the wide side of the English column on the left, had seized a favourable moment when the two brigades could not be supported by the cavalry and had hurled themselves, sabre in hand, towards their middle, and had inflicted on them the most considerable losses in men, cannon, and colours. I have also been told that in the storm coming from the right to the left, the d'Aumont Regiment which belonged to Touraine Brigade had had enough time to oppose a front to the enemy cavalry, that it had stopped it, and that it was this timely movement which had prevented the loss of this regiment in proportion to those which the Touraine Regiment, its chief of brigade, had suffered. The latter had not enough time to make the same evolution, and received the enemy in its left flank.

These various events on our right, and on our centre, had been successive and distant from the extremity of our left, where the cannonade from the enemy had seemed to double, and where the heads of the columns supporting their batteries had started to deploy, and to form in order of battle. The Comte de Guerchy, still considering Hahlen as the point of the main effort of the enemy, did everything he could to prevent them from penetrating there. The Comte de Lusace having already concentrated up the right of his Saxons to their left, and even reinforced with two battalions the village of Hahlen where Champagne was, had the Comte de Guerchy, who had ordered it, informed of this movement. The officer to whom the Comte de Lusace entrusted this report, had instructions to add to M. de Guerchy that if the fire of the battery of the enemy was to become superior to that of the artillery sited in front of the Du Roi regiment, then the Comte de Lusace offered to send the cannon of his right brigade there, and that he would come in the support at the head of the Saxons, and join the Du Roi Brigade as soon as M. de Guerchy would find it appropriate. The officer who commanded the artillery in front of the Du Roi regiment having replied that the fire of the enemy battery would not silence his own, and that he would manage without the reinforcement of cannon offered, M. de Guerchy only charged the officer sent by the Comte de Lusace with thanks for his offers, and asked him through the same officer to form his two Saxon Brigades in columns per battalion as soon as possible, the left one to the left, and the right one to the right, of the road leading from Minden to Hahlen at the entry of the village, and that as soon as this movement could be achieved, he planned to march forward and attack the enemy. The officer set off again from there to report of his message to the Compte de Lusace, who immediately began to execute it with the greatest swiftness.

While this was happening on the extremity of the left flank, the English infantry column, of which its head was already beyond the location of the first line, continued to follow with the same order, presented its right flank sideways, [from here the actions are those of the Comte de Lusace] and began to re-initiate combat, freeing the brigades of Aquitaine and Condé on his right, and giving an opportunity to the French cavalry squadrons to the right of Condé and Aquitaine to make a more successful charge, than the previous ones. He [de Lusace] only gave himself time to inform the Comte de Guerchy, who was present, of his decision and immediately executed it with the most brilliant success. The two volleys that the three Saxon battalions made with resolve, and in the greatest order against the flank that the enemy presented were deadly, and were followed by a surprise and a hesitation which communicated from the tail to the centre of the enemy column. The Comte de Lusace, having noticed this and seeing the French brigades which began to rally on his right, charged promptly by advancing on the column which was now retiring, and which lost more than two hundred paces of the ground that it had occupied, the Saxons marching on over their dead. But another corps of enemy infantry having debouched with some cannon, on the left flank of the Saxons, and the four battalions of these troops forming the rest of the brigade, which marched to join the first three in line, having been forced in battle at a right angle on the line of the first three to cover their left flank against the new attack, were unable to sustain themselves in this position, and their retreat once more uncovered the flank of the first three. That was the moment where our cavalry which, had it believed it had found, and which would effectively have found the moment to make a victorious charge if less shaken by the results of its first efforts, and of the losses it had suffered it had charged the enemy with the same confidence, came back a little too fast, and looking as if it would not return, had once more added to the disorder of the Brigades Condé and Aquitaine which were not yet entirely steadied, and which seeing themselves uncovered by the cavalry which they had had to their right, joined in following it in its retreat. The one [retreat] of the three Saxon battalions uncovered on both flanks was, of necessity, very hasty. However, the Comte de Lusace who had personally remained with the rightmost battalion had, despite the difficulty of this position, the chance to maintain it in good order, and without disunity, forming with this battalion, which he successively increased with those Saxons who could be rallied, the rearguard of the left, until the passage of the bridge on the small canal to the right of the village of Dützen, while the Brigades Du Roi, Champagne, and those of the Saxons which had been placed in the village of Hahlen were retiring by Hattenhausen and the brook of Hamelbeck, to return to our camp. At the same time, the entire right was making its own retreat to the town of Minden under the protection of the reserve of the Duc de Broglie which, after having formed the rearguard in this part, had the reserve repassing by the town to the right bank of the Weser.

By ten o'clock in the morning the whole army had returned to its camp, or at least the foot of the mountain on which the camp was sited. The enemy army had advanced up to the bank of the small canal which we had recrossed, and on which most bridges were still intact and at its disposal. It halted there, still fired a few volleys of cannon against us, rested on its arms, and the battle ended.

Before moving to matters concerning our retreat to Cassel by the right bank of the Weser, I owe myself a few reflections on the causes of such an unfortunate event and one which was so unnatural to foresee.

I do not regret what I have said above about the favourable occasions for fighting. If one had only been determined on a glorious defeat of the enemy of the King, and that we had let slip through our hands, and above all the one of the 29th June from the camp of Lipsprinck [sic, Lippspringe] on Stuckenbrock, nor of the fault that one had made after the surrender of Münster to have not advanced the totality or the greatest part of the reserve of the Marquis d'Armentières from Warendorp on Dissen, and Lübbecke, which seemed natural and necessary after the enterprise of the enemy on Osnabrück, and the retreat of the Volontaires de Clermont, the only corps we had to reconnoitre the movements which the enemy could perform on their right in this area. It is certain that by making this initiative, and by reinforcing, if one had considered it suitable with a brigade of the reserve of M. d'Armentières the corps of M. de Chevreuse charged with the blockade of Lippstadt, one would have forced without battle the enemy whose right one would have squeezed, to retire on Bremen, consequently to open to attempts the Electorate of Hanover which he would have left unprotected by his retreat, and to assure these successes, it would have cost us only to delay the capture of Lippstadt by ten days. I am unwilling to consider the necessity that forced the *Maréchal* to leave a secure camp, whose defences had held the enemy in check for fifteen days, to lose this advantage by marching against him.

I do not know exactly how long the siege of Lippstadt would have lasted, but I know that with the oat magazines which we had in Minden, the ovens established there, the flour transported there, and the foraging which we could have done on the right of the Weser, and even if the Erbprinz of Brunswick would have interrupted our communication with Herworden [sic, Herford] which could have lasted beyond the end of the expedition of M. d'Armentières on Lippstadt, we could easily have endured this for eight days, and it is unlikely that Lippstadt would have held longer.

Nor do I examine if it would not have been better (assuming that the concern about the corps of the Erbprinz and our communications was the reason which determined the Maréchal to give battle) to immediately form a corps decidedly superior to the forces of the Erbprinz's march towards Cooweldt, to drive him back with losses on the right of Prince Ferdinand, and dissuade him from harassing our convoys.

Finally, I do not enter into the discussion of the possibility, or impossibility, of success of the attack which the Duc de Broglie was charged with making on the entrenchments of Todenhausen and the left of the camp of M. de Wangenheim. On this I only have difficulty to conceive that one could attribute to a general who has won two battles, and who is generally renowned as too virtuous a citizen to sacrifice national glory, the baseness of a particular interest, that one can refuse to believe that he sanely judged what he had seen with his own eyes, and I positively know that the various reports which the Duc de Broglie had made, and made himself to the *Maréchal*, were done only after he had personally reconnoitred from the curtain, on the higher ground on which he established himself with his cannon, the entrenchments of Todenhausen, and the camp of M. de Wangenheim.

I consider the battle only in the part where it really occurred, that is to say, the ground where the troops charged, fought in the open and, in a word, manoeuvred. I leave aside the cannonade which was exchanged between the Duc de Broglie and Wangenheim, who reciprocally contained themselves, and I examine only what I think should have been done before the engagement, and then during the engagement, to achieve the success which we were seeking, and avoid the misfortune which has happened to us.

I believe we only have ourselves to blame for letting the wood extending across our front mask all the manoeuvres which would please Prince Ferdinand to have executed from the right to his left, while by making ourselves master of the edge of this wood on the side of the enemy, and by occupying instead of the village of Hahlen the one of Harthum, where the cannon established at the same place where the enemy placed his own against our left, would have sufficiently defended ourselves against the attempts that the enemy would have wanted to make on our left flank on the side of Rothenussen. By this I mean we would have clearly seen the dispositions of the enemy, and we could have made our own under the cover of the wood, to oppose him at the places where we would see fit, as he has been able to do himself by using the very same wood against our centre of cavalry, devoid of infantry.

The only objection that I can make to myself about the necessity of occupying the outer edge of this wood, which masked our front, is that the terrain beyond it might not have been as favourable to to our cavalry, but in the supposition that according to the disposition of the *Maréchal* de Contades, the Duc de Broglie had pushed M. de Wangenheim back on the left of Prince Ferdinand, should not this same cavalry have debouched towards Stemmer to follow the success of the Duc de Broglie? While on the heath, where it was posted with its nose against the wood, it could be useful only in the event of the retreat of M. de Wangenheim towards Hahlen, which could hardly be imagined, or in the case of the enemy debouching from the wood against our centre, which is what happened, but which we certainly had not predicted.

Another advantage we would have gained by first making ourselves master of this wood which was between the enemy and us is that this covered position would have moved the brigades Picardie and Belsunce under the command of the Chevalier de Nicolaï, on the hedges of the village of Codenhausen, where they would had distracted the attention of M. de Wangenheim, and eased the difficulty which prevented the Duc de Broglie from attacking on the main effort. Considering the passage of the cavalry through this wood, its ease was demonstrated by what the enemy cavalry was able to execute against the Brigades of Rouergue and Touraine. In short, the original battle plan had been to push M. de Wangenheim back onto Prince Ferdinand, while cutting off, if possible, the enemy from the Weser, and it seems that if we had made ourselves masters of the wood, as I have just explained, we could actually have driven Prince Ferdinand onto M. de Wangenheim, while dislocating him from the corps that the Erbprinz of Brunswick had under his command.

When one considers the army was on this ground from 5 o'clock, and that it was only at seven o'clock that the enemy started to emerge from the wood, and to cannonade the mill of Hartum, one does not presume to advance a forceful opinion in thinking that the wood and the village of Hartum were not occupied by the enemy, or that if they were, it certainly was not with sufficient forces to… [the account ends at this point].

Bibliography

Archival Sources

Archives Départementales de l'Aube

Xavier, Prince, Archives de la guerre de Sept ans et correspondance familiale : le fonds du prince Xavier de Saxe, EE81 and EE82.

The National Archives (TNA)

State Papers: 87: Secretaries of State: State Papers Foreign, Military Expeditions, Volumes 29 and 37.

National Army Museum (NAM)

NAM 1975-10-92. Lt Hugh Montgomery, Letter to his Mother, dated Camp at Paderborn 9 August 1759.
NAM 6807-142-13. Letter of an Officer Regarding the Battle of Minden.

Books

Almon, John (ed.), *Anecdotes of the Life of the Right Honorable William Pitt, Earl of Chatham: And of the Principal Events of His Time: With His Speeches in Parliament, from the year 1736 to the year 1778* (London: L. B. Seeley, 1797).

Anderson, F. *Crucible of War. The Seven Years' War and the Fate of the Empire in British North America, 1754-1766* (London: Faber & Faber, 2000).

Anon., *Advice to Officers of the British Army* (first published 1782, republished London: Jonathon Cape, 1946).

Anon., *The Trial of the Right Honourable Lord George Sackville at a Court-Martial held at the Horse-Guards, February 29, 1760, for an enquiry into his conduct, being charged in Disobedience of Orders, while commanded the British Horse in Germany* (London: Owen, 1760).

Archenholz, J.W. von, *Prussia and the Seven Years War 1756-1763* (Milton Keynes: Leonaur, 2016).

Arnold-Baker, C., *The Companion to British History* (Tunbridge Wells: Longcross Press, 1996).

Baugh, D., *The Global Seven Years War 1754-1763* (Longman: Harlow, 2011).

Blackmore, David, *Destructive & Formidable. British Infantry Firepower 1642-1765* (Barnsley: Frontline Books, 2014).

Blanning, T., *The Pursuit of Glory – Europe 1648-1815* (London: Penguin, 2007).

Blekwenn, Hans, *Altpreußiche Uniformen* (Dortmund: Harenberg, 1981).

Bobbit, P., *The Shield of Achilles. War, Peace and the Course of History* (London: Allen Lane, 2002).

Bradshaw, J. (ed.), *The Letters of Philip Dormer Stanhope, Earl of Chesterfield* (London: Swan Sonnerschein and Company, 1905).

Brewer, J., *The Sinews of Power* (Abingdon: Routledge, 1989).

Brocklesby, Dr., *Oeconomical and Medical Observations* (London: Becket and de Hondt, 1764).

Broglie, L. de, and Vernier, J. (eds.), *Correspondance inédite de Victor-François, Duc de Broglie, Maréchal de France, avec le Prince Xavier de Saxe, Comte de Lusace, Lieutenant-Général, pour servir à l'histoire de la guerre de la Guerre de Sept Ans* (Paris: Albin Michel, 1903-1904).

Cantlie, Lt. Gen. Sir N., *A History of the Army Medical Department* (Edinburgh: Churchill Livingstone, 1974).
Chartrand, R., *Louis XV's Army (1) Cavalry & Dragoons* (London: Osprey, 1996).
Chartrand, R., *Louis XV's Army (2) French Infantry* (London: Osprey, 1996).
Chartrand, R., *Louis XV's Army (3) Foreign Infantry* (London: Osprey, 1997).
Claude, I.L., *Power and International Relations* (Manhattan: Random, 1969).
Clausewitz, C.P.G. von (Trans. M. Howard, and P. Paret), *On War* (Princeton: Princeton University Press, 1989).
Cole, H.N., *Minden, 1759* (London: Charles Knight & Co., 1972).
Corbett, J.S., *The Seven Years War – A Study in British Combined Strategy* (London: The Folio Society, 2001).
Cormack, A., and Jones, A. (eds), *The Journal of Corporal William Todd 1745-1762* (Stroud: Sutton for the Army Records Society, 2001).
Duffy, Christopher, *The Army of Frederick the Great* (Newton Abbot: David & Charles, 1974).
Duffy, C. *The Military Experience in the Age of Reason* (London: Wordsworth Military Library, 1998).
Duffy, C. *The Military Life of Frederick the Great* (Fairfield: Atheneum, 1985).
Fortescue, The Hon. J.W., *A History of the British Army* (London: Macmillan, 1899-1930).
Fraser, D. *Frederick the Great* (London: Allen Lane, 2000).
Frearson, C.W. (ed.), *"To Mr. Davenport" being Letters of Major Richard davenport (1719-1760) to his brother during service in the 4th Troop of Horse Guards and 10th Dragoons, 1742-1760* (Society for Army Historical Research, Special Publication No.9, 1968).
Funcken, L. and F., *L'Unforme et les Armes des Soldats de la Guerre en Dentelle* (Tournai: Casterman, 1975).
Furneaux, R., *The Seven Years War* (London: C. Tinling & Co., 1973).
Gale, R.R., *A Soldier-Like Way. The Material Culture of the British Infantry 1751-1768* (Elk River: Track of the Wolf, 2007).
Grant, C.S., *Wargaming in History Volume 5, The Seven Years War* (Godmanchester: Ken Trotman Publishing, 2011).
Grossen Generalstabe, Kriegsgeschichtliche Abteilung II (ed.), *Die Kriege Friedrichs des Grossen, Dritter Teil: Der Siebenjahrige Krieg. 1756-1763* (Brelin: Mittler und Sohn, 1912).
Guy, A.J., *Oeconomy and Discipline. Officership and Administration in the British Army 1714-63* (Manchester: Manchester University Press, 1985).
Hogg, I.V., *Illustrated Encyclopaedia of Firearms* (Feltham: Newnes, 1978).
Holmes, R., *Redcoat – The British Soldier in the Age of Horse and Musket* (London: HarperCollins, 2001).
Hotham-Thompson, Sir Charles, *Operations of the Allied Army under the Duke of Brunswick 1757-1762* (London: T. Jeffreys, 1764) [reprinted Point Pleasant New Jersey: Winged Hussar Publishing, The Nafziger Collection, 2016].
Houlding, J.A., *Fit for Service: Training of the British Army, 1715-95* (Oxford: Oxford University Press, 1981).
Inglis, L., *Georgian London. Into the Streets* (Falkirk: Viking Penguin, 2013).
Jomini, Baron de, *Traité des Grandes Opérations Militaires*, 2nd ed. (Paris: Magimel, Paris, 1811).
Kennedy, P. *The Rise and Fall of Great Powers* (London: Harper Collins, 1989).
Knowles, Sir L., *Minden and the Seven Years' War* (Godmanchester: Trotman Publishing (reprint), 2010).
Lavery, B., *Empire of the Seas* (London: Conway Publishing, 2012).
Lebow, R.N., *Why Nations Fight* (Cambridge: Cambridge University Press, 2010).
Von Mauvillon, J., *Geschichte Ferdinands Herzog von Braunschweig-Lüneberg* (Leipzig: Dyk, 1794).
Mackesy, Piers, *The Coward of Minden. The Affair of Lord George Sackville* (London: Penguin Books Ltd, 1979).
McLynn, F., *1759, The Year Britain Became Master of the World* (London: Pimlico, 2005).
Mollo, J., and McGregor, M., *Uniforms of the Seven Years War 1756-6* (Poole: Blandford Press, 1977).
Otte, T.G., ed. *The Makers of British Foreign Policy from Pitt to Thatcher* (Basingstoke: Palgrave, 2002).
Pajol, C.P.V., *Les Guerres* sous Louis XV (Paris: Firmin-Didot, 1891).
Pocock, T., *Battle for Empire. The Very First World War 1756-63* (London: Caxton Editions, 2002).
Reid, S., *British Redcoat 1740-1793* (Oxford: Osprey, 1996).
Reid, S., *King George's Army 1740-93 (I)* (Oxford: Osprey, 1995).

Reid, S., *The Battle of Minden 1759 – The Impossible Victory of the Seven Years War* (Barnsley: Frontline Books, 2016).

Richmond, H.W., *National Policy and Naval Strength* (London: Longman's, Green and Co.,1928).

Sackville, Lord George, *Lord George Sackville's Vindication of Himself, in a Letter to Colonel Fitzroy* [pamphlet, misdated 2 August] (London: R. Stevens, 1759).

Savory, Lieutenant General Sir R., *His Britannic Majesty's Army in Germany During the Seven Years War* (Oxford: The Clarendon Press, 1966).

Saxe, Maurice Comte de, *Mes Rêveries. Ouvrage Posthume* (Amsterdam & Leipzig: Arkstee & Merkus, 1757).

Simms, B., *Three Victories and a Defeat. The Rise and Fall of the First British Empire.* (London: Penguin, 2008).

Smith, D., *Armies of the Seven Years War: Commanders, Equipment, Uniforms and Strategies of the 'First World War'* (Stroud: Spellmount, 2012).

Smith, D., *A New History of the Seven Years War. Volume 1: Power and Politics (1754-1757)* (Godmanchester: Ken Trotman Publishing, 2017).

Smith, D., *A New History of the Seven Years War. Volume 2: Years of Miracles (1758-1759)* (Godmanchester: Ken Trotman Publishing, 2017).

Steffen, Martin (ed.), *Die Schlacht bei Minden, Weltpolitik und Lokalgeschichte* (Minden: J.C.C. Bruns' Verlag, 2008).

Strachan, H., and Herberg-Rothe, A., *Clausewitz in the 21st Century* (New York: Oxford University Press, 2007).

Szabo, Franz A.J., *The Seven Years' War in Europe 1756-1763* (Harlow: Pearson, 2008).

Thompson, A.C., *George II* (Padstow: Yale, 2011).

Vormbaum, Friedrich, *Die Schlacht bei Minden 1759* (Minden: J.C.C. Bruns' Verlag, 1959).

Waddington, R., *La Guerre de Sept Ans. Histoire Diplomatique et Militair, Tome III: Minden, Kunersdorf, Quebec* (Paris: Firmin-Didot et Cie, 1867).

Walpole, H., *The Letters of Horace Walpole, (1749-59)* <https://www.gutenberg.org/cache/epub/4609/pg4609.html> (accessed 24 February 19).

Westphalen, F.O.W.H., *Geschichte der Feldzüge des Herzogs Ferdinand von Braunschweig-Lüneberg* (Nachgelassenes Manuscript von Christian Heinrich Philipp, Edler von Westphalen) (Berlin: Mittler & Sohn, 1871)

White, J., *London in the 18th Century. A Great and Monstrous Thing* (London: Bodley Head, 2012).

Wood, S. (ed.), *...By Dint of Labour and Perseverance... A journal recording two months in northern Germany kept by Lieutenant-Colonel James Adolphus Oughton, commanding 1st battalion 37th Regiment of Foot, 1758* (SAHR Special Publication No.14, 1997).

Woods, J., *Armies and Uniforms of the Seven Years War, Vol 1, Prussia, Britain and Allies* (Leigh-on-Sea: Partizan Historical, 2006).

Worsley, L., *Courtiers. The Secret History of the Georgian Court* (London: Faber & Faber, 2011).

Wylly, H.C., *History of the King's Own Yorkshire Light Infantry* (London: Humphries, 1926).

UK Government Publication

RCDS Handbook. *Thinking Strategically* (Shrivenham: British Crown Copyright, 2010).

Articles

Firth, Sir C. (ed.), 'The Battle of Minden – 1 August 1759', *Journal of the Society for Army Historical Research*, Vol 7, No.28 (April 1928), pp.126-128.

Gray, C., 'Future Warfare'. *RUSI Journal*, Vol.150, October 2005, pp.16-19.

Kroener, B.R., 'From Blenheim to Krefeldt. The Electorate of Hanover – A Continental Millstone'. *Strategic and Combat Studies Institute – The Occasional*, September 2004, pp.9-21.

'Neux' (pseud.), 'The Battle of Minden 1759', *Journal of the Society for Army Historical Research*, Vol.11, No.41 (January 1932), pp.48-50.

Rogge, C., 'Prussian 18th Century Artillery', *Smoothbore Ordnance Journal*. Issue 6 (May 2016), pp.23-60.

Papers and Theses

Carmichael, E.B., *To What Extent was Britain Able to Influence Her Strategy in the Face of the Events of the Seven Years War?* (Kings College London, MA Dissertation, 2010).
Land, J., *The Price of Empire: Britain's Military Costs During the Seven Years' War* (Appalachian State University, MA Thesis, 2010).
Sheffield, G., *Tommy and Fritz: Comrades in Arms? British Soldiers and their German Allies During the Long Eighteenth Century* (Oxford, The Strategic & Combat Studies Institute, The Blenheim Conference Papers, 2004).

Periodicals

The London Magazine: Or, Gentleman's Monthly Intelligencer.

Maps

Grossen Generalstabe, Kriegsgeschichtliche Abteilung II (Ed.), *Die Kriege Friedrichs des Grossen, Dritter Teil: Der Siebenjahrige Krieg. 1756-1763. Plan 27* (Berlin: Mittler und Sohn, 1912).
Roy W., *Plan de la Bataille de Thonhausen près de Minden* and insert *Journal des Mouvements de l-Armee Allie de sa Majeste Britiannique, aux Ordres de S.A.S. Mgr le Duc Ferdinand de Brunswic depuis le 14 Juillet jusqu'au 2me Aout 1759* (Unknown: Schley, 1760). Author's Collection, but a copy can be found on-line at Royal Collection K.Mil. RCIN 732112 <http://wwwmilitarymaps.rct.uk/the-seven-years-war-1756-63/battle-of-minden-1759-a-son-altesse-serenissime>.

Online Resources

Couture, R. (ed.), *Seven Years' War*, at <http://www:kronoscaf.com> (accessed 15 January 2019–31 October 2019).
Vial, J.-L., *Nec Pluribus Impar*, at <http://www.vial.jean.free.fr/new_npi> (accessed 15 January 2019–October 2019).